W9-CBE-710

Third Edition

Qualitative Research for Education

An Introduction to Theory and Methods

Robert C. Bogdan
Syracuse University

Sari Knopp Biklen
Syracuse University

Allyn and Bacon
Boston • London • Toronto • Sydney • Tokyo • Singapore

Vice President and Publisher, Education: Nancy Forsyth
Editorial Assistant: Cheryl Ouellette
Marketing Manager: Kathy Hunter
Editorial-Production Service: Omegatype Typography, Inc.
Manufacturing Buyer: Suzanne Lareau
Cover Administrator: Linda Knowles

Library of Congress Cataloging-in-Publication Data
Bogdan, Robert.
    Qualitative research for education : an introduction to theory and
methods / Robert C. Bogdan, Sari Knopp Biklen. — 3rd ed.
        p.   cm.
    ISBN 0-205-27564-8
    1. Education—Research.   2. Education—Research—Methodology.
I. Biklen, Sari Knopp.   II. Title.
LB1028.B56   1998
    370'.7—dc21   97-30859
                                                          CIP

Printed in the United States of America
10   9   8   7   6   5   02   01   00

Photo Credits: pp. 12, 13: Photographs by Jacob Riis. Courtesy of the Library of Congress. p. 15: Photograph by Lewis Hine. Courtesy of the National Archives. p. 17: Photograph by Marion Post Walcott. Courtesy of the Library of Congress. pp. 9, 18, 148: Courtesy of the Library of Congress. p. 45: Courtesy of Murray and Rosalie Wax. p. 92: Photograph by Andrejs Ozolins. pp. 142, 143: Photographs from the collection of Robert C. Bogdan. p. 144: Photograph by Miles Brothers. Courtesy of the National Archives. p. 145: Photograph by Henry W. Brown. p. 146: Courtesy of the Syracuse Development Center.

To our Families:
Janet, Yinka and Dan, Meg, Chet, and Jono
and
Doug, Noah and Molly

Contents

Preface

This is the third edition of *Qualitative Research for Education: An Introduction to Theory and Methods.* Educational research shifted between the first and second editions of the book in several ways. A field that had been dominated by measurement, operationalized definitions, variables, hypothesis testing, and statistics made room for a research agenda that emphasized description, induction, grounded theory, and the study of people's understandings—an approach to research we refer to as "qualitative." Dependence on qualitative methods for studying various educational issues deepened. Educational researchers who were trained in other research traditions regularly incorporated qualitative approaches in their teaching and their research. A growing number of educational researchers began to identify themselves as qualitative methods specialists. One had only to look at the funding patterns of government agencies, the programs of conventions, the titles of current books in the field, the advertisements for job openings, and the contents of the various education journals to know that qualitative research was flourishing. More educational research courses focused entirely on qualitative methods (Wolcott, 1983; Bogdan, 1983), and general research courses regularly incorporated this approach into their curricula.

Since the second edition these trends have continued. There is more enthusiasm for the approach now than ever before. Qualitative research can no longer be considered a marginal approach that mainstream researchers do not have to consider seriously. The number of sessions at recent meetings of the American Educational Research Association reporting on qualitative research has increased dramatically.

Since the second edition in 1992 new trends have emerged as well. Up until the early seventies the type of research discussed in this book was almost exclusively located within the disciplines of anthropology and sociology. At that time it began breaking out of those boundaries. In the early seventies the phrase "qualitative research" came onto the scene as a crossover designation for field research for people not wedded to a particular discipline (Filstead, 1970). Not belonging to any one tradition, the phrase heralded twenty years of increased influence, development, and cross fertilization. While some in the traditional disciplines resisted the use of the term, for most it united the old timers with those who are new to the approach.

While "qualitative research" gave affiliation to people in the 1970s and 1980s, in the 1990s shifts in the field began pulling adherents apart. The approach has attracted many who were trained in a more quantitative approach to research. They have championed a brand of qualitative research which is more structured and systematized than earlier methods, an approach which emphasizes qualitative technique more than a qualitative way of thinking. At the same time, other qualitative researchers were attracted by scholarship in the humanities which emphasized postmodern approaches to inquiry. These researchers de-emphasized the careful collection of field data and concentrated more on research as representation through writing, and on the politics of research.

It is during this period, when qualitative research is being stretched in different directions that we write this third edition. Since qualitative research is in the midst of turmoil and controversy, we have chosen to write a book that explains and incorporates some of the diverse trends while maintaining the stance taken in earlier editions. In our own work as researchers we have tried to do the same. There are many ways of doing and thinking about qualitative research. In this book we present ours. It is not the only way, or perhaps even the best way, to approach the craft. Our way is, however, consistent with the approaches of many others who practice it. We believe that the best way to learn qualitative research is to start with a particular tradition and branch out from there, exploring other approaches and eventually finding one, or inventing one, that represents your approach. We wish you the best in that endeavor.

In other professional areas such as nursing and the allied health fields, rehabilitation, social work, information studies, management, human development, and communications qualitative research has been embraced with an excitement that parallels what happened in education ten to fifteen years ago (Sherman & Reid, 1994; Ferguson, Ferguson & Taylor, 1992; *Journal of Qualitative Health Research*). Educational researchers have been pioneers and leaders in spreading qualitative research into these applied areas. Taking into account the growing interest in qualitative research in other professional fields we have broadened our discussion and examples in this edition to be more inclusive of people in fields linked to education.

In the preface to the first edition we stated our purpose: to provide a background for understanding the uses of qualitative research in education, to examine its theoretical and historical underpinnings, and to discuss specific methods for conducting research. Our purpose remains more or less the same in this edition. The second edition of *Qualitative Research for Education* reflected specific changes in the field. As new areas and issues—the relationship of gender studies and feminism to qualitative research, postmodernism, deconstruction, and the application of computer technology to the collection and analysis of qualitative data, and communication with in the field—emerged as important, we added material on these topics. These areas have continued to grow in importance and we have incorporated innovations and trends from them in this edition. While we have added these current trends we have maintained the introductory nature of the text. We want it to be useful primarily to those who are just starting out but we also want it to be useful as a handbook for those practicing research. We have updated the references in order to relate particular parts of the book to literature published after the second edition. In addition we have rewritten and expanded sections we felt could be improved by better examples or more explanation. Lastly we add short sections on topics not addressed in early editions, (e.g., triangulation, criteria for evaluating writing, and the presence of the author in the text), and reorganized some chapters to improve clarity and incorporate new material. This is most notable in the chapters on writing and applied research. We sometimes quote researchers who wrote at a time before there was widespread sensitivity to gender-biased language. We have left their words as they wrote them.

As we did in the original edition, we begin with a broad discussion of what qualitative research is and how it relates to education, looking at both the theoretical and historical concepts. In the next four chapters we apply the concepts to the actual practices of design, field-work, data collection, and data analysis. From there, we proceed to writing up findings. In the last chapter, we focus on a special set of cases in qualitative research in education—applied research. In this chapter we discuss evaluation, action, and practitioner research.

We have organized the book in a manner that parallels the process of doing research. Most people who teach qualitative research require students to do research projects as they read about the approach. Thus as the students read about design and getting started, they should be engaged in those activities in their own project. Similarly while they are collecting data and starting analysis, they should be reading those chapters. We suggest that people approaching qualitative research for the first time, whether or not they are taking a course, should first read the book over quickly to get a general understanding of the entire research process. Then, as they begin their own research, they should carefully read again the chapters related to the phase of the research they are doing at the time.

We have many people to thank. The National Institute of Education (grant number 400–79–0052) supported the inclusion study we discuss in the book. The study of the neo-natal unit in the teaching hospital was supported by a grant from the New York Bureau of Mental Retardation and Developmental Disabilities as well as Syracuse University's Senate Research Fund. Andrejs Ozolins wrote parts of the photography sections and helped choose the photographs in the book. Steven J. Taylor contributed to the chapter on applied research. Debra Gold helped with the literature review. TaShera Jenkins brought her computer talents to the production efforts as well. We thank them all.

We also acknowledge the valuable input of the following reviewers: Gail Delicio, Clemson University; Virginia Richardson, University of Arizona; and Linda Spatig, Marshall University.

Chapter 1

Foundations of Qualitative Research in Education

A man and woman sat in the upper level of a packed athletic stadium watching a big game of what was to be a winning season for an up-and-coming division I men's collegiate basketball team. Although it was difficult to distinguish them from the other enthusiastic and boisterous spectators, they were researchers engaged in a study of the home team—the socialization and education of male college athletes. Attending games was a minor part of their research work. They also hung out with and interviewed players, athletic staff, boosters, athlete's women friends, media personnel, and professors. In addition, they collected press reports and other written materials related to the team and players. They gained access to the locker room, the dormitories, and other places players spent their time. They followed several groups of players through their college years and beyond. The researchers maintained detailed written notes of what they observed and heard and conducted tape-recorded interviews which they transcribed. The result was a book which explored topics such as the relationship between athletics and academics, social class, ethnicity, and players' friendship and achievement, players' views of their college experience, and the social organization of collegiate athletics (Adler & Adler, 1991).

In another part of the United States, a researcher regularly visited a multicultural public elementary school where she spent long periods of time observing and carefully listening to boys and girls go about their day-to-day activities, in the classroom, on the play ground, in the gym, and in the lunch room, as well as in less supervised places. She was studying how children experience gender in school. The book which resulted from her work is rich in detail about the "gender play" among groups of children. She discusses and describes gender-related activities such as "chase and kiss," "cooties," "goin' with," and teasing (Thorne, 1993).

A researcher was interested in the academic achievement of African American adolescents, particularly in what she came to call the "logic" of responses of the students to their school. She spent time studying at a predominantly African American school in Washington, DC. Thirty-three students were her "key informants"; these students helped her to study the meaning systems at Capitol High. She explored how some students resisted school-sanctioned learning. She learned about the costs of doing well. She interviewed the students both formally and informally, looked at transcripts and other documents, and spent time hanging out at school and at the students' homes, churches, neighborhoods, and recreational center, even riding the bus with them, in order to find out how they made sense of their education. She found out that the theme of "acting white" was an important issue to these students; she came to look at success in terms that were more than academic (Fordham, 1996).

In a medium-size city a researcher regularly visited a city elementary school, interviewing and observing female teachers. She was studying her subjects' perspectives about their work, what they valued and criticized about their occupation, and how these views were manifested in their speech and actions. After she completed her work in the schools she read diaries and letters by female teachers archived in libraries. In addition, she examined published fictional accounts of teaching and other related material. In the book she published, she explored how teachers think about their occupation and how their thinking is related to images of teachers available in popular culture (Biklen, 1995).

These are examples of people conducting qualitative research for education. They exhaust neither the variety of strategies nor the range of topics. Other qualitative researchers look at old photographs from family albums and other sources to see how people with disabilities are presented (Bogdan, 1988); scrutinize brochures advertising educational safaris to understand how travel companies lure their customers (Casella, 1997); interview successful African American educators to understand their life struggles (Gordon, 1997). The educational experiences of people of all ages (as well as material that expands our knowledge of these experiences), in schools as well as out, can be the subject matter. Qualitative research for education takes many forms and is conducted in many settings.

Although researchers in anthropology and sociology have used the approach described in this book for a century, the term *qualitative research* was not used in the social sciences until the late 1960s. We use qualitative research as an umbrella term to refer to several research strategies that share certain characteristics. The data collected have been termed *soft*, that is, rich in description of people, places, and conversations, and not easily handled by statistical procedures. Research questions are not framed by operationalizing variables; rather, they are formulated to investigate topics in all their complexity, in context. While people conducting qualitative research may develop a focus as they collect data, they do not approach the research with specific questions to answer or hypotheses to test. They also are concerned with understanding behavior from the subject's own frame of reference. External causes are of secondary importance. They tend to collect their data through sustained contact with people in settings where subjects normally spend their time—classrooms, cafeterias, teacher's lounges, dormitories, street corners.

The best-known representatives of qualitative research studies and those that most embody the characteristics we just touched on are those that employ the techniques of *participant observation* and *in-depth interviewing*. The man and woman watching the basketball team and the researcher at Capitol High were engaged in participant observation. The researcher enters the world of the people he or she plans to study, gets to know them and earns their trust, and systematically keeps a detailed written record of what is heard and observed. This material is supplemented by other data such as school memos and records, newspaper articles, and photographs.

In addition to participant observation and archival research, the study of female teachers used in-depth interviewing. Sometimes termed "unstructured" (Maccoby & Maccoby, 1954), or "open-ended" (Jahoda, Deutsch, & Cook, 1951), "nondirective" (Meltzer & Petras, 1970), or "flexibly structured" (Whyte, 1979), the researcher is bent on understanding, in considerable detail, how people such as teachers, principals, and students think and how they came to develop the perspectives they hold. This goal often leads the researcher to spend considerable time with subjects in their own environs, asking open-ended questions such as "What is a typical day like for you?" or "What do you like best about your work?" and recording their responses. The open-ended nature of the approach allows the subjects to answer from their own frame of reference rather than from one structured by prearranged questions. In this type of interviewing, questionnaires are not used; while loosely structured interview guides may sometimes be employed, most often the researcher works at getting the subjects to freely express their thoughts around particular topics. Because of the detail sought, most studies have small samples. In some studies, the researcher draws an in-depth portrait of only one subject. When the intent is to capture one person's interpretation of his or her life, the study is called a *life history.*

We use the phrase *qualitative research,* but others use different terms and conceptualize the brand of research we present in this book slightly differently. Anthropologists have often used the term *field work* to refer to the kind of research we are describing (see Junker, 1960). Its use derives from the fact that data tend to be collected in the field as opposed to laboratories or other researcher-controlled situations. In education, qualitative research is frequently called *naturalistic* because the researcher frequents places where the events he or she is interested in naturally occur. And the data are gathered by people engaging in natural behavior: talking, visiting, looking, eating, and so on (Guba, 1978; Wolf, 1979a). The term *ethnographic* is applied to the approach as well. While some use it in a formal sense to refer to a particular type of qualitative research, one in which most anthropologists engage and which is directed at describing culture, it is also used more generally—sometimes synonymously—with qualitative research as we are defining it (Goetz & LeCompte, 1984).

Other phrases are associated with qualitative research. They include *symbolic interactionist, inner perspective,* the *Chicago School, phenomenological, case study, interpretive, ethnomethodological, ecological,* and *descriptive.* The exact use and definition of these terms, as well as words like *fieldwork* and *qualitative research,* varies from user to user and from time to time. We do not mean to suggest that they all mean the same thing, nor to imply that some do not have very exact meanings when used by particular people who belong to particular research traditions (Jacob, 1987; Tesch, 1990; Lancy, 1993; Smith, 1992; Wolcott, 1992). We prefer to use the term *qualitative research* to include the range of strategies that we call "qualitative." We will clarify some of the phrases we have just mentioned as we proceed with our discussion.

At this point we have merely introduced our subject matter. Next we discuss in more detail the characteristics of qualitative research. Then, before we explain its theoretical underpinnings, we place our subject in historical context.

Characteristics of Qualitative Research

Whether or not you have ever taken any kind of research methods course, you come to qualitative methods class already knowing about research. Media and popular culture, particularly television and radio news, as well as print media, explain the dangers of smoking, drinking while pregnant, driving without seatbelts, and other social problems as discoveries of science, or of scientific research. Charts and graphs illustrate the results of the research, and commentators and journalists employ words such as "variables," "populations," and "results" as part of their daily vocabulary. So, we come to think about research in terms of this vocabulary, even if we do not always know just what all of the terms mean. Whether or not we know how to determine sampling error, we know that this is part of the process of doing research. Research, then, as it comes to be known publicly, is a synonym for *quantitative* research.

Learning to do qualitative research means unlearning this social construction of "research," and opening oneself to the possibility of employing a different vocabulary and way of structuring the research process. While qualitative research shares with quantitative research an emphasis on disciplined data collection, it differs in other ways we will discuss later.

Some researchers "hang around" schools with notepads in hand to collect their data. Others rely on video equipment in the classroom and would never conduct research without it. Still others draw charts and diagrams of student–teacher verbal communication patterns. All of them, though, have this in common: Their work fits our definition of qualitative research and they study an aspect of educational life. In this section we elaborate on the common strands and show why, in spite of differences, their research fits in our category of qualitative research.

There are five features of qualitative research as we define it. All studies that we would call qualitative do not exhibit all the traits to an equal degree. Some, in fact, are almost completely lacking in one or more. The question is not whether a particular piece of research is or is not absolutely qualitative; rather it is an issue of degree. As we mentioned earlier, participant observation and in-depth interview studies tend to be exemplary.

1. *Naturalistic.* Qualitative research has actual settings as the direct source of data and the researcher is the key instrument. The word *naturalistic* comes from ecological approaches in biology. Researchers enter and spend considerable time in schools, families, neighborhoods, and other locales learning about educational concerns. Although some people use videotape equipment and recording devices, many go completely unarmed save for a pad and a pencil. Even when equipment is used, however, the data are collected on the premises and supplemented by the understanding that is gained by being on location. In addition, mechanically recorded materials are reviewed in their entirety by the researcher with the researcher's insight being the key instrument for analysis. In a major study of medical education, for example, researchers went to a mid-western medical school where they followed students to classes, laboratories, hospital wards, and the places where they gathered for social occasions as well: their cafeterias, fraternities, and study halls (Becker, Geer, Hughes, & Strauss, 1961). For a study of educational stratification in California (Ogbu, 1974), it took the author twenty-one months to complete the fieldwork of visiting, observing, and interviewing teachers, students, principals, families, and members of school boards.

Qualitative researchers go to the particular setting under study because they are concerned with *context*. They feel that action can best be understood when it is observed in the setting in which it occurs. These settings have to be understood in the historical context of the institutions of which they are a part. When the data with which they are concerned are produced by subjects, as in the case of official records, qualitative researchers want to know where, how, and under what circumstances they came into being. Of what historical circumstances and movements are they a part? To divorce the act, word, or gesture from its context is, for the qualitative researcher, to lose sight of significance. As one anthropologist described it:

> If anthropological interpretation is constructing a reading of what happens, then to divorce it from what happens—from what in this time or that place specific people say, what they do, what is done to them, from the whole vast business of the world's to divorce it from its application and render it vacant. A good interpretation of anything— a poem, a person, a history, a ritual, an institution, a society—takes us to the heart of that of which it is the interpretation. (Geertz, 1973, p. 18)

Whether they collect data on classroom interaction by videoing class sessions (Florio, 1978; Mehan, 1979), on the experiences of superintendents and teachers through interviewing (Chase, 1995; Weiler, 1988; Middleton, 1993; Casey, 1993), or on desegregation (Metz, 1978), literacy (Oyler, 1996), and adolescent identity formation in the high school (Eckert, 1989) by participant observation, qualitative researchers assume that human behavior is significantly influenced by the setting in which it occurs, and whenever possible, they go to that location.

2. *Descriptive Data.* Qualitative research is descriptive. The data collected take the form of words or pictures rather than numbers. The written results of the research contain quotations from the data to illustrate and substantiate the presentation. The data include interview transcripts, fieldnotes, photographs, videotapes, personal documents, memos, and other official records. In their search for understanding, qualitative researchers do not reduce the pages upon pages of narration and other data to numerical symbols. They try to analyze the data with all of their richness as closely as possible to the form in which they were recorded or transcribed.

Qualitative articles and reports have been described by some as "anecdotal." This is because they often contain quotations and try to describe what a particular situation or view of the world is like in narrative form. The written word is very important in the qualitative approach, both in recording data and disseminating the findings.

In collecting descriptive data, qualitative researchers approach the world in a nit-picking way. Many of us are locked into our "taken for granted" worlds, oblivious to the details of our environment, and to the assumptions under which we operate. We fail to notice such things as gestures, jokes, who does the talking in a conversation, the decorations on the walls, and the special words we use and to which those around us respond.

The qualitative research approach demands that the world be examined with the assumption that nothing is trivial, that everything has the potential of being a clue that might unlock a more comprehensive understanding of what is being studied. The researcher continually asks such questions as: Why are these desks arranged the way they are? Why are some rooms decorated with pictures and others not? Why do certain teachers dress differently from others? Is there a reason for certain activities being carried out where they are? Why is there a television in the room if it is never used? Why do similar behaviors on the part of different students elicit such different responses from the teacher? Nothing is taken for granted, and no statement escapes scrutiny. Description succeeds as a method of data gathering when every detail is considered.

3. *Concern with Process.* Qualitative researchers are concerned with process rather than simply with outcomes or products. How do people negotiate meaning? How do certain terms and labels come to be applied? How do certain notions come to be taken as part of what we know as "common sense"? What is the natural history of the activity or events under study? In studies of inclusion and integration in schools, for instance, the researchers examined teachers' attitudes toward certain kinds of children and then studied how these attitudes were translated into daily interactions with them and how the daily interactions then reified those taken-for-granted attitudes (Bruni, 1980; Rist, 1978). In interviews with female superintendents, a researcher showed how the administrators developed specific stories about their struggles over the course of their careers (Chase, 1995).

The qualitative emphasis on process has been particularly beneficial in educational research in clarifying the self-fulfilling prophecy, the idea that students' cognitive performance in school is affected by teachers' expectations of them (Rosenthal & Jacobson, 1968). Quantitative techniques have been able to show by means of pre- and post-testing that changes occur. Qualitative strategies have suggested just how the expectations are translated into daily activities, procedures, and interactions. A particularly brilliant rendition of the self-fulfilling prophecy in a kindergarten classroom is represented in a participant observation study of an African American kindergarten class in St. Louis. The children were divided into groups based on social and economic criteria within the first few days of school. The teacher interacted more with her top group, allowed them more privileges, and even permitted them to discipline members of the lower group. The day-to-day process of interaction is richly portrayed (Rist, 1970). This kind of study focuses on how definitions (teacher's definitions of students, students' definitions of each other and themselves) are formed.

4. *Inductive.* Qualitative researchers tend to analyze their data inductively. They do not search out data or evidence to prove or disprove hypotheses they hold before entering the study; rather, the abstractions are built as the particulars that have been gathered are grouped together.

Theory developed this way emerges from the bottom up (rather than from the top down), from many disparate pieces of collected evidence that are interconnected. The theory is grounded in the data. As a qualitative researcher planning to develop some kind of theory about what you have been studying, the direction you will travel comes after you have been collecting the data, after you have spent time with your subjects. You are not putting together a puzzle whose picture you already know. You are constructing a picture that takes shape as you collect and examine the parts. The process of data analysis is like a funnel: Things are open at the beginning (or top) and more directed and specific at the bottom. The qualitative researcher plans to use part of the study to learn what the important questions are. He or she does not assume that enough is known to recognize important concerns before undertaking the research.

   5. *Meaning.* "Meaning" is of essential concern to the qualitative approach. Researchers who use this approach are interested in how different people make sense of their lives. In other words, qualitative researchers are concerned with what are called *participant perspectives* (Erickson, 1986; see Dobbert, 1982, for a slightly different view). They focus on such questions as: What assumptions do people make about their lives? What do they take for granted? In one educational study, for example, the researcher focused part of his work on parent perspectives of their children's education. He wanted to know what parents thought about why their children were not doing well in school. He found that the parents he studied felt that the teachers did not value their insights about their own children because of their poverty and their lack of education. The parents also blamed teachers who assumed that this very poverty and lack of education meant the children would not be good students (Ogbu, 1974). He also studied the teachers' and the children's perspectives on the same issues to find some intersections and to explore the implications for schooling.

Qualitative researchers are concerned with making sure they capture perspectives accurately. Some researchers who use videotape show the completed tapes to the participants in order to check their own interpretations with those of the informants (Mehan, 1978). Other researchers may show drafts of articles or interview transcripts to key informants. Still others may verbally check out perspectives with subjects (Grant, 1988). Although there is some controversy over such procedures, they reflect a concern with capturing the people's own way of interpreting significance as accurately as possible.

   Qualitative researchers in education can continually be found asking questions of the people they are learning from to discover "what they are experiencing, how they interpret their experiences, and how they themselves structure the social world in which they live" (Psathas, 1973). Qualitative researchers set up strategies and procedures to enable them to consider experiences from the informants' perspectives. For some, the process of doing qualitative research can be characterized as a dialogue or interplay between researchers and their subjects.

Traditions of Qualitative Research in Education

The history of qualitative research in education in the United States, is rich and complex. It is rooted in early sociology and anthropology in the United States, but it also has ties to English and French intellectual traditions. Its development cannot be understood by looking only at academe, since larger social changes and upheavals have influenced it, as well as colonialism. In this section, we discuss the history of qualitative research in education, exploring disciplinary, continental, and ideological and political influences. They are intertwined, and we will try to keep them so in this discussion.

Disciplinary Traditions

Anthropologists and sociologists have always collected data in the field, attempting to understand how the particular peoples they studied made sense of their worlds. Bronislaw Malinowski was the first cultural anthropologist to really spend long periods of time in a non-western village to observe what was going on (Wax, 1971). He was also the first professional anthropologist to describe how he obtained his data and what the fieldwork experience was like. He laid the foundation for interpretive anthropology by his emphasis on grasping what he called the "native's point of view" (Malinowski, 1922, p. 25).

Malinowski insisted that a theory of culture had to be grounded in particular human experiences, based on observations and inductively sought (Malinowski, 1960). Malinowski's field approach, interestingly, seems to have developed accidentally. When he arrived in New Guinea with an extremely limited budget, World War I immediately broke out. His travel was curtailed, forcing him to remain in Australia and on the islands until the end of the war in 1918. This shaped the direction "fieldwork" would take.

Perhaps the earliest substantive application of anthropology to U.S. education was made by the anthropologist Margaret Mead (see, especially, Mead, 1942, 1951). Concerned particularly with the school as an organization and the role of the teacher, she employed her fieldwork experiences in less technological societies to dramatize the fast-changing educational scene in the United States. Mead examined how particular contexts—the kinds of schools she categorized as the little red schoolhouse, the city school, and the academy—called for particular kinds of teachers and how these teachers interacted with students. She argued that teachers needed to study, through observations and firsthand experiences, the changing contexts of their students' socialization and upbringing in order to become better teachers. The field research of anthropologists was an important source for the model of what is known as *Chicago sociology* (Douglas, 1976; Wax, 1971).

Chicago Sociology

The *Chicago School,* a label applied to a group of sociological researchers teaching and learning at the sociology department of the University of Chicago in the 1920s and 1930s, contributed enormously to the development of the research method we refer to as qualitative. While the sociologists at Chicago differed from each other, they shared some common theoretical and methodological assumptions. Theoretically, they all saw symbols and personalities emerging from social interaction (Faris, 1967). Methodologically, they depended on the study of the single case, whether it was a person, a group, a neighborhood, or a community (Wiley, 1979).

They also relied on firsthand data gathering for their research. W. I. Thomas, an early graduate, analyzed letters that Polish immigrants wrote to develop an insider's perspective on immigrant life (Thomas & Znaniecki, 1927; Collins & Makowsky, 1978). *The Polish Peasant in Europe and America* (Thomas & Znaniecki, 1927) concentrated on "the qualitative analysis of personal and public documents" and "introduced new elements into research and new techniques to study these elements which were not standard to empirical investigations in the traditional sense" (Bruyn, 1966, p. 9).

Robert Park, a leading figure in the Chicago School, came to the University after careers as a reporter, and a public relations representative focusing on issues of race for

Margaret Mead in Samoa, 1925, at age twenty-four with the daughter of a
Samoan chief. She was just beginning her celebrated field studies.

Booker T. Washington. Park brought some of journalism's practices, such as the importance
of being on site, to bear on research practices, moving the role of personal observation to
the forefront (Faris, 1967; Hughes, 1971; Matthews, 1977; Wax, 1971).

Chicago sociologists also emphasized city life. Whatever they studied, they did so
against the backdrop of the community as a whole, what Becker has called "the scientific

mosaic" (Becker, 1970b). Studies from Chicago sociologists illustrate both the interest in different aspects of ordinary life and an orientation to the study of ethnicity; publications on the Jewish ghetto (Wirth, 1928), the taxi-dance hall (Cressy, 1932), the boys' gang (Thrasher, 1927), the professional thief (Sutherland, 1937), the hobo (Anderson, 1923), *The Gold Coast and the Slum* (Zorbaugh, 1929), and the delinquent (Shaw, 1966; first published in 1930). In this emphasis on the intersection of social context and biography lies the roots of contemporary descriptions of qualitative research as "holistic." As a Chicago sociologist put it, "behavior can be studied profitably in terms of the situation out of which it arises" (Wells, 1939, p. 428). In addition, especially in the life histories Chicago School sociologists produced, the importance of seeing the world from the perspective of those who were seldom listened to—the criminal, the vagrant, the immigrant—was emphasized. While not using the phrase, they knew they were "giving voice" to points of view of people marginalized in the society.

This perspective emphasized the social and interactional nature of reality. Park, for example, in his introduction to a study of the methodology of a race relations survey on "Oriental-Occidental" relationships in California, suggested that the study was important because of its recognition "that all opinions, public or private, are a social product" (Bogardus, 1926). Many of the informants shared their perspectives on the difficulties they faced as Asian Americans:

> I thought I was American. I had American ideals, would fight for America, loved Washington and Lincoln. Then in high school I found myself called Jap, looked down on, ostracized. I said I did not know Japan, could not speak the language, and knew no Japanese history or heroes. But I was repeatedly told I was not American, could not be American, could not vote. I am heart sick. I am not Japanese and am not allowed to be American. Can you tell me what I am? (Bogardus, 1926, p. 164)

They not only emphasized the human dimension but studied those who had been pushed to the margins of society.

The Sociology of Education

The discipline of the sociology of education was predominantly quantitative except for the work of Willard Waller. Faculty in education were always concerned about the legitimacy of the field, and were concerned with such questions as, "Is educational sociology a science or can it become a science?" To become scientific, an editorial from the *Journal of Educational Sociology,* explained, research in educational sociology must become experimental. This view of the scientific school measurement movement reflected education's dominant concern of the times. This was "the heyday of empiricism" (Cronbach & Suppes, 1969, p. 43). The "scientific method" in education became identified with quantification.

While quantification represented the dominant school of thought in educational sociology (Peters, 1937; Snedden, 1937), exceptions did appear, notably in the work of Willard Waller (Willower & Boyd, 1989). Waller had studied for a master's degree under Ellsworth Faris in the Chicago Sociology Department, and his orientation to educational sociology was empirical but anti-quantitative, based on first hand involvement with the social world and concerned with how parts related to the whole.

In *Sociology of Teaching* (1932), Waller relied on in-depth interviews, life histories, participant observation, case records, diaries, letters, and other personal documents to describe the social world of teachers and their students. For Waller, the starting point of his book was his belief that "children and teachers are not disembodied intelligences, not instructing machines and learning machines, but whole human beings tied together in a complex maze of social interconnections. The school is a social world because human beings live in it" (Waller, 1932, p. 1). Waller called upon the methods of the "cultural anthropologist," the "realistic novelist," and what we would now describe as the qualitative researcher. His goal was to help teachers develop insight into the social realities of school life. For Waller, insight informed the scientific method, not the reverse (Waller, 1934).

The importance of Waller's discussion of the social life of schools and their participants rests not only on the strength and accuracy of his description, but also on the sociological concepts on which he depended. Among the foremost of these was W. I. Thomas's "definition of the situation" (Thomas, 1923), a clearly interactional concept that suggests people examine and "define" situations before they act on them. These "definitions" are what make situations real for us.

European Connections and the Social Survey Movement

Work in Britain and France, as well as other parts of Europe, during the nineteenth and twentieth centuries, reflected qualitative approaches to understanding people's lives, as researchers studied groups of people by living with them and trying to understand their perspectives. During the late 1800s, the Frenchman Frederick LePlay studied working-class families through the method that social scientists writing in the 1930s labeled "participant observation" (Wells, 1939). LePlay himself called it "observation" (Zimmerman & Frampton, 1935) and employed it to seek a remedy for social suffering. As participant observers, LePlay and his colleagues lived with the families they studied; they participated in their lives, carefully observing what they did at work, at play, at church, and in school. Published as *Les Ouvriers Europeans* (the first volume of which appeared in 1879), they described in detail the life of the working-class family in Europe.

Henry Mayhew's *London Labor and the London Poor,* published in four volumes between 1851 and 1862, consisted of reporting, anecdote, and description about conditions of workers and the unemployed. Mayhew presented life histories and the results of extensive, in-depth interviews with the poor.

The research of Charles Booth, a statistician who conducted social surveys of the poor in London beginning in 1886 (Webb, 1926), followed on the heels of a new urban literature. Booth's undertaking was of incredible proportions, lasting for seventeen years and filling as many volumes. His chief purpose was to discover how many poor there were in London and the condition of their lives. While his major concern was to quantitatively document the extent and nature of poverty in London, his work contained extensive and detailed descriptions of the people he studied. These descriptions were collected during the periods Booth lived, anonymously, among the people he surveyed. His goal was to experience firsthand the lives of his subjects (see Taylor, 1919; Webb, 1926; Wells, 1939).

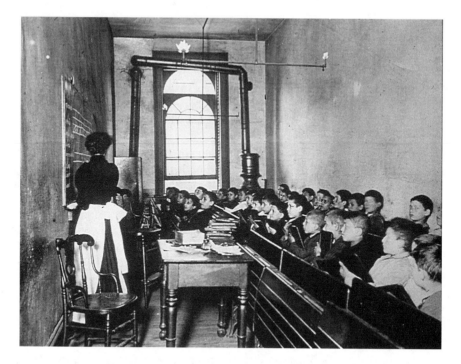

Teacher and pupils, New York City, 1890s. Photo by Jacob Riis.

One of the workers on Booth's colossal project was Beatrice Webb (nee Potter) who, along with her husband, went on to become a major figure in the Fabian socialist movement. A lifelong investigator of the sufferings of the poor and of social institutions, Webb's sympathy, commitment, and understanding arose from her first fieldwork experience. For the first time, she then understood what Roy Stryker (of the Farm Security Administration's "Photography Unit"), another documentarian of the poor, was later to write, "Individuals make up a people" (Stott, 1973, p. 53):

> I never visualized labor as separate men and women of different sorts and kinds. Right down to the time when I became interested in social science and began to train as a social investigator, labor was an abstraction, which seemed to denote an arithmetically calculable mass of human beings, each individual a repetition of the other, very much in the same way that the capital of my father's companies consisted, I imagined, of gold sovereigns identical with all other gold sovereigns in form, weight and color and also in value. (Webb, 1926, p. 41)

What were once abstractions became flesh and blood for Beatrice Webb through first-hand involvement with the subjects of her research. The Webbs later published a description of their methodology, which was widely read in the United States (Wax, 1971), and appears to be the first practical discussion of the qualitative approach (Webb & Webb, 1932). The lives of poor people in the United States at this time, particularly in urban centers, were also to be documented in similar ways.

On this side of the Atlantic, W. E. B. Du Bois undertook the first social survey in the United States. Published in 1899 as *The Philadelphia Negro,* this survey represented almost a year and a half of close study, including interviews and observations with informants living primarily, though not completely, in the city's Seventh Ward. The purpose of the research was to examine "the condition of the forty thousand or more people of Negro blood now living in the city of Philadelphia" (Du Bois, 1899 [1967], p. 1).

One of the most prominent social surveys was the Pittsburgh Survey, undertaken in 1907. While commentators at the time emphasized the statistical nature of these surveys (see, for example, Devine, 1906–1908; Kellogg, 1911–1912), the results of the Pittsburgh Survey, for instance, suggest that this emphasis may have reflected more on their emphasis of the "scientific method" than on the content of the actual reports. While the Pittsburgh Survey presents quantities of statistics on issues ranging from industrial accidents to weekly incomes, from the types and location of "water closets" to school attendance, it also bulges with detailed descriptions, interviews, portraits (sketched by artists in charcoal), and photographs.

Description ranged from educational planning—"School buildings in this city," said one of the experienced school officials of Allegheny, "are first built, then thought about"

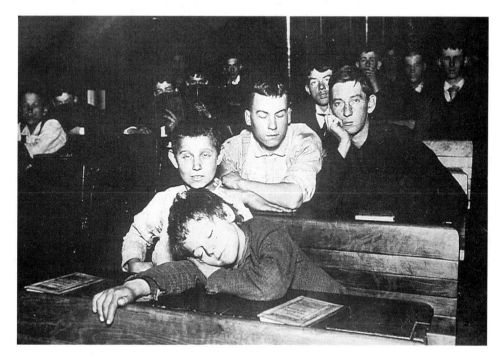

Night school in a 7th Avenue lodging house, early 1890s. Photo by Jacob Riis.

(North, 1909)—to problems that "duller" children encountered in school because of a first-grade teacher's approach to tracking. This teacher

> had 128 pupils one year and 107 the next. She divided the children into two classes. The brighter children came in the morning and were allowed to go on as fast as they could, "getting through" six to nine books in a year; the backward, a smaller number, came in the afternoon. They were worn out with play, the teacher was also worn, and the afternoon session was but two hours; so these children usually got through but one book a year. (North, 1909, p. 1189)

The students ended up dropping out to join the "ranks of uneducated industrial workers" (North, 1909).

All of these researchers on both sides of the Atlantic addressed from various standpoints (socialist, liberal, progressive muckraker) a variety of social concerns in the fields of education, human services, poverty, social welfare and urban life. Some of those who conducted this research were academics, anxious to distinguish their work from social welfare workers, but others were activists and social reformers. The work of both groups contributed, however, to including the perspectives or voices of traditionally underrepresented constituencies in the dialogue. When Frances Donovan (1920/1974) studied waitresses, for example, she did not undertake a work of social change, but indirectly contributed to representing a marginalized group of women's perspectives. Du Bois, on the other hand, did his work on the Philadelphia Negro in order to help effect social change. Ideological and political issues were also central to the traditions of the qualitative approach.

Ideological and Political Practices

In addition to disciplinary and geographic histories in the development of the qualitative approach as we talk about it today, there are ideological influences as well. That is, the doing of qualitative research reflects particular relationships to how power is distributed in a society. Who is studied? Who studies? What kinds of research projects get funded? How do funding and publishing patterns shift over time? What kinds of things carry social interest, and what strategies do researchers use to develop interest in particular areas? In the history of doing qualitative work, researchers have both extended the power of some groups over others, and resisted this power. There are, we would argue, a number of contradictions in the historical relationships of qualitative methods to progressive social change. On the one hand, some of the method's practices and representational strategies have been developed and exercised in the context of dominance and control, as enacted through educational and other institutions, of western countries over so-called third world countries, and, hence, connected to repressive practices. This charge has been directed, with some foundation, particularly at the field of anthropology. On the other hand, at least in the United States, there are strong indications that over the years, qualitative methods have been useful for and attractive to researchers who have been excluded from, or who are studying the perspectives of people excluded from, the mainstream. Groups such as women, African Americans, gays, and lesbians have been attracted to qualitative research because of the democratic em-

"Breaker Boys" working in the Ewen Breaker mine in South Pittston, Pennsylvania, 1911. Photo by Lewis Hine.

phasis of the method, the ease with which the method attends to the perspectives of those not traditionally included in mainstream research studies, and the strengths of the qualitative approach for describing the complexities of social conflicts.

Our account emphasizes what some might call the *transgressive* possibilities of qualitative methods. Connections between qualitative studies, especially abroad and within the discipline of anthropology, and the discourses of colonialism and post-colonialism have been discussed elsewhere (see for example, Vidich & Lyman, 1994; Pratt, 1985, 1986, 1992; Thomas, 1994; Clifford & Marcus, 1986). This discussion has been important in describing how western ethnographic studies of indigenous peoples have made them the "other" (Fabian, 1983; Bhaba, 1986, 1990, 1992). This history is particularly important for anyone interested in doing critical ethnography (Carspecken, 1996). Here, we attend to the contributions of qualitative methods to democracy and justice.

Ideologies and Social Change

The Depression in the United States created overwhelming and visible problems for a majority of citizens, and many scholars, including those hired by government agencies, turned to a qualitative approach to document the nature and extent of these problems. The Work Projects Administration (WPA), for example, produced informant narratives. *These Are Our Lives* contained oral biographies, life histories of black and white southern workers in three states (Federal Writers' Project, 1939). The authors were not social scientists; they were writers who needed work, but the method is sociological. Other forerunners of what we now call oral history included a folk history of slavery, a series of interviews with former slaves, collected in the mid-thirties (Botkin, 1945) and a collection of letters from union members to their union officers, "The Disinherited Speak: Letters from Sharecroppers," published in 1937 on behalf of the Southern Tenant Farmers' Union (Stott, 1973). This collection relied on the same kind of documents that Thomas & Znaniecki (1927) used for their mammoth study, *The Polish Peasant in Europe and America.*

Documentary photography examined the dimensions of suffering of dispossessed American people (see, for example, Evans, 1973; Gutman, 1974; and Hurley, 1972). The Roosevelt administration hired photographers who were out of work, and sent them all over the country to take pictures of daily life. Lewis Hine, Dorothea Lange, Russell Lee, Walker Evans, Jack Delano, Marion Post Wolcott, and John Collier were some of these photographers. When they wrote about their work, they described how they established rapport, worked to present the perspectives of those they photographed, and developed their interview methods (Collier, 1967; O'Neal, 1976; Stryker & Wood, 1973). Wolcott, for example, wrote about the importance of making "people believe you are not trying to ridicule them nor expose them or their living conditions" (O'Neal, 1976, p. 175). Americans were attracted to naturalistic approaches during this period, whether in literature, journalism, photography, or non-academic research, because it documented in personal, particular detail what the Depression meant for most Americans—the southern sharecropper, the northern worker, the homeless Okie.

Qualitative researchers also took up asymmetrical relations of power in gender relationships. In the 1940s, the sociologist, Mirra Komarovsky, completed a study of women in higher education that was to become an important document of feminist movement in the early 1970s. She conducted eighty in-depth interviews with women who were students at Barnard College and studied how cultural values intersected with women's sex role attitudes, noting the difficulty women described in being both "feminine" and "successful" (Komarovsky, 1946).

The 1960s brought national focus to educational problems, revived interest in qualitative research methods, and opened up educational research to this approach. During this period, educational researchers stopped depending completely on sociologists and anthropologists, and began to show interest in these strategies themselves. Their interest was supported by federal agencies which started to fund qualitative research.

The sixties were also characterized by upheaval and social change. Educators' focus turned to the experiences minority children encountered in schools. One reason for this was political: As cities burned and as leaders searched for ways to prevent future protests, they associated poor educational performance with black people's insistence that they receive inadequate services. Spokespeople within the civil rights movement insisted that the perspectives of those who suffered discrimination needed to be represented.

People wanted to know what the schools were like for the children who were not "making it," and many educators wanted to talk about it. A number of autobiographical and journalistic accounts of life in ghetto schools appeared (for example, Decker, 1969; Haskins, 1969; Herndon, 1968; Kohl, 1967; Kozol, 1967). These writers spoke from the "front lines," attempting to capture the quality of the daily lives of the children they taught.

A first-grade class near Montezuma, Georgia (FSA). Photo by Marion Post Walcott.

Federal programs, recognizing how little we really knew about the schooling of different groups of children, funded some research on these issues which used what is now generically labeled ethnographic methods. Qualitative research methods began to catch people's imagination.

Project True, undertaken in 1963 at Hunter College to understand different aspects of life in urban classrooms, relied on interviews with principals, teachers, parents, members of the Board of Education, and the community to examine school integration and the experiences of new teachers in urban schools (Eddy, 1969; Fuchs, 1966, 1969). They used participant observation to examine individual classroom experiences (Roberts, 1971), elementary schools (Moore, 1967), and the urban school in the context of the community (Eddy, 1967). As a group, the researchers worked from the standpoint that education had failed poor children, that the cities were in crisis, and that these old problems demanded to be studied in new ways.

Two other important qualitative studies addressed inequality and injustice. Eleanor Leacock (1969) investigated the meanings school authorities in different communities made of students' behaviors. The other major study on racial issues in education that used fieldwork methods was a project directed by Jules Henry which studied elementary schools in St. Louis (see Gouldner, 1978; Rist, 1970, 1973). Through his involvement in this project, Ray Rist, an influential researcher in the 1970s and 80s, began his research.

The audience for qualitative research in education grew in the 1960s. Not yet firmly established as a legitimate research paradigm, its status caused many graduate students to

A mother teaching her children numbers and the alphabet in her home, 1939.

face major hurdles if they chose to study a problem from this perspective. But qualitative approaches kindled excitement. Why did qualitative research begin to emerge from its long hibernation in education at this particular historical period?

First, the social upheaval of the sixties indicated to many that we did not know enough about how students experienced school. Popular accounts exposed for education what nineteenth-century muckraking revealed about social welfare.

Second, qualitative methods gained popularity because of their recognition of the views of the powerless and the excluded—those on the "outside." The qualitative emphasis on understanding perspectives of all participants at a site challenges what has been called "the hierarchy of credibility" (Becker, 1970c): the idea that the opinions and views of those in power are worth more than those of people who are not. As part of their typical research process, qualitative researchers studying education solicited the views of those who had never felt valued or represented. Qualitative research methods represented the kind of democratic impetus on the rise during the sixties. The climate of the times renewed interest in qualitative methods, created a need for more experienced mentors of this research approach, and opened the way for methodological growth and development.

Politics and Theory in the Academy

The academic disciplines of sociology and anthropology were in transition. Anthropologists found that fewer non-western communities were willing to allow them to conduct their research; funding for such studies diminished. The number of peoples that had not been significantly changed by contact with the west had declined, undermining the mandate to describe the cultures of the world before they were "spoiled." Anthropologists increasingly turned to studying urban areas and their own culture. Meanwhile, the political upheaval around issues of rights and privilege challenged the idea of studying "unspoiled" societies.

During the 1960s, the field of sociology, which for twenty years had been dominated by the ideas of structural-functionalist theory, turned to the writings of phenomenologists. Groups of researchers began doing what they came to call *ethnomethodology*. Others organized around the more established symbolic interaction tradition. Interest in qualitative methods was kindled by the publication of a number of theory and methods books. (Bruyn, 1966; Glaser & Strauss, 1967; Filstead, 1970; McCall & Simmons, 1969).

During the 1970s ideological conflicts also developed over the style and orientation of qualitative methods. One stylistic difference lay in the tension between the cooperative versus conflictual approach to research. Those researchers who belonged to the cooperative school generally believed that fieldworkers should be as truthful as possible with the subjects they studied. They held to the basic and optimistic assumption that people will grant access to a research site if they can. Followers of this perspective were those who tended to see themselves as descendants of the Chicago School (see Bogdan & Taylor, 1975). On the other hand, practitioners of the conflictual approach assumed that many subjects would want to cover up what they do; truthful and overt researchers would get less information. Particularly if he or she wanted to penetrate the world of big business, organized crime, or groups that were labeled deviant, a researcher should use covert means and not speak truthfully in explaining his or her presence. This perspective was clearly articulated by Douglas (1976).

Another stylistic difference is reflected in the attitude of the researcher toward informants or subjects under investigation. One group, again descendants of the Chicago School, might be said to have had an *empathic* perspective; that is, they called for sympathy and understanding toward those whom they studied. Hence, many of their research publications showed readers humanity in lives that at first glance seemed to make little sense. Proponents of this perspective were, in fact, charged with identifying too closely with those they studied, whether they were deviants, outcasts, or powerbrokers. At the other end of this continuum were those whose position seems to have reflected the view that "the sociology of everything is ridiculous." This perspective is reflected most clearly in the group called the ethnomethodologists (see, for example, Garfinkel, 1967; Mehan & Wood, 1975). Ethnomethodologists study how people negotiate the daily rituals of their lives, and in the process often put people's feelings on the sidelines. At the same time, ethnomethodological contributions to the study of gender have been significant, particularly in the construct of "doing gender" (e.g. West & Zimmerman, 1987).

Other ideological strands of the qualitative approach include *feminism, postmodernism* and *critical theory*. Feminist theory and practice intersected qualitative research starting in the late seventies and early eighties. First, feminism influenced the subjects that (feminist) qualitative researchers studied. Gender, constructed from a feminist perspective, emerged as a central topic in many qualitative research projects (Warren, 1988; Lesko, 1988; Lareau, 1987). Using participant observation, document analysis, life history research, and in-depth interviewing, qualitative researchers took seriously actors and categories of behavior that had previously received little, if any, attention. Feminism affected the content of the research, then, as researchers studied how informants made sense of how gender constructed their worlds as female teachers (Biklen, 1987, 1985, 1993; 1995; Middleton, 1987, 1993; Acker, 1989; Weiler, 1988; Casey, 1993; Foster, 1992, 1993, 1994), as food providers (DeVault, 1990), as students in female punk subcultures (Roman, 1988), as readers of romance novels (Radway, 1984), and as consumers and interpreters of medical knowledge about the body and reproduction (Martin, 1987). Additionally, qualitative researchers in education have more recently focused on the experiences of girls in middle schools (Finders, 1997; Research for Action, 1996), masculinity (Mac An Ghaill, 1994), adolescence (Fine, 1988, 1993) and sexuality (Tierney, 1994). Feminists have been important in developing emotion and feeling as topics for research (Hochschild, 1983). In addition, feminist approaches to qualitative methods are apparent in texts not specifically on gender, such as Oyler's study of a teacher changing her classroom pedagogy (1996), and in research on multiculturalism (e.g. Sleeter, 1993).

Second, feminism has affected methodological questions as well. Some of these effects emerged from a general questioning about the nature of feminist research methods in the sciences and social sciences (Harding, 1987; Reinharz, 1993), but practice also affected change. Oakley (1981), for example, worried about power in the interview relationship. Smith (1987) developed "institutional ethnography" as a feminist research strategy to foster a sociology for women instead of a sociology of women. We will discuss some of these issues in Chapter 3.

No matter what venue one uses to approach the intersection of feminism and qualitative research, mutual influences are significant. Feminists have moved the field of qualitative research toward greater concern with the relationships between researchers and their subjects (DeVault, 1990), as well as toward increased recognition of the political implications of research.

Rivaling feminist contributions to qualitative research in significance in the eighties and nineties—in some cases allied and in other cases antagonistic (Mascia-Lees, Sharpe, & Cohen, 1989) were those of the postmodernist sociologists and anthropologists (Marcus & Cushman, 1982; Marcus & Fischer, 1986; Clifford, 1983, 1988; Clifford & Marcus, 1986; Van Maanen, 1988; Denzin, 1989; Dickens & Fontana, 1994, Denzin & Lincoln, 1994; Brown, 1995). *Postmodernism* represents an intellectual position that claims we are living in a "post" modern period. "Post" carries at least two different meanings. The first is that the postmodern period is an actual historical time that differs from modernism. The second meaning is critical of the ideas represented by modernism. During modernism, beliefs in human progress through rationalism and science; the idea of a stable, consistent, and coherent self; and positivist approaches to knowing—beliefs that have held sway in the West since the enlightenment—were seen to explain the human condition. Postmodernists argue, however, that these foundations are no longer in place. The rise of the nuclear age, the growing gap between the rich and the poor, and the global threat to the environment have stripped away the possibility of human progress based on rationalism and caused people in many different areas of human life to question the integrity of progress. Architecture, art, fashion, and scholarship have all been shaped by the postmodern.

Postmodernists argue that you can only know something from a certain position. This assertion challenges the possibility of knowing what is true through the proper, that is, scientific, use of reason. It is a rejection of what Donna Haraway (1991) called "the view from nowhere." People do not reason or conceptualize outside of the self's location in a specific historical time and body; hence, this perspective emphasizes interpretation and writing as central features of research. Clifford and Marcus (1986), for example, called their collection on the poetics and politics of ethnography *Writing Culture.* Postmodernism has influenced qualitative methodologists to shift their focus to the nature of interpretation and the position of the qualitative researcher as interpreter. Rather than taking writing in the form of text in papers, manuscripts, articles, and books for granted, postmodern qualitative researchers make it an object of study. Postmodernists take the idea of a work as "scientific" and make that problematic, questioning what conventions and attitudes make a certain way of looking at the work, the discourse of science, scientific. In *Getting Smart,* for example, Patti Lather insisted that she could not use one explanation or story to account for the resistance of her students to a women's studies class (Lather, 1991a). Instead, drawing on Van Maanen (1988) she told four stories, or tales. We will examine the implications of this position more fully in Chapter 6.

The third important recent ideological influence on qualitative methods is critical theory. Critical theory, as the phrase implies, is critical of social organization that privileges some at the expense of others. Tracing a tradition to the Frankfurt School, it is less "a theory" than a group of theories which emphasize some similar features. First, critical theorists believe that research is an "ethical and political act" (Roman & Apple, 1990, p. 41) that always benefits a specific group. Critical theorists would rather benefit those who are marginalized in the society because they believe that the current way society is organized is unjust. Along these lines, critical theorists agree that their research should "empower the powerless and transform existing social inequalities and injustices" (McLaren, 1994, p. 168). Hence critical theorists who do qualitative research are very interested in issues of gender, race and class because they consider these the prime means for differentiating power in this society.

Qualitative researchers influenced by critical theory are interested in either how social values and organization get reproduced in schools and other educational institutions, or how people produce their choices and actions in the society (Weiler, 1988). Those studies whose emphasis is on reproduction examine how educational institutions sort, select, favor, disenfranchise, silence or privilege particular groups of students or people. Eckert (1989), for example, studied how schools reproduce social divisions among students based on social class so that some students were seen as "jocks," or good students, while others became "burnouts," or bad students. Those studies whose emphasis is on production are interested in how people negotiate these reproductive structures, how they act as agents in their own lives, sometimes resisting discrimination, sometimes setting up oppositional cultures, or wending their way through the maze of restrictions. Weis (1990) studied how working-class high school students negotiated an economic landscape without jobs, as well as how white working-class men think about whiteness and privilege when they no longer have access to industrial work (Weis, Proweller & Centrie, 1997). Some studies draw from both feminism and critical theory (e.g., Weiler, 1988), and postmodernism has influenced, to some degree, most discussions of method, objectivity, and power.

Qualitative research is influenced by these ideological perspectives in different degrees. Some have incorporated critical theory into the theory itself and called it *critical ethnography* (Carspecken, 1996). Other researchers have called on postmodernism to enable them to engage in *experimental ethnography* (e.g., Ellis, 1995b). And others go about their work because they are interested in specific issues and pay less attention to the methodological debates that are raging on campuses. The tremendous expansion of qualitative methods in education insures that it will engender even more methodological discussion.

Theoretical Underpinnings

The concern qualitative researchers have for "meaning," as well as other features we have described as characteristic of qualitative research, leads us to a discussion of the theoretical orientations of the approach. People use the word theory in many ways. Among quantitative researchers in education its use is sometimes restricted to a systematically stated and testable set of propositions about the empirical world. Our use of the word is much more in line with its use in sociology and anthropology and is similar to the term "paradigm" (Ritzer, 1975). A *paradigm* is a loose collection of logically related assumptions, concepts, or propositions that orient thinking and research. When we refer to a "theoretical orientation" or "theoretical perspective," we are talking about a way of looking at the world, the assumptions people have about what is important and what makes the world work. (Examples of theories other than those associated with qualitative research include: structural-functionalism, exchange theory, conflict theory, systems theory, and behaviorism.) Whether stated or not, whether written in what we have come to think of as theoretical language, or not, all research is guided by some theoretical orientation. Good researchers are aware of their theoretical base and use it to help collect and analyze data. Theory helps data cohere and enables research to go beyond an aimless, unsystematic piling up of accounts. In this section, we briefly examine the most influential theoretical underpinnings of qualitative approaches.

Most research approaches (other than qualitative research), trace their roots to positivism and the great social theorist, Auguste Comte. They emphasize facts and causes of behavior. While there are theoretical differences between qualitative approaches and even within single schools (Gubrium, 1988; Meltzer, Petras & Reynolds, 1975), most qualitative researchers reflect some sort of phenomenological perspective. There are many debates concerning the use of the word *phenomenology* and we use it in the most general sense. We start our discussion of theory by presenting the phenomenological perspective and clarifying some issues it raises. Next we discuss symbolic interactionism, a well-established particular type of phenomenological framework used extensively in sociology. We move on to talk of "culture" as an orientation, the interpretation of which is the undertaking of anthropologists. We also briefly introduce another sociological approach to the qualitative scene, ethnomethodology. Finally, we review contemporary trends in theory, those approaches that have more recently informed the work of many qualitative researchers and are influencing the direction of the methodology. Here we look at "feminist theory," "cultural studies," "textual and discourse analysis" and various trends that can be categorized as "postmodern." Our discussion does not exhaust the types. We have picked the most widely used and those most closely aligned with phenomenology (for further discussion see Guba & Lincoln, 1994; Kincheloe & McLaren, 1994; Olesen, 1994; Schwandt, 1994). Each of these theoretical positions interacts with the phenomenology so central to the quantative approach.

Phenomenological Approach

At the scene of a car accident a conversation occurred that illustrates two approaches people use to understand what happens around them. At an intersection where all the roads faced stop signs, two cars collided. The drivers were discussing what had happened when a police officer arrived on the scene. One driver took the position that the other had not made a full stop, while the other driver said that he had indeed stopped and that he had the right of way anyway. A reluctant witness was drawn into the debate who, when asked by one of the drivers for her account of the incident, said that it was hard to tell exactly what had happened from where she was standing. Phrases such as, "How could you say that?" "It happened right before your eyes." "Facts are facts. You didn't stop!" "You were looking the other way." were bantered about. The police officer was asked how she reconciled conflicting accounts. Her response was that contradictions occur all the time and that the parties involved were not necessarily lying since "it all depends on where you are sitting, how things look to you." The approach the police officer took to understand the situation is reflective of qualitative approaches that depend on a phenomenological point of view. They require a set of assumptions that are different from those used when human behavior is approached with the purpose of finding "facts" and "causes."

Some might argue, and we would too, that there are facts in such an accident case. If someone said that there were no stop signs, such an assertion could be checked on location. Some viewers' renderings are more accurate than others. If the accident resulted in a trial where one party was charged with causing the accident, we could garner evidence in support of guilt or innocence. Qualitative researchers would not say that this way to approach the situation is wrong; the legal system works on such logic. They would assert that such an approach is just one way of understanding the situation. Further, they would remind us that such an approach is only a partial telling of the occurrence. If you were interested in the dynamics of the encounter, in the behavior at accidents, in the ways people make sense of such incidents, and in the arguments they construct in explaining them, the "just the facts" approach would not be very illuminating.

Researchers in the phenomenological mode attempt to understand the meaning of events and interactions to ordinary people in particular situations. Phenomenological sociology has been particularly influenced by the philosophers Edmund Husserl and Alfred Schutz. It is also located within the Weberian tradition, which emphasizes *verstehen,* the interpretive understanding of human interaction. Phenomenologists do not assume they know what things mean to the people they are studying (Douglas, 1976). "Phenomenological inquiry begins with silence" (Psathas, 1973, p. 000). This "silence" is an attempt to grasp what it is they are studying. What phenomenologists emphasize, then, is the subjective aspects of people's behavior. They attempt to gain entry into the conceptual world of their subjects (Geertz, 1973) in order to understand how and what meaning they construct around events in their daily lives. Phenomenologists believe that multiple ways of interpreting experiences are available to each of us through interacting with others, and that it is the meaning of our experiences that constitutes reality (Greene, 1978). Reality, consequently, is "socially constructed" (Berger & Luckmann, 1967).

While there are various brands of qualitative research, all share to some degree this goal of understanding the subjects from participant perspectives. When we examine this proposition carefully, though, the phrase "participant perspectives" presents a problem. This problem is the rather fundamental concern that "participant perspectives" is not an expression informants use themselves; it may not represent the way they think of themselves. "Participant perspectives" is a way that people who do this kind of research approach their work; it is thus a research construct. Looking at subjects in terms of this idea may, consequently, force informants' experiences of the world into a mode that is foreign to them. This kind of intrusion of the researcher on the informants' world, however, is inevitable in research. After all, the researcher is making interpretations, and must have some conceptual scheme to do this. Qualitative researchers believe that approaching people with a goal of trying to understand their point of view, while not perfect, distorts the informants' experience the least. There are differences in the degree to which qualitative researchers are concerned with this methodological and conceptual problem as well as differences in how they come to grips with it. Some researchers attempt to do "immaculate phenomenological description"; others show less concern and attempt to build abstractions by interpreting from the data on "their point of view." Whatever one's position, qualitative analysis has to be self-conscious in regard to this theoretical and methodological issue.

While qualitative researchers tend to be phenomenological in their orientation, most are not radical idealists. They emphasize the subjective, but they do not necessarily deny a reality "out there" that stands over and against human beings, capable of resisting action toward it (Blumer, 1980). A teacher may believe he can walk through a brick wall, but it takes more than thinking to accomplish it. The nature of the wall is unyielding, but the teacher does not have to perceive "reality" as it is. He may still believe that he can walk through the wall, but not at this time, or that he had a curse put on him and, therefore, cannot walk through the wall. Thus reality comes to be understood to human beings only in the form in which it is perceived. Qualitative researchers emphasize subjective thinking because, as they see it, the world is dominated by objects less obstinate than walls. And human beings are much more like "The Little Engine That Could." We live in our imaginations, settings more symbolic than concrete.

If human perception is so subjective, one might ask, how do qualitative researchers justify saying they are researchers. Are not they subjective too? Most qualitative researchers believe there are people out there in the world who say and do things which the qualitative researcher can record. These records, or fieldnotes, are data. While they would not claim that the data they collect contain "the truth" or the only way of recording the empirical world, they do claim that their renderings can be evaluated in terms of accuracy. That is, there can and should be a correspondence with what the researcher said happened and what actually occurred. (If the researcher said informants were present and said something, they were in fact present and said these things.) Further, they strive to have their writing be consistent with the data they collect—not that they claim their assertions are "true," but that they are plausible given the data. In this sense qualitative researchers see themselves as empirical researchers. While this is true, most qualitative researchers see what they produce, research reports and articles, not as a transcendent truth, but as a particular rendering or interpretation of reality grounded in the empirical world. They believe that the qualitative research tradition produces an interpretation of reality that is useful in understanding the human condition. That is the logic in their claim to legitimacy.

Symbolic Interaction

As a review of history suggests, symbolic interaction has been around a long time. It was present in the Chicago School approach to research in the early part of this century. John Dewey, the pragmatist philosopher and educator, was at Chicago during the formative years of this theoretical perspective, and his writings and personal contact with such people as Charles Horton Cooley, Robert Park, Florian Znaniecki, and, most importantly, George Herbert Mead, contributed to its development. Mead's formulation in *Mind, Self, and Society* (1934) is the most cited early source of what is now called *symbolic interaction.* No agreement exists among social scientists about the use or importance of its various concepts. Most use it synonymously with qualitative research, but there are a few social scientists calling themselves symbolic interactionists who do quantitative research (i.e., the Iowa School of symbolic interaction). In our discussion we draw heavily on students of Mead's work: Herbert Blumer and Everett Hughes, and their students Howard S. Becker and Blanche Geer.

Compatible with the phenomenological perspective and basic to the approach is the assumption that *human experience is mediated by interpretation* (Blumer, 1969). Objects, people, situations, and events do not possess their own meaning; rather, meaning is conferred on them. Where the educational technologist, for instance, will define a television and VCR as devices to be used by the teacher to show instructional videos relevant to educational objectives, the teacher may define them as objects to entertain students when she runs out of work for them to do or when she is tired. Or, place the television with people who have had not contact with western technology and it may be defined as a religious icon to be worshipped (until the technology specialist arrives bringing, perhaps, new perceptions and possibly influencing some definitions). The meaning people give to their experience and their process of interpretation are essential and constitutive, not accidental or secondary to what the experience is. To understand behavior, we must understand definitions and the processes by which they are manufactured. Human beings are actively engaged in creating their world; understanding the intersection of biography and society is essential (Gerth & Mills, 1953). People act, not on the basis of predetermined responses to predefined objects, but rather as interpreters, definers, signalers, and symbol and signal readers whose behavior can only be understood by having the researcher enter into the defining process through such methods as participant observation.

Interpretation is not an autonomous act, nor is it determined by any particular force, human or otherwise. Individuals interpret with the help of others—people from their past, writers, family, television personalities, and persons they meet in settings in which they work and play—but others do not do it for them. Through interaction the individual constructs meaning. People in a given situation (for example, students in a particular class) often develop common definitions (or "share perspectives" in the symbolic interactionist language) since they regularly interact and share experiences, problems, and background; but consensus in not inevitable. While some take "shared definitions" to indicate "truth," meaning is always subject to negotiation. It can be influenced by people who see things differently. When acting on the basis of a particular definition, things may not go well for a person. People have problems and these problems may cause them to forge new definitions, to discard old ways—in short, to change. How such definitions develop is the subject matter for investigation.

Interpretation, then, is essential. Symbolic interaction, rather than internal drives, personality traits, unconscious motives, needs, socioeconomic status, role obligations, cultural prescriptions, social-control mechanisms, or the physical environment, becomes the conceptual paradigm. These factors are some of the constructs social scientists draw upon in their attempts to understand and predict behavior. The symbolic interactionist also pays attention to these theoretical constructs; however, they are relevant to understanding behavior only to the degree that they enter in and affect the defining process. A proponent of the theory would not deny, for example, that there is a drive for food and that there are certain cultural definitions of how, what, and when one should eat. They would deny, however, that eating can be understood solely in terms of drives and cultural definitions. Eating can be understood by looking at the interplay between how people come to define eating and the specific situations in which they find themselves. Eating comes to be defined in different ways: The process is experienced differently, and people exhibit different behaviors while eating in different situations. Teachers in a school come to define the proper time to eat, what to eat, and how to eat very differently from students in the same location. Eating lunch can be a break from work, an annoying intrusion, a chance to do some low-key business, a time to diet, or a chance to get the answers to questions on an examination. (We are not suggesting that these are mutually exclusive.) Some people's meals, for example, may serve as benchmarks for specific developments in their day. Here, eating takes on significance by providing an event by which one can measure what has or has not been accomplished, how much of the day one may still have to endure, or how soon one will be forced to end an exciting day.

Eating lunch has symbolic meaning with which concepts like drives and rituals cannot deal. The theory does not deny that there are rules and regulations, norms, and belief systems in society. It does suggest that they are important in understanding behavior only if, and how, people take them into account. Furthermore, it is suggested that it is not the rules, regulations, norms, or whatever that are crucial in understanding behavior, but how these are defined and used in specific situations. A high school may have a grading system, an organizational chart, a class schedule, a curriculum, and an official motto that suggests its prime purpose is the education of the "whole person." People act, however, not according to what the school is supposed to be, or what administrators say it is but, rather, according to how they see it. For some students, high school is primarily a place to meet friends, or even a place to get high; for most, it is a place to get grades and amass credits so they can graduate—tasks they define as leading to college or a job. The way students define school and its components determines their actions, although the rules and the credit system may set certain limits and impose certain costs and thus affect their behavior. Organizations vary in the extent to which they provide fixed meanings and the extent that alternative meanings are available and created.

Another important part of symbolic interaction theory is the construct of the "self." The self is not seen lying inside the individual like the ego or an organized body of needs, motives, and internalized norms or values. The self is the definition people create (through interacting with others) of who they are. In constructing or defining self, people attempt to see themselves as others see them by interpreting gestures and actions directed toward them and by placing themselves in the role of the other person. In short, people come to see themselves in part as others see them. The self is thus also a social construction, the results of persons perceiving themselves and then developing a definition through the process of interaction. This loop enables people to change and grow as they learn more about themselves through this interactive process. This way of conceptualizing the self led to studies of the self-fulfilling prophecy and provided the background for the "labeling approach" to deviant behavior (Becker, 1963; Erickson, 1962; Rist, 1977b).

A Story

To sum up our discussion of theory from the phenomenological and symbolic interactionist perspective, we end with an anecdote. If we had to give it a title, we would call this story "Forever."

One night at a dinner party a group of university faculty, including the dean of the law school, a physics professor, and a geology professor, all distinguished in their fields, began discussing the concept of "forever." The conversation began with someone making reference to the practice of having property leases drawn up in periods of ninety-nine years. Someone asked the dean of the law school whether the phrase wasn't the convention of the legal profession to refer to "forever." The dean said, "Yes, more or less, that's what it means." The geology professor suggested that in her field, "forever" refers to something quite different—the concept had more to do with how long the earth was expected to exist. The physics professor chimed in with the comment that in his field, "forever" really meant "forever."

Many children's stories end with the phrase, "And they lived happily forever after," another interpretation. Sometimes when children are waiting for their parents to take them somewhere, they complain that they have been waiting "forever." We have not exhausted all the possibilities, but the point is clear. Looked at from a number of perspectives, the word is rich in connotations. Each person referred to uses of the idea of "forever" in a very different world view. The child who says, "I have been waiting forever," finds it difficult to see the world from the point of view of a physicist, and the physicist dismisses the child's use of the concept with a knowing adult smile.

Some might attempt to resolve the discrepancy between the views of various users of the concept by calling for a more precise definition of the term—in other words, to create consensus by deciding on "real" definitions of the term. In discussion groups or in board meetings, this method might forestall misunderstanding, but qualitative researchers attempt to expand rather than confine understanding. They do not attempt to resolve such ambiguity by seeing the differences as "mistakes" and so attempt to establish a standard definition. Rather, they seek to study the concept as it is understood in the context of all those who use it. Similarly, when going to study an organization, one does not attempt to resolve the ambiguity that occurs when varied definitions of the word *goal* arise, or when people have different goals. The subject of the study focuses instead on how various participants see and experience goals. It is multiple realities rather than a single reality that concern the qualitative researcher.

Culture

Many anthropologists operate from a phenomenological perspective in their studies of education. The framework for these anthropological studies is the concept of *culture.* The attempt to describe culture or aspects of culture is called *ethnography.* While anthropologists often disagree on a definition of culture, they all count on it for a theoretical framework for their work. Several definitions help expand our understanding of how it shapes research. Some anthropologists define culture as "the acquired knowledge people use to interpret experience and generate behavior" (Spradley, 1980, p. 6). In this scheme, culture embraces what people do, what people know, and things that people make and use (Spradley, 1980, p. 5). To describe culture from this perspective, a researcher might think about events in the following way: "At its best, an ethnography should account for the behavior of people by describing what it is that they know that enables them to behave appropriately given the dictates of common sense in their community" (McDermott, 1976, p. 159). Researchers in this tradition say that an ethnography succeeds if it teaches readers how to behave appropriately in the cultural setting, whether it is among families in a African American community (Stack, 1974), in the school principal's office (Wolcott, 1973), or in the kindergarten class (Florio, 1978).

Another definition of culture emphasizes *semiotics,* the study of signs in language, and maintains that there is a difference between knowing the behavior and lingo of a group of people and being able to do it oneself (Geertz, 1973). From this perspective, culture looks more complicated and somewhat different: "As interworked systems of construable signs (what, ignoring provincial usages, I would call symbols), culture is not a power, something to which social events, behaviors, institutions, or processes can be causally attributed; it is a context, something within which they can be intelligibly—that is, thickly—described" (Geertz, 1973, p. 14). In this sense, there is interaction between culture and the meanings people attribute to events. The phenomenological orientation of this definition is clear.

Geertz borrowed the term "thick description" from the philosopher Gilbert Ryle to describe the task of ethnography. Geertz uses Ryle's example of a person blinking one eye, and examines the different levels on which such an act can be analyzed. Blinking can be represented as twitching, winking, pretending to wink (and so putting an audience on), or rehearsing winking. How and at what level one analyzes these behaviors constitutes the difference between thin and thick description:

> Between the…"thin description" of what the researchers (parodist, winker, twitcher…) is doing ("rapidly contracting his right eyelid") and the "thick description" of what he is doing ("practicing a burlesque of a friend faking a wink to deceive an innocent into thinking a conspiracy is in motion"), lies the object of ethnography: a stratified hierarchy of meaning structures in terms of which twitches, winks, fake winks, parodies, rehearsals of parodies are produced, perceived, and interpreted, and without which they would not (not even the zero-form twitches, which as a cultural category are as much non-winks as winks are non-twitches), in fact exist, no matter what anyone did or didn't do with his eyelids. (Geertz, 1973, p. 7)

Ethnography, then, is "thick description." When culture is examined from this perspective, the ethnographer is faced with a series of interpretations of life, of common-sense understandings, that are complex and difficult to separate from each other. The ethnographer's goals are to share in the meanings that the cultural participants take for granted and then to depict the new understanding for the reader and for outsiders. The ethnographer is concerned with representations.

A third conceptual handle on culture is suggested by the anthropologist Rosalie Wax (1971). In a discussion of the theoretical presuppositions of fieldwork, Wax discusses the tasks of ethnography in terms of understanding. Understanding, according to Wax, is not some "mysterious empathy" between people; rather, it is a phenomenon of "shared meaning." And so the anthropologist begins outside, both literally in terms of his or her social acceptance and figuratively in terms of understanding:

> Thus, a field worker who approaches a strange people soon perceives that these people are saying and doing things which they understand but he does not understand. One of the strangers may make a particular gesture, whereupon all the other strangers laugh. They share in the understanding of what the gesture means, but the field worker does not. When he does share, he begins to "understand." He possesses a part of the "insider's view." (Wax, 1971, p. 11)

An ethnographic study of a kindergarten class (Florio, 1978) examines how children entering kindergarten become insiders, that is, how they learn kindergarten culture and develop appropriate responses to teacher and classroom expectations.

Sociologists use culture as well to theoretically inform their qualitative studies. Becker's (1986b) description of culture also relies on shared meanings. Using the metaphor of a dance band, Becker suggests that if a group of individual musicians is invited to play in a dance band at a wedding, and if they show up and, having never met, can play the song in the key the leader announces (with the audience never guessing that they have never met), then they are relying on culture to do so. Becker suggests that culture is what enables people to act together.

It is the framework of culture, whatever the specific definitions, as the principal organizational or conceptual tool used to interpret data that characterizes ethnography. Ethnographic procedures, while similar if not identical to those employed in participant observation, do rely on a different vocabulary and have developed in different academic specialties. Recently, educational researchers have used the term *ethnography* to refer to any qualitative study, even within sociology. While people do not agree on the appropriateness of using *ethnography* as the generic word for qualitative studies (see, for example, Wolcott, 1975, 1990), there is some evidence to suggest that the sociologist and the anthropologist are coming closer in the ways they conduct their research and the theoretical orientation that underlies their work. As early as 1980 a well-known ethnographer declared that "the concept of culture as acquired knowledge has much in common with symbolic interaction" (Spradley, 1980). Some declare that the concept of "culture" as used by anthropologists asserts a structure, continuity, and pervasiveness of meaning among people that symbolic interactionists do not embrace. For symbolic interactionists meaning is much more to be found in the particular situation rather than in the group studied.

Ethnomethodology

Ethnomethodology does not refer to the methods researchers employ to collect their data; rather, it points to the subject matter to be investigated. As Harold Garfinkel tells the story, the term came to him while he was working with the Yale cross-culture area files which contained words like ethnobotany, ethnophysics, ethnomusic, and ethnoastronomy. Terms like these refer to how members of a particular group (usually tribal groups in the Yale files) understand, use, and order aspects of their environment; in the case of ethnobotany, the particular subject is plants. Ethnomethodology thus refers to the study of how people create and understand their daily lives—their method of accomplishing everyday life. Subjects for ethnomethodologists are not members of non-western peoples; they are citizens in various situations in modern society.

Garfinkel, giving what he calls a shorthand definition of the work of ethnomethodologists, says: "I would say we are doing studies of how persons, as parties to their ordinary arrangements, use the features of the arrangements to make for members the visibly organized characteristics happen (Garfinkel, in Hill & Crittenden, 1968, p. 12)." Ethnomethodologists try to understand how people go about seeing, explaining, and describing order in the world in which they live (Garfinkel, 1967). Ethnomethodologists have studied, for example, how people "do" gender (West & Zimmerman, 1987).

A number of educational researchers have been influenced by the approach. While their work is sometimes difficult to separate from the work of other qualitative researchers, it tends to deal more with micro-issues, with the specifics of conversation and vocabulary, and with details of action and understanding. Researchers in this mode use phrases such as "common-sense understanding," "everyday life," "practical accomplishments," "routine grounds for social action," and "accounts." After a period of increasing popularity in the late 1960s and through the 1970s interest in ethnomethology fell off in the 1980s. Many current theoretical critiques and concerns of empiricism raised by post-modernists were originally voiced by ethnomethodologists (Holstein & Gubrium, 1994). There is some evidence of a resurgence of interest in its application to education (Lynch & Peyrot, 1992). One issue to which ethnomethodologists have sensitized researchers is that research itself is not a uniquely scientific enterprise; rather, it can be studied as "a practical accomplishment." They have suggested that we look carefully at the common-sense understandings under which data collectors operate. They push researchers working in the qualitative mode to be more sensitive to the need to "bracket" or suspend their own common-sense assumptions, their own world view, instead of taking it for granted.

The Current Theoretical Scene: Cultural Studies, Feminisms, Post Modernism, and Critical Theory

Many researchers who are not primarily phenomenologists also do qualitative research but situate their work in a different conceptual framework. These frameworks include cultural studies, feminisms, post modernism, and critical theory.

We discussed some of the premises of these theoretical approaches in the historical section. Here, we describe some of the differences between these and phenomenological approaches.

Most qualitative researchers who identify as feminists, critical theorists, or postmodernists reject the idea that the world is "directly knowable"; it "cannot empirically present itself" as phenomenological accounts would suggest (Willis, 1977, p. 194). The world is not directly knowable for several reasons. First, all social relations are influenced by power relations that must be accounted for in analyzing informants' interpretations of their own situations. While the phenomenologist might say that a researcher can never assume how much one's position in the power structure is influential, these perspectives insist that power must always be taken into account to some degree, whether it is the informant's power or lack of it, or the researcher's. These groups may or may not be particularly interested in specific kinds of power. While feminists tend to be interested in the power of gender, including masculinity and femininity (Mac An Ghaill, 1994; Finders, 1997), for example, critical theorists and postmodernists may be as well, so the theoretical orientation of the researchers cannot be identified by the subject of their research (see McRobbie, 1994; Roman, 1997).

Second, they maintain that all research is informed by some theoretical understanding of human and social behavior; hence, it is not accurate to describe the analytical process as inductive. Researchers have ideas about, for example, race, or gender, before they enter the field, and these ideas are influential. They are not, however, binding. Roman and Apple (1990), for example, suggest that the "prior theoretic and political commitments" of the researcher are "informed and transformed by the lived experiences of the group she or he researches" (p. 62). These views, then, suggest that when qualitative researchers do research they engage in a kind of dialogue with their informants. Their own theoretical and ideological views are powerful, but these perspectives are also shaped by what they learn from their informants.

We have described these theoretical perspectives as if they were only different from each other, but that is somewhat artificial. People describe themselves as feminist postmodernists or as critical feminists, or even as feminist phenomenologists. While there may be some tension between these views, there are also similarities even between these different theories and symbolic interaction. Furthermore, all qualitative researchers are connected to the empirical world, since we must all deal with data. Theory emerges in published studies that, to different degrees, depend on data. Theory influences how we talk about our relationship to data and to the empirical world as well as what we imagine to be significant in what we understand.

On Methods and Methodology

One clarification related to theory before we move on. People often use the words *methods* and *methodology* synonymously or confuse the two. *Methodology* is a more generic term that refers to the general logic and theoretical perspective for a research project. *Methods* is a term that refers to the specific techniques you use, such as surveys, interviews, observation—the more technical aspects of the research. In good research, methods are consistent with the logic embodied in the methodology. (Beware of research methods books that only talk about technique and exclude the larger issue of methodology.) As you can gather from our discussion about theory, we are discussing "qualitative research" as a methodology. There is a logical connection between the techniques of participant observation and in-depth interviewing and phenemenological theory and inductive reasoning. If you want to understand the way people think about their world and how those definitions are formed you need to get close to them, to hear them talk and observe them in their day-to-day lives.

Some people employ some of the research methods we discuss in this book using different theoretical perspectives and approaches to analysis than the phenomenological. For example, some people go into natural settings like classrooms and observe but they structure their data gathering with observation guides. They may want to know how many times boys act aggressively or employ negative behaviors compared to girls. Before they start they define precisely what is aggressive and negative behavior and what constitutes an incident of behavior. While this might be called observational research, it is not an example of qualitative methodology. Similarly, many fields employ what they call the *case study* method. Some use the methodology of qualitative research. Others use observation and interviewing but are not concerned with understanding from the informants' point of view, or approaching the data with an eye to letting them teach you what is important. Often template-like instruments are used to guide the data collection and reporting. Other times theoretical approaches that neglect informants' meanings, such as systems theory, are employed. This is not qualitative research methodology as we define it.

Ten Common Questions about Qualitative Research

Hearing about qualitative research for the first time usually causes a number of questions to come to mind. We address ten questions others have raised that you may also have.

1. *Are qualitative findings generalizable?* When researchers use the term *generalizability* they usually are referring to whether the findings of a particular study hold up beyond the specific research subjects and the setting involved. If you study a specific classroom, for example, people want to know whether other classrooms are like the one you studied. Not all qualitative researchers are concerned with the question of generalizability as we have just defined it. Those who are concerned are very careful to state that explicitly. If they do a case study of a classroom, for example, they do not mean to imply in reporting results of the study that all classrooms are like that one.

Others who are concerned with generalizability, as we have discussed it thus far, may draw upon other studies to establish the representativeness of what they have found, or they may conduct a larger number of less intense studies to show the non-idiosyncratic nature of their own work. In a study of cheerleaders, for example, the researcher conducted intense participant observation and interviews at one school for six months, and then studied two other schools which served different populations so that she could be more sensitive to the significance of race and class in the lives of these young women (Swaminathan, 1997).

Some qualitative researchers do not think of generalizability in the conventional way. They are more interested in deriving universal statements of general social processes than statements of commonality between similar settings such as classrooms. Here, the assumption is that human behavior is not random or idiosyncratic. This, they state, is the basic premise of all of social science. Therefore, they concern themselves not with the question of whether their findings are generalizable, but rather with the question of to which other settings and subjects they are generalizable.

In the study of an intensive care unit at a teaching hospital, we studied the ways professional staff and parents communicate about the condition of the children. As we concentrated on the interchanges, we noticed that the professional staff not only diagnosed the infants but sized up the parents as well. These parental evaluations formed the basis for judgments the professionals made about what to say to parents and how to say it. Reflecting about parent–teacher conferences in public schools and other situations where professionals have information about children to which parents might want access, we began to see parallels. In short, we began concentrating on a general social process that appeared clearly in one particular setting. One tack we are presently exploring is the extent to which the findings of the intensive care unit are generalizable not to other settings of the same substantive type, but to other settings, such as schools, in which professionals talk to parents. The approach to generalizability as we have just described it is embraced by researchers who are interested in generating what is called a *grounded theory*.

Another way some qualitative researchers approach generalizability is to think that if they carefully document a given setting or group of subjects, it is then someone else's job to see how it fits into the general scheme of things. Even a description of a deviant type is of value because theories have to account for all types. They see their work as having the potential to create anomalies that other researchers might have to explain. Some of the explanation might entail enlarging the conception of the phenomena under study.

Before gorillas were studied by detailed observation in their own environments, doing what they naturally do, they were considered to be extremely aggressive and dangerous to humans and other animals. George Schaller went out and studied gorillas in their own environments and found out that they did not resemble the profiles drawn of gorillas in captivity. He observed them to be timid and shy, preferring to flee or avoid people rather than to attack. They would, however, rear up and beat their chests in a ritualistic warning when challenged. Questions about whether all gorillas are like that and under what conditions they are the way they have been described cannot be answered by such limited case-study research, but Schaller's gorillas have to be reckoned with in future discussions about gorilla behavior (Schaller, 1965; Waldorf & Reinarman, 1975).

2. *What about the researcher's opinions, prejudices, and other biases and their effect on the data?* Qualitative researchers, whether in the tradition of sociology or anthropology, have wrestled over the years with charges that it is too easy for the prejudices and attitudes of the researcher to bias the data. Particularly when the data must "go through" the researcher's mind before they are put on paper, the worry about subjectivity arises. Does, perhaps, the observer record only what he or she wants to see rather than what is actually there? Qualitative researchers are concerned with the effect that their own subjectivity may have on the data and papers they produce (LeCompte, 1987).

What qualitative researchers attempt to do, however, is to objectively study the subjective states of their subjects. While the idea that researchers can transcend some of their own biases may be difficult to accept at the beginning, the methods researchers use aid this process. For one thing, qualitative studies are not impressionistic essays made after a quick visit to a setting or after some conversations with a few subjects. The researcher spends a considerable time in the empirical world laboriously collecting and reviewing piles of data. The data must bear the weight of any interpretation, so the researcher must constantly confront his or her own opinions and prejudices with the data. Besides, most opinions and prejudices are rather superficial. The data that are collected provide a much more detailed rendering of events than even the most creatively prejudiced mind might have imagined prior to the study.

Additionally, the researcher's primary goal is to add to knowledge, not to pass judgment on a setting. The worth of a study is the degree to which it generates theory, description, or understanding. For a study to blame someone for a particular state of affairs, or to label a particular school as "good" or "bad," or to present a pat prejudicial analysis can brand a study as superficial. Qualitative researchers tend to believe that situations are complex, so they attempt to portray many dimensions rather than to narrow the field.

Further, as we discuss in detail in Chapter 3, qualitative researchers guard against their own biases by recording detailed fieldnotes that include reflections on their own subjectivity. Some qualitative researchers work in teams and have their fieldnotes critiqued by a colleague as an additional check on bias. It should be noted that we are talking about limiting observers' biases, not eliminating them. Qualitative researchers attempt to seek out their own subjective states and their effects on data, but they never believe they are completely successful. All researchers are affected by observers' bias. Questions or questionnaires, for example, reflect the interests of those who construct them, as do experimental studies. Qualitative researchers try to acknowledge and take into account their own biases as a method of dealing with them.

Some researchers and writers are so concerned about controlling their personal biases that it immobilizes them. Our advice is to lighten up. Acknowledge that no matter how much you try you can not divorce your research and writing from your past experiences, who you are, what you believe and what you value. Being a clean slate is neither possible nor desirable. The goal is to become more reflective and conscious of how who you are may shape and enrich what you do, not to eliminate it. On the other hand, do not be so head strong about who you are and what you believe that it leads to being unreflective and to losing your self-consciousness. It is fine to shape your study, but you need to be open to being shaped by the research experience and to having your thinking be informed by the data. The data argues with your general notions, so your thinking is necessarily shaped by the empirical world you are exploring. You need to be open to this and not defensive of what you bring to the research.

Subjectivity as a concern to qualitative researchers looks very different depending on who raises these concerns. Qualitative researchers may often feel defensive when talking with peers or colleagues accustomed to the quantitative mode because subjectivity is considered a problem. When talking with feminists or critical theorists, however, subjectivity is considered a part of all research and moreover, is an important aspect of the work. A researcher's standpoint can be considered an entry into the data. In *White Lies,* for example, a qualitative study of white supremacist literature (Daniels 1997), the author describes how her own identities, or standpoint, gave her "a particular angle of vision for analyzing white supremacist discourse and has also deeply affected me" (p. xiii). The importance of subjectivity for research is defined differently in these groups.

3. *Doesn't the presence of the researcher change the behavior of the people he or she is try-ing to study?* Yes, and these changes are referred to as *observer effect*. They are also called the "Heisenberg effect." This refers to Heisenberg's discovery that the heat of the electron microscope causes the electrons to move faster than they would if they were not under the microscope. So even using this expensive scientific equipment it is impossible to study something without having some effect on it. Almost all research is confounded by this problem. Consider surveys that try to gauge opinions. Asking people to sit down and fill out a questionnaire changes their behavior. Might not asking a person for his or her opinion create an opinion? Some experimental studies create a completely artificial world (in the laboratory) in which to observe people's behavior. Because other research approaches suffer from the problem does not mean that qualitative researchers take the issue of "observer effect" lightly. Throughout the history of qualitative methods practitioners have addressed themselves to this problem and have incorporated procedures to minimize it or take it into account.

Qualitative researchers try to interact with their subjects in a natural, unobtrusive, and nonthreatening manner. The more controlled and obtrusive the research, the greater the likelihood that the researcher will end up studying the effects of his or her methods (Douglas, 1976, p. 19). If you treat people as "research subjects," they will act like research subjects, which is different from how they usually act. Since qualitative researchers are interested in how people act and think in their own settings, they attempt to "blend into the woodwork," or to act so the activities that occur in their presence do not differ significantly from those that occur in their absence. Similarly, since interviewers in this type of research are interested in how people think about their lives, their experiences, and particular situations, they model their interviews after a conversation between two trusting parties rather than on a formal question-and-answer session between a researcher and a respondent. It is only in this manner that they can capture what is important in the minds of the subjects themselves.

Researchers can never eliminate all of their own effects on subjects or obtain a perfect correspondence between what they wish to study—the "natural setting"—and what they actually study—"a setting with a researcher present." They can, however, understand their effect on the subjects through an intimate knowledge of the setting, and use this understanding to generate additional insights into the nature of social life. Researchers learn to "discount" some of their data, that is, to interpret them in context (Deutscher, 1973). Subjects often attempt to manage impressions of researchers and their activities, especially during the early stages of the project (Douglas, 1976). Teachers, for example, might not yell at their students in front of you, or in other ways act more reserved. Knowing that you are seeing teachers' behavior before strangers is important to take into account. Principals may engage in behavior they consider principal-like, and in order to do this upset their normal routines. You can turn this to your advantage to learn what principals consider to be principal-like behavior (see Morris & Hurwitz, 1980). In their reaction to outsiders, people reveal as much as in their reactions to insiders, provided, of course, that you know the difference.

4. *Will two researchers independently studying the same setting or subjects come up with the same findings?* This question is related to the quantitative researchers' word *reliability*. Among certain research approaches, the expectation exists that there will be consistency in results of observations made by different researchers or by the same researcher over time.

Qualitative researchers do not exactly share this expectation (Agar, 1986, pp. 13–16; Heider, 1988).

Educational researchers come from a variety of backgrounds and have divergent interests. Some have studied psychology, others sociology, others child development, and still others anthropology or social work. Academic training affects the questions a researcher brings to an area of inquiry. In the study of a school, for example, social workers might be interested in the social background of the students, sociologists might direct their attention to the school's social structure, and developmental psychologists might wish to study the self-concept of pupils in the early grades. As such, social workers, sociologists, and developmental psychologists who pursue their interests in different ways may spend more time in some parts of the school than others, or may speak more to certain people than to others. They will collect different types of data and reach different conclusions. Similarly, theoretical perspectives specific to their fields will structure a study.

In qualitative studies, researchers are concerned with the accuracy and comprehensiveness of their data. Qualitative researchers tend to view reliability as a fit between what they record as data and what actually occurs in the setting under study, rather than the literal consistency across different observations. As the preceding discussion indicates, two researchers studying a single setting may come up with different data and produce different findings. Both studies can be reliable. One would only question the reliability of one or both studies if they yielded contradictory or incompatible results.

5. *How does qualitative research differ from what other people such as teachers, reporters, or artists do?* Let us take teachers first. Many intelligent laypeople are astute observers of their world, do systematic inquiries, and come to conclusions. Good teachers do this consistently. What they do is like qualitative research, but it is different in a number of ways. First, the observer's primary duty is to the research; he or she does not have to devote time to developing curricula, teaching lessons, and disciplining students. The researcher can thus devote full time and energy to taking it all in. Also, researchers are rigorous about keeping detailed records of what they find. They collect data. Teachers keep records too, but these are much less extensive and of a different sort. Further, researchers do not have as much of a personal stake in having the observations come out one way or the other. The teacher's life, career, and self-concept are always intimately tied to seeing what he or she is doing in a particular way. This is not to say that teachers cannot transcend this to do research or that researchers do not also have a stake in their studies. But for the researchers, success is defined by doing what certain others define as good research, not seeing what the teacher does in any particular way. Another way the researcher and the teacher differ is that the researcher has been trained in the use of a set of procedures and techniques developed over the years to collect and analyze data. Many of these are described in this book. Finally, the researcher is well-grounded in theory and research findings. These provide a framework and clues to direct the study and place what is generated in a context.

What about reporters? Some people link qualitative research with journalism disparagingly. We do not. As the short history we presented suggests, some traditions of qualitative research are linked to journalism. Journalists share some of the goals and standards social scientists have, and some produce research of greater social science value than those who flaunt their academic credentials and titles (Levine, 1980a). While this is so, we do believe that academic researchers in general do work in a different way than journalists (Grant, 1979). Journalists tend to be more interested in particular events and issues and tend to have a bias toward the newsmakers. Journalists work under deadlines. Rather than spending years collecting data and carefully analyzing it, they usually write with less evidence; they shoot from the hip. They also tend to write for a different audience and their work is more directed at telling a story than at analyzing it. Journalists also are not necessarily grounded in social theory. Therefore, they do not address their findings to theoretical questions. Of course, journalists also are interested in selling papers and this puts some constraints on what they can say and how they write. Sometimes, however, the line separating social science research and good investigative journalism is nonexistent (see Douglas, 1976; Levine, 1980a).

What about artists? Some novelists and poets are very keen observers of the human scene. Again, they may not be as formal or as rigorous as qualitative researchers in their data-collecting techniques, and they may take greater license with the data they do collect. Much of what they have to say, however, is of interest to social scientists. Some people fall between the cracks of social science and art. They write in a very involving style while drawing from social science traditions in what they say (Coles, 1964; Cottle, 1976a). Social scientists probably have a lot to learn from novelists and essayists. They had best not set themselves apart, but rather try to understand what it is that they can learn from them to improve their own trade (see Eisner, 1980).

6. *Can qualitative and quantitative approaches be used together?* Yes, some people do use them together (Cronbach et al., 1980; Miles & Huberman, 1984, 1994; Reichardt & Cook, 1994). It is common, for example, in designing questionnaires to do open-ended interviews first. Qualitative data can be used used to supplement, validate, explain, illuminate, or reinterpret quantitative data gathered from the same subjects or site (Miles & Huberman, 1994). There are studies with both qualitative and quantitative components. Most often, descriptive statistics and qualitative findings have been presented together (Mercurio, 1979). While it is possible, and in some cases desirable, to use the two approaches together (Fielding & Fielding, 1986), attempting to carry out a sophisticated quantitative study while doing an in depth qualitative study simultaneously is very difficult. Researchers, especially novices, trying to combine good quantitative design and good qualitative design have a difficult time pulling it off, and rather than producing a superior hybrid, usually produce a piece of research that does not meet the criteria for good work in either approach (Locke, Spirduso & Silverman, 1987, p. 96). The two approaches are based on different assumptions (Smith & Heshusus, 1986). While it is useful to have an interplay of competing data, often such studies turn out to be studies in method rather than in the topic the research originally started out to study.

7. *Is qualitative research really scientific?* In the past, educational researchers modeled their research after what they saw the so-called "hard scientists" doing. Some saw measurement as synonymous with science, and anything straying from this mode was suspect. The irony is that scientists in the hard sciences (physics and chemistry, for example) do not define science as narrowly as some of those who emulate them. Nobel prize–winning physicist P. W. Bridgeman has this to say of the scientific method: "There is no scientific method as such.… The most vital feature of the scientist's procedure has been merely to do his utmost with his mind, no holds barred" (Dalton, 1967, p. 60). Dalton (1967) says that "many eminent physicists, chemists, and mathematicians question whether there is a reproducible method that all investigators could or should follow, and they have shown in their research that they take diverse, and often unascertainable steps in discovering and solving problems" (p. 60). More recently, feminist researchers studying the history of science have brought to light how major scientific breakthroughs occur serendipitously or even by people refusing to be constrained by methodological orthodoxy.

Some people may use an extremely narrow definition of science, calling only research that is deductive and hypothesis-testing scientific. But part of the scientific attitude, as we see it, is to be open-minded about method and evidence. Scientific research involves rigorous and systematic empirical inquiry that is data-based. Qualitative research meets these requirements, and in this book we describe some of the conventions in this scientific tradition that define what rigorous and systematic investigation entails.

8. *What is the goal of qualitative research?* As we have suggested, there is variety in the work done under the rubric of qualitative research. All qualitative researchers do not share the same goal. Some approach their work in an attempt to develop grounded theory. Others emphasize the creation of sensitizing concepts. Description is another objective. If we included applied qualitative research in our discussion of goals the variety in objectives would be greater still. While differences between various approaches to qualitative research exist, researchers operating in the qualitative mode do have some shared understanding about the purpose of their work. Unlike quantitative researchers, qualitative researchers do not see themselves as collecting "the facts" of human behavior, which when accumulated will provide verification and elaboration on a theory that will allow scientists to state causes and predict human behavior. Qualitative researchers understand human behavior as too complex to do that and see the search for cause and prediction as undermining their ability to grasp the basic interpretive nature of human behavior and the human experience.

The qualitative researchers' goal is to better understand human behavior and experience. They seek to grasp the processes by which people construct meaning and to describe what those meanings are. They use empirical observation because it is with concrete incidents of human behavior that investigators can think more clearly and deeply about the human condition.

Some qualitative researchers (including some feminist and action researchers) who study people who have been marginalized also hope to empower their research informants (Roman & Apple, 1990; Lather, 1988). They engage in dialogue with their informants about their analysis of observed and reported events and activities. They encourage informants to gain control over their experiences in their analyses of them. Here the goal is promoting social change.

9. *How does qualitative differ from quantitative research?* Many authors have elaborated the different assumptions, techniques, and strategies of qualitative as opposed to quantitative research. Most of those writing about the qualitative approach define it in contrast to quantitative (Bruyn, 1966; Rist, 1977a). Although a certain amount of comparison is unavoidable, we have attempted in this book to concentrate on describing what qualitative research is and how to do it rather than presenting what it is not. We refer you to others for examination of the differences (see Campbell, 1978; Eisner, 1980; Guba & Lincoln, 1982; Lincoln & Guba, 1985; Smith & Heshusius, 1986).

While we have not been comprehensive in discussing the qualitative/quantitative distinction, Figure 1-1 summarizes the characteristics of both approaches. This chart also serves as a useful summary of the points we have raised in this chapter, many of which we elaborate in the pages that follow.

10. *Which research approach is better, qualitative or quantitative?* While this may strike you as a silly question many people new to research seem deeply concerned with it. Perhaps this is because they see people associated with one approach discrediting the other. There are a number of positions on this question. By far the most widely held is that there is no best method. It all depends what you are studying and what you want to find out. If you want to find out what the majority of the American people think about a particular issue, survey research which relies heavily on quantitative design in picking your sample, designing and pretesting your instrument, and analyzing the data is best. If you want to know about the process of change in a school and how the various school members experience change, qualitative methods will do a better job. Without a doubt there are certain questions and topics that the qualitative approach will not help you with, and the same is true of quantitative research.

People who think this way see choices of research approaches as pragmatic—pick the right one for the job. While this is the popular position, some strongly aligned with one research tradition or the other take less of a cooperative stance. They say their method is best and the other is basically flawed. While this may remind you of an argument between kids about who is the toughest, the argument can involve more than pure self-aggrandizement. People can have strongly held beliefs about the basic nature of human behavior which they lay claim to when explaining why they hold the position they do. They say that the best method of studying human behavior, or anything else for that matter, is the one which is consistent with the basic nature of the subject matter. If you tried to study microorganisms with a telescope or the stars with a microscope you would not get very far. The approach you would be applying just does not fit the subject matter. Similarly, some qualitative researchers believe that meaning and interaction are so basic to human behavior that to use methods that do not make these qualities central distorts the very thing you are trying to understand. Some quantitative researchers say that without precise measurement and systematic hypothesis testing no advances can be made in studying human behavior and the way they go about operationalizing variables and the like is very consistent with the way the universe is organized and humans behave.

Unfortunately the way the university is set up, with its propensity for specialization, some people who take strong stances do so without a deep knowledge about what they are against. But this does not diminish the fact that some who are well read in a variety of approaches take a position on which research approach is best.

This issue raises another question: How do you respond to people who are critical of qualitative research? Beware of argumentative types, especially those who have not read anything about qualitative research and who are basically hostile to it. Let them talk because they are not their strategy when they control the conversation by insisting that you use their vocabulary rather than the one you suggest. Encounters with people like this can

FIGURE 1-1   Characteristics of Qualitative and Quantitative Research

Qualitative	Quantitative
Terms/Phrases Associated with the Approach	
ethnographic	experimental
documentary	hard data
fieldwork	outer perspective
soft data	empirical
symbolic interaction	positivist
inner perspective	social facts
naturalistic	statistical
ethnomethodological	scientific method
descriptive	
participant observation	
phenomenological	
Chicago School	
life history	
case study	
ecological	
narrative	
interpretive	
Key Concepts Associated with the Approach	
meaning	variable
common-sense understanding	operationalize
bracketing	reliability
definition of situation	hypothesis
everyday life	validity
negotiated order	statistically significant
understanding	replication
process	predication
for all practical purposes	
social construction	
grounded theory	
Theoretical Affiliation	
symbolic interaction	structural functionalism
ethnomethodology	realism, positivism
phenomenology	behaviorism
culture	logical empiricism
idealism	systems theory
Academic Affiliation	
sociology	psychology
history	economics
anthropology	sociology
	political science
Goals	
develop sensitizing concepts	theory testing
describe multiple realities	establishing facts
grounded theory	statistical description

Continued

FIGURE 1-1 *Continued*

Qualitative	Quantitative
Goals (Continued)	
develop understanding	show relationship between variables
	predication
Design	
evolving, flexible, general	structured, predetermined, formal, specific
hunch as to how you might proceed	detailed plan of operation
Written Research Proposals	
brief	extensive
speculative	detailed and specific in focus
suggests areas research may be relevant to	detailed and specific in procedures
often written after some data have been collected	thorough review of substantive literature
not extensive in substantive literature review	written prior to data collection
general statement of approach	hypotheses stated
Data	
descriptive	quantitative
personal documents	quantifiable coding
fieldnotes	counts, measures
photographs	operationalized variables
people's own words	statistics
official documents and other artifacts	
Sample	
small	large
nonrepresentive	stratified
theoretical sampling	control groups
snow ball sampling	precise
purposeful	random selection
	control of extraneous variables
Techniques or Methods	
observation	experiments
participant observation	survey research
reviewing various documents, etc.	structured interviewing
open-ended interviewing	quasi experiments
first person accounts	structured observation
Relationship with Subjects	
empathy	detachment
emphasis on trust	short-term
equalitarian	distant
subject as friend	subject–researcher
intense contact	circumscribed
Instruments and Tools	
tape recorder	inventories
transcriber	questionnaires

Continued

FIGURE 1-1   *Continued*

Qualitative	Quantitative
Instruments and Tools (Continued)	
computer	indexes
	computer
	scales
	test scores
Data Analysis	
ongoing	deductive
models, themes, concepts	occurs at conclusion of data collection
inductive	statistical
analytic induction	
constant comparative method	
Problems in Using the Approach	
time consuming	controlling other variables
data reduction difficulties	reification
reliability	obtrusiveness
procedures not standardized	validity
difficult to study large populations	

be frustrating, even upsetting—especially if the person is your superior in the organization (a senior professor in you department, for example). Suggest readings for them. Send them articles you feel are particularly good and relevant. One way to win someone over or to succeed in spite of their apparent disapproval is to do good work. Exhaust yourself doing research and writing that gets recognized by outside sources—publish, get funding, be asked to speak on panels—not on engaging in combat with someone with whom you can not win. If you do well, he or she will come around; that has been our experience. It is also useful to find other people in your area or on your campus who do or who are interested in qualitative methods. There is strength in numbers.

Ethics

Like the words *sex* and *snake, ethics* is emotionally charged and surrounded with evocative and hidden meanings. Nothing is more indicting to a professional than to be charged with unethical practices. While the word conjures up images of a supreme authority and absolutes, ethics in research are the principles of right and wrong that a particular group accepts at a particular time. Most academic specialties and professions have codes of ethics that set forth these rules (see, for example, American Sociological Association, 1989). Some codes are thoughtful and help sensitize members to dilemmas and moral issues they must face; others are narrowly conceived and do more to protect the professional group from attack than to set forth a moral position.

Two issues dominate traditional official guidelines of ethics in research with human subjects: informed consent and the protection of subjects from harm. These guidelines attempt to insure that:

1. Subjects enter research projects voluntarily, understanding the nature of the study and the dangers and obligations that are involved.
2. Subjects are not exposed to risks that are greater than the gains they might derive.

These guidelines are usually implemented through the use of forms that the researcher fills out in which he or she gives a description of the study, what will be done with the findings, possible dangers to the subjects and other pertinent information. The subject's signature on this form is taken as evidence of informed consent. Committees on human subjects, often referred to as "institutional review boards," now exist in most colleges, universities, and other places researchers are employed; they review proposals, checking that the proposed research insures proper informed consent and safety for the participants. They also ask for information that allows them to weigh the risks that subjects might face against the gains they and the larger society might accrue.

These bureaucratic responses to the concern for exploitation and harm of subjects were precipitated by public exposés of research projects that endangered their human subjects in extraordinarily blatant ways. It was discovered, for example, that upon admission at Willowbrook State School the mentally retarded residents were injected with hepatitis virus as part of a study on vaccines (Rothman & Rothman, 1984). In another part of the country, headlines revealed that, without their knowledge, a group of men known to have syphilis were not treated for their condition. Still other experimental subjects were lied to while they participated in and watched what they thought was the electric shocking of other human beings who were actually actors working for the project. It is clear that such abuse must be stopped.

The relationship between the present regulations and what qualitative researchers do is less clear (Duster, Matza, & Wellman, 1979; Thorne, 1980; Wax, 1980; Taylor, 1987). Over the years there have been proposals for a specific code of ethics for qualitative researchers (Cassell, 1978b; Cassell & Wax, 1980; Lincoln, 1995; Punch, 1986; Curry & Davis, 1995). Many qualitative researchers have come to the conclusion that the relationship between researcher and subject is so different in the qualitative and quantitative approaches that following established procedures on informed consent and the protection of subjects seems little more than ritual. In the research for which these guidelines were established, subjects have a very circumscribed relationship to the researcher; they fill out questionnaires or participate in specific experiments. Institutional review board policies were developed on the medical model. The subjects can be told explicitly the content and possible dangers of the study. With qualitative research, on the other hand, the relationship is ongoing; it evolves over time. Doing qualitative research with subjects can be more like having a friendship than a contract. The subjects have a say in regulating the relationship and they continuously make decisions about their participation. While the regulations seem to reflect the studies in which the exact design is completed prior to entering the field, in qualitative research no such designs exist. In submitting a research proposal to human subjects committees, for example, only a "bare bones" description of what will occur can generally be included. This raises the issue of whether institutions force students doing qualitative studies to be unethical by filling out forms that were designed to protect human subjects in quantitative research. If students have to make up interview questions because they do not know before entering the field what questions they will ask, for example, they can be pressured to lie on the form.

Furthermore, qualitative researchers who are critical of the current guidelines question the extent to which subjects can truly be informed. Most people with college educations are not sophisticated enough in such esoteric subjects as qualitative research to ever really know what it means to be a subject in such a study. Furthermore, much of what qualitative researchers do is not all that different from what regular citizens do as they go about their work. Reporters observe and do interviews. So do novelists and others. Should qualitative researchers have less freedom to interact with people than others? After all they are not giving injections or other life altering treatments.

Much research has a tradition of insensitivity to the lives of the people in the studies. In addition to the studies we mentioned earlier, many black and white people were angry at Moynihan's findings in his study of poor African American families. It is not clear, however, that institutional review boards can have any effect on the politics of research. But qualitative researchers can work to change how the members of institutional review boards understand qualitative methods.

While regulations about informed consent and protection of human subjects, as they are traditionally formulated, may not fit the qualitative mode of doing research, ethical issues are of concern (Burgess, 1984). Although qualitative researchers have not developed a specific written code of ethics, conventions have been established regarding ethics in fieldwork (Punch, 1986). As we suggest in Chapter 4, different styles and traditions of fieldwork operate on different ethical principles. We make specific suggestions related to ethics in other chapters, but here we want to lay out some general principles by which the majority of mainstream fieldworkers abide in their research. They apply more specifically to people who are conducting basic research. As we will suggest in Chapter 7, the following ethical principles may be irrelevant to some forms of applied research, particularly to what we call *action research.*

1. Unless otherwise agreed to, the subjects' identities should be protected so that the information you collect does not embarrass or in other ways harm them. Anonymity should extend not only to writing, but also to the verbal reporting of information that you have learned through observation. The researcher should not relate specific information about individuals to others and should be particularly watchful of sharing information with people at the research site who could choose to use the information in political or personal ways.

2. Treat subjects with respect and seek their cooperation in the research. While some advocate covert research, there is general consensus that under usual circumstances the subject should be told of your research interests and should give you permission to proceed. Get written consent. Be particularly sensitive and diligent in explaining yourself and getting consent when studying people who are vulnerable to manipulation such as people labeled mentally disabled or who are very young or very old or who lack formal education. Researchers should neither lie to subjects nor record conversations on hidden mechanical devices.

Rosalie Wax on the Pine Ridge Reservation, South Dakota, 1963, with members of the Sioux family she discusses in *Doing Fieldwork.*

3. In negotiating permission to do a study, you should make it clear to those with whom you negotiate what the terms of the agreement are, and you should abide by that contract. If you agree to do something in return for permission, you should follow through and do it. If you agree not to publish what you find, you should not. Because researchers take the promises they make seriously, you must be careful as a researcher to be realistic in such negotiations.

4. Tell the truth when you write up and report your findings. Although for ideological reasons you may not like the conclusions you reach, and although others may put pressure on you to show certain results that your data do not reveal, the most important trademark of a researcher should be his or her devotion to reporting what the data reveal. Fabricating data or distorting data is the ultimate sin of a scientist.

While we have provided ethical guidelines, as with all rules, there are exceptions and complications so that in many cases the rules seem extraneous or difficult, if not impossible, or even undesirable to employ. There are times, for example, when people do research in which the subjects' identity is difficult or impossible to hide. Further, the people involved may state their indifference to publication of their names or may even insist on being identified. The rule of anonymity may be reconsidered.

Some situations pose difficult dilemmas because they place the researcher in a position where his or her obligations as a researcher conflict with those of being a good citizen. You may, for example, see government corruption and misuse of funds when studying a school. In studies we have done in state institutions for mentally retarded people, we witnessed the physical abuse of the residents. What is the ethical responsibility of researchers in these cases (Taylor, 1987)? Should they turn their backs in the name of research? In the case of the physical abuse, the solution may seem obvious at first: Researcher or not, you should intervene to stop the beatings. In some states it is illegal not to report abuse. That was our immediate disposition. But, through our research, we came to understand that abuse was a pervasive activity in most such institutions nationally, not only part of this particular setting. Was blowing the whistle on one act a responsible way to address this problem or was it a way of getting the matter off our chests? Intervention may get you kicked out. Might not continuing the research, publishing the results, writing reports exposing national abuse, and providing research for witnesses in court (or being an expert witness) do more to change the conditions than the single act of intervention? Was such thinking a cop out, an excuse not to get involved? Such dilemmas are not easily resolved by a list of rules.

While people may make up guidelines for ethical decision making, the tough ethical decisions ultimately reside with you, with your values, and with your judgments of right and wrong. As a researcher you have to know yourself, your values and your beliefs, and be familiar with the principles other researchers have used in making such decisions (Punch, 1994). You have to know how to define your responsibility to other human beings and what that responsibility is when you are put in contact with their suffering (Taylor, 1987). Qualitative research allows for that contact. For many qualitative researchers, ethical questions do not reside narrowly in the realm of how to behave in the field. Rather, ethics are understood in terms of their lifelong obligations to the people who have touched their lives in the course of their research (Curry & Davis, 1995).

People doing research have always been concerned with taking more from the subjects than they give (Whyte, 1992). Researchers write dissertations that lead to career advancement or books that result in promotion and royalty checks. What the subjects get from the arrangement is not as clear. In recent years this issue has reared its head regularly in discussions about ethics. Exploitation of subjects has been a burning topic in a number of fields. Feminist scholars have been most prominent in keeping this topic before the research community. Some researchers are plagued with guilt about it. A number of responses have surfaced in defense of the apparent lack of reciprocity. One is an appeal to the larger contribution research makes to society—although subjects may not get anything directly, the understanding that comes from research improves the larger world. Some claim that the subjects do receive benefits, albeit minor. As any person benefits from being in a relationship, subjects benefit from the time and attention they receive. Feeling this is not enough, some researchers do things for their subjects that bring more tangible help such as sharing royalties, advocating for them or assisting them with legal and other problems (Liebow, 1967; Lincoln, 1995; Curry & Davis, 1995).

In addition to lack of direct reciprocity there is concern that the researcher may use the subjects in other ways. Most prominent here is the concern that researchers get to write and talk about what they have learned but the subjects do not have a chance to speak back or to provide their own interpretations of what their lives are like. The subjects thus may get misrepresented and in some cases demeaned (Fine, 1994a). While we will discuss practices designed to mitigate this more fully later, some researchers have developed new practices in which the researcher and subject are more partners in the study; where the social scientist gives up some of his or her authority and lets the subjects have a say. In addition, conventions have developed in writing qualitative research where it is incumbent on the researcher to tell more about themselves, their backgrounds, and their politics so it is apparent to the reader that what they are reading is written from a particular position (McLaughlin & Tierney, 1993).

Another ethical concern related to the one just discussed but even more complicated is that researcher findings, in the hands of people with power, might lead to actions that could hurt subjects (or people in similar circumstances), and/or lead to social policy or public attitudes that counter the wishes or intentions of the researcher. When Laud Humphries published his famous study of the sexual activities of gays in public rest rooms, for example, some accused him of providing information to the police who could use it to increase surveillance and arrests of male homosexuals. Studies of truants might lead to truancy laws that would restrict young peoples' freedom. What the researcher might think of as a sympathetic portrayal of people living in a housing project might be read by others as proving prejudices about poor people being irresponsible and prone to violence. While you can never be sure of how your findings will be received and used, the political ramifications and implications of your work must be carefully thought through. To do otherwise is to be irresponsible—some might say unethical. If you lack experience in such matters seek out people who might be more sensitive to what might be done with your work and ask their advice about tone, emphasis, and potential consequences. Often researchers are reluctant to directly address what they see as the policy and action implications of their research. Avoiding the task is not the solution. Not interpreting the implications your own work allows others freer reign in doing it for you.

As our discussion begins to suggest, being an ethical and responsible researcher is more difficult than it first appears. Filling out required forms may help you think through some ethical issues and dangers but it is no substitute for evaluating and being in touch with your own values, for continually taking your subjects' welfare and interests to heart, and incorporating them into your practice.

What Is to Come

Having provided you with a general introduction to the foundations of qualitative research, our goal in the rest of the book is to provide guidance on "how to do it." Although people seasoned in the approach will find it useful, reminding them of certain issues and clarifying particular aspects that have been obscure elsewhere, we write for the novice, the person taking an introductory course in qualitative research in education.

The rest of the book is shaped by the five characteristics we have discussed in this chapter. We first consider the issue of research design, emphasizing the inductive nature of the approach. Chapter 3 is concerned with fieldwork. The field-based nature of the research enterprise and the dominance of the researcher as the instrument is clear throughout this discussion. In Chapter 4 the descriptive nature of what qualitative researchers collect is central to our discussion. Here we describe various forms data can take and present some suggestions for their collection. Returning to the inductive character of the approach, we deal extensively with data analysis in Chapter 5. The narrative, descriptive nature of qualitative analysis guides the discussion on writing and disseminating findings in Chapter 6. Because of the applied concerns of educational research, we have devoted a separate chapter, Chapter 7, to the description of applied and evaluation research.

Chapter 2

C h a p t e r 2

Research Design

We have a friend who, when asked where she is going on vacation, will tell you the direction she is traveling and then concludes with, "I'll see what happens as I go along." Another friend makes detailed plans, with all the stops (including restaurants) and routes set in advance. "Design" is used in research to refer to the researcher's plan of how to proceed. A qualitative educational researcher is more like the loosely scheduled traveler than the other.

Qualitative researchers proceed as if they know very little about the people and places they will visit. They attempt to loosen themselves from their preconceptions of what they will find—what the people will be like and what will go on in the setting. Similarly, although they may have a general idea of how they will proceed and what they are interested in, to state exactly how to accomplish their work and what specific questions they will pursue would be presumptuous. Plans evolve as they learn about the setting, subjects, and other sources of data through direct examination. A full account of procedures is best described in retrospect, a narrative of what actually happened, written after the study is completed. To repeat, a detailed set of procedures is usually not formed prior to data collection. Qualitative researchers avoid going into a study with hypotheses to test or specific questions to answer. They believe that shaping the questions should be one of the products of data collection rather than assumed a priori. The study itself structures the research, not preconceived ideas or any precise research design. Their work is inductive.

Our advice is to hang loose. This is the hardest recommendation for some people to hear. Beginning researchers are often anxious about doing their first study. Some of this worry is just the feeling you get trying something new, but it is more than just that. "Research" is intimidating and, if you are new at this, you often wonder if you are up to such an important sounding enterprise. One strategy some impose to deal with this anxiety is to try to control the unknown by imposing the structure of one's preconceived ideas. For example, if you were to go into a "typical" class that is alleged to have children labeled "disabled," you might want to frame the study as one of "inclusion" before you stepped through the classroom door. Before, that is, you knew what the people you would observe were about. Some people generate a list of questions prior to entering the field to allay their fears.

Try to resist this desire to be in control. See what is going on. Hear the people involved with the class talk about what they are doing. Spend time there. Ask very basic questions like: "What's going on here?" "How do the people in the study think about what they are doing?" "How does what I see fit with how others talk about it?"

Qualitative researchers have a design; to suggest otherwise would be misleading. How they proceed is based on theoretical assumptions (that meaning and process are crucial in understanding human behavior, that descriptive data are what is important to collect, and that analysis is best done inductively), on data-collection traditions (such as participant observation, unstructured interviewing, and document analysis) and on generally stated substantive questions. In addition, all researchers bring their own specific backgrounds to a study. This often includes training in a particular field, knowledge of substantive topics, a particular standpoint, and theoretical approaches. This shapes what approaches are taken and what issues are focused on. These markers provide the parameters, the tools, and the general guide of how to proceed. It is not that qualitative research design is nonexistent; it is rather that the design is flexible. Qualitative researchers go off to study carrying the mental tools of their trade, with plans formulated as hunches, only to be modified and remolded as they proceed (Janesick, 1994).

Traditional researchers speak of the design of a study as the product of the planning stage of research. The design is then implemented, the data collected and analyzed, and then the writing is done. While qualitative studies have stages, the work is not as segmented. Design decisions are made throughout the study—at the end as well as the beginning. Although the most intensive period of data analysis usually occurs near the end, data analysis is an ongoing part of the research. Decisions about design and analysis may be made together. This chapter on design contains information that will be helpful in understanding fieldwork and analysis; similarly, Chapters 3 and 5 ("Fieldwork" and "Data Analysis") contain useful ideas about design.

This general description of design we have just provided is the common ground that most qualitative researchers stand on, but not all qualitative researchers embrace design as we have described it. Some are more structured (Miles & Huberman, 1994). They may choose a question, who to interview, where and when to observe, and prepare interview schedules prior to doing field work. More experienced researchers, who have done prior research related to their current interests, are likely to have more specific questions in mind. Those doing evaluation and contract policy research often use a more structured approach in that they need to negotiate the scope and nature of their work with those who hired them. So too do those doing multiple-case research where there is more than one fieldworker and there is concern of having comparable data across cases. But others are even less structured, drifting through data without ever consciously formulating a plan or a question. The particular tradition they are working from affects where they stand; so do research goals and research experience (see Janesick, 1994; Morse, 1994 for discussions). This is true of all aspects of qualitative research.

This chapter is about design. Our discussion begins with the factors to consider in choosing a topic to study. We then discuss design as it relates to specific types of "case" and "multiple data source" studies. In pursuing the topic of design as it relates to multiple data source studies, we present two designs that have been used to generate grounded theory: analytic induction and the constant comparative method.

Choosing a Study

People reading this book are most likely either enrolled in a course where one of the requirements is a research project, or you are about to launch your first major study that will, you hope, become your thesis or dissertation. Many people starting out in qualitative research get bogged down with the questions: "What should I study? Where should I do my field work?" There are no "right" answers to these questions. While decisions are important, they are not right or wrong. If you decide on one school or one class over another, your study may turn out differently, but not necessarily better or worse. The exact decisions you make are not always crucial, but it is crucial that you make some decision. Also, a decision to start a study by going to a particular place does not mean that you are committed to the site forever. Think of your first attempt as an exercise in learning by doing as well as an exploration into the feasibility of doing a study in the location you choose. Your first study should also be thought of as an opportunity to explore a topic area so as to get your bearings if you should undertake a larger endeavor.

Experienced researchers often have a research agenda. They have thought about how they want to spend their research life—what they would like to study and what they hope to accomplish. They look for opportunities to carry out that work. Some are so clear that they refuse research opportunities because they do not fit into their overall plan. For the novice researcher, however, the question of what to study is more perplexing. A research agenda is developed from a number of sources. Often a person's own biography will be an influence in defining the thrust of his or her work. Particular topics, settings, or people are of interest because they have touched the researcher's life in some important way. Others get started in an area because a professor or someone else they know is doing related research. Sometimes it is even more idiosyncratic: an opportunity arises; you wake up with an idea; you are out doing what you normally do and you come across some material that strikes your fancy. However a topic comes to you, whatever it is, it should be important to you and excite you. This is particularly true if it is going to be your thesis, dissertation or other large effort. Self-discipline can only take you so far in research. Without a touch of passion you may not have enough to sustain the effort to follow the work through to the end, or to go beyond doing the ordinary. If someone asks you to undertake a study, be sure it is of sufficient interest to you to maintain your spirit. Of all the thousands of topics and data sources in the world, do not burden yourself with one you are likely to find boring.

While the choices are endless, some advice is in order. First, be practical. Pick a study that seems reasonable in size and complexity so that it can be completed with the time and resources available. Also take into account your own skill which, at this time, is likely to be untested and underdeveloped. We will have more specific suggestions later about practicality in relation to particular kinds of studies. But the general advice we give to the novice is: "Think small." Qualitative research tends to take a lot of time; it is labor-intensive research. Try to limit the number of hours you clock in and the number of pages of data you review. Try to get a good concentration of information rather than widely scattered pieces.

As you can see from the examples we have given, thinking small means thinking about limitations. It is not the equivalent of making the research project very specific. Questions that are very specific are difficult for the qualitative researcher because the issues posed may not arise in the time available for studying them. An example of a question that is *too specific* would be, "How do residence hall advisors employ strategies of Total Quality Management with first semester college freshman?"

The location of your data sources can be critical. Before starting a project it may not matter that you have to travel across town to a school or to another city to look at official documents, observe a class or interview teachers. But, as you get into your work, travel can become burdensome. It drags the work out, limiting your access and therefore your involvement. Without your data source close by, you cannot spontaneously jump in and out of the field.

The second suggestion is that when you are learning the method, study something in which you are not directly involved. If you teach at a school, for example, do not choose that school as a research site. In spite of the fact that successful studies have been accomplished by people who were personally involved in the places they studied (see, for example, McPherson, 1972; Rothstein, 1975), we advise you, the novice, to pick places where you are more or less a stranger. "Why? Don't I have a jump on an outsider studying my own school? I have excellent rapport and I have guaranteed access." This may be true and at times these may be sufficient reasons to ignore our advice, but, especially for a first study, the reasons not to are also compelling. People who are intimately involved in a setting find it difficult to distance themselves both from personal concerns and from their common-sense understandings of what is going on. For them, more often than not, their opinions are more than "definitions of the situation"; they are the truth. Since a major part of your goal is to study what people take for granted, it is important that you not take the same perspectives for granted.

Others in the setting in which you are doing your research, if they know you well, are not used to relating to you as a neutral observer. Rather, they see you as a teacher or as a member of a particular group, as a person who has opinions and interests to represent. They may not feel comfortable relating to you as a researcher to whom they can speak freely. A teacher, for example, studying his or her own school, might not expect the principal to be straightforward in discussing evaluations of fellow teachers or decisions that he or she is making about hiring and firing. Conducting a study with people you know can be confusing and upsetting. Becoming a researcher means more than learning specific skills and procedures. It involves changing your way of thinking about yourself and your relations with others. It involves feeling comfortable with the role of "researcher." If people you know are your research subjects, the transition from your old self to your researcher self becomes indistinct.

Additionally, ethical issues may arise when you study your colleagues, peers, or people over whom you have some kind of authority in a setting. Principals, who have very busy schedules and are also getting higher degrees, may try to save time by studying their own schools. How could you ever be certain that the teachers were not coerced into cooperating with your study? Your authority, in this case, is probably insurmountable as a form of coercion, even if you have good relationships with teachers. A university minister we know, who was interested in student religious cults, felt that he could never study such a group on his own campus because of the ethical implications, and so had to make the trip to another campus for his project.

We are providing advice based on years of experience supervising research projects and teaching qualitative research, but our suggestions are not rigid. You, the novice, might think that you are sufficiently sophisticated or have a relationship with colleagues such that you do not have to worry about these issues. So be it. Give it a try; if it works, great; if it does not, we do not promise not to say "we told you so."

It is fine to have general interests: gender relations, multiculturalism, inclusion, empowerment, collaborative learning, life-long learning, but try not to be too abstract to start. Translate theoretical and conceptual interests into concrete behavioral and setting descriptions and use these to locate a place to collect data. Ground your abstract concerns in people, places, and situations. Thus, in pursuing an interest of gender relations you might go to a little league baseball team that you have heard is composed of both boys and girls. Or perhaps you might study cheerleaders at a local high school (Swaminathan, 1997), or the experiences of young men and women attending their high school proms (Best, 1997). Brainstorm possibilities and then eliminate some on practical or other grounds. Doing this often helps you become clearer about your interests and thus narrows the options. The possibility of studying a little league team might make you confront the decision of what age group interests you.

Another bit of advice: Have preferences, but do not be single-minded in your choices. In the beginning you never know what you are going to find. While it is fine to have general preliminary plans—such as "I will study teacher/teacher friendships"—do not rigidly adhere to such plans. You may discover that teachers at the school you decide to go to observe do not form friendships with other teachers, or that the word "friendship" does not capture the complexity of the relations they do have. Treat your initial visits as exploratory opportunities to assess what is feasible. If you have a particular interest you may choose subjects or settings where you think these will be manifest, only to find them not there. Be prepared to modify your expectations and change your design, or you may spend too much time searching for "the right place to study" when it might not exist.

We have discussed choosing a study as if it does not matter what you choose. Qualitative researchers generally share the belief that you can drop a qualitative researcher off anywhere and he or she will come back with important findings. This position contrasts with the novice's fear that only a "great" site will produce worthwhile findings. There may be some truth in the qualitative researcher's optimism, but all sites are not as easy or as interesting to research.

Some topics and settings are difficult to study because those that grant you permission to be there ("gatekeepers") or the subjects themselves are hostile to outsiders. Under those circumstances it can take months to acquire permission and extensive time to get cooperation. As a novice researcher, you may want to avoid such settings. Deciding what to study always involves assessing who is involved and taking into account the feasibility of access. Who, for example, are the gatekeepers of the files (or of the settings and subjects in which you are interested) and what is the likelihood you can get to them? In Chapter 3, in which we cover researcher relationships, we will discuss "getting in" and negotiating initial relationships with sponsors and subjects. We leave the question of access until then.

In addition to considerations of access, a study's potential significance is something to consider. Some research is relevant to issues that are of crucial importance to education or to the society as a whole. In addition, certain topics and sites have been studied over and over again, while others are relatively unexplored. While interests are paramount, you may want to take into account the state of the field in which you work and the salient issues of our time in choosing a research problem. Students often underestimate the time it takes to do a major research project (one that results in a product as large as a dissertation). They begin their work at the height of interest in a topic only to find that when they finish it is passé. Those who anticipate trends or spot enduring issues are more likely to accomplish work that generates interest than those who do not.

To summarize our suggestions for picking a study:

1. Be practical. Pick something of reasonable size and complexity, that you have easy access to and that is close by.
2. Study something with which you are not directly involved.
3. Be open and flexible.
4. Study something that is interesting to you.
5. Study something that you think might be important.

Case Studies

Thus far we have discussed the first problem: choosing a study. One of the suggestions was to be practical in choosing a topic and a data source that are compatible with your resources and skills. It is no accident that most researchers choose for their first project a case study. A *case study* is a detailed examination of one setting, or a single subject, a single depository of documents, or one particular event (Merriam, 1988, Yin, 1989; Stake, 1994). Case studies vary in their complexity; both novices and experienced researchers do them, but characteristically they are easier to accomplish than multisite or multisubject studies (Scott, 1965). Start with a case study. Have a successful first experience and then move on, if you choose, to the more complex.

The general design of a case study is best represented by a funnel. The start of the study is the wide end: The researchers scout for possible places and people that might be the subject or the source of data, find the location they think they want to study, and then cast a wide net trying to judge the feasibility of the site or data source for their purposes. They look for clues on how they might proceed and what might be feasible to do. They begin to collect data, reviewing and exploring them, and making decisions about where to go with the study. They decide how to distribute their time, who to interview, and what to explore in depth. They may throw aside old ideas and plans and develop new ones. They continually modify the design and choose procedures as they learn more about the topic of study. In time, they make specific decisions on what aspect of the setting, subject, or data source they will study. Their work develops a focus. They formulate questions. The data collection and research activities narrow to particular sites, subjects, materials, topics, questions, and themes. From broad exploratory beginnings they move to more directed data collection and analysis. This process is more fully discussed in Chapter 5.

There are many different types of qualitative case studies (Werner & Schoepfle, 1987a, 1987b; Ragin & Becker, 1992). Each type has special considerations for determining its feasibility for study as well as the procedures to employ.

Historical Organizational Case Studies

These studies concentrate on a particular organization over time, tracing the organization's development. You might do a study, for example, of a "free school," tracing how it came into being, what its first year was like, what changes occurred over time, what it is like now (if it is still operating), or how it came to close (if it did). You will rely on data sources such as interviews with people who have been associated with the organization, observations of the present school, and existing documents including various written records and even old photographs. If your intention is to do this type of study, do some preliminary checking on who is available to interview and what documents have been preserved. Many times historical organizational case studies are not possible, simply because the sources are insufficient for a minimally acceptable piece of work. The determination in your initial inventory of people and documents that sufficient material exists provides a starting point as well as the design for your data collection.

Observational Case Studies

In these studies the major data-gathering technique is participant observation (supplemented with formal and informal interviews and review of documents) and the focus of the study is on a particular organization (school, rehabilitation center) or some aspect of the organization. Parts of the organization that become foci in organizational studies typically are the following:

1. A particular place in the organization—a classroom, the teachers' room, the cafeteria, the office of the dean of students.
2. A specific group of people—members of the high school basketball team, teachers in a particular academic department, staff of an educational travel organization (Casella, 1997), resident advisors in a dormitory.
3. Some activity of the school—curriculum planning or courtship.

Often studies use a combination of these listed aspects for their focus. In a study of high schools, for example, Cusick (1973) focused on sociability (an activity) among students (a group). While observational case studies often include an historical treatment of the setting, this is supplementary to a concern with the contemporary scene.

The researcher often will choose an organization, such as a school, and then focus on some aspect of it. Picking a focus, be it a place in the school, a particular group, or some other aspect, is always an artificial act, for you break off a piece of the world that is normally integrated. The qualitative researcher tries to take into account the relationship of this piece to the whole, but, out of necessity, narrows the subject matter to make the research manageable. Detaching a piece to study distorts, but the researcher attempts to choose a piece that is a naturally existing unit. (The part that is chosen is one that the participants themselves see as distinct and the observer recognizes as having a distinct identity of its own.)

The researcher has to examine the organization to see what places, groups, or programs offer feasible concentrations. After visiting a school a few times you should be able to determine the choices. A good physical setting to study is one that the same people use in a recurring way. In public schools, of course, you can count on classrooms, an office, and usually a teachers' lounge, but even here you cannot be certain these are feasible to study. Some schools, for example, do not have a teachers' lounge. In other schools, classrooms may not be the physical units that organize pupils and teachers.

When we talk about "a group" in an organization as the focus of study, we are using the word sociologically to refer to a collection of people who interact, who identify with each other, and who share expectations about each others' behavior. Teenagers often form friendship groups. Faculty members of a particular department at a particular college often are a group. Members of a basketball team usually are also. People who share characteristics such as age, race, sex, or even organizational position may not, however, share "group" membership. Such characteristics may provide the basis of friendship or collegiality, but the people who share such characteristics do not necessarily form a group. People often enter a setting planning an observational study of, for example, "Chicano teachers," only to find out that Chicano teachers in the particular school they have chosen do not spend their time together and apparently do not hold group identity. Before you make a decision to study a group, you have to know the informal structure of the school.

Individuals who share a particular trait but do not form groups can be subjects in a qualitative study, but interviewing is usually a better approach here than participant observation (see, for example, Kiang, 1995). What they share will emerge more clearly when you individually solicit their perspectives rather than observe their activities. Similarly, sharing the same organizational positions does not necessarily mean that people form a group. All science teachers in a high school have something in common, but in certain schools their contact may be so irregular that they do not form a group. In another school, however, the science department might have regular meetings, eat lunch together, and make a good unit to study.

In choosing a setting or group as the focus of an observational case study, keep in mind that the smaller the number of subjects the more likely you are to change their behavior by your presence. Obviously, hooking up with two students who have a romantic relationship, if such a hook-up were tolerated, would change what went on significantly. A larger number of subjects, on the other hand, usually makes it easier to be unobtrusive. It is keeping track of everyone and managing all the data and relationships present that becomes difficult. For your first study, try to pick a setting or a group that is large enough so that you do not stand out, but small enough so that you are not overwhelmed by the task. This simple rule regarding the size of a setting does not always work however. Schools provide some unique and challenging rapport problems that defy the rule. Although there may be twenty-five people in a setting of an elementary school classroom, for example, there is only one adult. Adding the researcher as the second adult may alter the relationships and make it difficult for the observer to be unobtrusive. (For discussions of this concern, see Fine & Glassner, 1979; Smith & Geoffrey, 1968.)

Life History

In this form of case study, the researcher conducts extensive interviews with one person for the purpose of collecting a first person narrative (Helling, 1988). When this type of interviewing is done by historians it is referred to as *oral history* (Taylor & Bogdan, 1984, esp.

Ch. 4). Historians who do this kind of work often interview famous people (presidents, social movement leaders, and generals) to get the details of history from those who participated in it. When they interview less famous people (domestics or farmers, for instance), they are more interested in how history appears from the point of view of the "common person." Sociological or psychological first person life histories collected through case study interviewing are usually directed at using the person as a vehicle to understand basic aspects of human behavior or existing institutions rather than history. Here, the concept of "career" is often used to organize data collection and presentation. *Career* refers to the various positions, stages, bench marks and ways of thinking people pass through in the course of their lives (Hughes, 1934). Researchers talk about a person's total career or particular dimensions of it. Goffman, for example, studied the career of the mental patient referring to the person's changing identity as he or she experienced the process of being labeled and then treated as "mentally ill" (Goffman, 1961). Sociological life histories often try to construct subjects' careers by emphasizing the role of organizations, crucial events, and significant others in shaping subjects' evolving definitions of self and their perspectives on life. Feminist approaches to life history tend to emphasize the lived experience of the narrator and how that relates to the intersection of gender, race and social class (see, for example, Behar, 1990; Chase, 1995; Middleton, 1993).

The feasibility of a life-history case study is mostly determined by the nature of the potential subject. Is the person articulate and does he or she have a good memory? Has the person lived through the kinds of experiences and participated in the types of organizations or events you want to explore? Does he or she have the time to give? Researchers who do these kinds of case studies usually fall into them. They do not decide on the "type" of subject they want to interview and then go out looking for an example. Rather, they meet a person who strikes them as a good subject and then decide to pursue it. The feasibility and design of such a study is usually determined either on the basis of initial conversations or during the first few interviews. At the onset of a life-history study, when the subject and the interviewer do not know each other well, discussion usually covers impersonal matters. Over time, the content becomes more revealing, the researcher probes more closely, and a focus emerges. Life-history interviews can involve over one hundred hours of tape-recorded meetings and over a thousand pages of transcripts. While some life-history interviews are directed at capturing the subjects' rendering of their whole lives, from birth to present, others are more limited. They seek data on a particular period in the person's life, like adolescence or elementary school, or on a particular topic, like friendships or courting. For discussions of the life-history method, see Becker, 1970b; Denzin, 1978, Ch. 10; Dollard, 1935; Plummer, 1983. For oral history see McAdoo, 1976; and Shumway & Hartley, 1973; Langness & Frank, 1981; Reinharz, 1992, pp. 126–144; Smith, 1994.)

Documents

We have been using the term *document* to refer to materials such as photographs, videos, films, memos, letters, diaries, clinical case records, and memorabilia of all sorts that can be used as supplemental information as part of case study whose main data source is participant observation or interviewing. While their use as an auxiliary is most common, increasingly, qualitative researchers are turning to documents as their primary source of data. This move has come about in part by the influence of discourse theory developed in literature departments or in cultural studies, but others are finding them useful as well.

We will discuss documents more extensively in our chapter on data but, by way of an introduction, there are three main types of documents to consider:

1. *Personal documents:* those produced by individuals for private purposes and limited use such as letters, diaries, autobiographies, family photo albums and other visual recording. Personal documents, or *narratives,* as they are often referred to, have become of particular interest to feminist scholars who are interested in understanding women's "lived experience";

2. *Official documents:* produced by organizational employees for record-keeping and dissemination purposes such as memos, newsletters, files, yearbooks, and the like are used to study bureaucratic rhetoric. Even official documents such as the *Congressional Record* and the *Pentagon Papers* are the exclusive source of data for some.

3. *Popular Culture documents:* these are produced for commercial purposes to entertain, persuade, and enlighten the public such as commercials, TV programs, news reports, or audio and visual recordings. They are of particular interest to qualitative researchers interested in media studies, and also to those influenced by cultural studies, critical theory and various forms of postmodernism. Photographs of all types have a substantial researcher clientele as well.

While we are discussing this form of research under the heading of qualitative research, the extent to which a particular study fits the definition that we presented in the first chapter depends on the specifics of how the research was conducted and how elastic your definition of qualitative research is. Documents clearly fit the criteria of using data rich in description but to what extent the researcher uses them in a manner that is naturalist, inductive, and concerned with the process of meaning construction for those who produce them or use them has to be examined in each case. Studies in which the researcher imposes his or her own predetermined categories and theory on the text, and/or is not concerned with what the narrative means to the people who create it or read it represents a kind of qualitative method, an example of which is what sociologists call *qualitative content analysis* (Daniels, 1997; Fields, 1988). But these studies do not always take up the kind of qualitative approach we feature in this book, which emphasizes how people make meaning of data. We discuss examples of qualitative approaches to found texts in Chapter 4.

An important issue in thinking about the question of design for some studies using documents is the question of availability. As with subjects for life histories, researchers often come across this type of material serendipitously: they find a box in the attic filled with a great aunt's family papers, or they come upon file cabinets filled with old school records. For those on the prowl for such material, check out the holdings of special collections and other archives in libraries. The Library of Congress, for example, is a treasure trove of documents of all kinds. They have slave narratives, the photographs from the Works Progress Administration, and a huge collection of Matthew Brady's Civil War photos, to name a few well-known collections. But to find a stash of interesting material is not enough. Before you get seriously involved in a study you need to assess the depth and breadth of the material. In addition, you will need to find out more about how it was produced, for what purposes, what supplementary materials might be available to be used in conjunction with your find, and who else, if anyone, has used the material before you and for what purposes.

You need to start playing with the questions concerning the possibilities of the materials. What is it that I can find out that can not be revealed using other materials or even doing a different type of study altogether? Is there enough there? Is it worth it? It is often difficult to make such assessments objectively. Certain types of documents have a personal appeal to the researcher. They get in touch with the past through a diary of a distant relative who happened to be a teacher, or they become nostalgic about the past through old year books. You need to be somewhat cold-hearted when making decisions about starting document studies. Doing it solely for your own personal enjoyment is different from wanting to write an acceptable thesis or publishable manuscript. The material has to have research potential.

While the problem with doing studies using personal and official documents as your primary resource is often not being able to find them and having too few, for other projects, popular culture studies in particular, the issue is having too much. Of all the thousands of hours of commercial videos, films, and popular records as well as the millions upon millions of printed words and pictures that appear each day in the media, how do you ever narrow down the scope to make your task manageable. Remember! Think small. Most people who read research do not expect the researcher to cover the universe. Pick a particular program, or a particular event and work on it intensely rather than spreading yourself too thin. Again, try to think about the possible outcomes of the study and then think of ways of narrowing down your data set that would be consistent with these. When confused try any approach. See how it works, what happens, and then think about it and regroup.

We want to remind you of an issue we raised earlier related to assessing the potential of particular studies with documents. If you are interested in qualitative research you need to carefully assess your study in terms of the limitations it possesses for understanding the context that produced the material and the meaning of the material to those who produced and/or use or used it. Personal documents can and have been used much in the same way as life histories have, as data to try to understand the perspective of the author, how they make sense out of their world, themselves, and others and how these meanings were shaped. While with the life history the researcher is more active in shaping the tale and in creating the context of its production, personal documents are often produced by the author and deposited someplace only to be "found" later by the researcher. Thus, the context in which they are produced is elusive, with the intentions and thinking of the author often a mystery. A good deal of laborious collaborative work needs to be done to understand how, or if, the text reveals the perspective of the author. As interesting as some texts appear to be, without information to put it in context, it may not have very much potential as a qualitative study.

In a somewhat different vein, some researchers sit and watch videos of films and then do an analysis of the content. This may involve elaborate coding and a great deal of systematic work and may present important and interesting findings about the depiction of violence, sexuality, gender and racial stereotypes, and other issues of broad concern. If you are doing research employing the kind of qualitative methods we describe in this text, such analysis may be part of your work but that is not enough. You need to gather data on questions such as: How do people who watch videos make sense out of them? What do they see in them? How do they fit into their lives? How do people who produce, promote and sell videos think about their work and the content of what they sell?

Other Forms of Case Studies

There are many other forms of case studies. Some researchers do community studies. These are similar to organizational or observational case studies, except the study focuses on a neighborhood or community rather than on a school or other organization (Classics include Gans, 1967; Whyte, 1955; Lynd & Lynd, 1929; 1937). Another form of case study has been termed *situation analysis.* In this type, a particular event (the expulsion of a student from school, for example) is studied from the points of view of all the participants (the student, his or her friends, the parents, the principal, the teacher that initiated the action). *Microeth-nography* is a term used in several ways, but most often it refers to case studies done either on very small units of an organization (a part of a classroom) or on a very specific organizational activity (children learning how to draw). While educational anthropologists usually employ this label, ethnomethodologists claim it as well (see Erickson, 1975; Smith & Geoffrey, 1968).

Case Study Design Issues

A few general issues concerning design within the confines of the case study approach need discussion. We referred to one in the first chapter in the discussion of generalizability. People who are in search of a setting or a subject for a case study often feel in a quandary about whether to look for a so-called "typical" situation (one that is similar to most others of the type) or an "unusual" one (clearly an exceptional case). Let us say that you decide to study an urban third-grade class. Should you attempt to find out beforehand what the average size of third-grade classes in U.S. cities is, the average years of experience third-grade teachers have, and the typical racial and ethnic composition of third-grade classes, and then choose your class on those bases? Or should you pick a class in which the teacher is trying a new reading program or a new grouping arrangement, or perhaps select the only class in the city that has a child with Down syndrome? Should you choose a teacher with a reputation for excellence or one who seems to be having problems?

All the characteristics we have already mentioned that might be associated with the third grade suggest that it is difficult to pick a third-grade class that you could say is typical. Even so, some people will try to pick a setting that is not so demonstratively different to forestall the possible charge that it is an oddball case. Researchers who choose to go the "typical case" route are concerned about generalizability as it is traditionally defined. They want to learn something about third-grade classes in general through studying one class. As we have suggested, they are likely to be challenged in making such decisions and, therefore, either do not make them or leave it up to the readers to come to their own conclusions concerning generalizability. Some researchers lay claim to generalizability on the basis of the similarity of their case study to others reported in the literature.

Purposely choosing the unusual or just falling into a study leaves the question of generalizability up in the air. Where does the setting fit in the spectrum of human events? This question is not answered by the selection itself, but has to be explored as part of the study. The researcher has to determine what it is he or she is studying; that is, of what is this a case? Most qualitative researchers are skeptical of conventionally defined categories anyway and do not assume that things called by the same name or having the same superficial characteristics are necessarily similar. They feel that the researcher should examine assumptions about what belongs in categories rather than having these assumptions determine the research design. As we said at the start of this chapter, some decisions are not good or bad in themselves; they are just a matter of choice. The "typical" or "unusual" decision is probably one of those kinds of decisions.

We have discussed the general approach researchers take in case-study design, but we have not discussed internal sampling. By *internal sampling* we mean the decisions you make once you have a general idea of what you are studying, with whom to talk, what time of day to observe, and the number and type of documents to review. We will discuss sampling at greater length in other chapters. Narrowing the focus of your study will, in many cases, make it possible to examine the entire population of interest; that is, you will talk to everyone in the group, all the people in the setting, or review all the documents present. If you cannot see everything and talk to everybody, you want to make sure that you sample widely enough so that a diversity of types are explored. You want to understand the range of materials and the range of perspectives present. You also make choices, however, on the basis of the quality of the data produced. As we discuss in Chapter 4, some subjects are more willing to talk, have a greater experience in the setting, or are especially insightful about what goes on. These people become key informants and often you will talk with them, compared to other subjects, a disproportionate amount of time. There are dangers in relying exclusively on a small number of subjects, but you should not approach internal sampling with the idea that you have to spend the same amount of time with everyone. Similarly, with documents and other material, some pieces of data are simply richer and deserve more attention.

In regard to time sampling, the time you visit a place or person often will affect the nature of the data you collect. Schools are different at the start of the year than at the end. Similarly, the morning routine in the class can be quite different from the afternoon. Documents collected at one historical time are different from those collected at another. What time periods the data represent will depend on the time constraints the researcher faces as well as his or her research interests. If the focus is a particular class, you may want to sample widely from different times of the day, week, and year. If you decide to study a playground before the school day begins, the sampling concerns differ.

Like most decisions qualitative researchers must make, those relating to choice of informants and allocation of time are always made in the context of the study. These choices must make sense for your purposes in your particular situation. They logically flow both from the premises of the qualitative approach and from the contingencies of the study as these become apparent in the course of the work. Often the researcher steps back to ask, "If I do it this way, what am I missing? What am I gaining?" The more aware you are about the ramifications of the choices, the better chances you have to choose wisely.

Another design issue involves the amount of time you should set aside for a case study. In many instances you know how much time you have or want to devote to the study and you design the study with those limits in mind. You narrow the study, trying to get a piece that you can manage to complete in the time you have set aside. You may, for example, say that you want to complete data collection in four months and set aside two days a week to devote to the work. As is most often the case, after collecting data for a while you get a sense that you underestimated the time you need. You adjust for the mistake by either increasing the amount of time per week you work on it, extending your time line, or narrowing your focus more.

Some people start studies by devoting a certain amount of time per week to them and leaving the question of how long they will take up in the air. In this approach (and to some extent, in adjusting schedules for studies where the time limit is predetermined), qualitative researchers gauge when they are finished by what they term *data saturation,* the point of data collection where the information you get becomes redundant. Of course, you always learn more by staying in the study, but eventually you reach a point of diminishing returns. It is the period where you learn a decreasing amount for the time you spend. The trick is to find that point and bow out. Of course, if you do not have a clearly defined goal you can go on and on, switching your focus and collecting data more or less randomly. One difficulty in case studies is that the subject matter continually changes. When something new happens in the setting that is of interest, the temptation rises to redefine the goals and to continue the study. Be flexible, but to do analysis and to complete the study, you have to define a finishing point. You should realize that most researchers collect too much data. They have more data than they can ever analyze. The data for a typical dissertation study usually runs 700 to 1,500 pages of fieldnotes or interview transcripts.

We have provided a general overview to the case-study approach. Great diversity exists within the types of case studies we have discussed. One important distinction has to do with whether the researcher is interested in substantive or theoretical conclusions. A more substantively focused study on a classroom, for example, would be one that attempted to understand the dynamics of classroom behavior and the relationship between teacher and pupils. You also could use the classroom, however, to study more basic social processes such as the negotiation of order between the various parties. In the first case, you are using qualitative research to tell you something about schools; in the latter, the classroom provides a place to conduct research to generate theory about human relationships in general. That the research setting is a classroom is of primary importance in the first instance and is relatively unimportant in the second.

Most people think all case studies are descriptive. Although they tend to be descriptive, there are a variety of goals and forms they can take—the theoretical and abstract, as well as the very concrete (Stake, 1994). (For examples of case studies, see Becker, Geer, Hughes, & Strauss, 1961; Eckert, 1989; Peshkin, 1986; Oyler, 1996; Finders, 1997; Chang, 1992; Quint, 1994; Raissiguier, 1993).

Multi-Case Studies

When researchers study two or more subjects, settings, or depositories of data they are usually doing what we call *multi-case studies.* Multi-case studies take a variety of forms. Some start as a single case only to have the original work serve as the first in a series of studies or as the pilot for a multi-case study. Other studies are primarily single-case studies but include less intense, less extensive observations at other sites for the purpose of addressing the question of generalizability. Other researchers do comparative case studies. Two or more case studies are done and then compared and contrasted (see, for example, Lareau, 1989; Research for Action, 1996; Wells, 1996; Lightfoot, 1978; McIntyre, 1969). Multi-case studies follow most of the suggestions already made. If you are conducting additional data collection to show generalizability or diversity, your concern should be picking additional sites that will illustrate the range of settings or subjects to which your original observations might be applicable. If you are doing a second case study to compare and contrast, you pick a second site on the basis of the extent and presence or absence of some particular characteristic of the original study. If integration is your focus, for example, you may want to examine an urban, racially balanced third-grade class if you studied a suburban third grade where the number of traditionally under-represented students was minimal.

When they do multi-case studies, most qualitative researchers do not do fieldwork at more than one site at a time. They do their fieldwork for one case and then move to the next. Occasionally they may return to earlier sites to collect additional data, but the field work is not carried out simultaneously. The reason for this is mainly that doing more than one site at a time can get confusing. There are too many names to remember, too much diverse data to manage. After you finish your first case, you will find that in multi-case studies subsequent cases are easier; they take less time than the first. Not only have you improved your technique, but also the first case study will have provided a focus to define the parameters of the others.

Multi-Site Studies

There are research designs used in qualitative research that call for multiple site and subject studies that are considerably different than the ones we have discussed so far. They employ a different logic than the multi-case–study approach because they are oriented more toward developing theory (Corbin & Strauss, 1990; Strauss & Corbin, 1990) and they usually require many sites or subjects rather than two or three. Those who do them must have both experience in thinking theoretically as well as some skills in data collection prior to embarking on the studies. This type of research project is difficult to accomplish for a first undertaking. We provide a brief description of two of these approaches, however, not only to give you some idea if you do want to attempt them, but also to make you familiar with the range of designs that comprise qualitative research. While you may not want to conduct a complete study using these models, many elements of these designs can be incorporated into case studies.

Modified Analytic Induction

Analytic induction is an approach to collecting and analyzing data as well as a way to develop and test a theory. It has had a long and controversial history (Becker, 1963; Denzin, 1978; McCall & Simmons, 1969; Robinson, 1951; Turner, 1953); however, the version of the approach we present here differs somewhat from the way early practitioners employed it (Cressey, 1950; Lindesmith, 1947; Znaniecki, 1934). The procedure of analytic induction is employed when some specific problem, question, or issue becomes the focus of research. Data are collected and analyzed to develop a descriptive model that encompasses all cases of the phenomena. The procedure has been used extensively in open-ended interviewing, but it can be used with participant observation and documented analysis as well.

To be concrete, we will illustrate the procedure with a hypothetical study. Jonah Glenn is interested in teacher effectiveness. He thinks that some teachers do a better job at teaching than others and is interested in understanding why (Blase, 1980). That is his general topic and focus. He starts his study with an in-depth interview of one teacher whom someone has recommended as particularly "effective." He has a long, open-ended, tape-recorded discussion with the teacher. He encourages her to talk about her career, her thoughts about teaching and how they have changed over time, and about the question of effectiveness.

During the interview, the teacher describes in detail her disillusionment during her first few weeks of teaching, when her optimism (concerning what she thought she could accomplish, her plans about how she would conduct herself, and the nature of her relationship with students) confronted "the reality" of her new job. A teacher for twenty years, she describes a variety of issues: the ups and downs of her career, the changing definitions about her role, some of her first teaching experiences, the relationship of her work to her personal life, and what a good teacher is all about for her. In addition, she discusses schools she has taught in and how particular aspects of them contributed to her satisfaction, as well as to her performance in class. She describes her current position and evaluates it in relation to her perceived effectiveness. As a supplement to the interview, Jonah visits the teacher's school and observes her in action.

From that initial interview and observation, Jonah Glenn develops a loose descriptive theory of teacher effectiveness. It consists of a career-stage model in which effectiveness is defined differently at various periods in the teacher's career. The problems faced and decisions made about how to meet them are included in the theory. It also integrates the teacher's personal life with her professional life to explain effectiveness. Particular aspects of schools and the teacher's relationships with others also are included. The theory consists of prepositional statements and a diagram of career and career contingencies as they relate to effectiveness. In addition, his formulation defines effectiveness and explains its dimensions. After Jonah has sketched out his theory, he picks a second teacher to interview. In picking the first few teachers, Jonah used the *snowball sampling technique;* that is, he asked the first person he interviewed to recommend others. He interviewed the second in a similar open-ended manner, withholding the theory he developed on the basis of his first interview.

After the second interview, Jonah rewrites and modifies the theory to fit the new case. He continues choosing and interviewing new people, modifying the theory to fit each new case. After a few interviews, Jonah chooses subjects he hopes will provide examples of negative cases, teachers who he thinks will not fit the evolving model. The first few interviews, for example, were all done with teachers born and raised in the city in which they were working. He suspects that mobile teachers have different career patterns and define effectiveness differently. Jonah purposely seeks out mobile teachers to test his theory. He proceeds in this manner, picking new subjects, enlarging the theory, until he no longer comes across any case that does not fit the theory. At the conclusion of the study, he has a theory about effective teachers.

Often theories developed in this manner include some statements that describe all the teachers interviewed and other statements that apply only to certain "types" of teachers. The "types" emerge as part of the theory you develop. Thus the theory contains a typology of teachers and shows how the types differ from each other in regard to careers, perspectives, and ideas about effectiveness.

The hypothetical study just presented would probably not go exactly the way we described it. Often you start out with a question and conduct an interview only to learn that the way you have been thinking about the topic does not match the data you are getting. Teachers may not, for example, think in terms of effectiveness. Typically, the first few interviews result in the formulation of the questions or the problem rather than in specific propositional statements. In addition, although the strategy of the design is to conduct interviews until you find no cases that your theory does not fit, this task is too large for most researchers to accomplish in the time they have. Thus some researchers limit their study by tightly defining the population the theory is encompassing. You could decide, for example, to interview teachers in only one school. The theory you develop then would be a theory of teacher effectiveness for the teachers in that school. Similarly, some researchers, prior to the study, decide on the number of subjects they know they will have the time and resources to interview. They develop a theory based on that number, making no claim for the inclusiveness of their work.

Not only is the theory modified during the research process to fit all new facts that arise, but the research question also can be redefined (narrowed) to exclude the cases that defy explanation by it. By choosing what categories to include or exclude, you also control the breadth of the work by limiting the theory's scope.

The type of design we are discussing does not allow you to say anything about distribution frequency of the particular types included in your theory. You might find, for example, that to understand teacher effectiveness it is important to think in terms of the effectiveness of beginning teachers, mid-career teachers, and near-retirement teachers. This research procedure ensures that a variety of types of subjects are included, but it does not tell you how many or in what proportion the types appear in the population. The method of sampling in analytic induction is *purposeful sampling.* You choose particular subjects to include because they are believed to facilitate the expansion of the developing theory. This is not *random sampling,* that is, sampling to ensure that the characteristics of the subjects in your study appear in the same proportion they appear in the total population.

Robinson (1951) summarized this modified version of analytic induction as follows:

1. Early in the research you develop a rough definition and explanation of the particular phenomenon.
2. You hold the definition and explanation up to the data as they are collected.
3. You modify the definition and/or explanation as you encounter new cases that do not fit the definition and explanation as formulated.
4. You actively seek cases that you think may not fit into the formulation.
5. You redefine the phenomenon and reformulate the explanation until a universal relationship is established, using each negative case to call for a redefinition or reformulation.

The design does not follow the funnel model we presented earlier. The analysis indeed becomes more encompassing as new cases are presented, although the developing theory usually becomes more refined.

The steps just outlined represent a method of thinking about and working with data. Most qualitative studies borrow parts of the general procedure and employ it more casually. The term *working hypothesis* is sometimes used by participant observers, and some of the procedures of analytic induction are closely aligned to that.

The Constant Comparative Method

As we have suggested, designs of all qualitative studies involve the combination of data collection with analysis. This is clear in the modified version of analytic induction we presented. Analysis and data collection occurred in a pulsating fashion—first the interview, then the analysis and theory development, another interview, and then more analysis, and so on—until the research was completed. In most forms of case studies, the emerging themes guide data collection, but formal analysis and theory development do not occur until after the data collection is near completion. The *constant comparative method* (Glaser & Strauss, 1967; Strauss, 1987; Strauss & Corbin, 1994) is a research design for multi-data sources, which is like analytic induction in that the formal analysis begins early in the study and is nearly completed by the end of data collection. As you will see in our discussion, the constant comparative method differs from analytic induction in a number of respects.

We start with a hypothetical and somewhat simplified example of how an educational researcher might proceed using this complicated approach. Mary Schriver is about to arrive at an elementary school to begin a rather lengthy study using the constant comparative method. While she has no investment in any specific topic, she is interested in teachers, so she decides (and has received permission) to observe in the teachers' lounge. Her plan is to start there and see what emerges. The first day on the site is awkward, but in spite of all the self-conscious introductions and explanations of what she is doing there, she does have a chance to hear many conversations teachers have with each other. She is struck immediately by how much of the talk that goes on is about other people: Teachers talk about students, other teachers, and administrators. The tone of the talk varies from humor to anger, and some of the conversations halt when certain people enter the room. The next day, Ms. Schriver returns to the same room and hears more of the same kinds of conversation. She decides to study this talk and tentatively labels it "gossip." From then on, Mary concentrates her data-collecting activities on incidents of gossip. She tries to get material on the diversity of kinds and types. Although the teachers' lounge is central to her activities, as she gets to know the teachers she leaves the room with them to collect data in other places, both in and out of school. She learns of special places, less conspicuous than the teachers' lounge, where particular teachers meet and talk together. She listens to those conversations.

She begins to examine how people talk about each other only to discover that "gossip" is only one type of a larger category she has come to call "people talk." As she works, her data suggest to her a number of areas for exploration. They include: the members of the school staff who engage in people talk; the content of people talk, for instance, the persons discussed; the levels of intensity of people talk; and the behavior that stems from people talk. As she collects data on these different issues, she begins to delineate other types of people talk besides gossip. She begins to see, for example, that certain types of people talk only occur between teachers who define themselves as "close." She labels this "friendship people talk." Other types of people talk occur in mixed groups—"mixed group people talk."

She notes the wide variety of subjects of people talk: the central office staff, the principal, teachers in friendship groups, teachers not in groups, students who are high achievers, and students who are low achievers. Some of the people talk she notices is "bad news" people talk and some is "good news" people talk.

Mary examines the data, coding and reworking it in an attempt to see the connections between who talks and what is talked about, in order to understand the dimensions of people talk. All through this work she writes about what she discovers and attempts to expand her category by drawing models and writing about it. A theory of people talk is developing, but it is limited to the one setting. While she has stayed in one school, Mary has located herself in different places in the school and has talked with different groups to enlarge the number of incidents observed and to get at new properties and dimensions of the general category people talk.

As part of Mary's emerging theory she also begins to see that who talks to whom and what is said in regard to people talk relates to ongoing patterns of friendship as well as formal hierarchy in the whole school district. After observing in the original school she goes to another, purposely picking one that has recently opened in the same district. The idea behind her choice is that friendship patterns in this new school may differ, providing a good setting to enlarge the emerging theory of people talk. Similarly, Mary then chooses an open-space private school, which prides itself in its participatory decision-making structure, as a likely place to collect more incidents of teacher talk to enlarge the theory.

In each of the new sites she chooses, she limits her data collection to incidents related to people talk, trying to develop new dimensions of the category and working to integrate the new dimensions into the emerging theory, thus enlarging it. Up to this point she has regularly been writing about the data she collects with a mind to working out aspects of the theory of people talk.

We leave Mary here, but if we continued with her on her research journey we would see her pick new sites to broaden her theory while integrating the new material back into the developing theory. She may go on doing this for as many as forty sites. The decision to stop would be based on her assessing that she has exhausted the dimensions of the categories—the point of "theoretical saturation"—and has developed a theory of people talk in schools. (She could go on to enlarge her category and develop a theory of people talk in general.)

Glaser (1978) recounts the steps in the constant comparative method of developing theory as follows:

1. Begin collecting data.
2. Look for key issues, recurrent events, or activities in the data that become categories of focus.
3. Collect data that provide many incidents of the categories of focus, with an eye to seeing the diversity of the dimensions under the categories.
4. Write about the categories you are exploring, attempting to describe and account for all the incidents you have in your data while continually searching for new incidents.
5. Work with the data and emerging model to discover basic social processes and relationships.
6. Engage in sampling, coding, and writing as the analysis focuses on the core categories.

As Glaser notes, although you can talk about the constant comparative method as a series of steps, what has just been described goes on all at once, and the analysis keeps doubling back to more data collection and coding.

The procedure we described is complex and requires an ability to think analytically (categories and their properties are difficult to grasp), but it is an important way of controlling the scope of data collecting and making multiple-site studies theoretically relevant. The constant comparative method, although it may rely on descriptive data to present the theory, transcends the purposes of descriptive case studies. Although those who formulated the constant comparative method (Glaser & Strauss, 1967) suggest their approach is applicable to any kind of data, it is most often used in conjunction with multiple-site, participant observation studies.

Additional Issues Related to Design

Proposal Writing

Prior to conducting research, people are often asked to write a formal statement about what they will study, what they will actually do, and a justification of its importance. These are called *proposals*. Students write them for their professors or for dissertation committees; researchers write them to potential funders (Morse, 1994). As you might guess, those who choose a qualitative research design sometimes have a difficult time describing what they are going to do prior to conducting their research (see Locke et al., 1987; Dobbert, 1982; Krathwohl, 1988, p. 135). This often creates problems, especially when those who want to see the proposal are not familiar with the evolving nature of the qualitative design (Burgess, 1984, pp. 34–35).

Proposals for qualitative studies are usually shorter than those for quantitative research. Because you do not know exactly what you will do, a detailed discussion of methods is not feasible. The long review of the literature is often absent as well. You are not sure exactly what literature will be relevant at the beginning stages of a study, since the literature depends on the themes you discuss. (Some experienced qualitative researchers counsel neophytes not to review substantive literature prior to collecting data even if they are sure which literature is relevant. Reviewing the literature might be too influential in determining themes and focus and thus curtail inductive analysis—an important advantage of the qualitative approach. Others encourage students to explore research they think might be relevant early on so they can direct their research to unexplored or contentious areas. We will return to this issue in the chapter on analysis.)

Qualitative proposals are handled in two ways. The first, the approach we prefer, is to do some fieldwork prior to writing the proposal. Anselm Strauss (1987), speaking of qualitative research proposals, decisively states: "No proposal should be written without preliminary data collection and analysis" (p. 286). After spending some time in the field, you are in a much better position to discuss what your plans are and what might be in your data. You can discuss design and emerging themes in more detail. Of course, you will not be sure of the outcome of the study or exactly how you will proceed with the rest of the study, but you are in a better position to make educated guesses. In addition, the discussion you engage in can be much more concrete and therefore much more likely to satisfy the curiosity of the proposal readers (Strauss, 1987).

This pre-proposal data-collecting approach we champion often conflicts with the long tradition of how dissertation research is done in some university departments. In fact, we have met professors who are incredulous at such a suggestion. Some departments even require the research methods and the review of the literature chapters of a dissertation to be completed before the doctoral student approaches a subject. Of course professors and departments that have such requirements think they are upholding high standards and helping students complete their dissertations in a timely and structured way. Such rules need to be changed because they are detrimental to doing good qualitative research and they ask students to compromise the logic of the research approach they have chosen.

A second choice is to write a proposal without preliminary observations or interviews. Such a proposal is necessarily highly speculative; at best it is a rough guess about how you are going to proceed and what the issues to examine might be. This type of proposal is more of an exercise to show those who read it that you are conversant with the qualitative research literature and are imaginative in your thinking about the issues than an actual concrete description of what you will do. These proposals can provide an opportunity for you to review the theory and methods literature, but are often not very helpful in conceptualizing the study. People who are not familiar with the qualitative approach often criticize such proposals as being too vague and not stating research questions or hypotheses clearly enough. On the other hand, there is a danger that in order to fill the pages with something, you will do more written speculation and armchair theorizing than is healthy. Not only can this be a waste of time, but it can be detrimental to the research project. Theorizing and speculating can frame what you are doing too rigidly, erecting barriers to discovery. This kind of frame can act as a hypothesis to which you become prematurely committed.

It is important that those who read your proposal, be they professors on your thesis committee, or reviewers for funding agencies, know about qualitative design. It is difficult to please them if they are not familiar with the dilemmas involved in writing such a proposal. In an attempt to educate reviewers, some writers of qualitative research proposals explain in the introduction to the text what stage they are in their research and why the proposal is written the way it is. They also refer readers who are not familiar with the qualitative approach to informative literature. While novices might be reluctant to be assertive about such touchy matters, some reviewers appreciate the coaching.

Proposals for qualitative studies differ significantly from each other, but there are commonalities. There are specific questions all good proposals address. The answers to the questions vary in length and the detail in which they are discussed. They are not always answered in the order we present them here.

1. What are you going to do?
2. How are you going to do it?
3. Why are you doing it?
4. How does what you are going to do relate to what others have done?
5. What are the ethical issues involved in your study, and how will you handle them?
6. What is the potential contribution (to basic research and/or practice) of your work?

A list of references consulted in doing the proposal is also included. In addition to these questions, people who have done preliminary data collection prior to writing the proposal address the following:

1. What have you done already?
2. What themes, concerns, or topics have emerged in your preliminary work? What analytic questions are you pursuing?

It is common for researchers who have done preliminary data collection to provide a tentative outline of the monograph they will produce.

In answering the first two questions, "What are you going to do?" and "How are you going to do it?," you should include information about where you are going to do your study, who your subjects will be, how you will decide what subjects to include, how much time you expect to spend doing which activities (interviewing, participant observation), what other data you will include, and how will you do the analysis. You also address what particular problems you might face in carrying out your study and how you will overcome them.

Proposals also often contain broad research questions, that is, questions that help frame the focus of your study. Research questions are not interview questions. They are not, in other words, the questions you would put to informants to discover their perspectives. Rather, they are open-ended questions that attempt to portray some of the terrain you will explore.

The proposal is not the blue print for what you will do. Rather it points you in the direction you will travel. While one knows the general outline of what is likely to happen, the particulars are vague. We begin inquiry with questions like, "What is the meaning of teachers' work to teachers?" (Biklen, 1985), and know that we will refine the question as we know more about how the teachers we study think. We know neither how it will eventually be framed nor which specifics will emerge. The chapters that follow will provide information that will help you understand this process and how to proceed.

Those involved in reviewing qualitative proposals must understand that these proposals are not fixed contracts from which the researcher cannot deviate. Qualitative proposals are much looser than quantitative proposals; they are educated speculations about the form the research is taking and the direction the study is likely to go. The openness of the qualitative proposal provides for researcher flexibility, but it also involves risk. Neither you nor the people that accept your proposal have a clear picture of the particulars or the final product. Whether the end product will meet the standards of a competent piece of work depends much more on how the study is executed and the conceptual and writing skills of the researcher than on the specifics of the research plan. It is no wonder that reviewers of qualitative proposals tend to rely heavily on the authors' past accomplishments in judging the likelihood of success of the proposed project. This leads some proposal writers to discuss their prior training, experience, and other preparation in qualitative research and relate that to the task under consideration.

Interview Schedules and Observer Guides

We have discussed research design as an evolving process, one in which the questions to be asked and the data to be collected emerge in the process of doing research. There are times, however, when researchers enter the field with an interview schedule or an observational guide (Schneider & Conrad, 1980). In keeping with the qualitative tradition of attempting to capture the subjects' own words and letting the analysis emerge, interview schedules and observation guides generally allow for open-ended responses and are flexible enough for the observer to note and collect data on unexpected dimensions of the topic.

Schedules and guides are most commonly used in multi-subject studies and multi-site team research work, that is, in participant observation studies where a number of researchers are working at different sites. Schedules and guides are used primarily to gather comparable data across sites. If in each site or with each subject similar data are collected, you can make some statements concerning the distribution of facts that you gather. While this is important in certain studies, concern with following a schedule rather than with understanding the data can undermine the major strength of the qualitative approach. Qualitative studies that report how many people do this and how many people do that, rather than generating concepts and understanding, are not highly regarded by qualitative researchers. More accurately, they are a poor use of qualitative resources when such data can be collected more easily and cheaply using other methods.

Team Research and the Lone Ranger

The great majority of qualitative research has been what is termed *Lone Ranger research;* that is, the researcher single-handedly faces the empirical world, going off alone to return with the results. More and more qualitative research, however, is undertaken in teams. Some classic qualitative educational research studies, in fact, were accomplished with teams. *Boys in White* (Becker et al., 1961) and *Making the Grade* (Becker et al., 1968), the first, a study of medical students, the second, a study of university undergraduates, used three and four researchers to collect the data. Unless you become part of a funded study, you are more likely to do a study alone, but you should know that team research can be satisfying and productive. As with every team effort, it is important to be linked to people with whom you feel comfortable—people who work as hard as you and who share your values and your understanding of the division of labor in decision making. (For further discussion of team research see Chapter 7.)

Qualitative Research and Historical Research

What is the relationship between historical research and qualitative research? As you can see from the discussion so far, in some studies qualitative researchers use the same source material (data) as historians. In most studies such materials are just part of the information base and often supplement participant observation and interviewing data. But in others, qualitative researchers rely almost exclusively on historical material. They use the logic and techniques from the qualitative tradition to do their work. When Ron Casella studied the history of educational travel as a part of his dissertation research, he described himself as studying historical materials from a symbolic interactionist perspective (Casella, 1997). These researchers emphasize meaning and process and are inductive in their approach. Should they be considered historians? Although there are many different approaches to doing history, there are historians who concentrate on meaning and use inductive thinking in their work. They are not trained as qualitative researchers but think like them. Should these historians be considered qualitative researchers?

In some ways it is a matter of semantics and in others it is a matter of academic politics and convention. People trained as qualitative researchers using historical material usually identify as qualitative researchers. Similarly people trained as historians embrace that discipline. Some people who use historical material but were trained in another discipline call what they do "interdisciplinary." But this suggests that they are merely combining two or more disciplines. Some prefer to think of what they are doing as "transdisciplinary." They are not combining two or more sets of disciplinary techniques and conventions; they have different concerns, they write for different audiences and they produce a new form of scholarship (Biklen, 1995; Bogdan, 1988).

Concluding Remarks

Our discussion of design does not provide precise instructions or a formula to plan your work from beginning to end. We have given some suggestions and presented some of the ways qualitative researchers think about design issues. The next chapter, concerned with fieldwork, should further help you incorporate the qualitative way of thinking about research into practice.

Chapter 3

Fieldwork

Fieldwork sounds earthy. It is the way most qualitative researchers collect data. They go to where the people they will study—their subjects or informants—are and spend time with them in their territory—in their schools, their playgrounds, their hangouts, and their homes. These are the places where subjects do what they normally do, and it is these natural settings that the researcher wants to study. As time is spent with subjects, the relationship becomes less formal. The researcher's goal is to increase the subjects' level of comfort, encouraging them to talk about what they normally talk about and, eventually, to confide in the researcher. Researchers build trust by making it clear that they will not use what they are finding to demean or otherwise hurt people.

In one way researchers join the subjects' world, but in another way they remain detached. They unobtrusively keep a written record of what happens as well as collect other forms of descriptive data. They attempt to learn from the subjects, but don't necessarily emulate the subjects. They may participate in their activities, but on a more limited basis, and they do not compete for prestige or status. They learn how the subjects think, but they do not think like the subjects. They are empathetic, but also reflective.

Fieldwork refers to being out in the subjects' world, in the way we have described—not as a person who pauses while passing by, but as a person who has come for a visit; not as a person who knows everything, but as a person who has come to learn; not as a person who wants to be like them, but as a person who wants to know what it is like to be them. You work toward winning their acceptance, not as an end, but because it allows you to pursue your research goals (Geertz, 1979, p. 241).

Some will charge us with distortion for romanticizing the relationships qualitative researchers have with their subjects (see Douglas, 1976; Johnson, 1975). It might be said that the relationship captured by fieldwork holds best for participant observation and, even there, the ideal as we have described it is never reached. Further, it could be charged that in other forms of qualitative research (interviewing and document analysis, for example) the term *fieldwork* does not apply. There is truth in these charges, but it is important to understand how the idea of fieldwork relations sets the tone for most qualitative research.

To achieve quality fieldwork is the goal in establishing relations, whether the research method be participant observation, interviewing, or searching documents. In interviews, the researcher often makes repeated visits to his or her subjects, sometimes interviewing them for many hours in their own homes or other places they normally spend their time. In addition, researchers doing interview studies often supplement this form of data collecting with observations of subjects in their natural setting. Even with less extensive interviewing, the emphasis is on equality, closeness, and informality in the relationship rather than on authority and control by the researcher and formality in the encounter. Even when working with case records and archival material, the researcher, where feasible, develops a fieldwork relationship with the keepers of the material and those that produced them. This relationship maximizes access and brings the keepers and producers of the records into the study, too. They can lead you to an understanding of the context in which the materials you are studying were produced. As we will discuss in Chapter 4, most qualitative studies involve more than one data-gathering technique. Rarely does one do a qualitative study that does not involve fieldwork.

In this chapter we discuss fieldwork. Our focus is on how you, as a researcher, should conduct yourself—from gaining access to leaving the field—and the issues involved in maintaining and establishing rapport.

Gaining Access

The first problem to face in fieldwork is getting permission to conduct your study. Some circumvent this problem by doing covert research, the collection of data without their subjects' knowledge. They might, for example, get jobs at a school or enroll as students without announcing to the school what they are doing. Although some excellent research has been conducted undercover (e.g., McPherson, 1972), our advice to the novice is use the overt approach. (With the requirement that research proposals must be approved by institutional review boards, it is doubtful that research using a covert approach would be permitted.) Make your interests known and seek the cooperation of those you will study. Under most circumstances, if permission is well negotiated, doing research openly provides the advantage of release from the duties of being a regular participant and, therefore, the freedom to come and go as you wish. It is difficult to conduct research, for example, if you have to be the teacher to thirty-two third-graders. The overt role also gives you greater access to the range of people in the setting. The teacher's role may not put you in a good position to interview a principal concerning his or her candid views of, say, corporal punishment or the merits of IQ testing. Lastly, and most important for some, lying is not only awkward, but offensive. A related point is that getting caught in misrepresentation is not only embarrassing, but devastating to rapport.

The position we have just taken in regard to covert research, as well as the style of research we present in our discussion on fieldwork, is not embraced by all those who do qualitative research. It is probably the most widely used approach and, although there is no name for it, might be termed the *cooperative style*. Some have critiqued this approach and called for researchers to be more confrontational and deceptive (Douglas, 1976; Garfinkel, 1967; Adler & Adler, 1987). Other researchers, such as feminist methodologists, have advocated for a less hierarchical relationship between interviewer and informant, and sometimes, shared decision making and authorship (Reinharz, 1992). The cooperative style has its origins in anthropology as well as the Chicago School of sociology tradition of conducting fieldwork. (See Geertz, 1979, pp. 225–243, for a discussion of the limitations.) At times even people working in these traditions have used a covert approach, but usually only under circumstances in which the overt approach was not feasible. Ethnomethodologists, on the other hand, have a history of using the confrontational approach, believing that by disturbing people's everyday world they can reveal what we take for granted.

You have decided on the study you would like to do. How do you get permission? There are a number of ways to proceed (Burgess, 1984, pp. 38–50). Which one you choose depends on who you are, what you want to study, and what you hope to accomplish. But, for purposes of illustration, let us assume you are interested in doing a participant observation study in a local elementary school. (The general logic and approach we explain here applies to all kinds of bureaucratic organizations, not just schools.) No two school systems are organized exactly the same. Most have specific procedures to follow in giving approval to researchers. In negotiating entry, the first step is to find out something about the hierarchy and rules of the particular school system. Ask people—a professor, a friend, or someone else who knows the system—for advice on how to proceed. Consult a few people, if they are available. You might even try calling the secretary at the intended school. Do not say that you are calling to ask for permission to do research; limit your set of questions to how you would go about getting permission if you decided on this step. Use your imagination to come up with leads.

In making these preliminary inquiries, you are interested in getting knowledge not only of the formal system, but also of the informal system. You are looking for tips, like the name of someone in the system who is particularly receptive and helpful. If you get such advice, and it seems reasonable, call or visit the person to discuss what you are thinking about and to hear what the individual has to say.

You may be sent to the school principal; often principals have an important say in these matters. Although not the ultimate authority, their influence is felt in a variety of ways. If there are some forms to be filled out for a district committee that approves all research, the principal's support carries a great deal of weight. He or she is often the key gatekeeper. The principal usually will not go to bat for you unless he or she knows that the teachers involved are supportive. Meeting and talking with teachers and others you plan to involve in the study may be a necessary step in getting approval. If you know you want to study a particular teacher's class, for example, seeing the teacher and getting an endorsement for your project before you see the principal is advantageous. Only in large, funded research projects do researchers start at levels higher than the building principal. Permission is almost never granted at the central office level without consulting down the hierarchy.

Even if permission is granted from up high without first checking with those below, it behooves you to meet those lower on the hierarchy to seek their support. Your arrival on the scene with a research permission slip from the central office is likely to ruffle feathers, unless you do the necessary work first to court your potential subjects. While you may get official permission, your study may be sabotaged by the subjects. Getting permission to conduct the study involves more than getting an official blessing. It involves laying the groundwork for good rapport with those with whom you will be spending time, so they will accept you and what you are doing. Helping them to feel that they had a hand in allowing you in will help your research.

Qualitative researchers are in a somewhat unique position when negotiating entry in that many people are not familiar with the approach. For more than a few people, research means controlled experiments or survey research. This perception can cause problems in communicating with gatekeepers, but it also offers some advantages. When people are told, for example, that you plan to spend time on the premises in an unobtrusive way, that you are not going to require people to fill out forms, answer specific questions, or alter their normal routine, the response often is, "then you are not really doing formal research." The researcher is consequently given an opportunity to negotiate entry with a low profile. We mean that the people in the school—the teachers, the principal, and the other staff—do not treat what you are doing as research and therefore do not require you to follow official sanctioning procedures. They may just let you proceed or perhaps follow a less complicated entry procedure. You can almost slip into the setting. When seeking research approval, you can facilitate this kind of entry by offering a low-key explanation and not insisting on playing the researcher role.

Novice researchers are often students conducting their first qualitative project as a requirement for a course. After hearing these students' explanations of their assignments, school personnel often treat the request as they would any request for a student placement. If you manage to get in this way, fine—fine, that is, if what is expected of you is not stifling. You should avoid taking on specific responsibilities such as tutoring students or being put in a position where school personnel have a great deal of control over your time and mobility.

The informal method of gaining access raises the question of when and under what conditions would-be qualitative researchers should seek approval from institutional review boards (IRBs). (These are the committees we discussed in Chapter 1 that universities and other organizations have to review proposals in regard to protection of human subjects. They are also know as "human subjects committees.") There is not a uniform policy on this. Some IRBs do not want to review qualitative proposals from people who are learning to do observation and interviewing as part of a class. They see this work as a research simulation—pretend research—rather than a full-blown project. Similarly, they treat preliminary interviews and observations for a research project you might do in the future as pre-research activity. It is only when you get to the point that you begin collecting data that has a real chance of resulting in a thesis, dissertation, or a publication that they want to review the proposal. Other boards and committees have stricter interpretations of the regulations requiring everyone, no matter how preliminary, no matter that it is an exercise for an introductory research class, to file a request for approval. There is also disparity regarding which board should review your proposal, the one at the site you are studying, or the one at your university. Most universities insist on reviewing your proposal even if the other site does as well. *Check with your professor or the chair of the IRB at your institution for clarification on these matters.*

Most college students are not perceived as threatening by gatekeepers or potential subjects. They understand that professors require educational placements; anyway, they feel that it is a good idea for people to learn firsthand what the world is like. In short, they are usually receptive to students. It is a good idea to emphasize that you are a student and seek their sympathetic cooperation. Many students starting their careers as qualitative researchers have come back to school to receive advanced degrees after having established themselves in careers. Some have gained considerable success, having won awards and high positions. When you are trying to gain access it is a good idea to play down your status rather than flaunt it. People are often cautious and guarded around high status people. This does not mean you should lie. If you are asked directly about positions you have held and other aspects of your background you should share this information, but in as low-key a way as possible.

There are other ways to negotiate a low-profile entry. Some people use friends inside the system to slip them in. A low-profile entry is usually expedient, but, for some, it provides ethical dilemmas similar to those involved in doing covert research. They feel that if they do not emphasize that they are doing research, they will misrepresent themselves. We do not feel this way. If you do, you will have to use the more official approach to seek approval.

Going through the formal procedures that some bureaucratic systems require can be a long, frustrating process. Typically, there will be weeks, if not months, between initiating the request and gaining approval. Many school districts have committees to review proposals. The teachers' union may have to review it as well. Some districts have application forms. If the district is large, it will have an office in charge of research. The people there will give you suggestions on processing the application and also will help in other ways. At times, approval is a mere formality. We have had staff allow us to start research unofficially before receiving official sanction. Ask if there is any way to speed up the approval process. If you are going through the procedures, try to get an estimate of the time it will take and the likelihood that you will be approved before you start. Because getting permission can take time, it is smart to begin negotiating well in advance of your projected starting date.

While we have been talking about gaining access as if it was something that only occurred at the beginning of your study, throughout many studies permission will have to be sought and cooperation gained as you move out into new territories and meet new people. In explaining yourself at the start of the study and during its course, subjects will have questions, many of which will recur. Following is a list of common questions with suggestions about how to respond.

1. *What are you actually going to do?* A general rule to follow in answering all questions is to be honest. Do not lie, but do not be too specific or lengthy in your explanations. Novices are often amazed at how little people want to know. Do not use a lot of research jargon. You will scare or turn off people. You might want to start by saying something like: "What I want to do is something called participant observation. It would involve visiting your classroom a few times a week. I want to try to understand what it is like to be a teacher." If you are pushed to be more specific, try to be helpful, but explain that what you will do evolves as you proceed. In your explanation emphasize that you want to learn from them but do not be solicitous to the point of being patronizing.

2. *Will you be disruptive?* This is a common concern of school personnel. They fear that your presence will interfere with their routines and work. It is important to allay these fears. Share with them how it is important in this kind of research to be unobtrusive and non-interfering with what people normally do. Part of being successful is being non-disruptive. Assure them that you will not be making excessive demands and that you will attempt to be sensitive to their problems and requirements. Share with them your intention of fitting your schedule around theirs.

3. *What are you going to do with your findings?* Most people ask this question because they fear negative publicity or the political use of the information the researcher gathers. As we suggested in our discussion on ethics (Chapter 1), you should come to a decision about how you intend to use the material and share that with your subjects. If you have short-term interests, like writing a term paper, mention that fact and tell them who will read it. Tell them that you do not plan to use anyone's name and that you will disguise the location. If you have long-term interests, such as writing a dissertation, mention this possibility, but we suggest you hold off asking permission for that until you have established relationships at the site. Think of your early observations as a pilot study. After subjects have the chance to know you better, and after you have assessed the setting's possibilities for the large project, then renegotiate your position. If you are not sure what you will do with your findings, explain this and assure them you will discuss your plans with them after your work gets underway.

4. *Why us?* People often want an explanation of why they or their organizations were singled out for study. If you have heard positive comments about them that helped direct your choice, tell your subjects. Say, for example, "I was told that you had a lot of insights about teaching, and that is in part why I came to see you." "I'm looking for experienced teachers to talk with; that is why I approached you." "I heard that interesting things are happening here in the area of remedial reading."

Unless you have come to see a particular group whose reputation is exemplary, it is usually important that you communicate to people in the setting that you are not so concerned about the particular people in the study, or the particular organization where you may be collecting data. Rather, your interests center on the general topic of teachers, or education, or whatever specific aspect you are pursuing. You are not a reporter looking into Salem High. You are an educational researcher trying to study Salem High so that you can better understand education.

5. *What will we get out of this?* Many school personnel expect reciprocity. They figure that if they provide you access, they should get something in return. You should decide what it is you are prepared to give. Some want feedback about what you find, a report, or even a meeting with you after the work has been completed. Some people, of course, want nothing. Try not to promise too much. A meeting or a short general summary of what you find may be in order, but we advise against a lengthy report. If you are doing the project as a requirement for a course avoid committing yourself to sharing your term paper with your subjects. Promising your report may inhibit what you say and how you say it because it could make you tense worrying about who will read what you write.

When people find out that the research involves fieldnotes, they sometimes request to see them. Downplay the notes. Do not tell your subjects that you try to remember their every word. Never promise to show your fieldnotes to subjects. Knowing you are going to share the fieldnotes with your subjects restricts what you put in them.

Sometimes school personnel want you to provide services to the school in return for access. You might help out, but be sure that what you agree to do does not overly restrict your research.

Although much of what we have said about gaining access best fits participant observation studies, much of it can be applied to other types of qualitative studies as well. Gaining access to official educational documents often involves the procedures we have discussed here. In most interview studies, each respondent has to be asked to cooperate individually, but often your subjects will share some organizational affiliation. They may be teachers in a particular school or parents attached to a particular parents' group. When this is the case, you may have to seek permission from the organization as well. You can avoid going through the organization by approaching subjects as individuals (not as members of the organization). While this is often most expedient, at times organizational sanction becomes necessary. Lists of potential subjects with their addresses, for example, may lie in the hands of the administration. Organizational members will at times defer to the administration in deciding whether to participate. Staff of educational organizations are often paternalistic about their students. They are very reluctant to allow researchers to interview them, fearing the disapproval from the students or, in the case of youngsters, from their parents. Requesting permission from the school to interview students often results in a complicated set of procedures that includes getting the parents' written permission as well as going through the formal research-sanctioning channels. Many gatekeepers appreciate avoiding such problems. They prefer that the researcher deal with the student and parents as if they were not members of the particular school. Others become concerned when you go directly to the subjects and their guardians, feeling that it is their responsibility to protect their privacy. As with research design choices, at times there are no right answers or correct approaches.

In some forms of qualitative research the data you seek are, at first glance, open and available. For example, some historical societies not only allow researchers to look through their materials but provide special personnel and services to help. Even in these situations, some of what we have said about gaining access applies. It is important to understand the structure of the historical society and its personnel before going. In certain historical societies, for example, some workers are more helpful than others. There are particular collections of materials that archivists only make available to certain select visitors. Finding out how to become one of "the chosen few" is an important part of gaining access. In certain local historical organizations researchers from out of town are not welcomed without someone vouching for the sincerity of their interests as well as their character. In this case, gaining access requires a sponsor.

As you can see, negotiating permission is tricky. We offer three bits of advice.

1. *Be persistent.* Often the difference between the person who gets in and the person who strikes out is how long and how diligently he or she is in pursuit.
2. *Be flexible.* If your first idea of how to proceed seems ill-conceived, come up with a different plan or a new approach.
3. *Be creative.* Often gatekeepers appreciate a new idea. One researcher we know, in a manner that fits his personality, brought small gifts (single flowers, buttons) to subjects. Holiday greeting cards are not out of the question, and although they may not get you in, they may keep the door open.

First Days in the Field

You have gotten permission and you are ready to start at full speed. The first days in the field can be rough if you do not have a sense of humor and if you are not prepared to make mistakes. Rosalie Wax, a distinguished educational qualitative researcher in the anthropological tradition, has this to say about participant observation in general:

> The person who cannot abide feeling awkward or out of place, who feels crushed whenever he makes a mistake—embarrassing or otherwise—who is psychologically unable to endure being, and being treated like, a fool, not only for a day or week but for months on end, ought to think twice before he decides to become a participant observer (Wax, 1971, p. 370).

We think that this view is more representative of the novice's or the researcher's first days at a new site than of the lifelong experiences of the qualitative researcher. Becoming a qualitative researcher is like learning to perform any role in a society (teacher, parent, artist, college student). Not only do you have to learn the technical aspects of how to do it, but you have to feel that the role is authentic for you. During the first times out, novices have not had experiences to draw on and they feel uncomfortable with the label of "researcher." They are not sure that they want to be associated with that title or, in other cases, they do not know if they are worthy of such a lofty sounding label. In addition, they do not understand that feeling uncomfortable is part of doing this kind of work. Like any role, that of researcher grows more comfortable with practice. While it may be particularly difficult at first, being a researcher grows on you.

A researcher describing her first observation experience can give you a sense of how disconcerting the first days in the field can be. She had decided to observe a college extension course for engineers:

> I remember walking in there and seeing all those men. I sat down and everyone seemed to be talking at once. I felt so out of place. I panicked. Should I try to remember what everyone was saying, I said to myself? As soon as I started focusing on remembering I got more nervous. I gave that up and decided to just sit quietly and passively to see what happened.

This was not the end of her awkwardness. During the class, the instructor used a word with a double meaning, connoting the lewd and sexual. The men in the class smiled with him. The person sitting next to the researcher turned toward her to catch her reaction. As she put it, "I remember half smiling." At the end of the class the instructor introduced the observer and explained her research intentions to the class. Afterwards, she got up and said a few words; then the instructor turned, paused, and said reluctantly, "Well, I'll guess we'll get used to you." And they did. And she got used to them. While never "one of the boys," she developed sufficient rapport to carry out her study, which explored the similarities and differences between on-campus and off-campus university offerings.

Another researcher interested in studying the training of para-professionals in a medical laboratory tried to get a parking-lot ticket stamped by the secretary at the front desk. Upon handing in the ticket, the researcher was told by the secretary, "We don't stamp salesmen's tickets." The researcher replied, "I'm not a salesman. I'm a researcher and will be visiting here often." The secretary looked up and said, "We don't stamp researchers' either."

During the first few days in the field you begin to establish rapport, you "learn the ropes," you become comfortable and work at making the subjects feel comfortable with you. It is a time when you are confused—even overwhelmed—with all the new information. There is much to learn. The feeling of incompetence pervades. Subjects' comments, some like the ones just quoted, weigh heavily; they are taken as signs of rejection or even hostility. It is a time of paranoia.

Here are some suggestions to make your first days in the field less painful:

1. Do not take what happens in the field personally. What you are going through is a typical part of the fieldwork process.
2. Set up your first visit so someone is there to introduce you. One of the people who gave you permission can do it or can direct you to someone else. Ask someone to facilitate your entrance.
3. Do not try to accomplish too much the first few days. Ease yourself into the field. Make your first day a short visit (an hour or less); use it as a time to get a general introduction and overview. There are so many new faces and things to learn; go slow. You will have to take fieldnotes after completing each visit to the field. Taking in too much may mean that you will not have enough time to write it all down.
4. Remain relatively passive. Show interest and enthusiasm for what you are learning, but do not ask a lot of specific questions, especially in areas that may be controversial. Ask general questions that will provide your subjects an opportunity to talk.
5. Be friendly. As you are introduced to people, smile and be polite. Say "hello" as you pass people in the hall. The first days in the field, subjects will ask why you are there. Repeat what you told the gatekeepers, more or less, but try to use abbreviated explanations. Most of the suggestions on how to behave in the field parallel the norms governing nonoffensive behavior in general. In order to be a good researcher you have to know and practice those skills.

The first few days in the field represent the first stage of fieldwork. The feelings of awkwardness and not belonging that characterize this stage often end with some clear indication of acceptance from the subjects. An invitation to a social event or a request to participate in some activity usually reserved exclusively for participants are indicators. Being told that you were missed on a day you did not show up is another. Gradually, people in the setting call you by your name and seem to seek you out rather than ignore or avoid you.

The Participant/Observer Continuum

To what degree and in what ways should researchers participate in the activities of the setting? Gold (1958) has discussed the spectrum of possible roles for observers to play. At one extreme is the complete observer. Here, the researcher does not participate in activities at the setting. He or she looks at the scene, literally or figuratively, through a one-way mirror. At the other end is complete involvement at the site, with little discernible difference between the observer's and the subject's behaviors. Fieldworkers stay somewhere between these extremes (Adler & Adler, 1994).

Exactly what and how much participation varies during the course of a study. During the first few days of participant observation, for example, the researcher often remains somewhat detached, waiting to be looked over and, hopefully, accepted. As relationships develop, he or she participates more. At later stages of the research, it may be important once again to hold back from participating. Too much participation can lead to the researcher getting so involved and active with subjects that their original intentions get lost. (See Levine, 1980b, for a description of how an attempt to expose the fakery of shamans was subverted this way.)

The correct amount of participation and how you should participate have to be calculated with the particulars of your study in mind. Some observers of classrooms have situational constraints that allow them to partake little in classroom activities; they choose to sit in the back of the room and take it all in (Rist, 1978; Smith & Geoffrey, 1968). Others negotiate more active roles like volunteering in the classroom (Lareau, 1989). Those who do join activities face the dilemma of choosing how to participate. They ask themselves: "Should I act like a teacher?" "Should I do what the kids are doing?" "How about acting like a teacher's aide?" None of these choices may feel right. There may be pressure, some brought about during negotiating access, for the second adult in the classroom to function as a teacher's helper. As we already suggested, a certain amount of this type of participation can work, but you must be on your guard not to let it dominate your time. In addition, be aware that when acting as a helper, the children will define you in a particular way. Annette Lareau did participant observation in two classrooms in two schools. In one school she was able to take minor roles, like helping the students clean up when they finished their art projects. In the other school, she was placed in a more supervisory role with the students and felt uncomfortable, particularly with regard to discipline (Lareau, 1989).

As with much of our discussion of fieldwork relations, we can inform you of some of the issues and provide some suggestions, but there are many aspects of fieldwork that you have to work out for yourself. Because there has not been extensive writing on the various forms of fieldwork in the various settings in which researchers work, there is a great deal of opportunity to publish methods papers in which you share your experience and advice with others.

Questions concerning how much, with whom, and how you participate tend to work out as the research develops focus. If, for example, your goal becomes understanding a classroom from the students' point of view, you may choose to participate more with them than with the teacher. If you decide to spend a great deal of time with the participants, such as the students, it is important that other participants understand that you are not purposefully slighting them. Share with the teacher your strategy of focusing on the children so he or she does not feel ignored or offended. While participation in the classroom itself may be awkward, studies of classrooms are often enlarged to include interviews or observation sessions with the teacher outside this setting. Participation becomes less problematic.

Balancing participation and observation can be particularly trying in other situations as well. We have found that small groups whose members make a purposeful attempt to be inclusive and participatory are particularly difficult. In sensitivity groups, encounter groups, support groups, recovery groups, co-operative groups, share groups and other similar situations the pressure is on for everyone to become a full-fledged participating member. There is pressure to act like they act. There is the danger that if you hold back they will judge you as critical of what they are doing and saying. Field workers feel guilty being on the margin, especially if they share the values of group members. Even in less intense group activities tough and awkward decisions arise. One observer was studying a training course for teachers in which teachers were learning how to teach students "prosocial behavior." As part of the training, the teachers were asked to role play a disruptive group of students in a classroom. This occurred early in the observer's research and he was at a loss to know what to do. Should he pass when it came to his turn? How should he act if he chose to participate? How visible should he be? He felt lucky observing the session because the teachers revealed their ways of thinking about disruptive students by performing, but the situation created anxiety for him. When it came to his turn he decided to role play, but he chose to play a sullen student rather than a gregarious one. By making this choice, he participated, but did not draw attention to himself.

As the last example suggests, how you participate depends on who you are, your values, and your personality. You can adjust your typical behavior to the research task, but what you feel comfortable doing sets some parameters for how you will behave. People who are very outgoing have to temper their gregariousness, but even when they exhibit this kind of restraint they still may participate more than people who normally are more quiet. The very shy person might have to practice being more assertive in initiating conversations and introducing himself or herself. There is no "right" personality for fieldwork.

Becoming a researcher means internalizing the research goal while collecting data in the field. As you conduct research you participate with the subjects in various ways. You joke with them and behave sociably in many ways. You may even help them perform their duties. You do these things, but always for the purpose of promoting your research goals. You carry with you an imaginary sign that you hang over each subject and on every wall and tree. The sign says, "My primary purpose in being here is to collect data. How does what I am doing relate to that goal?" If what you are doing does not relate to collecting data, you should take that as a warning that you may be slipping out of role. This does not mean, however, that you have to spend every minute in the field systematically pursuing leads. Sometimes establishing good rapport requires hanging out and just plain socializing with your subjects. You might even go to a movie or out for a drink. Going to a movie may not produce a great deal of data, but the idea is that the activity may enhance your rapport and put you in a better position to collect data in the future.

Doing Fieldwork in Another Culture

In one sense all qualitative research is done in another culture. But studies you do vary in the degree to which the people you study share your language, customs, and other aspects of every day life. While your study at the school around the corner should be approached as if it were another culture, there are places you study that are radically different from your own background. This "border crossing" may raise some particular problems for fieldwork. Doing fieldwork in another country often means being in a different culture but in multicultural America you may find dramatic differences within the same city or even neighborhood.

There are some special considerations to keep in mind. All cultural groups do not share the middle-class American's definition of *research* or *researcher.* While it may be quite clear and unambiguous what these terms mean to you, your subjects may not share your understanding. Although asking them to sign an informed consent form may provide the opportunity to discuss what you are up to, their signature does not assure a meeting of the minds. While *research* may be a nebulous term for most, for some it may conjure up images of what is done in a laboratory, or as an instrument of government repression. It is common for subjects to view it as an activity for which they should get paid. While perfect correspondence in meaning is unlikely in any study, it is important to understand how your subjects see you and to try to curtail any troubles and misunderstandings that might arise, as well as to interpret the data in the context of how subjects define the relationship. In the eyes of subjects researchers are often seen in images of other roles they are familiar with: extension worker, social worker, or even spy. Sometimes, translating the concept of researcher into comparisons they are familiar with can be helpful. At times it may be easier for your subjects to understand you as an author who has come to write a book, for example, than a researcher.

In different cultures there are different rules about human communication and relationships. For example, in some cultures people are suppose to be quiet around authority figures. Or it may not be proper to share beliefs and opinions with people outside the group. Many cultures have different notions of privacy from middle-class Americans. Individual interviews with strangers might be common in your world but in other places it may be unacceptable. It is easy to misinterpret rapport and other aspects of fieldwork relations if you are not familiar with these cultural variations. Try to find out about these by discussing them with others. Do not assume that the way you are being treated, or that peoples' reluctance to do things your way, is a reflection on you. Interactions often reflect differences in the way things are done. Adjust, because your fieldwork has to take these into account. Your style has to be appropriate and adaptive to the style and customs of those you study. Your methods need to take into account indigenous ways of relating and knowing.

Researcher Characteristics and Special Problems with Rapport

In addition to understanding general aspects of the culture you are studying you have to understand how your personal characteristics and status might affect your fieldwork relationships with individual subjects you encounter. To subjects, you are likely to be seen not just as a researcher. You may, for example, be identified as a middle-aged, white, divorced woman with a working-class background, or a never-married African American male in his late twenties with an Ivy League education. You may be from another part of the country and your style so differs that it is noticeable (one of us did work in Georgia and was seen as too energetic, fast talking, and quick for the local culture). Or, your sexual orientation may be different from many of the people you are studying. On the basis of such identifiers, or markers, you may be defined as dangerous, insignificant, or untrustworthy.

Who you are to the various subjects and what that means to them is important to try to figure out when negotiating fieldwork relations as well as for interpreting the data you gather. (Also, some characteristics are not visible to subjects. What you should reveal about yourself and the implications of that information need to be considered when negotiating fieldwork relations.) While we do not want to minimize the effect of who you are on your subjects, we would not make any categorical statements about the effect of, say, being a woman studying an all male setting, or being an African American studying an all white group, or any other such arrangement. There is a lot of room to break out of definitions subjects might have for "people like you" and, as with any situation, when you first meet a person their personal characteristics tend to be more important in defining them than later on in the relationship. You may have to be more reflective in thinking about how to handle yourself and precisely what role to play if who you are has special meaning to your subjects.

For the purposes of an example we look briefly at special considerations adults might have when their subjects are children. The young present special rapport and conceptual challenges (Fine & Sandstrom, 1988). Most people see childhood as an absolute category rather than as a social construction. Researchers are not immune from this view (James & Prout, 1990). Adults have a difficult time taking what children say seriously (Morrow, 1995). Also, grown-ups tend to take charge with juveniles, directing conversations and even joking with them in particular ways. Adults tend to evaluate children's behavior and feel responsible for them more than they do for their age peers. If you have such adult habits and you want to study children, you need to break out of your patterns. Kids are use to being treated "like children" and they are ready for it. They have developed particular strategies in dealing with the full grown; they may seek their approval, withdraw, or even conspire to mislead (Bluebond-Langner, 1978). An alternative is to participate with the children not as an authority figure (an adult), but as a quasi-friend (see Fine & Glassner, 1979; Mercurio, 1972, Michaels, 1994). It is difficult for children to accept adults as equals, but you can move toward being a tolerated insider in children's society. Observers we have known have had varying degrees of success in doing unobtrusive observations with children. One observer studied kindergartners and first-graders and participated with them, acting as they did, when they worked and played. She felt that by doing what they did (drawing, playing games), and refraining from "helping them," the children came to act more naturally in front of her. Another observer, studying a "free school," felt that his conversations with the children were always stilted by the fact that he was perceived as an adult and therefore as an outsider. He went out of his way to enter into the children's world. The children he was interested in were ten to fourteen years old. He went out for sodas with them and did other things they did, but his efforts came to no avail. He even tried to bribe them. Age—not only when you are an adult and the subjects are children but even when you are in your twenties and you want to interview school district superintendents—has to be taken into account when trying to establish fieldwork relationships.

Class and status differences are also significant in fieldwork relationships. Brenda Solomon studied women who were or had been on welfare and were trying to get off it by learning to be nurses aides. She sat in on their classes and thought frequently about how to connect with them across these differences in their educational statuses. One strategy she developed concerned test taking. When the women took exams, she took them also. She always did poorly, and could be corrected by the students. As she wrote in her field notes (1996):

> *Mrs. R. instructs us to put our books and notebooks under the desk for a second abbreviation test. We each go up to Mrs. R.'s desk to get the test. I take it too. (I took it during the last program I attended and it seemed to be fun for everyone to see how many I MISSED. I consider this an important strategy in laying out my*

weaknesses for the group to poke fun at.)…I understand my poor performance on
the test to be helpful to me in connecting with the group.

Brenda is comfortable when her test comes back with the teacher's red writing all over it, especially after April, one of the students, says to her in front of the class, "You better not get them all right and make us look bad!"

While we cannot discuss all researcher characteristics and how they might affect rapport with subjects, several are particularly significant. One is gender. Gender is a central organizing identity in U.S. culture and male and female researchers will be treated differently by their subjects and will come to know different aspects of the worlds they study (Warren, 1988, p. 5). Traditionally, women studying all-male settings, for example, were forced into stereotypically sexist female roles such as the cute airhead, the gofer, the object for sexual conquest, and the object of gender joking (Warren, 1988; Easterday, Papademas, Shorr, and Valentine, 1977). There is also the question of access. Male ethnographers have had their access limited by their sex. Back (1993) was accused by the young adolescent men he studied in south London of making sexual advances whenever he tried to speak with a few young women. And Abramson (1993) reported his difficulty in studying domestic work because of the spaces unavailable to him.

Some researchers have pointed to the close relationships women interviewers establish relatively easily with other women while such intimacy eludes male interviewers (Devault, 1990; Oakley, 1981). Lillian Rubin, takes the position that women interviewers are more effective in getting men to open up about intimate topics than men, because men have patterns of relating to each other that may curtail such personal talk (Rubin, 1976). Many feminists articulate the politics of power that reside in the relationships between researcher and informant and work to create non-heirarchical relationships that are more reflexive about that power (Fine, 1994b). Along with the issue of rapport is how it gets represented in writing. Feminists have paid significant attention to the "emotional dimensions" of doing research (Fonow & Cook, 1991, p. 9).

The meaning of skin color and ethnic background are pronounced in many segments of the United States and may have a particularly powerful significance for particular subjects. Subjects are likely to make assumptions about you and feel more or less comfortable around you based on skin color and ethnic background or how you relate to such issues. You need to work through how you might react to racial stereotyping and social isolation and other forms of racism encountered in the field.

Skin color, race, and cultural identity sometimes facilitate, sometimes complicate, and sometimes erect barriers in fieldwork. This seems to be true both when researchers are studying people within their same ethnic group, or when they are studying people in another group. Signithia Fordham, an African American woman, studied African American high school students' meanings of success. She described herself experiencing both "estrangement and identification" through her identity as an African American woman (1996, p. 36). The tension between estrangement and identification often emerged through the questions that "haunted" her. How would the shared histories of her informants and herself affect the research process? Would she be positioned to speak for African American students? Would she have to relive her own schooling experiences when she studied the students at Capital High? How would the students relate to her? (pp. 36–37). Michele Foster had fewer feelings of distance from her informants because she was able to draw on the history of her own family's community involvement when she interviewed African American teachers (Foster, 1994). Guadalupe Valdes (1996), studied the experiences of Mexican immigrant families with American schools. She shared a common ethnic background with her informants:

> *Like the families I was studying, I had experienced sadness in leaving Mexico, in knowing that I would not go back. I had also raised children in this country. Like the mothers I was studying, I too had had questions and doubts about how strict to be and about how much of my own upbringing I could impose on my "American" children. (p. 11)*

She did not share the same class background, however, because unlike the poor families she studied, she had come from a "family of means" and so had experienced a very different class structure. While she was both an insider and outsider to the people she studied, she eventually came to take on the role of "godmother," a reciprocal role. While there are some shared identities when studying within cultural communities, there are also divisions.

Racism is significant when European American researchers study people from traditionally under-represented groups. Researchers construct and confront it differently. Mitchell Duneier (1992), who studied a group of African American men who frequented a cafeteria in Chicago, wrote very little about how race worked in his relationship with Slim and his contemporaries. He did describe how his own white privilege worked when describing an incident of his own insensitivity to the African American photographer who took the pictures for the book.

The social construction of race affected one of the authors of this text in her study of elementary school teachers. Several of the African American teachers did not want to be interviewed for the study. While the researcher had successfully cajoled some of the European American teachers who were hesitant to participate, she did not do so with the African American teachers. She acted more stiffly and did not work as hard to engage their participation. She also misread cues that one African American teacher shared about her family history because she could only read the cues in light of a white middle-class model. When the teacher, with whom the researcher had a good relationship, always greeted her with questions about her children, and gossip about her own, the researcher categorized this dialogue as part of rapport-building, and hastened to change discussions down to the "real" issues. She did not see the significance of the teacher's talk about her children, and missed opportunities to build on these connections. None of the other teachers in the school had children in daycare. This teacher and the researcher did. This common bond could have served as an entry to talk in much greater detail about the social supports this woman drew on to manage her career. This opportunity was lost because the researcher read the cues only in terms of her own culture.

What about disability, a factor most people do not think of in relation to relationships? Being able-bodied and studying people labeled "disabled" can create tensions and misunderstandings, especially if you have never examined your assumptions about physical and mental differences (Goode, 1994) and you are with people who identify with particular disability rights groups. Political consciousness is particularly high among members of the deaf community who declare themselves a separate culture with a separate language that wants to stay that way. Being a person with a disability doing research with people who do not share your difference can create other difficulties. These need to be faced and factored in. Some of the most creative and challenging work in the field of disability studies attempts to understand the perspectives of people who have been defined as having severe and profound developmental disabilities. This work involves innovation and persistence (Goode, 1992; 1994; Ferguson, 1994; Biklen & Moseley, 1988; Taylor, Bogdan & Lutfiyya, 1995).

Lastly, while not to the same extent that people have been interested in gender and race, a few researchers have focused on special problems of studying people in positions of authority and power, those with privilege, the so-called *elite* of society (Hertz & Imber, 1993). Elite settings can be particular difficult to penetrate and, once you are there, it may be difficult to break down the barriers to get behind the scene without being co-opted. There are the personal implications and reprisals when researchers write critically about people in power.

Some characteristics in some settings make establishing rapport easier. Being closer in age to your subjects or being the same gender may facilitate rapport. But this does not mean that your characteristics always exclude you from studying people who are different from you. These differences just have to be taken into account and strategies have to be worked out to convert potential difficulties into advantages.

Be Discreet

The hope of "cooperative" fieldworkers is that they will blend into the setting, becoming a more or less "natural" part of the scene. A number of strategies facilitate this acceptance. Appearance is one. People choose to wear clothes that communicate who they are. We do not suggest that you desert your personal style, but that you be aware of what your dress means to subjects. If you are in a place where people dress casually, wear casual clothes also. In a school, the formality of your dress can say something to others about who you are and with whom you identify. Administrators might wear suits or dresses, teachers might be less formal, while students and custodial staff might wear T-shirts and jeans. Beware of the unspoken dress codes and, if they do not make you feel too uncomfortable, dress in a manner that seems appropriate for your status in the situation. Do not imitate your host's dress pattern unless you feel at ease with it and you think they will too.

If you conduct your research in a systematic and rigorous way and develop trust, you soon will become privy to certain information and opinions about which even all insiders might not be aware. It is important, however, not to display too much of your knowledge while talking with subjects, since they may feel uncomfortable being in the presence of a "know-it-all." Do not discuss anything that has been told to you in private by one subject with another. You want to be regarded as a person with discretion. Even if you encounter people whose beliefs and opinions are inaccurate—even silly in the light of what you know—do not go out of your way to correct them by displaying that knowledge. One researcher reported that his acceptance by the teachers in the school in which he observed was eased in large part by his reputation as a trustworthy person; while they were not always certain of exactly what he was up to, "at least he didn't gossip" (Smith & Geoffrey, 1968).

The suggestion to refrain from gossiping carries over to talks with people who are not your subjects. Although it is important to discuss with your colleagues or your professor the problems you are facing and what your study is yielding, avoid being flippant with the information you have. It should not, for example, be the topic of a conversation at a party. Ask yourself, when discussing your experience with others, "What would the people in the setting I am studying think if they heard me talking?" If you think they would be embarrassed, it is a good idea to restrain yourself. What you say might get back to your subjects and seriously affect your relationship with them. It can fracture trust.

While many teachers find people who observe their classes both non-disruptive and an interesting addition, they also have suggested that it can be a strain to perceive themselves as continually being watched. Feeling like they are in a fish bowl can be difficult enough for teachers, but learning that they are the center of a discussion in a university class simply intensifies their uneasiness. Students doing fieldwork in schools with teachers must continually pay attention to this concern. As one cooperating teacher told a researcher placed with her, "the professors say that they have student teachers observe us to learn, but it really seems like they criticize us. I feel inadequate enough to serve all these different kids, and the last thing I need is more criticism. They are not in here with thirty-one kids all day." (See Sarason et al., 1966, pp. 74–97, for a discussion of the issue.)

The fieldnotes you keep will likely contain harmless information about what you are learning. Since they also will contain quotations from people, as well as your own personal reflections, it is important to be careful with this material. Be sure you do not misplace your notes where someone in the setting you study may find them. Also, for the sake of anonymity, use fake names for the people about whom you are writing, change the name of the school (if you are studying a school), and adjust other information that might tell a reader where and from whom you have been collecting data.

Although in the overt approach your subjects know your research intentions, after you build rapport the fact that you are a researcher fades from their minds. You try to encourage them to take you for granted and not to be self-conscious around you. Taking extensive fieldnotes is an intrinsic part of doing qualitative research. We will describe this in detail in Chapter 4. The procedure we suggest is that the notes be taken after you leave the site at the end of an observation period. We recommend that you try to refrain from writing notes in front of the subjects. There are times, however, when note-taking is quite appropriate. These are times when the people in the setting are taking notes themselves. While attending classes, high school students often take notes. Medical students often take notes on morning rounds. It would be quite appropriate for you to take notes at these times. Also, when an informant explains some elaborate, detailed information, taking notes in front of him or her will not be upsetting. When a school principal, for example, describes the organizational chart of the school, it would be perfectly acceptable to take out a pad and jot down notes. In fact, administrators and people in high places often expect note taking when they talk. Taking notes when interviewing them can even enhance rapport.

Subjects are often very curious about what it is that you are writing down. They try to peek. Make sure that anything you put down on paper is of such a nature that you would not mind your subjects seeing it. If you write notes, do not act like you are recording secrets or uncomplimentary information by holding your pad at an angle that makes it obvious that you do not want others to see.

Try not to walk around with pad and pencil continually in hand, but if you feel you must, jot down a note here and there. One strategy observers sometimes employ during an observation period is to retreat to a private place (like the toilet) and write down some headings or phrases that will help recall. If you do this, make sure you do not carry yourself like a detective and spook your subjects.

Researching in Politically Charged and Conflict-Ridden Settings

It is not uncommon for human service organizations to have dissension and political wrangling. The level can be from mild to intense. Debates on policies and procedures often rage in schools, hospitals, welfare offices and other such settings; staff and clients can be distrustful of each other and those who visit from the outside. This can pose particular problems for the researcher. When the trust level is low, when people are sensitive to particular topics, when there are strong barriers between insiders and outsiders, when the subjects feel they have a lot to gain or lose by what they say and with whom they speak, or when there are clearly delineated factions and subgroups, the researcher needs to tread with care. If you sense you are in such an environment slow down, be particularly low key until you figure out who is against whom and what the struggles are about. Listen carefully and talk very little. If you ask questions phrase them carefully.

In organizations with conflict people may vie for your allegiance, wanting you to identify with one side or the other. They may try to convince you that the way they see things is right and you should join them in the struggle against those they define as the enemy. Although as a strategy it is trying at times, and close to impossible at others, in general it is best to remain neutral. If you identify with one side, it will be difficult to understand or to have access to the people on the other side. While it is often difficult to do and organizations where there is conflict can be the most challenging in fieldwork relations, try to be friendly to all. Spread yourself around, spending time with various people. Have a sympathetic ear to all sides and do not talk about one group in front of the other.

If, on the other hand you are not studying an organization as a whole, but are researching a particular group across sites, like maintenance workers on different college campuses who are trying to organize a union, or African American student groups charging their universities with racism, it then becomes important for you to be identified with the group you are studying.

While conflict in a school or other organization may cause special difficulties for the researcher, it can provide a unique opportunity for an astute observer to understand the dynamics of confrontation and negotiation. During times of conflict, people most overtly reveal their perspectives on what is important to them. Therefore, studying an organization in conflict can be a particularly productive experience.

Conflicts may also be less intense and confined to a small segment of the organization. Often teachers disagree with each other about how to resolve daily problems. Some researchers in an elementary setting, for example, found that certain teachers disagreed on why pupils had been placed in "resource rooms." A first-grade teacher reported to the researcher that her pupil needed to be in the resource room because he had a ''learning disability.'' The teacher in the resource room, however, felt that the pupil had a "behavioral problem," not an academic one. "He acts up and the teacher sends him to me." These two teachers interpreted the child's behavior quite differently, and their contrasting perspective fueled much debate and argument. Following these kinds of controversies, hearing the various sides in the dispute, provided important data to the researcher.

Feelings

In our introductory chapters we mentioned the researcher's own feelings and prejudices as possible sources of bias. In the preceding chapter we discussed how qualitative researchers record their feelings as a method of controlling bias. Here, we approach the topic of feelings in a different light—for their positive impact on research. Feelings are an important vehicle for establishing rapport and for gauging subjects' perspectives (Johnson, 1975). Feelings are not something to repress (Ellis, 1991). Rather, if treated correctly, they can be an important aid in doing qualitative research (Rosaldo, 1989).

We now recount two research experiences that illustrate the use of feelings to generate understanding. The first time an observer visited a cafeteria of a junior high school where she was conducting research, she became overwhelmed with a feeling that things were out of control—"chaos" is how she described it: the deafening noise, the smell of steamed foods and garbage cans, the pushing and yelling. She felt almost immediately after arriving that if she did not leave, she would scream. Teachers in the study described similar feelings when they first went to the cafeteria. In fact, one teacher came up to the observer amidst the chaos and said, "How's your head? This is some zoo." Later, when the observer was in the teachers' room, someone mentioned the cafeteria. The observer indicated that being there for one period had almost "wiped her out." Teachers began discussing how it was for them the first few weeks on cafeteria duty. But they assured her, "You'll get used to it. Some of us actually enjoy it now." Sharing her feelings with the teachers enabled her to get in touch with theirs.

In a teaching hospital, on the intensive care unit for infants, interns had a very difficult time finding arteries in which to place needles in their tiny patients. (Many of them were premature infants, some weighing as little as a pound.) This meant they had to stick the infant time and time again until they got blood. The first few times he watched this process, the observer had trouble controlling his feelings of compassion for the babies as they cried, twisted, and turned from their apparent pain. After a while, however, the observer found it less difficult to watch these procedures. Interns seldom showed any emotion except exasperation at not being able to accomplish their tasks. Parents, however, reacted to the children's treatment by becoming noticeably upset. The observer shared his feelings with the interns, and they were able to talk about how difficult this process had been for them at first and how they had developed techniques to control it. One technique was to insist to themselves that what they were doing was helpful to the baby. They further discussed how the infants they were treating tended to lose their personhood in their eyes and that how losing feeling was upsetting to them. Their patients were becoming objects to treat. But they felt they could not afford to cringe at needle procedures. They also realized how parents felt about their babies' pain and had explanations to give them to ease these feelings: The undeveloped nerves were not like adults' and the infants would not remember.

As these two accounts suggest, the researcher's feelings can be an important indicator of subjects' feelings and, therefore, a source for reflecting. They also can help formulate questions to get at subjects' experiences. In this sense, the observer's emotional reactions are a source for research hunches. If carefully sorted out, selectively presented, and appropriately expressed, they also can be a wonderful avenue for building rapport. (Of course, if your feelings are counter to your subjects', if shown, they might create hostility.) Becoming part of a group, after all, means that you can share insiders' reactions (see Everhart, 1977).

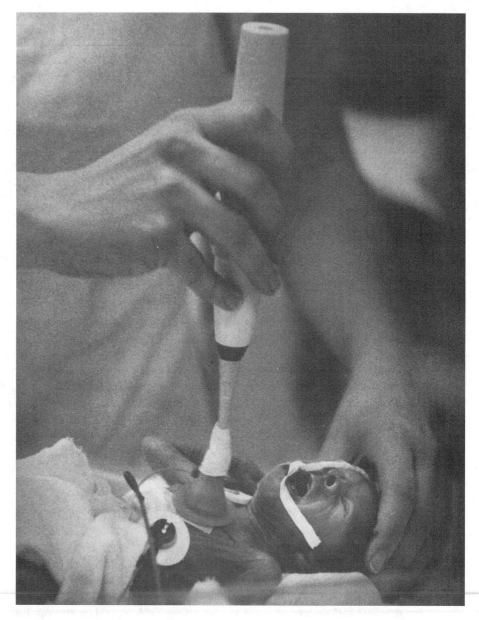

Cardiac arrest on a neonatal unit. The medical instrument is fashioned from an electric toothbrush. Photo by Andrejs Ozolins.

Many people in schools say that outsiders can never know "what it's really like" to be a teacher. This refrain refers, in part, to the inability of the outsider to know the frustration, the anger, the joy, and the feelings of accomplishment teachers experience. We do not want to suggest that you, the researcher, can come to feel all these things in the way that the teacher or any other group of subjects does, but you can experience some of them and develop empathy. Being there on a bad day when tension fills the air, or on the last day of school when people say their goodbyes, you can share part of the teachers' emotional world and you can feel closer to them and they to you.

Another topic related to feelings, but somewhat different, has to do with the stress and strains of being a researcher. Fieldwork can be physically and emotionally draining. It is people and labor intensive. It is difficult balancing being friendly and warm while remaining reflective and instrumental. While fieldwork requires a significant amount of socializing, many researchers report being lonely and feeling estranged from the people they are studying as well as from their own friends and family. Some find it difficult to resolve ethical issues, and they feel guilty about not intervening or about being too judgmental. Beginning researchers, in particular, entertain a lot of self doubt: Do I have what it takes? Am I really thinking inductively? Is my data rich enough? Experienced researchers are not immune from such doubts.

Be aware of the stress and strain fieldwork can produce and try to do things to eliminate some of it. Take a day or two off and in other ways break your routine. Try not to be so single minded about your research that you neglect other parts of your life.

How Long Should an Observation Session Be?

As we suggested, for the first few days limit the sessions to an hour or less. As your confidence and knowledge of the setting increase, so can the hours you spend at any one time. With the exception noted in the next paragraph, you should not stay in the field for periods longer than your memory or the time you have available to take notes after the session allows. Fieldwork is often more fun than doing the notes, so there is a tendency to stay in the field longer than you should. Fieldwork takes discipline. Practice restraint—remember the sign.

Sometimes, after being in the field a few times, researchers feel that they have not had enough time with the subjects to have established sufficient rapport. They may decide to spend a longer period, a whole day for example, even though they know they cannot possibly record the data that would result. In this case, they are willing to sacrifice detailed notes for the rapport gained. This is reasonable.

Interviewing

Most of us have conducted interviews. The process is so familiar we do it without thinking. An interview is a purposeful conversation, usually between two people but sometimes involving more (Morgan, 1988), that is directed by one in order to get information from the other. In the hands of the qualitative researcher, the interview takes on a shape of its own (Burgess, 1984; Fontana & Frey, 1994).

In qualitative research, interviews may be used in two ways. They may be the dominant strategy for data collection, or they may be employed in conjunction with participant observation, document analysis, or other techniques. In all of these situations the interview is used to gather descriptive data in the subjects' own words so that the researcher can develop insights on how subjects interpret some piece of the world.

In participant-observation studies, the researcher usually knows the subjects through interacting with them before interviewing so the interview is often like a conversation between friends. Here the interview cannot easily be separated from other research activities. When the subject has a spare moment, for example, the researcher might say, "Have you got a few minutes? I haven't had a chance to talk with you alone." Sometimes an interview has no introduction; the researcher just makes the situation an interview. In a study one of the authors did of a neonatal unit in a hospital, he would go to the unit late at night when there were very few people visiting because he knew this would be a good time to do informal interviews with nurses about how they saw the doctors and their communication with parents. Particularly toward the end of a study, however, when specific information is sought, the participant observer sets up specific times (appointments) to meet with the subjects for the purpose of a more formal interview. This also is true of qualitative studies involving archival and document research.

In studies that rely predominantly on interviewing, the subject is usually a stranger. (It is common in studies that involve long-term interviewing with one or very few subjects, however, for the researcher to be acquainted with the subject before the research begins.) A good part of the work involves building a relationship, getting to know each other, and putting the subject at ease (Whyte, 1984, esp. Ch. 6).

Most interviews begin with small talk. Topics can range from baseball to cooking. The purpose this chit-chat serves is to develop rapport: You search for common ground, for a topic that you have in common, for a place to begin building a relationship. In situations where the subject knows you, you usually get right down to business, but in situations where you and the subject are strangers, you may have to break the ice. In some cases, this takes some time; in long-term interview projects it may take a whole interview session, although feminist researchers have commented on the ease with which women informants have opened up to women researchers conducting in-depth interviews (DeVault, 1990; Stacey, 1988; Lather, 1988; Finch, 1984; Oakley, 1981).

Early in the interview you try to briefly inform the subject of your purpose, and make assurances (if they are necessary) that what is said in the interview will be treated confidentially. Many subjects feel self-conscious at first, contending in a self-effacing manner that they have nothing important to say. In these cases, the interviewer must be reassuring and supportive. Less often, the potential subject will be challenging, questioning your methods and the soundness of the study. In those cases, you must stand your ground without being defensive.

Qualitative interviews vary in the degree to which they are structured. Some interviews, although relatively open-ended, are focused around particular topics or may be guided by some general questions (Merton & Kendall, 1946). Even when an interview guide is employed, qualitative interviews offer the interviewer considerable latitude to pursue a range of topics and offer the subject a chance to shape the content of the interview. When the interviewer controls the content too rigidly, when the subject cannot tell his or her story personally in his or her own words, the interview falls out of the qualitative range.

At the other end of the structured/unstructured continuum is the very open-ended interview. The researcher, in this case, encourages the subject to talk in the area of interest and then probes more deeply, picking up on the topics and issues the respondent initiates. The subject plays a stronger role in defining the content of the interview and the direction of the study in this type of interview (Mischler, 1991). Some call this type of interview a *guided conversation* (Rubin & Rubin, 1995).

Some people debate which approach is more effective, the structured or the unstructured. With semi-structured interviews you are confident of getting comparable data across subjects, but you lose the opportunity to understand how the subjects themselves structure the topic at hand. While such debates may enliven the research community, from our perspective you do not have to take sides. You choose a particular type to employ based on your research goal. Furthermore, different types of interviews can be employed at different stages of the same study. At the beginning of the project, for example, it might be important to use the more free-flowing, exploratory interview because your purpose at that point is to get a general understanding of a range of perspectives on a topic. After the investigatory work has been done, you may want to structure interviews more in order to get comparable data across a larger sample or to focus on particular topics that emerged during the preliminary interviews. (For another discussion of structure and types of interviews, see the section on analytic induction in Chapter 2.)

Good interviews are those in which the subjects are at ease and talk freely about their points of view (for a comprehensive discussion, see Briggs, 1986). Good interviews produce rich data filled with words that reveal the respondents' perspectives. Transcripts are filled with details and examples. Good interviewers communicate personal interest and attention to subjects by being attentive, nodding their heads, and using appropriate facial expressions to communicate. The interviewer may ask for clarification when the respondent mentions something that seems unfamiliar, using phrases such as, "What do you mean?" "I'm not sure I am following you." "Could you explain that?" The interviewer also probes the respondent to be specific, asking for examples of points that are made. When asking the respondent about the past, for example, the interviewer suggests that he or she think back to that time and try to relive it. The interviewer may ask the respondent to quote what was said at particular times. People being interviewed have a tendency to offer a quick run-through of events. Informants can be taught to respond to meet the interviewer's interest in the particulars, the details. They need encouragement to elaborate.

Certainly a key strategy for the qualitative interviewer in the field is to avoid as much as possible questions that can be answered by "yes" or "no." Particulars and details will come from probing questions that require an exploration. "Were you a good student in elementary school?" can be answered in one word if the respondent so chooses, but "Tell me about what you were like as a student in elementary school," urges description. As a corollary, interviewers need not fear silence. Silences can enable subjects to get their thoughts together and to direct some of the conversation. Unless subjects are talking at length about subjects the researcher has no interest in—yesterday's ball game—it is a poor habit for interviewers to interrupt subjects and change the direction of the conversation.

Not all people are equally articulate or perceptive, but it is important for the qualitative researcher not to give up on an interviewee too quickly. Some respondents need a chance to warm up to you. Information in the qualitative interview project is cumulative, each interview building on and connecting to the other. It is what you learn from the total study that counts. While you might learn more from some interviews than from others, and while you cannot get the same intensity from everyone with whom you speak, even a bad interview contributes something.

It has been our experience to misjudge the quality of data we get from interviews. Often what you think is a wonderful interview turns out to be disappointing when you read the transcript. The reverse is also true, interviews perceived to be bad produce good transcripts. This occurs, we believe because judgments of the interview itself are more a function of how you feel about the subject and how comfortably the conversations proceed; and this may not tell much about the content of the information received.

There are no rules that you can always apply across all interview situations, but a few general statements can be made. Most important is the need to listen carefully. Listen to what the people say. Treat every word as having the potential to unlock the mystery of the subject's way of viewing the world. If at first you do not understand what the respondent is getting at, ask for clarification. Question, not to challenge, but to make clear. If you cannot understand, assume that you are at fault. Assume the problem is not that the subject does not make sense, but that you have not been able to comprehend. Return and listen and think some more. Interviewing requires flexibility. Try different techniques, including jokes or sometimes gentle challenges. Sometimes you might ask respondents to elaborate with stories and sometimes you might share your experiences with them.

While we have said that some qualitative interviewing is more like a conversation than a formal, highly structured interchange between a subject and a researcher, there are many ways the good qualitative interview is not like a typical conversation. Too often people involved in conversations do not concentrate intensely on what the other person is saying. They are busy trying to impress the other, or criticize their logic, or relate what they are saying to their own life experiences or preconceived notions. Often people do not give the person they are talking to their full attention. They are easily distracted or bored. Often status conventions reign in typical conversations. The person of lower status defers to the person of higher status. All of this gets in the way of giving the person you are talking to your full undivided attention and treating them as the experts of what you are interested in finding out—how they think. Good interviewing involves deep listening.

Very few studies had been done asking people labeled mentally retarded about their experiences when Bogdan and Taylor (1994) began doing life history interviews with ex-state school residents (state schools were the name given to institutions in which people labeled mentally retarded were placed). The work they read reported that people labeled mentally retarded said they were are not retarded. Earlier researchers interpreted this as meaning that their subjects were lying, covering up or "in denial" (Edgerton, 1967). Prior researchers had taken the classification of mental retardation as the truth, so those who were labeled in this way but who said they were not retarded were understood to be making false claims. The people Bogdan and Taylor interviewed also said they were not retarded, but rather than taking their utterances as fabrications, they listened carefully, probing what their subjects meant when they said they were not retarded. What emerged was a much richer understanding of how their subjects thought. For example, those interviewed talked about the prejudice and stereotypes attached to the word "retarded" and felt they were not as bad as the concept implied.

They refused to be discredited. Further, the subjects had been in institutions with other people labeled mentally retarded, some of whom could not talk and take care of their basic bodily functions. As their subjects saw it, they had much more in common with the interviewers than with the severely impaired people with whom they had been grouped. Rather than dismiss their subjects' views by applying the psychological concept of "denial," the researchers took them seriously and began to question the efficacy of applying the term to their subjects. Through listening carefully to their subjects they began questioning the system of classifying human beings as normal and abnormal rather than further reifying the classification.

The goal of understanding how the person you are interviewing thinks is at the center of the interview. While a loose interview guide might provide some structure for the encounter, getting all the questions answered or all the areas covered is not the purpose of the interview. The researcher has to be captive to the larger goal of the interview—understanding—not to the devices, gimmicks, questions, or the like that were invented as strategies and techniques of obtaining information. The researcher must always be prepared to let go of the plan and jump on the opportunities the interview situation presents. For example, Bogdan, in the study of people labeled mentally retarded cited earlier, went to a subject's home to start an interview. The researcher had prepared by writing down a list of potential questions to ask. No sooner did he get to the site and greet Pattie, his subject, when he was asked to sit down. He looked around. On the table were three framed photos, next to a record player with a stack of records nearby. Pattie opened the refrigerator and offered Bogdan a soda, commenting that there was nothing else in the refrigerator and what a difficult time she was having shopping. The subject began talking about the difficulties she was having adjusting to life outside the institution. He then asked about the framed pictures. This unleashed long explanations of who each of the people in the photographs were, and how she thought about them in relation to her present situation. The researcher then commented about the records and the kind of music the subject liked. This resulted in a long explanation of her musical tastes and her present social life. By this time, close to two-and-a-half hours had gone by, and it was time for the interview to end. The researcher had begun to understand Pattie's current life, what was important to her and the difficulties she was having. It had gone well even though none of the questions on the original list were asked directly.

How do you invite your subjects to think deeply and express themselves fully and in-depth about their experiences and perspective? Good listening usually stimulates good talking. Other forms of positive reinforcement work too. Being empathetic by expressing appropriate feelings when subjects tell about the ups and downs of their lives, good eye contact, and showing the informants that you take them seriously all contribute to getting the subject to open up.

An approach to open-ended interviewing we find effective and feel comfortable with is one in which you treat the person you are interviewing as an expert. Explain yourself to the person and describe in a general way what you are interested in and why you are interviewing him or her. For example, if you are interested in high school teachers and their careers, you might start off with something like this:

> I am interested in finding out more about the careers of high school teachers. Ms. Smith suggested that you might be a good person to talk to. Right now this is for a class I am

taking but I am very interested in the topic and will probably will go on to do my dissertation on it. I don't know exactly what my focus will be yet, and I'm hoping I'll learn more about that from talking with you. Later, I'm going to ask you about your ideas about teachers and their careers, but I'd like to start by asking you to tell me about your own career as a teacher.

We like this approach for a number of reasons. The first is that it lets the subject in on the study. It is a personal and inviting approach. In addition, it sets the interview up in such a way that it establishes the subject as the one who knows and the researcher as the one who has come to learn. Third, it tells the interviewee that you respect his or her ideas and opinions. You do not just want them to tell their story but instead are encouraging them to share their own ideas and observations. When you approach interviewing in this way you are likely not only to get good descriptive material but also to generate more abstract ideas about how to think about your topic.

In quantitative research the emphasis is on standardized procedures in collecting interview material. When filling out questionnaires with subjects, for example, researchers are supposed to act the same in all the interviews. They are instructed to follow the standard protocol—dress the same, recite the standard, memorized introduction, read the questions exactly the same way each time, do not provide additional information if the subject asks questions, and so on. The belief is that if you standardized the stimulus you know better what to make of the responses because you have controlled for researcher variation. As you have already gathered, the qualitative approach to interviewing is considerably different. Qualitative researchers do not believe that by standardizing procedures you will get more valid answers. They believe that the very wording of the question will evoke different responses among different respondents. The words have different meanings to different subjects. Thus, the subjects are not responding to the same question. For example, if you ask a factory assembly line worker and a surgeon: "Do you like your job?" both may say that they like their jobs very much. The surgeon most often is responding to the question thinking about the intrinsic nature of the job—what he or she actually does, and the gratification he or she gets from that. The factory worker, on the other hand may be thinking about the extrinsic aspects of work—the pay, the health and retirement benefits, and what consumer goods can be bought with what is left over from the pay check after the basics have been paid for.

Qualitative researchers believe that reading the same question to each subject assures nothing about the response. They believe that each subject needs to be approached somewhat differently. The goal is to get each subject to feel relaxed and open and to talk about the topics in a meaningful way, exploring the different meanings of words and questions. Thus in order to get at the subject matter the qualitative research method advocates adapting how you dress, present yourself, and ask questions in order to fit the research situation you are in. To be flexible means responding to the immediate situation, to the informant that is sitting before you, not to some predetermined set of procedures or stereotypes. In his dissertation research with Chicago school teachers, Becker (1951) reported how he used different approaches with different teachers. He felt that with the young, new teachers he could be more direct about their political feelings. With the older teachers, on the other hand, he had to be more circuitous.

You can usually tell a good interview by looking at the transcript. If the parts labeled "subject" are long and those designating the interviewer are short, you usually are looking at good, rich interview material. If the subject's paragraphs are interrupted and there are long sections where the researcher's comments go on beyond a couple of lines, chances are the interview is weak.

What about situations where the person you are interviewing appears seriously stressed or emotional? Researchers should avoid hurting those they are interviewing by aggressively trying to push them to talk about topics that may be upsetting, hurtful, or humiliating. Most researchers do not have clinical training and may not be able to recognize a person who is experiencing deep depression or other psychological states that make subjects feel vulnerable. While you should not fear subjects expressing themselves, do not push. If you are worried about the person's state of mind, do what any sensitive, responsible person would do when in the presence of someone you recognize as needing help. Be supportive. Encourage them to seek help.

Some discussion among qualitative researchers has centered on whether the interview takes the form of persuasion or seduction; that is, do we persuade or seduce people into talking and revealing themselves? Finch (1984), for example, worries about the "extreme ease" with which women researchers can get information from their female informants, particularly if these women have had few opportunities to talk about the issues central to their lives that are raised by the researcher. The interviewer has to be careful not to exploit that trust (Stacey, 1988). One way researchers can counterbalance this concern is to emphasize the importance of self-disclosure when interviewing (DeVault, 1990; Lather, 1988).

As we suggested with the example of doing interviewing with a former state school resident, photographs and memorabilia can serve as stimuli for conversation. When doing interviews in people's homes or in the classroom, ask them about objects and pictures hanging on the walls or displayed in the room. In a study of parents' thoughts about their child's development, a researcher purposely asked parents if they had any pictures of the child. The interviews were conducted at the home and most parents were delighted to get out the family photograph album. The pictures then served as a protocol to structure the conversation. Request pictures, ask about trophies displayed, and inquire about other objects you see around you.

If you ask people to share part of themselves with you, it is important that you not be judgmental or they will feel demeaned. Even if a teacher's racist comments about his or her students upset you, for example, you must control your reaction by reminding yourself that the purpose of the research is to learn people's perspectives, not to instruct your subjects. While you may feel value conflicts with the views you hear, you want to encourage your respondents to say what they feel. You are not there to change views, but to learn what the subjects' views are and why they are that way. Often subjects hold stereotypic views, for example, of what university people are like. Many feel that all university types are "super-liberals" or "radicals," and therefore may be reluctant to talk if their views are conservative. It is important to create an atmosphere where they can feel comfortable expressing themselves. Subjects often may begin to open up with a phrase like, "You people up at the University don't think this way, but you haven't had the experiences that I've had...." "You may think that what I am saying is a lot of bunk, but...." "There's a big difference between what you read in those books and what you learn first hand...." It is difficult, on the other hand, to form a good relationship with respondents if you neither respect their views nor feel free to express any of your own.

Group interviews can be useful in bringing the researcher into the world of the subjects. In this situation, a number of people are brought together and encouraged to talk about the subject of interest (Morgan, 1988). You might bring teachers, parents, or principals together to talk about their work or about those who work with their children. Usually this is a good way of getting insights about what to pursue in individual interviews. When reflecting together on some topic, subjects often can stimulate each other to talk about topics that you can explore later. Group interviews also can be a cue to the language teachers, principals, or aides might share. Group interviews are particularly useful if you are studying adolescents' perspectives on particular issues. While you may have to handle issues that arise about being cool, about put downs, and about issues of appropriate language use that may arise in mixed-gender groups, young people are often stimulated to talk more expansively when others of their age join them.

Researchers have widely adopted focus groups as a research tool (Stewart & Shamdasani, 1990). Their use began in market research to test and develop products. Evaluation and policy researchers discovered their effectiveness, and they are now part of the arsenal of many types of research. Focus groups are group interviews that are structured a particular way and have specific, well-defined goals. Usually they consist of eight to ten people and a facilitator. A topic is introduced and participants are encouraged to comment on it in turn and then as part of a dynamic group dialogue.

Problems with focus groups and group interviews of all kinds include controlling the person who insists on dominating the session and keeping the conversation on topic. An additional problem arises when the group interviews are tape recorded. Unless the cassettes are transcribed very soon after the session, the interview will be difficult to reconstruct. Recognizing who is speaking and the likelihood that several people will speak at once contribute to making transcription difficult.

Using a tape recorder during interviews raises some special considerations for fieldwork relations. We will discuss the use of tape recorders in Chapter 4, but here we focus on their implications for the researcher–subject relationship. If you choose to use a tape recorder, ask respondents if they mind. The point in the encounter where you ask permission can be touchy. Either out of shyness or out of fear of being turned down, many people have a difficult time raising the issue. Never record without permission. Force yourself to ask. Some subjects simply will not care if the interview is recorded. Others will ask what you intend to do with the tapes. They want assurance that private information they share with you will not be revealed to others at their expense. In addition, some people think that once their words are recorded on tape, the tapes could come back to haunt them (or get them in trouble if, for example, they revealed something illegal they did). They need reassurance. Some subjects simply will say "no," and you must accept their wishes. For short interviews that are part of a participant observation study, you should take fieldnotes after the session. In long interviews you may jot down notes to supplement your memory. Sometimes people will change their minds as they begin talking. Provide the opportunity for people who originally refuse to change their minds.

What place should the tape recorder have in the relationship between subject and researcher? Edward Ives (1974), an oral historian and recorder of folklore, suggests that when interviewing, the tape recorder should be thought of as a third party that cannot see. When subjects gesture or show size with their hands, these nonverbal cues have to be translated into verbal language so that the tape recorder can play them back for typing. The interviewer tries not to feed respondents answers or make them feel uncomfortable with their own thoughts. During an interview focusing on sexual development in elementary school, an informant stated that she thought she had started developing secondary sex characteristics in the third grade. Later she said, "It must have been at the end of the fourth," to which the researcher replied, "That sounds a little more like it." This statement signified to the informant that the interviewer distrusted her, and later she stated that she was having trouble remembering things because she had been confused by the researcher's "doubting." The interviewer's thoughtless remark, which measured the respondent against some imaginary guideline of "normal development," had caused the interviewee to feel distrusted (Biklen, 1973).

Good interviewers need to have patience. You often do not know why respondents reply as they do, and you must wait to find out the full explanation. Interviewers have to be detectives, fitting bits and pieces of conversation, personal histories, and experiences together in order to develop an understanding of the subject's perspective.

Visual Recording and Fieldwork

Researchers engaged in qualitative research vary considerably in the degree to which they use a camera while doing fieldwork. We will discuss more fully the various visual material and how it is used in the next chapter, which focuses on data. Here we discuss visual material as it relates to the topic of fieldwork.

While a few researchers rely extensively on still and video footage, even employing visual recording as the prime data collecting approach, most do not. Cameras have significant potential as a data collecting aid but many qualitative researchers shy away from them. Some just do not feel competent with a camera because they have not mastered the technical aspects of the equipment. Some who are proficient do not want to be bothered with something else to do, feeling that they are more trouble than they are worth. Also, some researchers associate the camera with tourism and voyeurism, "isms" from which they want to distance themselves. Many share the opinion that the camera makes research in the field more visible, something they wish to avoid.

A camera can be used in an uncomplicated and unobtrusive manner, for example, to take inventories of objects in a setting. Objects and settings that contain more information than it is convenient to record in written form—the bulletin board, the contents of a book case, the writing on the blackboard, and the arrangement of furniture—can be recorded on film for later study and analysis. These can be taken at any convenient time, when people are not around, and this sort of picture taking can certainly be postponed to give you a chance to carefully conduct your interviews or observations. You can also postpone taking photos until you have established a comfortable relationship with your subjects so that they will not be threatened by your visual recordings. The researcher can keep notes on what inventory he or she wants to have photographed, or what categories of detail may be too numerous or ambiguous to record verbally and will need to be visually available later. The pictures can be taken quickly whenever the opportunity arises, and it takes little technical expertise.

But most people want to take pictures of other things besides bulletin boards and book cases. They want to photograph people in action; they want a visual record of how their subjects look in their natural setting. They want these as a record to help them remember and to help manage their data. They also want them to include in monographs so the reader will have illustrations to better grasp who the subjects are. Mitchell Duneier (1992) hired a photographer to take the pictures of Slim and his fellow diners for his book, *Slim's Table*. If the intention is to get more than an inventory of objects things can become more complicated.

All the interpersonal issues related to observation and interviewing re-emerge in a special variation relating to photography. The presence of an observer changes the setting to be observed; the presence of a photographer also changes it, but in different, often more dramatic ways.

People can become accustomed and indifferent to anything in their environment, and a photographer is no exception. By being "always" present and familiar, the photographer eventually ceases to be a special stimulus. One photographer remembers being in a classroom long enough that, when a new child entered and asked who he was, she was curtly told, "Oh, he's just the photographer," and no further attention was paid to his activities. This indifferent familiarity can set in amazingly quickly. In some settings, such as with groups of active young children, the photographer can cease to be a novelty in as little as fifteen minutes and slip into oblivion in a half an hour. In other settings, it may take two or three days of returning for hour-long sessions before people cease responding to the camera and begin to be "themselves." This "extinction time" must be reckoned with in designing any study focused on typical events, and enough time must be allowed for it. It should be evident that the photography site visits have to be scheduled close enough so that the process of becoming familiar and ignored does not have to be repeated each time.

The second way for the photographic researcher to become invisible is by distraction. If there are sufficiently engaging activities going on in the setting, subjects will pay little attention to the camera. However, usually it is important to make arrangements and come to an understanding that the regular activities should proceed. Often, when a photographer arrives on the scene, people wonder what they "should do." As long as this uncertainty is unresolved, they may be reluctant to proceed as usual. If someone is clearly in charge, such as a teacher in a classroom, the researcher should arrange that, at the time of his or her introduction to the setting, the purpose of the visit be defined as nonintrusive ("He just wants to see what we do every day" or "We won't pay any attention to her."). In less structured settings, it is best if an insider can be found to perform the introductions and "decontaminate" the researcher by explaining that the subjects are not "supposed to do" anything special. In the rare event that no one is available to present and define the nature of the photographic visit, the researcher should be sure to answer the questions many subjects will have even if they do not verbalize them ("Who are you?" "What are you doing?" and, most important for the study, "What do you want me to do?"). As the photographer proceeds to work, the subjects will gradually do the same.

Most of these remarks relate to studies that involve groups of people in defined settings. Some of the suggestions would not be useful in studies focusing on individuals and/

or where the subjects move about through various activities and places. It would be virtually impossible for a photographer to become "invisible" if he or she were the only other person in the room besides the subject. It also would be impossible, or very difficult, to remain invisible if the subject or subjects passed through other settings where other people were not cognizant of the purpose and nature of the photography. In general, these situations indicate the limits of the photographic researcher's ability to work invisibly. It would not be too difficult for an observer to accompany a subject through an entire day's activity from breakfast to supper, including shopping and visiting, as well as periods of solitude. But to do so with a camera, photographing every episode, would quickly become grotesque and anything but unobtrusive. The point is that, as with any method of research (or anything else), there are limits beyond which it is unproductive or silly to press. This is not to say a qualitative researcher would never want to photograph a subject shopping for groceries or riding a bus, but that the intensity and unobtrusiveness of photography (that is, the method's thoroughness and validity) is diminished in certain settings. In designing a study, these limits should be recognized and compensated for.

To take pictures in the field at events when your subjects are taking pictures often makes it an unobtrusive thing to do. Graduations, family gatherings, athletic competitions and other special activities bring out the cameras. These are times when subjects look on each other with pride, when they see themselves as being at their best. These are public times, times when they purposely dress to be on display. The researcher taking pictures at these times is often greeted warmly and filming is interpreted as a affirming act, as long as it is done within the conventions of normal picture taking.

Some of the problems associated with the researcher taking photographs or video can be minimized by having an experienced photographer who understands qualitative research as part of a research team or brought in for shoots. Of course, having a photographer can add additional problems—negotiating such arrangements with subjects is one—but not as many as you might think. One reason for advocating for a special role of photographer in a project is that often a good photographer is not a good observer; moreover, often a photographer interacts poorly. It may seem paradoxical to say that the photographer does not observe well—after all, is not a photograph the best possible observation of the scene? In fact, it is a human observer who can be sensitive to and recall (within limits, of course) the entirety of a scene. A photographer works very differently. The two operations basic to photography are framing (deciding what to include in the picture and from what perspective) and timing (deciding when to trip the shutter). It is not that the one research method is better than the other, but that they are very different ways to gather data. A good photographer can isolate and freeze relationships or behaviors in a way that cannot be recreated verbally; but a human observer can give a sense of the entire fabric of events that cannot be conveyed photographically. Thus a collaboration may be the ideal way to conduct some studies.

While we have mainly been talking about visual recording as a problem in establishing rapport or workable fieldwork relations, some have advocated that taking pictures can be a means of enriching relations. For example, taking pictures and then sharing them—even giving pictures to subjects—can bring you closer together. Showing your subjects pictures you have taken of them or of events related to them can stimulate good conversation and produce rich data.

Triangulation

Recently the word *triangulation* has been used widely in discussions of qualitative research. The subject index of a recent book on qualitative research includes seventeen references to the term (Denzin & Lincoln, 1994). It has gotten so that it is difficult to find a qualitative research dissertation were the author does not evoke the word in an attempt to convince the reader that his or her work is carefully done. Unfortunately the word is used in such an imprecise way that it has become difficult to understand what is meant by it. The term originally comes from the application of trigonometry to navigation and surveying. You can not locate your precise position on a map by taking your bearing on only one object in the distance. That only locates you on a line. You need a bearing on a second object as well. Then you can locate yourself at the intersection of the two bearings. Your location plus the other two points can be treated as the points of a triangle by which, if you have the distance of one side, you can calculate the length of the other sides.

Triangulation was first borrowed in the social sciences to convey the idea that to establish a fact you need more than one source of information. For example, to be confident that a train arrived in a certain station on a certain day you need more than the entry from the diary of a person who was on the train. (The person might have been inaccurate.) If you had the train schedule plus the diary you could be more confident. Still better would be the train schedule plus the diary, plus a report in a newspaper covering the arrival. When triangulation made its way into qualitative research it carried its old meaning—verification of the facts—but picked up another. It came to mean that many sources of data were better in a study than a single source because multiple sources lead to a fuller understanding of the phenomena you were studying. Others expanded its use to include using multiple subjects, multiple researchers, different theoretical approaches in addition to different data-collecting techniques. We advise against using the term. It confuses more than it clarifies, intimidates more than it enlightens. If you use different data-collecting techniques—interviewing, observation and official documents, for example—say that. If you collected data from many subjects about the same topic, say that. If more than one researcher collected the data, say that. In short, describe what you did rather than using the imprecise and abstract term *triangulation*. (For a discussion of the term see Blumer, 1967; Bryman, 1988; Denzin, 1978; Glesne & Peshkin, 1992.)

Leaving the Field

During the first days in the field you feel awkward and unwanted. As time progresses you begin to feel more comfortable, a part of the scene. Then comes the point when you have accomplished what you set out to do and you have to leave. Leaving can be difficult (Maines, Shaffir & Turowetz, 1980). Usually you become interested in and fond of the people you came to study. You may feel as if you are deserting them, especially if they were working under adverse conditions, or are poor and have limited opportunities to change their situation. The feeling hangs on that if you leave you will miss something important—some new piece of data that will lead to a new insight. While there are many reasons one can use to argue against leaving the field, there comes a time when procrastination must end.

Rather than abruptly ending this phase of their research, many people ease out of the field by coming less frequently and then eventually stopping altogether. This transition is probably psychologically helpful to both researchers and subjects. Often, researchers stop data collection only to find later that more fieldwork is needed, thus requiring them to return to the field. To prepare for this contingency, it is important when stopping fieldwork to leave the door open for such returns. Depending on the bargain you negotiated with the gate-keeper, there may be some obligations to keep, such as delivering a report or discussing your experience with organizational members before you say goodbye.

Many fieldworkers report that they maintain ties with the people with whom they were involved, returning to the research sites periodically to keep up with subjects' activities and situations. Sometimes subjects become lifelong friends. Qualitative researchers have reported that they enter and leave a site periodically, studying the same people and places longitudinally.

Chapter *4*

Qualitative Data

A person walking in a field sees a yellow bird as it plucks a red berry from one bush only to go to another bush, drop the first berry, and pick a second. If the observer is an ornithologist studying feeding habits, he or she might be keeping detailed notes—collecting data. If the person is an educational researcher just out for a holiday stroll, the details go unnoticed and are not written down. Similarly, archeologists call data what others consider rubbish. (Ancient garbage dumps are a favorite location for this form of research.) A school principal's memo can be valuable data if the researcher approaches it as if it were and if he or she understands its potential. As a miner picks up a rock, turning it to look for gold, so must a researcher look for the worth of information encountered in the research process. In one sense, then, ordinary events become data when approached with a particular frame of mind—that of a researcher.

The term *data* refers to the rough materials researchers collect from the world they are studying; they are the particulars that form the basis of analysis. Data include materials the people doing the study actively record, such as interview transcripts and participant observation fieldnotes. Data also include what others have created and the researcher finds, such as diaries, photographs, official documents, and newspaper articles.

Data are both the evidence and the clues. Gathered carefully, they serve as the stubborn facts that save the writing you will do from unfounded speculation. Data ground you to the empirical world and, when systematically and rigorously collected, link qualitative research to other forms of science. Data involve the particulars you need to think soundly and deeply about the aspects of life you will explore.

In this chapter, we discuss data and data collection. This topic is intimately tied to our discussion of fieldwork (see Chapter 3), but our emphasis here is more on the content and the mechanical aspects of gathering data.

Some qualitative studies rely exclusively on one type of data, interview transcripts, for example, but most use a variety of data sources. Although we will be discussing different types of data separately, it should be kept in mind that seldom are they found isolated in research. We start with a lengthy discussion of the mainstay of qualitative research—fieldnotes.

Some Friendly Advice

Before we start giving detailed information about fieldnotes and other forms of qualitative data we offer a word of advice. Pledge to keep your data physically well-organized, develop a plan about how you are going to do it, and live up to your vow. When you are in the field and the data are coming at you from all sides, it is easy to be sloppy about storing it. Confusion about the location of files and about other aspects of your data gets upsetting later and hinders analysis. With the current state of computer technology and the advantages computers offer in entering and managing data, all fieldnotes and interview transcripts should be typed and stored using a state-of-the-art word processing program and filing system. Most qualitative computer data analysis software does not require special procedures or formatting for entering the data. You can type your notes and transcripts as you would any text in a good word processing program. If you decide to use a qualitative data analysis program and there are special formatting requirements, the text files you create can easily be transformed to meet these requirements when you are ready to do analysis. While it is advantageous to know what software you are going to use in analysis prior to starting a study, this is usually unrealistic for the novice. The decision can be put off. If you do know the program you are going to use, consult the manual about text entry.

As with any information stored in a computer, be sure you back up your files. We may be old-fashioned, but we always feel more comfortable also having a hard copy of what is in the computer for safe keeping. The specifics of your study will shape your filing system. But for general advice: Create a separate file for each set of fieldnotes you write and for each formal interview you transcribe. Name files in a way that you can easily ascertain what is in them. Put fieldnotes and interview transcriptions in separate files. Try to keep files arranged in the directory in the order they were collected.

Documents that you find in the setting also constitute data that need to be saved. Whether you enter them into the computer depends on the nature of the material, how much you have, and how you might use them. These considerations will help you to decide whether scanning them for computer use makes sense. Usually it does not. Such found data are often not uniform in size, or are of a type that makes scanning laborious and time-consuming. The same goes for pictures and photographs. In contradiction to what some computer people tell you, good scanning equipment is expensive, tedious to use well and takes a tremendous amount of storage if you want good images. Thus, in unfunded projects, most found material has to be managed using manila folders and other paper products and filing cabinets. If you keep a hard copy of your data, you can still keep the chronological order of your collection by inserting the documents between pages of fieldnotes.

Fieldnotes

After returning from each observation, interview, or other research session, the researcher typically writes out, preferably on a computer, what happened. He or she renders a description of people, objects, places, events, activities, and conversations. In addition, as part of such notes, the researcher will record ideas, strategies, reflections, and hunches, as well as note patterns that emerge. These are *fieldnotes*—the written account of what the researcher hears, sees, experiences, and thinks in the course of collecting and reflecting on the data in a qualitative study.

The successful outcome of a participant observation study in particular, but other forms of qualitative research as well, relies on detailed, accurate, and extensive fieldnotes. In participant observation studies all the data are considered to be fieldnotes; this term refers collectively to all the data collected in the course of such a study, including the fieldnotes, interview transcripts, official, documents, official statistics, pictures, and other materials. We are using the term here in a narrower sense.

While researchers know that fieldnotes are central to participant observation, some forget that they can be an important supplement to other data collecting methods. In conducting taped interviews, for example, the meaning and context of the interview can be captured more completely if, as a supplement to each interview, the researcher writes out fieldnotes. The tape recorder misses the sights, smells, impressions, and extra remarks said before and after the interview. Fieldnotes can provide any study with a personal log that helps the researcher to keep track of the development of the project, to visualize how the research plan has been affected by the data collected, and to remain aware of how he or she has been influenced by the data.

In our discussion of other forms of data (later in this chapter), we will briefly discuss specific aspects of fieldnotes that are unique to these techniques. Here we concentrate on the fieldnotes taken in conjunction with a participant observation study. While we pick the fieldnotes from participant observation to discuss, much of what is said here is directly relevant to fieldnotes written in conjunction with other approaches, such as interviewing.

A set of fieldnotes collected as part of a study of a program that includes students with disabilities in an urban high school is reproduced as Figure 4-1. These notes were taken after the sixth observation at the school. They have been slightly rewritten and edited for the purposes of this book. We include these notes to provide an example of rich data and to illustrate the discussion that follows. We suggest that you read through Figure 4-1 quickly before you go on, and then refer to it as you read. As our discussion indicates, there are many styles of fieldnotes. The notes in Figure 4-1 are offered as an example of one approach.

A word of encouragement before we go on. Looking at the fieldnote example in Figure 4-1, you might be thinking that it is impossible to write so much from one short observation—that your memory, your writing ability, and/or your energy are not enough to meet the challenge. Take heart; do not quit before you give it a try. Some of you will only go out once and never complete a set of notes; for others, however, the discipline and skill that taking fieldnotes promote will be stimulating. Some people actually get hooked on observing and note-taking. Your ability to record notes will increase; the apparently impossible nature of the task will seem quite manageable if you can get through a few sets.

We have already recommended that all fieldnotes be typed into a computer using a common, up-to-date word-processing program. Windows programs enable you to use a mouse when you make changes to or shift your text. Recording data is not speedier, but marking, coding, copying and moving text are significantly faster. Sometimes we meet people starting a study who tell us that they cannot type or that they are computer illiterate. It is difficult for us to imagine being able to do qualitative research without these skills. Take a crash course or choose another calling. In Chapter 5 we will discuss the other benefits of using the computer in data sorting and analysis.

FIGURE 4-1 Example of Fieldnotes

Date: March 24, 1980

Joe McCloud

11:00 a.m. to 12:30 p.m.

Westwood High

6th Set of Notes

THE FOURTH-PERIOD CLASS IN MARGE'S ROOM

I arrived at Westwood High at five minutes to eleven, the time Marge told me her fourth period started. I was dressed as usual: sport shirt, chino pants, and a Wool-rich parka. The fourth period is the only time during the day when all the students who are in the "neurologically impaired/learning disability" program, better known as "Marge's program," come together. During the other periods, certain students in the program, two or three or four at most, come to her room for help with the work they are getting in other regular high school classes.

It was a warm, fortyish, promise of a spring day. There was a police patrol wagon, the kind that has benches in the back that are used for large busts, parked in the back of the big parking lot that is in front of the school. No one was sitting in it and I never heard its reason for being there. In the circular drive in front of the school was parked a United States Army car. It had insignias on the side and was a khaki color. As I walked from my car, a balding fortyish man in an Army uniform came out of the building and went to the car and sat down. Four boys and a girl also walked out of the school. All were white. They had on old dungarees and colored stenciled t-shirts with spring jackets over them. One of the boys, the tallest of the four, called out, "oink, oink, oink." This was done as he sighted the police vehicle in the back.

> O.C.: This was strange to me in that I didn't think that the kids were into "the police as pigs." Somehow I associated that with another time, the early 1970s. I'm going to have to come to grips with the assumptions I have about high school due to my own experience. Sometimes I feel like Westwood is en-tirely different from my high school and yet this police car incident reminded me of mine.

Classes were changing when I walked down the halls. As usual there was the boy with girl standing here and there by the lockers. There were three couples that I saw. There was the occasional shout. There were no teachers outside the doors.

> O.C.: The halls generally seem to be relatively unsupervised during class changes.

Continued

FIGURE 4-1 *Continued*

Two African American girls I remember walking down the hall together. They were tall and thin and had their hair elaborately braided with beads all through them. I stopped by the office to tell Mr. Talbot's (the principal) secretary that I was in the building. She gave me a warm smile.

O.C.: I feel quite comfortable in the school now. Somehow I feel like I belong. As I walk down the halls some teachers say hello. I have been going out of my way to say hello to kids that I pass. Twice I've been in a stare-down with kids passing in the hall. Saying, "How ya' doin'?" seems to disarm them.

I walked into Marge's class and she was standing in front of the room with more people than I had ever seen in the room save for her homeroom which is right after second period. She looked like she was talking to the class or was just about to start. She was dressed as she had been on my other visits—clean, neat, well-dressed but casual. Today she had on a striped blazer, a white blouse and dark slacks. She looked up at me smiled and said: "Oh, I have a lot more people here now than the last time."

O.C.: This was in reference to my other visits during other periods where there are only a few students. She seems self-conscious about having such a small group of students to be responsible for. Perhaps she compares herself with the regular teachers who have classes of thirty or so.

There were two women in their late twenties sitting in the room. There was only one chair left. Marge said to me something like: "We have two visitors from the central office today. One is a vocational counselor and the other is a physical therapist," but I don't remember if those were the words. I felt embarrassed coming in late. I sat down in the only chair available next to one of the women from the central office. They had on skirts and carried their pocketbooks, much more dressed up than the teachers I've seen. They sat there and observed.

Below is the seating arrangement of the class today:

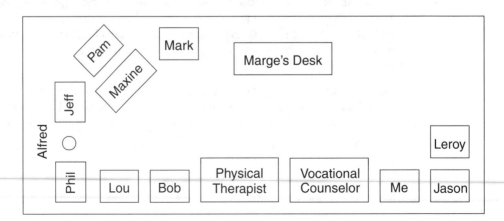

FIGURE 4-1 *Continued*

Alfred (Mr. Armstrong, the teacher's aide) walked around but when he stood in one place it was over by Phil and Jeff. Marge walked about near her desk during her talk which she started by saying to the class: "Now remember, tomorrow is a fieldtrip to the Rollway Company. We all meet in the usual place, by the bus, in front of the main entrance at 8:30. Mrs. Sharp wanted me to tell you that the tour of Rollway is not specifically for you. It's not like the trip to G.M. They took you to places where you were likely to be able to get jobs. Here, it's just a general tour that everybody goes on. Many of the jobs that you will see are not for you. Some are just for people with engineering degrees. You'd better wear comfortable shoes because you may be walking for two or three hours." Maxine and Mark said: "Ooh," in protest to the walking."

She paused and said in a demanding voice: "OK, any questions? You are all going to be there. (Pause) I want you to take a piece of paper and write down some questions so you have things to ask at the plant." She began passing out paper and at this point Jason, who was sitting next to me, made a tutting sound of disgust and said: "We got to do this?" Marge said: "I know this is too easy for you, Jason." This was said in a sarcastic way but not like a strong putdown.

O.C.: it was like sarcasm between two people who know each other well. Marge has known many of these kids for a few years. I have to explore the implications of that for her relations with them.

Marge continued: "OK, what are some of the questions you are going to ask?" Jason yelled out "Insurance," and Marge said: "I was asking Maxine not Jason." This was said matter of factly without anger toward Jason. Maxine said: "Hours—the hours you work, the wages." Somebody else yelled out: "Benefits." Marge wrote these things on the board. She got to Phil who was sitting there next to Jeff. I believe she skipped over Jeff. Mr. Armstrong was standing right next to Phil. She said: "Have you got one?" Phil said: "I can't think of one." She said: "Honestly Phil. Wake up." Then she went to Joe, the white boy. Joe and Jeff are the only white boys I've seen in the program. The two girls are white. He said: "I can't think of any."

She got to Jason and asked him if he could think of anything else. He said: "Yeah, you could ask 'em how many of the products they made each year." Marge said: "Yes, you could ask about production. How about Leroy, do you have any ideas Leroy?" He said: "No." Mr. Armstrong was standing over in the corner and saying to Phil in a low voice: "Now you know what kinds of questions you ask when you go for a job?" Phil said: "Training, what kind of training do you have to have?" Marge said: "Oh yes, that's right, training." Jason said out loud but not yelling: "How much schooling you need to get it." Marge kept listing them.

O.C.: Marge was quite animated. If I hadn't seen her like this before I would think she was putting on a show for the people from central office.

Continued

FIGURE 4-1 *Continued*

Marge continued: "Now you got all these questions down? Have you got them on cards? Can you all ask at least one question when we are out there? Don't ask the same question that the person in front of you asks, but do you all have a question that you could say? Now you know that Mrs. Sharp likes you to ask questions and you'll hear from her after, if you don't ask them. You are all excused through the fifth period tomorrow. If we get back late, I'll excuse you for first period lunch and you can eat lunch during the second period."

I looked around the room, noting the dress of some of the students. Maxine had on a black t-shirt that had some iron-on lettering on it. It was a very well-done iron-on and the shirt looked expensive. She had on Levi jeans and Nike jogging sneakers. Mark is about 5'9" or 5'10". He had on a long sleeve jersey with an alligator on the front, very stylish but his pants were wrinkled and he had on old muddy black basketball sneakers with both laces broken, one in two places. Pam had on a lilac-colored velour sweater over a button-down striped shirt. Her hair looked very well-kept and looked like she had had it styled at an expensive hair place. Jeff sat next to her in his wheelchair. He had one foot up without a shoe on it as if it were sprained. Mr. Armstrong (Alfred) had on a white, shiny shirt opened two buttons in the front. He had on light-colored dress pants, the kind without a belt. Phil had on a beige sweater over a white shirt and dark pants and low-cut basketball sneakers. The sneakers were red and were dirty. He had a dirt ring around the collar. He is the least well-dressed of the crowd. Joe had on a regular white old t-shirt and jeans. His long blondish hair was uncombed. He has acne on his face and is over six feet tall. He had on jogging sneakers that were clean and new-looking. He was the only boy who had on jogging sneakers. The rest had basketball sneakers. Jim is probably 5'9" or 5'10". He had on a red pullover. Jason had on a black golf cap and a beige spring jacket over a university t-shirt. He had on dark dress pants and a red university t-shirt with a v-neck. It was faded from being washed. Jason's eyes were noticeably red.

O.C.: Two of the kids told me that Westwood High was a fashion show. I have a difficult time figuring out what's in fashion. Jason used that expression. He seems to me to be the most clothes-conscious.

Marge said: "OK, we are going to have the test now." She went and handed out a sheet of problems. On one side it was a blank check with some instructions about what to put on it. There was also a deposit ticket and a balance sheet of a checkbook with a lot of figures below. They were supposed to put all the figures in the right place, balance the checkbook, and write out a check as well as write out a deposit slip. A great bulk of the period was spent doing that. Marge said: "Get started—remember this is a test." Maxine asked her a question. She said: "Remember this is a test. I can't tell you that." Jason said: "At least can you tell us how to spell a word? How do you spell twenty?" Marge ignored this. She came up to Leroy and said: "Leroy, you are supposed to use a pencil not a pen. If you make a mistake,

Continued

FIGURE 4-1 *Continued*

you can't erase it. Where is the pencil that you have?" He looked toward Jason and Jason gave Leroy back his pencil and then Marge gave Jason a pencil from her desk. She went over to the other side of the room. Bob was using a pen also. She said: "Bob, a pencil not a pen." A few times Jason said: "Miss Katz, Miss Katz," trying to get her to come over and help. He got Mr. Armstrong's attention and asked him some questions about writing out the deposit slip. Armstrong said: "If I answer that question, I'll be answering the test for you."

I leaned over to the person who was the vocational counselor and asked her about her job. She said she had been working for the city for two years but she was also in graduate school at the University. I asked her the reason for the visit. "I heard about this program. I want to explore if L.D. (Learning Disabled) kids are eligible for counseling. I hadn't seen this group so I wanted to come out and take a look, see what kinds of services they were getting and what they might get." I asked about the lady who was with her and she said that she was a physical therapist who was just coming along with her to see if there were any services that physical therapists could give. She was new to the district.

> O.C.: I really felt these women were out of place here. Their dress wasn't appropriate and they were like bumps on a log.

During the testing, Marge was walking around the room looking at what they were doing. She said, "You're all so smart. Now all you need is money to put into the bank." Three or four times during the test she used the phrase: "You're all so smart" in praise of them.

At one point, Marge looked around and said, "Where's Mac? Oh, yes, I told him not to come without his mother. Well, that's what you get, he's not here and I guess his mother couldn't come."

Marge came over and talked to the vocational counselor. The vocational counselor asked: "What about mainstreaming the kids?" Marge responded: "Oh, they're in the regular classes with the other kids. This is the only class they are together." The counselor said: "What about gym and Jeff?" Marge said: "They're in the regular gym period. Jeff can use the pool. It's designed so the handicapped can use it." The counselor said: "Do any of the children get any kind of therapy outside of class?" Marge said: "Jeff goes to the C.P. (Cerebral Palsy) clinic once a week." When Marge was talking, she whispered but her voice did carry and I was sure that Jason who was sitting next to me could hear everything that she was saying. The vocational counselor said: "I was watching Bob over there. He has almost a primitive grasp of the pencil." Marge said: "Oh, they all have that. The writing is a real problem not just reading."

Marge said: "Before this class was formed, most of these kids were not labeled L.D. or if they were labeled, they were emotionally disturbed. There was really no place for them. I mean, they would have them in this program or that program but not one that really is what they needed."

Continued

FIGURE 4-1 *Continued*

At this point, she was raising her voice and I was sure that Jason could hear her say: "Emotionally disturbed."

O.C.: I wonder if the students are as sensitive to these labels as I am. I feel terrible if they are used in front of the students.

The vocational counselor said: "Are there other kids besides those in wheel-chairs that could use the therapy?" Marge said: "I don't really know. What kinds of things are you thinking about doing?" The vocational counselor said: "Oh, consultation, physical therapy. We can't perform miracles but there are certain things we can do. I remember a C.P. kid's parents saying that the first word our child said was car. Now how can she tell him he can't be a mechanic?"

O.C.: This comment came out of nowhere. I couldn't figure out what it was hooked to. I got the feeling that the vocational counselor was nervous. She was young and Marge was being nice but not warm.

At some point during the class, Marge said in a voice that interrupted the class: "I forgot to hand this out to my homeroom. (Her homeroom is made up of typical students.) Oh, how could I be such a jerk." She was holding up a sheet of paper. Jeff asked: "What's it about?" Marge said, "A summer program, it's about visiting colleges. Visiting colleges that you might be interested in." Jeff gestured with hand as if he wasn't interested.

O.C.: This is the second reference that Marge made to colleges today. It really makes you wonder how college-oriented secondary school is. I wonder how the kids feel when they hear the word "college" said.

Marge started talking to the vocational counselor about some troubles with the way the schools were set up. She said: "The problem is the stupid credits plus the tests they have to take in order to get a diploma. You are almost forced to put them in academic subjects when that's not what they need. They ought to have some competency-based programs where you can measure them against life skills and have something to give them at the end of the program. They shouldn't be in here four years wasting their time." The vocational counselor asked what kind of subjects the students were in. Marge said: "There'll be a kid who's in here who is in biology. We will have somebody who is in algebra." The vocational counselor said, "Wow, that's something. Do you ever need things like a computer?"

O.C.: The vocational person didn't follow up on Marge's concerns.

Marge said with a little anger: "Well, if we had a computer, we could use it. We do have cassettes and we try to make those available." The vocational counselor said: "We are getting some computers down in the office. I can't promise that you will be able to use one but they are on order." Marge said: "Now one of the kids does hand in printed stuff. His mother does the typing. He wants to go to college. I don't

Continued

FIGURE 4-1 *Continued*

see it unless he takes her along with him." Marge lowered her voice and said: "He's not realistic. He wants to be a forester."

Marge continued to talk to the vocational counselor: "Most of the kids are in C.E.T.A. Now C.E.T.A. is not a career but at least it's a job, something for them to do. The problem is the diplomas. They can go through and take all their credits and then not get a diploma. Only E.M.R.'s (Educable Mentally Retarded) can get adaptive diplomas. My kids, they can take their minimum competency test orally but they're going to have to pass all parts of it, the writing and the reading and math. I don't want to be pessimistic but next year I know that none of my kids will pass it."

All this time while they were talking, perhaps fifteen or twenty minutes, everyone was very, very hard at work. Mr. Armstrong went from place to place and people were asking him questions. He wouldn't give any information to help solve the problems they had. He would only clarify what the instructions were.

The two women from the downtown office left thanking Marge and saying: "We'll get back to you." Actually, the one woman hardly said a word. After they left the room, Marge said to the class: "Those two women were from the downtown office. One is a vocational counselor and the other one is a physical therapist. I would have introduced you, but I didn't know one of the lady's names and it was embarrassing. Joe McCloud (pointing to me) is sitting over here. You know he is visiting regularly. He's interested in classes like this. He's from the University."

Marge said: "Do the adding and subtracting the best you can do. If you did this at home, you would have your own calculator and it would be a lot easier."

O.C.: Most of the kids in the class are poor. I can't imagine them having a calculator but I think she was saying that to be encouraging.

Mr. Armstrong came over to Leroy and said: "What do you have this for? This is a test." Leroy looked up with a smile on his face and said, "Well, I wanted to learn how to do it." Apparently Leroy was using a book to work on his test which he wasn't supposed to do. It ended with that.

Jason finished and handed in his test and said: "I got one hundred, this was easy." He asked if he could go to the bathroom and walked out with Marge saying: "Five minutes." A short time later he came back and he had the pencil in his mouth. Marge said, "What are you doing with my pencil in your mouth?" Jason said: "I'm holding it." She said: "Give it to me." He took it out of his mouth and gave it to her and Marge said: "Look at this you have got your teeth marks in my pencil. Nice way to return it."

O.C.: The tone of this was mild anger but not confrontational—Marge has a relationship with Jason where she is very direct with him but they are old friends.

Continued

FIGURE 4-1 *Continued*

Marge collected the papers and Jason said: "Let's see who has got them wrong. I know I ain't got none wrong." As she collected the papers Marge said to Jeff: "Now, you can finish this during the sixth period and some of you can finish this tomorrow."

O.C.: This gave me the impression that it was a pretend test, not the real thing.

Jason said: "How can they finish it tomorrow if we are leaving at 8:30 on the bus? Marge said, "Some of the people come in other periods than the fourth period."

The bell rang and everybody began to leave. I can't remember who was wheeling Jeff out or if he was doing it himself but Philip noticed Jeff's leg up and said: "What happened. You sprung you leg?" Meaning you sprained your leg. Marge said: "Sprung your leg, very good Philip. Try sprained." Mark and Laura chuckled.

O.C.: Marge talks in a joking way because of the tone of her voice. I don't think of it as a put-down. It is more joking. The tone of her voice is not hostile and the kids do seem to like her. She is the same way with the kids who are not in the program. The kids joke back with her.

Everybody left and Mr. Armstrong came over; so did Marge. They sat down next to me and we began to talk. I asked about where Mac was. Marge said: "Mac's a real problem. He just doesn't come. In the other program that he was in, he didn't come. I keep trying to talk to the father but I can't get him. I can't get the mother. I called the other day and Mac was on the phone. I heard his mother say that she couldn't come to the phone because she was too tired. The father works all day and then is a minister at night. They live on Hollow Street." I asked: "What kind of minister is he?" Marge said: "Alfred, maybe you know."

O.C.: Alfred lives in Mac's neighborhood.

Alfred said: "It's a full-time church and everything. It is just very small."

I asked: "Why were the people from the central office here?" Marge said: "Well, she said that she was going to come at 10:30 and then she didn't come until almost 11:45. At 10:30, I could have talked to her. I had some free time. I didn't want to say you can't come in, so I told her to come in and sit down. I don't know if she saw very much. I don't know what she is going to do."

I asked Marge what she felt about the central office and she said: "They don't know I am here. They don't know I exist." I said: "Who do you report to down there?" She said: "Well, not really anybody. Joe Carroll is the person. But Bullard is the one who is in charge of Special Ed. Let me see, Carroll is in charge of some special programs, I guess new programs that they are getting started. I really don't know what Bullard does. For sure, he doesn't make any decisions. I go to see Carroll. He's the supervisor of special programs."

Continued

FIGURE 4-1 *Continued*

I asked if the people come up and see the program. She said: "Well, Claire Minor who is a teacher on special assignment came once to see if we were alive and well but I haven't seen her since. I called Carroll once because I needed something and he came in, but he didn't initiate coming up. They don't come to see what I am doing. They don't know what I am doing. I don't mind. They must think that I am okay and I can handle my own thing but if there were new teachers, maybe they would come in but for sure, they ought to find out what's going on and what they are doing. I feel that if I had a problem, I could get help but they're really not on top of what I am doing. You will hear people talk. You can't get a decision on anything."

I said: "Can you give me some examples of not getting decisions?" She said, "Well, Jeff, now I have been calling down to that office to try to get a special bus for him so he could go with us to Rollway and I can't get Mike down there. He is going to wind up not going because we don't have the bus."

I asked for any other examples. She said: "At the beginning of the year with the aide. The aide I had, he quit and I called down and told them and Carroll told me that I wasn't going to get an aide this year. They said that I was going to share an aide with the resource teacher across the hall. Now that is kind of impossible because she has the same setup that I do. You can never tell how many kids are going to be in her class or my class so I went crazy. I screamed and yelled. Finally, I went to see Mr. Talbot, the principal. He's really good at screaming and yelling but he didn't seem to get anywhere either. Finally, I mentioned Teachers' Association. I told them that I was going to call T.A. That finished it. They are really afraid of the union. Before you know it, I got a call and they said they were sending up Alfred. That was around October 1st. This is supposed to be a pilot program. How can they have a pilot program if they don't have an aide for it? Yes, then they called me when I mentioned the union and they said that there was a young man for me."

I asked Marge about how the program began. I said that I hadn't gotten that clear last time. She said: Let me see, you know Leroy, you see Leroy. Well, he's the lowest functioning guy in the class. He's on five years probation for robbery and some assault, too. I had Leroy at the beginning of last year. Lou Winch tested him and found him to be neurologically impaired. Nobody knew that he had any problems. He just went along and wasn't getting anything. There was a teacher on special assignment and she couldn't believe that he had come up through school functioning at the level he does now. He was labeled emotionally disturbed. He is very very suspicious. Even if you raise your voice, he gets all excited. One time in the library, I mentioned his probation officer and he started yelling at me telling me, "Don't tell this in front of everybody." It's like nobody knows. Everybody knows that he has a parole officer. They put Leroy through the district committee. They said they needed a program for kids like this and they talked to Lou about it and then I volunteered. I also had Mel in the resource room. I was a resource room teacher last year. I hope you meet Mel before you go. He hasn't been coming in." Alfred said: "Yeah, he has got a job in some food store."

Continued

FIGURE 4-1 *Continued*

Marge said: "Anyway, people started talking about needing a program. Lou Brown at Miron Junior High has more of a self-contained classroom for neurologically impaired and learning disabled kids and we knew some of those kids would be coming here. So there was a need and so it just happened."

I mentioned how hard I thought the kids worked on their test. She said: "Yeah, you give them a task and they will stick to it. Now they don't get it all right. Like Leroy for example, instead of signing his name he signed sweater and pants."

I mentioned that Mark looked fairly sharply dressed and that he had an expensive shirt on. She said: "That's not the way he always looks. The other day he had on a shirt that looked a wreck. I went to his house. It is on East Street. They've moved now. Mark has never been in a regular class, always Special Ed. At Rosetree he was in with Alfred and his program. The Committee on the Handicapped, which was local then, looked at him and they encouraged his mother to develop a lawsuit because there was really no program to meet his needs. His mother didn't have to do very much before they said that there was going to be this program available for him. I mean it wasn't like the committee officially told her to start a lawsuit. It's kind of, they say it on the side. Mary Willow is the person who Alfred used to work with and she's really good."

Marge started talking about Luca Meta who I have not met. She said: "Now there is a boy who shouldn't be in here. His father put the old squeeze on Bullard and he wanted a special class for him so here he is. Luca doesn't need living skills. He seems to get something out of the vocational program but then he says that he wants him to be a forester. Well, I don't know about it."

I told Marge and Alfred that I had been to the Westwood High School play on Saturday night. I asked them about the kids that were in the play in relation to the kids in the special program. I asked generally about friendships in the high school. She said: "Well the way I think about it is that there's the very top and there's the very bottom. We really don't have a middle. Now that's my impression. Now you noticed there was only one black person in the play. Black kids like to come here because there are lots of other blacks. Some of the other schools don't have as many. But they really don't intermingle the way you would think. Thursday was the fifties day. Everybody was supposed to get dressed up like the fifties. The play was kind of like a fifties play. Very, very few of the blacks would dress up. They don't stay strictly to themselves but at lunchtime you go into the cafeteria, the whites are eating with the whites, the blacks with the blacks. Now the black middle-upper class mix with the white. That's different."

At one point, Marge told me that she had volunteered to coach the volleyball team. She said, "I have to get used to talking with kids at a different level. I always talk so slowly here and don't use big words. The volleyball team ought to be good. I play myself and it will give me a chance to practice."

We continued talking about the very top and the very bottom. Marge said: "The teachers that I talk to say that in their classes there is a mixture of those who can do the work and those who can't do the work." I ask whether they had the kids

Continued

FIGURE 4-1 *Continued*

on welfare from the inner-city and then professional class people. She said: "Yes, that's pretty much the way it is."

It's not very clear when this was said, but I remember at one point, she said: "The L.D. label gets you a better class." Meaning that having an L.D. class got you more of the less-troublesome kids.

I don't know what got this started but she started talking about the social background of the kids in the class. She said: "Pam lives around here right up there so she's from a professional family. Now, Maxine that's different. She lives on the east side. She is one of six kids and her father isn't that rich. As a matter of fact, he's in maintenance, taking charge of cleaning crews. Now, Jeff, he lives on Dogwood. He's middle class." I asked about Lou. She said: "Pour Lou, talk about being neurologically impaired. I don't know what to do about that guy. Now he has a sister who graduated two years ago. He worries me more than anybody. I don't know what is going to become of him. He is so slow. I don't know any job that he could do. His father came in and he looks just like him. What are you going to tell him? What is he going to be able to do? What is he going to do? Wash airplanes? I talked to the vocational counselor. She said that there were jobs in airports washing airplanes. I mean, how is he going to wash an airplane? How about sweeping out the hangars? Maybe he could do that. The mother is something else. His mother thinks that Lou is her punishment. Can you imagine an attitude like that? I was just wondering what could she have done to think that she deserved Lou?

"Now Luca Meta, he is upper class all the way. Leroy, there's your low end of the spectrum. I don't know how many kids they have but they have a lot. His mother just had a kidney removed. Everybody knows he is on parole. Matter of fact, whenever there is any stealing in the school, they look at him. He used to go to gym and every time he went, something was stolen. Now they don't let him go to gym anymore. His parole officer was down. He won't be here next year."

By this time it was about 12:00 and I mentioned going and setting up another time. She said: "You could come anytime you want. We're having a Tuesday trip." I said I probably would come the fourth period on Wednesday. She said something about them starting to read ads for apartments.

She said: "By the way, I was talking and maybe you overheard me about what we need is a competency-based program here. I have already finished a competency-based program if they ever took it. It is silly to have kids spend four years sitting here, when it makes no sense in terms of them. They ought to be out working. If they're not going to graduate, what they ought to have is some living skills like what we did with writing the checks. People aren't going to teach them that out in the world so they could do that. Once they had enough skills, living skills, to make it on their own then they ought to go out. There is no sense to this."

At one point, she was talking about Philip's family. She said: "Now that is a nice family. He's a very nice boy, middle-class boy."

Sometime during my visit I asked about the armed services as a possible career. She said: "That is another problem. Most kids can't pass the test to get into

Continued

FIGURE 4-1 *Continued*

the armed services. There was a show on 'Sixty Minutes' about how they get kids in by cheating. They can't get a diploma. They can't get in the army. I wish there would be some way to let them cheat with these kids because these kids could really use the diploma. If Phil doesn't get a diploma, he's going to feel very, very bad but I don't see how he can get it. Pam, it will destroy her. It will devastate her if she doesn't graduate. She has a group of friends who are going to get diplomas. She's on the track team."

We left the room. Alfred and Marge walked up the empty hall with me. I asked her how the kids felt about being in this class. She said: "Well, it varies. It really bothers Pam. Like she failed history and she has to go to summer school. The reason she failed it was she wouldn't tell them that she was in this program so she didn't get any extra help and then she failed." Marge walked me to the door. Alfred dropped off at the teachers' room.

On the way to the door she said: "Remember that boy I told you about who's going to be in here? The dentist's son, the Swenson boy? Well, I have been hearing stories about him. I come to find out that he is really E.M.H. (Educable Mentally Handicapped) and a hyperactive kid. I really am going to have my hands full with him. If there is twenty in the program next year, I really am going to need another aide." I said good-bye and walked to my car.

ADDITIONS

The night before last I met a woman at a party who teaches at Westwood. She asked me what I was doing at Westwood. I explained. She said she hadn't had that many kids from the program in her class. She did say that she had Luca and he is very good. I remember her saying something like: "He can't read very well but he's intellectually up with the other kids in the class." She said he wrote a report for her that was typed. She said she had Leroy in a class but she didn't see much of him. I said that some time I would set up a meeting to talk to her.

> O.C.: This morning I was up talking with Hans about the inclusion study. We began talking about Jones Markey School and how perhaps having more than one or two handicapped kids in a class made it easier for the handicapped kids. As we talked I began to realize that maybe a lot of what we are seeing in regard to hostility toward inclusion has very little to do with the kids or inclusion. Perhaps those schools that are undergoing strain and transition are the ones who are most anti-inclusion. Inclusion should not be understood as a thing that people are for or against. It should be understood that at different times schools face different problems. At Macri Jr. High one teacher sees the special education class being there as an example that the school is going to close down. The principal may see it as an indication that it is going to remain. Special Ed can alleviate or cause problems in the way it is perceived. It is very important.

There is at least one important fringe benefit in doing fieldnotes. It can improve the quality and speed of your writing. Any writer will tell you that a most effective way to learn to write is by writing often. People seldom have the opportunity to write page after page of concrete description. Even the amount of writing required in the most demanding college courses is small compared to what you are asked to do here. The nice thing is that fieldnotes are not like most required writing. It is expected that the fieldnotes will flow, that they will come from the top of your head and represent your particular style. In addition, you are encouraged to write in the first person. No one will scrutinize them for poor sentence construction or spelling; they should simply be thorough and clear. In addition, you will not have the problem of having nothing to write about. What you have seen in the field will become the source of endless sentences and paragraphs. Some people have been liberated from their fear of writing and of the one-half-page-per-hour speed limit they operate under by being given the writing opportunity that doing fieldnotes provides.

The Content of Fieldnotes

As our definition suggests, fieldnotes consist of two kinds of materials. The first is *descriptive*—the concern is to provide a word-picture of the setting, people, actions, and conversations as observed. The other is reflective—the part that captures more of the observer's frame of mind, ideas, and concerns. We discuss these two aspects of fieldnotes separately.

Descriptive Fieldnotes

The descriptive part of the fieldnotes, by far the longest part, represents the researcher's best effort to objectively record the details of what has occurred in the field. The goal is to capture the slice of life. Aware that all description represents choices and judgments to some degree—decisions about what to put down, the exact use of words—the qualitative researcher strives for accuracy under these limitations. Knowing that the setting can never be completely captured, he or she is dedicated to transmitting as much as possible on paper, within the parameters of the project's research goals.

When we say that the researcher attempts to be as descriptive as possible, we mean that whatever he or she observes should be presented in detail rather than summarized or evaluated. For example, rather than saying, "The child looked a mess," you might choose something like, "The child, who was seven or eight years old, wore faded, muddy dungarees with both knees ripped. His nose was running in a half-inch stream down to his mouth, and his face was streaked clean where he had rubbed it with his wet fingers." Rather than saying, "The class was festive," describe what was hanging on the walls and ceilings, what was on the bulletin board, what sounds and movements were there. Whenever you can, quote people rather than summarizing what they say.

It is particularly important in working on description not to use abstract words (unless, of course, you are quoting a subject). Do not, for example, say that the teacher was in front of the room "teaching." What was he or she actually doing and saying? Be specific. If the teacher was talking, quote and describe it. You might be interested in when and under what conditions teachers use the word *teaching* to describe their own behavior, but you should avoid using such a term yourself. Generally, replace words and phrases like *disciplining, playing, tutoring, practicing, nice person, good student,* and *doing nothing* with detailed renderings of exactly what people are doing and saying and what they look like. You want to cut into the world you are observing, and abstract words will lead you to gloss over rather than to dissect.

It may be difficult to abandon superficial or overly evaluative description. We have provided questions in the Appendix at the end of this book that may be helpful in bringing you to a deeper level of inquiry. We provide them to sensitize you to some aspects of schools you might study, but not as a set of questions to carry with you and to which you seek answers. The questions serve to increase curiosity and to broaden your range of vision.

As you can see by examining the fieldnotes in Figure 4-1, the descriptive aspects of the fieldnotes encompass the following areas:

1. *Portraits of the subjects.* This includes their physical appearance, dress, mannerisms, and style of talking and acting. You should look for particular aspects of people that might set them apart from others or tell you about their affiliations. Because the set of notes included in Figure 4-1 is the sixth in a study, the descriptions of people are not as extensive as they would be in an earlier set of notes. This is because the people in the setting have been described earlier. After the first full description, only changes are noted in subsequent fieldnotes.

2. *Reconstruction of dialogue.* The conversations that go on between subjects are recorded as well as what the subjects say to you in private. The notes will contain paraphrases and summaries of conversations, but, as we have suggested before, you should strive to make the subject's own words bountiful. Quote your subjects. You should be particularly concerned with writing down words and phrases that are unique to the setting or have a special use in it. Gestures, accents, and facial expressions also should be noted. Novice researchers are often troubled because they do not know exactly when to put quotation marks around dialogue in the fieldnotes. It is understood that you will not capture exactly, word for word, what the subjects have said. Rather than indicating an exact, literal, word-for-word rendering, quotation marks mean that the conversation is a close approximation of what was said. If you think you have captured the words fairly accurately, put quotation marks around them. If you are not sure of what the subject has said, before the quotation indicate that you are not sure that it is accurate. Use a phrase such as, "Joe said something like" and then write your transcription. If you really are unsure, note this and then summarize what you remember.

3. *Description of physical setting.* Pencil drawings of the space and furniture arrangements are useful in notes. Verbal sketches of such things as the blackboard, the contents of bulletin boards, the furniture, and the floors and walls also may be included. You also should try to capture the sense of the building or location where you are observing. What image, for example, does the school you are studying project as you approach it?

4. *Accounts of particular events.* The notes include a listing of who was involved in the event, in what manner, and the nature of the action.

5. *Depiction of activities.* For this category you include detailed descriptions of behavior, trying to reproduce the sequence of both behaviors and particular acts.

6. *The observer's behavior.* In qualitative research, the subjects are the people interviewed and found in the research setting, but you should treat yourself as an object of scrutiny as well. Because you are the instrument of data collection, it is very important to take stock of your own behavior, assumptions, and whatever else might affect the data that are gathered and analyzed. Much of the material that is discussed in the section on reflective fieldnotes is directed at this concern, but the descriptive part of the notes also should contain materials on such things as your dress, actions, and conversations with subjects. Although you attempt to minimize your effect on the setting, always expect some impact. Keeping a careful record of your behavior can help assess untoward influences.

"Rich data" or "rich fieldnotes" are phrases used by experienced fieldworkers to refer to fieldnotes that are well-endowed with good description and dialogue relevant to what occurs at the setting and its meaning for the participants. Rich data are filled with pieces of evidence, with the clues that you begin to put together to make analytical sense out of what you study.

Reflective Fieldnotes

In addition to the descriptive material, fieldnotes contain sentences and paragraphs that reflect a more personal account of the course of the inquiry. Here you record the more subjective side of your journey. The emphasis is on speculation, feelings, problems, ideas, hunches, impressions, and prejudices. Also included is material in which you lay out plans for future research as well as clarify and correct mistakes or misunderstandings in your fieldnotes. The expectation is that you let it all hang out: Confess your mistakes, your inadequacies, your prejudices, your likes and dislikes. Speculate about what you think you are learning, what you are going to do next, and what the outcome of the study is going to be. The purpose of reflection here is not therapy. Although some people indicate that fieldwork has therapeutic benefits, the purpose of all this reflection is to improve the notes. Because you are so central to the collection of the data and its analysis, and because neither instruments nor machines nor carefully codified procedures exist, you must be extremely aware of your own relationship to the setting and of the evolution of the design and analysis. In order to do a good study, you must be self-reflective and keep an accurate record of methods, procedures, and evolving analysis. It is difficult to get the right balance between reflective and descriptive material. Some researchers go overboard on the reflective side and end up writing autobiographies. It is important to remember that the reflections are a means to a better study, not an end in themselves.

The reflective parts of fieldnotes are designated by a notational convention. The set of notes in Figure 4-1 uses parentheses and the notation of "O.C.," which stands for *observer's comment*. As you can see in our example, observer's comments are scattered throughout the notes. At the end of a set of fieldnotes, the author also will take time to contemplate the day's experience, speculate about what he or she is theorizing, jot down additional information, and plan the next observation. From time to time, not as part of any particular set of notes, the researcher will write additional "think pieces" about the progress of the research. These longer pieces, added to or placed at the end of a set of notes, are called *memos* (Glaser & Strauss, 1967). It should be noted that some researchers, particularly those trained in some anthropological traditions of qualitative research, prefer to keep descriptive and reflective parts of the notes completely separate (Werner & Schoepfle, 1987a, 1987b, p. 32). They keep two sets of notes, entering their personal reflections in a field diary.

We have already given you some idea about what the reflective part of fieldnotes includes, but we categorize the materials to elaborate and clarify. Observer's comments, memos, and other such materials contain:

1. *Reflections on analysis.* At this time, speculate about what you are learning, the themes that are emerging, patterns that may be present, connections between pieces of data, additional ideas, and thoughts that pop up. Long reflections that focus on analysis are referred to as *analytic memos* (Glaser & Strauss, 1967). The importance and role of your comments and memos are more thoroughly discussed in Chapter 5. Illustrations of these types of reflections can be found in that chapter as well as in Figure 4-1.

2. *Reflections on method.* Fieldnotes contain material about procedures and strategies employed in the study and decisions made about the study's design. It is also the place to include comments on your rapport with particular subjects as well as the joys and problems encountered in the study. Particular problems you are having with a subject or some other dilemma may be a topic of such reflection. Include your ideas about how to deal with the problem. Assess what you have accomplished and what you have yet to do. Your reflections on method will help you think through the methodological problems you face and make decisions about them. When you are finished with your research experience, these methodological discussions will enable you to write an account of what you did.

3. *Reflections on ethical dilemmas and conflicts.* Because fieldwork involves you in the lives of your subjects, relational concerns between your own values and responsibilities to your subjects as well as to your profession continually arise. We discussed some of the ethical dilemmas in Chapter 1. Observer's comments and memos not only help you to keep a record of these concerns, but also aid you in working them out.

4. *Reflections on the observer's frame of mind.* Although they work to be open to the perspectives of the people they study, qualitative researchers generally enter their projects with certain assumptions about the subjects and the setting they are studying. Some of these preconceptions relate to religious beliefs, political ideology, cultural background, position in society, experience in the schools, race, or gender. The list could go on. Like everyone else, qualitative researchers have opinions, beliefs, attitudes, and prejudices, and they try to reveal these in their notes by reflecting on their own way of thinking. Of particular interest are encounters you have while collecting data that provide breakthroughs to new ways of thinking about prior assumptions. Early in the research these can come fast and furiously. What you thought just does not hold up to the empirical world you are studying (Geer, 1964). Subjects with mental retardation are not as dumb as you thought, adolescents are not as crazy as you knew they were, schools you thought you would hate you like, schools you thought were terrific tarnish, and programs you thought did certain things do not.

   The first reflections usually are entered into the notes prior to entering the field. Here, you depict, as fully as possible, assumptions about what is out there and expectations for the outcome of the study. When they are put up front in your notes, they can be confronted and compared with what emerges in the course of the study.

As an observer, you should be concerned with your own presumptions. We think your fieldnotes will reveal, however, that some of these initial thoughts and assumptions become fragile as they confront the empirical evidence you encounter in the field. Qualitative research requires long-term contact with people and places. The evidence that continually amasses can overwhelm groundless assumptions. Reflections facilitate and document this process.

5. *Points of clarification.* In addition to all the heavy pondering we suggest you do, as an observer you also add sentences in the notes that are simply asides, or that point out or clarify something that might have been confusing. You correct informational errors that were recorded at other times. You might note, for example, that you do not know how this happened, but in the previous observation session you confused the names of two teachers. Then you go on to correct that error.

Before we move on to other aspects of the fieldnotes, it is important to understand that qualitative researchers are not naive. They know that they can never reach a level of understanding and reflection that would result in pure notes, that is, notes that do not reflect the influence of the observer. Their goal is to purposefully take into account who they are and how they think, what actually went on in the course of the study, and where their ideas came from. They are dedicated to putting this on the record in order to accomplish a better study.

All research methods have their strengths and limitations. Some say that the weakness of the qualitative approach is that it relies too heavily on the researcher as the instrument. On the other hand, others say that this is its strength. In no other form of research are the processes of doing the study and the people who do it so consciously considered and studied as part of the project. The reflective part of fieldnotes is one way of attempting to acknowledge and control observer's effect. The reflective part of fieldnotes insists that research, like all human behavior, is a subjective process.

The Form of Fieldnotes

Before we move on from the content of fieldnotes to the process by which fieldnotes are collected, we want to offer some suggestions with regard to the form of the notes and then answer some questions you might have at this point.

The First Page

While the exact form and content may vary, we suggest that the first page of each set of notes (by set we mean those notes written for a particular observation session) contain a heading with such information as when the observation was done (date and time), who did it, where the observation took place, and the number of this set of notes in the total study. As we will discuss, you should strive to record fieldnotes the same day as the observation, but if that is impossible, the date the observation was recorded should also be given. We also like to give a title to each set of notes (like "Second Interview with the Principal," or "Observing the University Senate Meeting," or "The First Class of The Semester"). The title is a quick reminder of the session—a handle to grasp what the set is about. The headings help you keep the notes in order and maintain a record of the conditions under which the notes were taken; they also make retrieval of information easier.

Paragraphs and Margins

Most methods of analyzing qualitative data require a procedure called *coding*. (See Chapter 5 on Data Analysis.) Coding and other aspects of data analysis are more easily accomplished if the fieldnotes consist of many paragraphs. When writing notes, every time a change occurs—in the topic of a conversation, when a new person enters the setting, or whatever—start a new paragraph. When in doubt, start a new paragraph. Another way to make your notes useful for analysis is to leave large margins on the left-hand side of the page. This provides room for notations and coding. Some methods of coding require pages in which the lines down one side are numbered. Before you start taking fieldnotes you should read through Chapter 5 to see the analytical options that might affect the form of your notes.

Thinking about these issues, and with an eye to the fieldnotes in Figure 4-1, you might be wondering: How long should a typical set of fieldnotes be? How much detail should I include? How long will the fieldnotes of a total study run?

The many different styles of fieldwork and the different goals of particular studies affect the answers. If you have a more specific focus, your notes may be shorter and there may be fewer of them. Also, as you become more experienced, you will tend to do ongoing analysis in the field and less copious, random note-taking than at first.

Researchers usually take more extensive notes during the first few visits to a new site. It is during this period that the research focus is usually most unclear, and so the observer has not decided what is important in the setting. As a researcher, you cast the net widely, taking copious notes, and often spending many more hours writing than observing. As the focus narrows to particular themes, or you do more directed observations to fill in the picture, you may reverse your earlier practice and spend many more hours observing than writing.

What you observe often affects the quantity of the fieldnotes you take after a particular session. When studying a college class, for example, you would probably not take notes on the content of the lectures (exactly what is being said in anatomy class, for instance). Rather, you would note the questions asked, the comments students made to each other, the general form of the lecture, key phrases or words the professor used to describe the assignments, and other such materials. Thus an hour lecture may not yield as many pages of notes as an observation of a twenty-minute bull session after class in the student lounge.

We offer two examples to show what researchers thought was relevant. In one study we conducted we were interested in how residents and interns learned to talk to parents as they went about their training in a pediatric department of a teaching hospital. We would attend long case conferences in which a single patient was discussed, but take only a few pages of notes after such a session. Not only was the discussion too technical to follow in its medical dimensions, but what was of importance to us—the fact that the parents were seldom brought up—could be ascertained without hours of note taking on tracheotomy, Turner's syndrome, and other such matters.

In a study of a class where women were getting certified to become nurses' aides, the researcher found that in addition to the subject matter of taking care of bodies, the women were also taught a particular view of professionalism. Her notes reflect the necessary details to show this:

> Mrs. R. [the teacher] then goes on to discuss "primary nursing." "Primary nursing," she tells them, "is patient oriented. Usually, 1 RN, 1 LPN, 1 NA and 8–10 patients…Using this type of care, the RN can go with the doctor, listen to what he says—there are a lot of doctors around who will ask the nurse what she thinks; another thing, she can remember what he says and ask at the end, 'Now, did you want to order that?,' kind of to remind him. This is the ideal way to do it." (Solomon, 1996)

Here, the teacher's actual comments were important.

You would probably take account of the content of an elementary school faculty meeting if you were studying teachers. While you might not be interested in the exact characteristics that differentiate Houghton Mifflin from Open Court basal reading series, you will be interested in who leads the discussion and what information is presented and in what ways. You may find it important to understand what about the content of these contrasting basal series attracts different teachers. Additionally, the content of the principal's remarks to the teachers, while perhaps intrinsically interesting, can be important because you learn from it something about the principal and his or her relationship to the school staff.

The Process of Writing Fieldnotes

You have been in the first-grade classroom for close to an hour. There has been a lot going on. Twice, while the children were working, the teacher came over to you and explained her worries about what will happen to these children next year. She was very explicit about some of the children. The children seem much less conscious of your presence and you believe you are watching them play as they normally do. You have taken a lot in and you know you must leave in order to have time to write out your fieldnotes before your evening plans. You feel tense from concentrating so hard on remembering. Anxiety wells up as you wonder if you are up to the laborious task ahead. You say your goodbyes, walk out the door, and head for your car. You would rather do other things than take notes. You think of stopping at a friend's or going to a store, but you put those thoughts aside. Sitting in the car, you quickly jot down a topical outline of what you have observed. You include key phrases and important topics and you list the sequence of events that occurred. You fight the urge to give in to the idea that, "Now that I have an outline of my observation, I could do the complete fieldnotes any time."

You return to your apartment. You sit alone in a quiet room with your computer. You resist the temptation to call a friend who is working on a similar study to tell her what happened today. You stay at your computer and, working from your outline, you start to reconstruct with words the hour-long observation. You do it chronologically, trying to actually relive the events and the conversations. Thoughts of mistakes or missed opportunities break the line of your reconstruction. These reflections are written down as observer's comments.

You started your writing at one o'clock in the afternoon and by three o'clock you look up, not knowing where the time has gone. You forgot to eat. While it was difficult forcing yourself to sit down and get started, now it is difficult to leave your chair. The sentences run from your fingers in a way they never do when you are working on something else. You have lost your self consciousness about your writing and the words flow. You are sorry now that you made the date for dinner. You would hate to leave this without finishing, and yet you wish you were done with it so the burden of having to finish would be lifted. You work harder and you finish by five o'clock, leaving just enough time to get ready.

While in the shower you keep going over in your mind what you learned today and how it connects with other things. You remember having left the conversation you had with John, the teacher's aide, out of the notes. As soon as you get out of the shower you return to your computer and record the conversation along with some other ideas you had. You get up for the last time, resolving that enough is enough. You stick to it with the exception of jotting down a note or two on your napkin over dinner. The next morning you enter those scribbles with the set you completed the day before.

While we do not know how typical this account of writing up a set of fieldnotes is, it rings true to us. It highlights many of the struggles and practices involved in completing the job.

One problem everyone worries about is memory. Memories can be disciplined. More important and more immediately helpful in making the most of the ability you presently have, however, are some helpful hints to employ while writing up fieldnotes. The person in our story illustrates some of them:

1. Get right to the task. Do not procrastinate. The more time that passes between observing and recording the notes, the poorer your recall will be and the less likely you will ever get to record your data.
2. Do not talk about your observation before you record it. Talking about it diffuses its importance. In addition, it is confusing because you begin to question what you put down on paper and what you said to your colleague.
3. Find a quiet place away from distractions and with adequate equipment to record and get to work.
4. Set aside an adequate amount of time to complete the notes. It takes practice to accurately judge how long completing a set of notes will take. Especially for your first few times out, give yourself at least three times as long to write as to observe.
5. Start by jotting down some notes. Sketch out an outline with key phrases and events that happened. Some people draw a diagram of the setting and use it to walk through the day's experience. Like our friend, some people write down notes immediately after leaving the field and then work from them. Others write fuller outlines when they get to their computer.
6. Try to go through the course of the observation session chronologically. While some people do their notes topically, the natural flow of a chronology can be the best organizing outline.
7. Let the conversations and events flow from your mind onto the paper. Some people actually talk through the conversations as they write.
8. If, after you have finished a section of the notes, you realize that you have forgotten something, add it. Similarly, if you finish your set of notes and then remember something that was not included, add it to the end. Don't be concerned about getting everything the first time through. There is always time later to add.

9. Understand that note-taking is laborious and burdensome, but, as the Vermont farmer said when talking about winter on a warm day in spring, "It's a sweet suffering. It's like you paid for spring."

We have discussed writing up fieldnotes as though researchers always did them on the computer. Although less and less common, some people use a typewriter, but in addition, it is common for experienced fieldworkers to speak their notes into a Dictaphone or tape recorder. This can be an effective way to record notes quickly, but observers often forget that in order for the material to be coded and analyzed, it has to be transcribed. If you must type your own tapes, the process of getting material down on paper will take more time than typing them out in the first place. Transcribing tapes is laborious, which is a good explanation for the high fees freelance typists charge per page for this job.

If you do have secretarial services, the recording method can work quite well. Unless the project you are working on is heavily funded, however, you will rarely have such secretarial support. Even if you are lucky enough to have the money to pay someone to transcribe the notes, it is usually very difficult to find an experienced typist who will do the job as you want. Typists are not as accurate in transcribing tapes as the person who took the notes. Researchers often like to read over sets of notes soon after the observation session in which they were taken. Seldom can professional typists keep up with the pace of an ongoing study.

As you can see, we advise that you type or write out your own notes. Although time consuming, the typing and writing of notes has advantages. It can improve your writing, and when you do your own notes you get to know your data better. When you are collecting data in the setting, the knowledge that you must write up notes after you leave forces you to concentrate while gathering evidence. Reliving the experience line by line as you write out the notes intensifies concentration further. The note taking thus encourages the observer to replay the events: seeing and hearing things a second time should improve recall. The process also helps the observer to internalize, to commit to memory, what has been observed. The computer preserves the data, but the researcher's mind stores the thought process used to recall the data. This is like an extra source of data.

The fieldnotes in Figure 4-1 were written after a formal observation session. But fieldnotes also are written after more casual encounters. If you go to a party, for example, and have a conversation with a teacher about what school means to him or her, you might go home and write notes on the conversation. Phone conversations you have with the subjects during the course of the study should go in the notes. Very often the first set of fieldnotes reports the initial telephone call you make to inquire about access.

Fieldnotes should be detailed and descriptive but should not rest on assumptions that the researcher makes about the setting. A student realized, for example, that he did not know if the sentence he wrote in his first set of fieldnotes of his emergency room observations reflected a relationship or his assumptions. He had written, "Her husband stood up." He changed it to read, "The man who was with her stood up." He also learned how to capture detail. He revised this sentence, "I turned to the girl on my right," to read, "The girl on my right who was dressed in a brown flannel shirt and blue jeans, looked to be about eleven years old. She sat with her hands clasped on her lap, her head tilted back, and her eyes closed. I turned to speak to her." His notes reflected greater observation but fewer assumptions.

Transcripts from Taped Interviews

Some researchers take extensive fieldnotes after an interview to record their subject's statements. They rely on their recall rather than on a tape recorder. But long interviews are difficult to recapture fully. When a study involves extensive interviewing or when interviewing is the major technique in the study, we recommend using a tape recorder. We shall call the typed interviews *transcripts*. Transcripts are the main data of many interview studies. In Chapter 3 we went into some detail on the process of conducting tape-recorded interviews. Here we briefly take up some technical matters and offer some warnings. Some of the hints given in the previous section on participant observation fieldnotes apply to transcripts.

The Form of Transcripts

In Figure 4-2 we include the first page of an interview conducted with a woman in her forties in which she reflects on her years as an elementary school teacher. This interview was undertaken as a part of a larger study that examined female elementary school teachers' perspectives on their work. The form in which transcripts are typed varies (see Ives, 1974; Wood, 1975). The page we provide here illustrates a typical format.

As with fieldnotes, a heading at the start of each interview helps to organize your data and to retrieve specific segments when you want them. Here, the heading consists of the person interviewed, the time the interview occurred, the site of the interview, and any other information that might help you to remember the content of the interview. In studies where there are multiple subjects and where you conduct more than one interview with the subjects, it is useful to mark the headings indicating which interview this is with the subject. As with fieldnotes, titles can be helpful, especially when you are doing life-history interviewing. Choose titles that summarize the material covered in that interview, for example, "Early Life," "The First Day of School," or "The Year with Mrs. Brown."

In typing the transcripts be sure that every time a new person speaks, you start a new line, noting on the left who the speaker is. (In the example, "I" stands for the interviewer.) The transcript should, paralleling the interview, be dominated by the subject's remarks. That does not mean that your questions and comments are not included. It is necessary to have such material to weigh the respondent's remarks appropriately. When a subject talks for a long stretch of time, break the monologue into frequent paragraphs to facilitate coding. In addition, leave room in the left-hand margin for coding and comments.

Tape recorders can create the illusion that research is effortless. Aside from the short fieldnotes describing the setting and subject, the interviewer usually does not have to worry about extensive writing after the session. Because of this, the researcher might think that the machine does all the work. As we warned in our discussion on recording fieldnotes, accumulating tapes of interviews without an adequate system to transcribe them can spell the project's failure. Before you gain some practice, it is difficult to estimate how long transcribing takes. It is easy to let recording sessions go on too long, providing you with more dialogue on tape than you can possibly transcribe.

If you choose to record and transcribe interviews, a good rule to follow is "think short." Qualitative interviews are, of course, supposed to be open-ended and flowing. We do not mean that you should force the interview into a short answer format. Rather, we suggest that you limit the interview's length. Pick a reasonable number of subjects and spend an

FIGURE 4-2 Interview Transcript (Excerpt)

Interview with Kate Bridges

Date: January 9, 1981

Kate Bridges agreed to let me interview her for my project. She is on sabbatical from the Vista City Elementary School this semester and is leaving for California in a little while. I invited her over for lunch and she enthusiastically accepted. She had a lot to say.

I: How do you feel about talking while we eat?

K: I'd love to eat and talk if you don't mind.

I: Great! Let's get to it then. How long have you been teaching?

K: I started in 1971. I loved it for the first twenty years. I say, you really got me at a turning point here.

I: Great!

K: I felt that teaching was a calling. I mean it wasn't just a piece of work that I fell into that was good for being a mother and everything. I was standing at the window of my dorm room in my junior year and I was looking out at this beautiful garden and all of a sudden it came to me that I should be a teacher.

I: Uh-huh.

K: I knew. I just knew. And there's never been any question in my mind. There still isn't a question in my mind about being a teacher. The question for me is: Is it possible to be a teacher in the circumstances that are existing in the public schools here?

I: Yeah?

K: And being the kind of teacher that you want to be.

I: Yes.

K: As I think of the alternatives for teaching, I can't think of myself in any other career. I can think of a million things that I can do that I have thought of, like family counseling. I have friends going into that and we have talked about maybe doing it together. If I was starting over again at twenty I can imagine that might be another field, and I can imagine doing a lot of things that I enjoy. But for something that I really want to do, I come to teaching, and primary school teaching at that. I like teaching little kids. My mother was a fifth grade teacher for twenty years starting when I was in high school. She's recently retired and she always felt that it wasn't good enough.

I: That teaching wasn't good enough?

Continued

FIGURE 4-1 *Continued*

> K: That teaching in elementary school wasn't good enough. She thought she should teach in high school or college.
>
> I: The status issues.
>
> K: Yeah. Right. Exactly. She said to me recently, "Why don't you go on to become a college teacher?" I don't want to go into college teaching. I'm not remotely interested in college teaching. I might enjoy supervising student teachers. I have done that in the past.
>
> I: Yeah.
>
> K: But what I really want to do is teach these nine-year-old kids.

amount of time in each interview that makes sense in terms of the work involved in transcribing it. You do not want the respondent's discussion to wander all over the field, but to center on a particular area. You should figure that a one-hour interview, when typed, amounts to twenty to forty typewritten pages of data. If you plan to transcribe the tapes yourself, this will mean hundreds of hours of your time. If someone else is typing it, it can mean great expense to you.

We have a few suggestions about recording equipment (see Ives, 1974; Wood, 1975). Good recording equipment is invaluable. It does not have to be expensive, but it should be easy to operate, in good repair, and capable of making clear tapes. Because many of the expensive tape recorders are designed to capture music, they do more than you need. Since the tonal quality of the tape matters little (unless, for example, you are recording how a teacher uses folk music in classes), an expensive recorder designed to record music is rarely necessary.

The tape recorder must be in good working order. You need to practice with your equipment before you do your first interview and check your equipment both before and during each interview. While intrusive, this equipment check can be handled casually and is worth it in the long run. We have lost too many interviews because of equipment malfunction that occurred when we took it for granted that the equipment was working. We have been particularly plagued with problems with battery-operated recorders. The frustration of trying to type barely audible tapes is costly. You can forestall these and other problems by making certain in advance that your equipment is well cleaned and in good condition, or by borrowing or buying a new tape recorder. It is worthwhile paying attention to the quality of the tapes you buy as well.

The placement of the microphone during the interview is important in getting clear recordings. Test that you are getting a distinct recording of your voice and the voice of the subject. Try different placements to see which is best. One of the authors did a long tape-recorded interview in which the tape recorder was placed under the chair of the interviewer. Thinking that locating it there would be best because it was out of sight, the resulting tape was inaudible. Do not try to hide the recorder. It may interfere with the reception and may distract the subject more than a visible machine.

If you plan to do any transcribing yourself, try to use a transcriber. (It is worth buying one if you can scrape up the money.) A transcriber does not do the typing for you but it considerably reduces the time it will take. A transcriber is the playback part of a tape recorder with foot pedals to control stopping, rewinding, and starting the machine. Some models have special features to slow down the voice or adjust the number of lines the machine will jump when the pedal is pushed. New computer programs which enable you to "dictate" your notes through a microphone and then convert them into text in the computer are very promising for qualitative researchers.

If someone is typing the transcript for you, you ought to work closely with that person in order to make certain that the work is accurate. Capturing the punctuation that gets at the meaning of what you heard is especially difficult, so considerable difference can arise when two typists type the same transcript. The most accurate rendition of what occurred, of course, is on the tape. If you have the money to buy enough tapes, we recommend that you save the tapes so that you can check on the finished transcripts.

Because of the extensive time and expense involved in transcribing interviews, people working without research funding often take shortcuts. One shortcut is to type transcripts yourself, but leave out a lot of the material that does not address your concerns. While there are some dangers involved in this shortcut, the risks are often worth the gains. Another alternative is to transcribe the first interviews more or less completely (when we say "completely" we mean it would be all right to leave out long discussions of recipes and baseball) and then narrow what you transcribe in later interviews. As the study goes on, you should have a better idea about your focus and be more selective in what you type.

Documents

The data we have discussed thus far consist of materials the researchers have a major hand in producing. They write the fieldnotes and conduct the interviews that become the transcripts. Another form of data are the documents we briefly discussed in Chapter 2. These can be categorized as personal documents, official documents, and popular culture documents. Sometimes these documents are used in connection with, or in support of, the interviews and participant observation. Documents the subjects write themselves or are written about them such as autobiographies, personal letters, diaries, memos, minutes from meetings, newsletters, policy documents, proposals, codes of ethics, statements of philosophy, yearbooks, news releases, scrapbooks, letters to the editor, "Dear Abby" letters, newspaper articles, personnel files, and students' case records and folders are included in the data. Other documents can be found in the files of organizations, the desk drawers of principals, the attics of buildings, and in the archives of historical societies.

The quality of this type of material varies. Some of the materials provide only some factual details such as the dates meetings occurred. Others serve as sources of rich descriptions of how the people who produced the materials think about their world. Subject-produced data are employed as part of studies where the major thrust is participant observation or interviewing, although at times they are employed exclusively.

More recently, researchers have become particularly interested in the documents themselves, and may use interviews or participant observation as supplementary data to see how the documents get interpreted by real people instead of by an imaginary audience. Some researchers have taken to studying audio and visual material from the mass media: talk shows, popular records, MTV and other videos, soaps, and the like. Popular culture documents can be found on the shelves of the local video store or are available through flicking your remote or pressing some buttons on your radio, television, or VCR. The major task is to locate and get access to the material or, as in the case of mass media, deciding what to study out of the vast array of material available.

We will now review different kinds of documents as data.

Personal Documents

In most traditions of qualitative research, the phrase *personal documents* is used broadly to refer to any first-person narrative that describes an individual's actions, experiences, and beliefs (Plummer, 1983; Taylor & Bogdan, 1984). The criterion for calling written material *personal documents* is that it is self-revealing of a person's view of experiences (Allport, 1942). The aim of collecting such materials is to "obtain detailed evidence as to how social situations appear to actors in them and what meanings various factors have for participants" (Angell, 1945, p. 178). Used this way, personal documents include materials collected through interviewing. Thus, much of the data we discussed as transcripts would be considered personal documents. Here, however, we discuss only materials that the subjects themselves have written.

Personal documents that the subjects write themselves are usually discovered rather than solicited by the researcher. On occasion, researchers do ask people to write for them or get others to help them produce such materials. Clifford Shaw (1966) asked juvenile delinquents with whom he worked to put down on paper their life stories, which he later used for his research. Teachers frequently ask students to write compositions about certain aspects of their lives (for example, "My Family" or, more commonly, "What I Did During the Summer"). While raising ethical issues, teachers might be helpful in directing children to write on topics a researcher is studying. With the help of teachers, one Swedish researcher collected children's descriptions of how they envisioned their future family life (Hallden, 1994). Another researcher got 700 descriptions of what teenagers did each day after school. Jules Henry reports findings based on 200 school children's written responses to the question: "What do you like most and what do you like least about your father (and mother)" (Henry, 1963). Each year the Nordic Museum in Stockholm asks villages in the Swedish countryside to write essays on various aspects of the community. One researcher is working with material in which respondents were asked to describe people who lived in their town who were unusual or different and how they were treated. In a study of how teachers' home and school lives interact, teachers were requested to keep journals for a year to give to the researcher—and they did (Spencer, 1986). An advantage of soliciting compositions is that the researcher can have some hand in directing the authors' focus and thereby get a number of people to write on a single event or topic.

We want to discuss briefly some types of personal documents that are unsolicited by the researcher.

Intimate diaries

As Allport (1942) has stated, "The spontaneous, intimate diary is the personal document par excellence" (p. 95). He was referring to the product of a person who keeps a regular, running description and reflective commentary of the events in his or her life. Allport's image of the intimate document reflects his portrait of a young girl or woman writing in detail about various aspects of adolescent life she is experiencing for the first time. While this characterization may be a stereotype, it is also reflective of a type of diary. Adults with families and jobs may have less time to reflect on their lives and record these thoughts. Whatever the source of the diary, educational researchers have not been known to employ them in their own research. Because a diary is usually written under the immediate influence of an experience, it can be particularly effective in capturing peoples' moods and most intimate thoughts. Diaries, of course, are not lying around for the taking. The very intimacy that makes them so valuable also keeps them out of the hands of strangers.

Diaries can surface in the course of interviewing or participant observation. Subjects with whom you have developed relationships may spontaneously mention that they now keep a diary or have kept one in the past. It may take courage on your part to ask, "How would you feel if I read it?" But the effort may be the only way these kinds of documents will be revealed to you. Whether you see it will depend on your rapport with the subject as well as the personal value of the diary to the writer. Chances are, if the document is mentioned by an informant, the subject is toying with the idea of showing it to you, so you ought to pursue it.

While it may seem like a ridiculous suggestion, one way of locating diaries is to place an ad in a newspaper or publicly announce in other ways your interest in looking at certain kinds of materials and the uses you have in mind for them (Thomas & Znaniecki, 1927). You may be surprised that people will be willing to share their most intimate thoughts with persons who can establish their trustworthiness as well as their pure research interests.

Historians are researchers who depend heavily on diaries and other personal documents. They find these materials in local historical societies and various archives as well as in the boxes of memorabilia that people store in their attics. For educational researchers, teachers' diaries that record in detail first teaching experiences, problems with students, and other such materials are important finds.

There are other materials that are similar to diaries, but much less intimate. There are special-purpose logs such as those teachers might keep. Lesson plans with accompanying notes are interesting, especially if they contain personal comments. Also, parents sometimes keep developmental diaries of the growth and progress of their children. Some go as far as to make weekly entries about what the child is doing. This kind of material can be an important source of understanding how parents perceive their children and their expectations for them. Travel logs and other kinds of written records of peoples' activities, although not as intimate or revealing as a diary, can provide some hints about what life is like for the people you are interested in studying.

Personal Letters

Personal letters between friends and family members provide another source of rich qualitative data. These materials can be especially helpful in revealing relationships between people who correspond. When the letter represents an attempt by the author to share his or her problems and dilemmas, it can provide insights about the author's experiences. Many people go away to school or travel to take up jobs in educational institutions. The letters written home describing their lives and the nature of their experiences offer rich data about the educational system. Much of what has been said about locating diaries applies to letters as well, although letters are a more common form of communication than diaries. The increased use of the phone and electronic mail for communicating may discourage letter-writing, however, this data source may soon be useful only to people with historical interests.

Although they should not be classified as personal, letters written to the editors of newspapers about school issues are another possible source of information for the qualitative researcher. Another are the more personal letters written to the likes of Ann Landers and Dear Abby. Perusing such materials can give you some insight, for example, about problems adolescents face. It should be kept in mind, of course, that the published letters are not randomly selected. They represent the choice of the person writing the column or the columnist's staff.

Autobiographies

Published autobiographies provide a readily available source of data for the discerning qualitative researcher (Denzin, 1989). Virtually thousands of such documents get published and most contain extensive discussions of peoples' educational experiences. There are autobiographies written by school dropouts, great teachers, world leaders, adolescents, scholars, doctors, check forgers, drug addicts, and ordinary people. Autobiographies range considerably from the intimate and personal (containing materials such as are found in rich diaries) to the superficial and trivial.

With all personal documents it is important to understand the writer's purpose in producing the document. The autobiographer's purpose can vary widely. Some reasons to engage in such a task include:

1. Special pleading for oneself or a cause
2. Exhibitionism
3. Desire to give order to one's life
4. Literary delight
5. Securing personal perspective
6. Relief from tension
7. Monetary gain
8. Outside pressures to write it
9. Assisting in therapy
10. Redemption and social reincorporation
11. Scientific interest
12. Public service and example
13. Desire for immortality (Allport, 1942, p. 69)

The motivation will affect the content of the document. An autobiography, rich in detail, written for the purpose of telling the person's own story as he or she experienced it, parallels the role a key informant would play for a researcher. It can be an introduction to the world you want to study. Autobiographies by particular categories of people, ethnic minorities, for example, particularly sections of the work force that describe their schooling, can introduce the researcher interested in this issue to the range of educational experiences the particular group encountered.

Novels should not be ruled out as a potential source of qualitative understanding, although they are more troublesome than autobiographies because discerning accurate description from imaginative portrayal is difficult. (See Eisner, 1980, on artistic understanding.) They cannot be taken as the truthful representation of an author's experiences. They can, however, provide insight when they are about a segment of society the author has first hand knowledge of.

Official Documents

Schools, and other organizations, like groups and companies produce documents for specific kinds of consumption. Bureaucratic organizations, in particular, have reputations for producing a profusion of written communications and files. Most people talk disparagingly about these mounds of paper and might look askance at us for calling these official documents "data." We are talking about such things as memos, minutes from meetings, newsletters, policy documents, proposals, codes of ethics, dossiers, students' records, statements of philosophy, news releases, brochures, pamphlets, and the like. These materials have been viewed by many researchers as extremely subjective, representing the biases of the promoters and, when written for external consumption, presenting an unrealistically glowing picture of how the organization functions. For this reason, many researchers consider them unimportant, excluding them as data. It is precisely for these properties (and others) that qualitative researchers look upon them favorably. Remember, qualitative researchers are not interested in "the truth" as it is conventionally conceived. They do not search for the "true picture" of any school. Their interest in understanding how the school is defined by various people propels them toward official literature. In these papers researchers can get access to the "official perspective," as well as to the ways various school personnel communicate. Much of what we term *official documents* are readily available to the researcher, although some are protected as private or secret. We will briefly discuss some types of official documents, their use, and special problems you may encounter obtaining them.

Internal Documents

These are memos and other communications that are circulated inside an organization such as a school system. This information tends to follow the hierarchical course, circulating downward from the central office to teachers and staff. Information flows the opposite way, of course, but it rarely equals the downward tide. Minutes of department meetings and other such gatherings are often passed along horizontally. Internal documents can reveal information about the official chain of command and internal rules and regulations. They also can provide clues about leadership style and potential insights about what organizational members value. While secret memos exist, secret information is not, by and large, passed along in written form. If a researcher has established good rapport, he or she will have access to most internally produced documents.

External Communication

External communication refers to materials produced by organizations for public consumption: newsletters, news releases, yearbooks, the notes sent home, the public statements of philosophy, advertisements for the open-house programs, brochures, and pamphlets. As we suggested earlier, this material is useful in understanding official perspectives on programs, the administrative structure, and other aspects of the organization. It should be kept in mind that, increasingly, school systems hire public relations experts to produce such materials, so they do not necessarily flow directly from the pens of those in charge. Most likely, though, school administrators review and approve the documents. You may be able to put external documents to better use if you know something about who produced them and for what reasons—in other words, if you know the social context. Some external documents are good indicators of school systems' strategies for increasing fiscal support, while in other cases they represent a direct expression of the values of those who administer the schools.

Usually external documents are easy to get. In fact, they are often produced in quantities that far exceed their demand. Very often administrative offices will maintain scrapbooks and files to keep these materials as they are issued over the years. Scrapbooks may contain local newspaper coverage of school-related events. Casella (1997) sent away for trip brochures listed in the back of the *New York Times* travel section for his research on educational travel brochures. Daniels (1997) first set up a post office box under a pseudonym when she requested pamphlets and other publications of white supremacist groups. But when they requested a donation, she felt she could not ethically donate money to a cause she despised, so she used the collection in the archives of the organization Klanwatch instead. Ask the organization you want to study to see such holdings because they can save you time.

Student Records and Personnel Files

In addition to the official documents already discussed, schools keep individual files on every student and, in most cases, on each employee. The files on students are particularly elaborate and important. They include psychological reports, records of all testing, attendance, anecdotal comments from teachers, information about other schools attended, and profiles of the family. This file follows the child throughout his or her school career.

Traditional researchers often use such case records to conduct research, but many take the position that they are not very helpful because they do not give accurate information about the child. Qualitative researchers would agree with this wholeheartedly. While they might occasionally want to retrieve a test score or a list of teachers from a file, by and large qualitative researchers approach student records not for what they tell about the child, but rather for what they reveal about the people who keep the records (psychologists, administrators, teachers). Taylor's study of bureaucratic texts (1996) traces the "injustices of bureaucratic texts" from the welfare, criminal justice, and health care systems through the lives of five people. In this framework, the information the files contain—the letters, the teacher's comments, the test scores—represent perspectives on the child. They present one side of the picture. They seldom contain unaltered quotations from the students or their parents. Juxtaposing a student's records with interviews with the student or the parents can prove to be revealing.

Popular Culture Documents

Qualitative researchers have shown increasing interest in using these methods to study popular culture. Popular culture documents include videos (Schoonmaker, 1994), educational and feature films (Ellsworth, 1988; Farber & Holm, 1994; Giroux & Simon, 1989; Kennard, 1990; McRobbie, 1991; Trudell, 1990; Whatley, 1991), rock and roll (Holm & Farber, 1994; Rowe, 1995; Willis, 1990), magazines (Holm, 1994; Lutz & Collins, 1993; Provenzo & Ewart, 1994; McRobbie, 1991) television (Bacon-Smith, 1992; Livingstone & Lunt, 1994; Press, 1991; Schwoch, White & Reilly, 1992; Willis, 1990), romance novels (Radway, 1984; Christian-Smith, 1988, 1990), and advertisements (Barthel, 1988; Kellner, 1991; O'Barr, 1994). These documents, as we said earlier, have been studied in two ways: first, as texts, where the transcripts of the shows, lyrics, and films are treated as fieldnotes; and second, as part of studies where the interpretations of the viewers are a central part of the project.

Feminists, critical theorists, and scholars of mass communications first became interested in popular culture documents as texts because of the significant role of media in people's meaning-making processes. If media and popular culture are part of our "symbolic interactions," then if we study these texts we learn about one influence on how people make sense of their everyday lives. Researchers were interested in how, for example, television, magazines, advertisements and other popular cultural forms affected how women thought about femininity, how men thought about masculinity, or how youth made sense of class and race. The purpose of the research was to make visible "messages," or social constructions in the texts. These messages might include, for example, how cigarette smoking was constructed as healthy in advertisements (Kellner, 1991), how romance novels for adolescent girls constructed femininity (Christian-Smith, 1988), or how social class was constructed in the film *Dirty Dancing* (Giroux & Simon, 1989). Because the texts had never been studied systematically for these concerns before, these interpretations were interesting and provocative.

Such work suggests, however, that the representations in these films, ads, and magazines will be taken up, engaged and absorbed by the spectators as they are read by the investigators. The spectator, in other words, will respond to the codes in the popular culture document unproblematically. While early research examining representations in popular culture documents was significant because it used interpretive strategies to examine these representations, it was clueless about how individual readers, film and television viewers, or listeners to rock and roll made sense of the texts. Research needed to reflect how spectators might take up one part of a show as the creators wanted them to while resisting another part, or even ignoring significant features. A new generation of researchers studied, more ethnographically, how women enacted being fans of *Star Trek* and other science fiction shows (Bacon-Smith, 1992), how they talked about the television shows they watched (Press, 1991; Willis, 1990), and how they thought about renting and viewing videos (Schoonmaker, 1994). This kind of research emphasizes the possibility of "being surprised" (Willis, 1980, p. 90) as it brings together the researcher's reflexivity, the paradigm in which the research was conceptualized, and the spectators' perspectives. Researchers who draw on symbolic interaction or cultural studies as their paradigm believe that studying responses to cultural documents are key.

If you are interested in using popular culture documents in your research, the following guidelines may be useful:

1. *How interest groups read popular culture documents.* In this kind of research you will have two kinds of fieldnotes, the documents themselves, and the interview transcripts or participant observation fieldnotes written from your interviews or observations with a particular group that is engaged with this popular culture form. You might watch a particular soap opera, like *General Hospital,* and construct fieldnotes from the shows, considering each show a separate set of fieldnotes. You read these fieldnotes, and look for themes, ideas, vocabulary, and perspectives which seem prominent. You may then interview women, or men and women, who watch this show about their viewing habits, their understanding of the program, their changing interest or involvement with different characters. Or, if you do not like soap operas, but are interested in popular culture, you might watch a particular situation comedy for their representations of race, and then interview a certain group of people who watch that show. Lutz and Collins (1993), analyzed how *National Geographic* represented non-western peoples by looking at the text and the photographs to see how these views were produced. They also interviewed editors at the magazine to see how they made sense of their work. In addition, they interviewed white readers of *National Geographic* to see how they interpreted the magazine's construction of non-western people.

   2. *Your pleasure is significant.* It is very difficult to do this kind of research if you do not like the popular culture form that you are studying. Therefore, choose a project that utilizes a form that you enjoy, that gives you pleasure. One of the significant aspects of popular culture as topic of consideration is that particular forms may teach things we do not like, but we may also experience pleasure at the same time. Any study must account for both of these aspects. You should not study wrestling if you do not like this sport, or soap operas if that kind of television turns you off. The reflexivity of this kind of research benefits from your own reflection on a form which may both entertain you and make you feel critical. Students doing qualitative projects on popular culture have chosen the forms of popular culture that they are willing to spend significant amounts of time viewing or reading, like *Seventeen* magazine, "On the Road," an MTV show, or the Oprah Winfrey show. Pleasure, yours as well as informants', is connected to popular culture.

   3. *Decisions about emphasis.* Each study will probably not emphasize the text of the show, magazine, or film equally with the interviews or observations. While you may not know when you begin the research which aspect of the research interests you most, you should decide this partway through data collection. Your research will probably emphasize either the lived experience of the spectators, as they engage with the popular culture documents, if that aspect of your data interests you most, or the textual analysis, if that is where your interest lies. Some researchers talk to television viewers, and write very little about the shows themselves, outside of what their informants say about them. Andrea Press (1991), for example, has a short chapter called, "Work, Family, and Social Class in Television Images of Women: Prefeminism, Feminism, and Postfeminism on Prime-Time Television," but the most substantial part of the book explores how working-class and middle-class women interpret the shows. Schoonmaker (1994) hardly discusses the videos themselves, emphasizing instead how store owners and clients think about the videos. Other studies focus much more on the shows, ads, or song lyrics, as well as on their informants' views. Trudell (1990) describes the film, and the curricular materials that accompany the film for the teachers' use, and then discusses the reactions of the students.

   4. *Individual or group interviews and observations.* If you are interested in particular groups, you may want to consider watching a television show with the group, and then talking with the group about the show. Whether you meet with your informants in groups or individually depends on the project and on the group. When Radway (1984) studied readers of romance fiction, she did participant observation with Dot and the Smithton readers, a group that had formed to evaluate romance fiction for other women. These women already met together before Radway began her research, so they composed a natural group. Her study was of the group and the texts. It is also possible to bring together groups of adolescents, for example, to watch films, videos, or television and to engage in dialogue with them about what they see. We know a teacher who showed the films of John Singleton to African American students after school, and listened to them talk about what they saw in the films. We know another student who asked an adolescent woman to bring together some of her friends who read magazines like *Seventeen,* and *YM* to talk about how they read, what they see, and what images they resisted or responded to in their reading experiences.

5. *Systematic organization of textual data.* When you use popular culture documents as evidence, you need to be systematic in your management of the data. You need details from the shows, films, or advertisements, in the same way that you need details when you interview or observe informants. If you are using television shows for your data, it is most helpful to record the shows on video so that you can create transcripts for them at slower speeds. If you are using magazines or advertisements, you should copy them so that you can see them many times and develop ways to code them for vocabulary and themes. You may want to scan them into the computer for use with a software analysis program.

Photography

Photography has been closely aligned with qualitative research and, as we shall explore here, it can be used in many different ways. Photographs provide strikingly descriptive data, are often used to understand the subjective, and are frequently analyzed inductively.

Almost from its advent, photography was employed in conjunction with social science research. One of the early photographers who did social photographic documentaries was John Thomson, whose book *Street Life in London,* a portrayal of London's poor, was published in 1877 (Thomson & Smith, 1877). A decade later in New York City, Jacob Riis's photographic essay on immigrants included portraits of the interiors of dilapidated schools. He educated people about urban conditions (Riis, 1890). Lewis Hine, a sociologist, was one of the first social scientists to use a camera to show the American people poverty in their own country. His photo documentaries of child labor were influential in passing the first child labor laws and legislation directed toward compulsory education. He said, "If I could tell the story in words, I wouldn't need to lug a camera" (Stott, 1973).

While social science and photography have been linked for a long time (Edwards, 1992), it is only recently that photos have captured the attention of a significant number of researchers (Becker, 1986b; Wagner, 1979; Ball & Smith, 1992; Harper, 1994) and theorists (Bolton, 1989; Chaplin, 1994; Becker, 1995). The journal *Visual Sociology,* is devoted to the exploration of photography and social science and we recommended it to you if you want to pursue photography and qualitative research beyond what is said here. This interest in photography has been controversial. Some claim that photography is virtually useless as a way of objectively knowing because it distorts that which it claims to illuminate (Sontag, 1977; Tagg, 1988). Others counter with the claim that it represents a significant research

A one-room school class in the Northeastern United States, circa 1905. From the collection of Robert C. Bogdan.

breakthrough, since it allows researchers to understand and study aspects of life that cannot be researched through other approaches; they echo Hine's suggestion that images are more telling than words or the cliché that a picture is worth a thousand words.

While a few argue these extreme positions, most social scientists neither accept nor reject photography outright; they ask, "What value does it have for me and how can I make use of it in my own work?" They ask these questions in relation to specific research problems and with particular photographs in mind.

Photographs that might be used in qualitative educational research can be separated into two categories: those that others have taken and those that the researcher has a hand in producing.

Found Photographs

Photographs that fall under this category are available because others have taken them (Dowdell & Golden, 1989). Historical societies have large collections and there are many private collectors of antique photographs as well (Mace, 1990). Many schools and human service agencies have extensive collections of photographs, often going back to the laying of the cornerstone. Some universities have a person, "the university archivist," who is in charge of the institution's holdings related to its own history. This person can show you a rich array of photographic and other visual materials. Close by and readily available, this

Teacher Edith McWilt and her first-grade class, New Port, New York, 1918. From the collection of Robert C. Bogdan.

resource is seldom tapped as data. Yearbooks, class pictures, and amateur photos taken at annual events and outings near and far are available for the asking. Students often have their own photo collections, some of which they carry with them in purses or wallets. Newspapers keep photo libraries, although access to this material is often limited. County planning offices keep aerial photographs of all the land that falls within their jurisdiction. Some of this data can be found at flea markets and garage sales. Try local post card collectors and antique paper clubs and shows. The *Post Card Collector* is a national magazine of post card collectors that has articles about various kinds of post cards, including photographic ones, and where to find them. There are similar publications for other forms of visual material. The possibilities are endless and fun to pursue. We are, and have been for at least a hundred years, a photographic society.

Photos that turn up in a setting under study can provide a good sense of individuals no longer there or what particular events in that setting were like. As suggested, schools often keep photo collections, yearbooks. and, sometimes, albums that offer their own visual history. Photos that staff may have taken of former students or co-workers portray some sense of what these people were like despite your never having met them. While not a substitute for having been there, photos can offer one historical rendering of the setting and its participants. Further, such photos can be incorporated into research reports to communicate this perspective.

Public school in Valdez, Alaska, October, 1902. Photo by the Miles Brothers.

While photos provide a general sense of a setting, they can also offer specific factual information that can be used in conjunction with other sources. Pictures taken at retirement parties, for example, can show who attended and indicate something about seating arrangements, hinting, perhaps, at the informal structure. Aerial photos of a community under study can suggest relationships between population distribution, geographic location, and the educational system.

While photos do give factual information, it is important to understand that photos researchers find or are given were taken for a purpose or from a particular point of view. In order to use them more than superficially, we have to know the purpose and the frame of mind of the photographer (Fancher, 1987). In this way, a photo is like all other forms of qualitative data: To use it, we must place it in a proper context and understand what it is capable of revealing before extracting information and understanding (Fox & Lawrence, 1988). One of the authors began a study of the history of exhibiting people with physical anomalies in the side show by visiting repositories of circus memorabilia. The data he came across consisted mainly of publicity photographs that the exhibitors sold to supplement their incomes. At first the photos were examined as if they were a source of information about the people exhibited. As the researcher began reading candid memoirs and autobiographies of various showmen he came to understand that exhibits were presented in fraudulent ways in photographs to attract customers. The pictures came to be seen not as accurate portrayals of people with disabilities but as stylized presentations of exhibits to enhance

Miss Blanche LaMont with her school at Hecla, Montana, October, 1893. Photo by Henry W. Brown.

their value as entertainment commodities. Thus the study turned out to be a look at how the exhibits were promoted, not who they were personally (Bogdan, 1988)

Photos can represent the photographer's own view of what was important, the orders he or she was given from a superior, or the demands of people who were the subjects. While some might contend that this may place them in the realm of the subjective and may detract from their "factual" worth, it does provide another use of photos, one that is much in line with the qualitative perspective; that is, when we study photos, we ascertain clues about what people value and the images they prefer—how they like to be pictured and how they picture others. Approached in this way, photos are visual rhetoric. Looking at photographs and other visual material in an attempt to understand how oppressed groups were pictured by those subordinating them is of great interest to those in post-colonial studies (Alloula, 1986; Graham-Brown, 1988; Sharpe, 1993; Said, 1993), African American Studies (Lyon, 1992; Durham, 1991; Willis & Dodson, 1989) and women's studies (Kozol, 1994; May, 1988), to name of few areas of academic interest (see also, Graebner, 1990; Squiers, 1990). While photos may not be able to prove anything conclusively, when used in conjunction with other data, they can add to a growing pile of evidence (Bogdan, 1988).

Craftsmaking at an institution for the retarded, 1920s.

Photographs serve another function as well. They may present anomalies, images that do not fit the theoretical constructs the researcher is forming. When photographic images are not compatible with a developing analysis, they can push the analysis and insights further than they might originally have gone. In the study of freak shows discussed earlier, for example, the researcher expected to find people with disabilities degraded when he began his study. While some of the images he came across supported that perspective, others did not clearly illustrate what he expected. Many of the pictures seemed to elevate the status of the exhibits. Midgets, for example, were often depicted as royalty and as unusually talented. These images forced reconsideration. In a study we did of photographs taken in the 1920s at a state school for the mentally retarded, we noted how all the pictures presented the students as clean-cut, well-mannered, middle-class youngsters. This image stood in dramatic contrast to what professionals were saying during this period about people with retardation. The time was the height of the eugenics movement when professionals agreed that mentally handicapped people were society's rogues—a terrible danger to everyone's well-being. Our attempt to think through the contradiction between the written words and the pictures facilitated a multidimensional discussion of these issues.

Researchers also use photographs to probe how people define their world; they can reveal what people take for granted, what they assume is unquestionable. Schools and human service agencies, for example, often taken photos to release to the press in conjunction with events they sponsor. They also photograph students and clients for inclusion in the agency's official records. Study may elicit organizational assumptions about students and clients revealed in the photos: What are the clients wearing when they are photographed? In what positions are they posed? When we examined photos taken for fund-raising campaigns by one agency whose clients are defined as mentally retarded, for example, we found that the clients were often cast in the role of children, clowns, or as helpless.

In the next few paragraphs we provide a historical note about the photographic craft, collecting crazes, and the range of images left for us to ponder. We focus on older images that you may come across in your research or other travels but might not know about.

Although the first photographs made for commercial purposes—for sale—go back to the 1840s and the daguerreotype, it was not until the 1860s that there was a proliferation of photos among the population at large. Prior to 1860 you could get your picture taken, but the technology was such that multiple copies could not be made. With that problem solved, the commercial possibilities for photographs escalated, and their availability soared. The first wildly popular format for selling these new images was called the *carte de visite*. The name derives from their similarity to French visiting cards. The photos were glued to a light piece of cardboard, 2 ½" by 4", and sold by photographers and photographic distributors. It was common for people to have pictures taken of themselves and their families and to put them in albums to show when guests came. But albums contained images of others as well—of war heroes, clergy, politicians, presidents and their families, royalty, authors, stage personalities (including freaks), and other well-known people. While there are carte de vistes of scenery and objects, people's portraits dominated the form. These images were so popular, so collectable, that some people were said to be struck with *cardamania,* the inability to stop buying and collecting them. The carte de visite style was replaced by the larger (4 ½" by 6 ½") cabinet card in the 1870s and 1880s. Cabinet cards were also mainly portraits and their use was much the same as their smaller predecessor. By the turn of the century the cabinet card craze subsided. The cabinet card was not replace by any particular format, instead a wide range of photographic types and sizes came into use.

One of the most popular photographic formats in the first quarter of the twentieth century was the picture post card. In the United States, picture post cards came into large scale use by 1905 due to changes in postal laws which made their use allowable and cheap. They were enormously widespread in the United States and in other parts of the western world. People bought them to keep as well as to send. Everyone who could read or write seemed to collect them. The great majority were commercially produced. Large firms printed them in bulk on printing presses but the most interesting were those produced as photographs by local craftspeople. These richly document small town life and its people. Post cards of schools—inside and out, classes, sports teams, and graduations abound. Some post cards were made by amateurs. By the turn of the century, Kodak was producing cameras that the person in the street could use and then have their snap shots turned into post cards. While post cards were not mainly a portrait format, in the hands of local photographers and amateurs, they were. If you have old family pictures, look on the back. You are likely to see the printed words "post card."

Carte de viste, cabinet, and post cards were small. There were much larger photos produced as well. Rather than displayed in albums, many of these were hung on walls as

Normal School graduates posing with their diplomas, circa 1905.

decorations in homes and civic and commercial buildings such as schools, court houses, libraries, fire stations, factories, summer camps, armories and fraternal halls. One format that was widely popular and of special interest to the qualitative social scientist is the panoramic group photo (sometimes called yard-long photographs). By the turn of the century a camera had been invented in which the lens mechanically moved in a horizontal arc panning the scene and moving the light across the unexposed film, resulting in an elongated image of large proportion. Some cameras took pictures in a 180 degree arch producing pictures over six feet long and 10 inches high containing hundreds of people. (Most were of smaller size and with fewer people.) As with most early photographs, the negatives used for the panoramic photo were the same size as the final print. Unlike most contemporary photos, which are enlargements from small negatives, these old time photographs are amazingly clear and detailed. When you look at them you often get the feeling of actually looking at people from another era in the face. While more or less out of use by the 1950s, for half a century people loved the format. Photographers responded by producing a large legacy of photographic images of celebrations, meetings, outings and almost every other planned social event—weddings, graduations, birthdays, class trips, conventions, building dedications, retirement parties, etc.

The most common way for photographers who took group panoramics to make a profit was by selling individual copies to those in the picture. Many of these pictures turn up at house and garage sales and in antique shops after being rescued from basements and attics after being in storage for years. The format has not been a collector's choice because of its size. There are a number of archives that have large collections of panoramic photos taken by local craftspersons including the works of McAllister in northern Vermont (Borsavage, 1979) and Goldbeck (Burleson, 1986) in Texas. Many of these images are of subjects related to education and the human services.

There were other photographic formats. The stereocard, for example, had a long history and was produced in large numbers by commercial firms for entertaining the masses who looked through stereo viewers to see the scenes reproduced in three dimensions. While not as visually dramatic as the group panoramic, there were other group photos taken with wide angle lens. While we could go on, the nature of this book allows only a sampling from the rich history of photographic images and an introduction to their possibilities as data. We have just scratched the surface of possible uses of available photographs. Locating and using them takes imagination and care (Dowdell & Golden, 1989).

Researcher-Produced Photographs

In the hands of an educational researcher, the camera can produce photos for use in some of the ways already discussed. They can simplify the collection of factual information. Researchers can take aerial photographs, for example, to better grasp population distribution and its relationship to school location. One social scientist we know was asked to help city planners work out plans to redesign a downtown public square. To get a sense of how people use space at given times during the day, a camera with a device that automatically took a picture every ten minutes was placed in a window of a building facing the square. The camera was aimed to include the entire area each time the shutter opened and closed. Such a technique might easily be employed in conjunction with other methods to study the use of playgrounds, college quads, or various indoor spaces.

Perhaps the most common use of the camera is in conjunction with participant observation (English, 1988; Walker, 1993; Preskill, 1995). In this capacity it is most often used as a means of remembering and studying detail that might be overlooked if a photographic image were not available for reflection. Photographs taken by researchers in the field provide images that later can be closely inspected for clues to relationships and activities. Insignia and pins indicating organizational affiliations, the appearance of people who attended particular events, seating arrangements, office layout, and contents of bookcases can be studied and used as data when the camera is employed as part of the data-collecting technique. Complete photographing of a classroom can facilitate conducting a cultural inventory.

Another way a camera can be used as a research tool occurs when the researcher gives the camera to subjects, asking them to take the pictures. While we have not used this technique ourselves, those who have suggest that it can be a way to gain insight into how the subjects see their world. In one project, cameras were strapped to a wheelchair in an apartment complex designed for handicapped individuals. These photos, taken as the person in the wheelchair moved through the complex, were used to sensitize architects to how their designs appeared from the position of those who were using them.

Photos taken by researchers or chosen by researchers and shown to subjects can be used as a stimulant for data gathering (Schwartz, 1989). In one study, the researcher was trying to understand how typical students (non-disabled children) thought of children with severe disabilities who had been mainstreamed into their classes. The children were interviewed and asked to discuss other students in their classes (Barnes, 1978). Rather than naming the children or describing them, the researcher showed slides to the children and asked them to describe and discuss the students pictured there. In another study in which geographers were trying to understand how various people thought about particular kinds of environments, wilderness pictures of forest areas were projected on a screen and groups of urban dwellers, including inner-city elementary school students, were asked to discuss them.

Photographs as Analysis

Thus far we have discussed photographs as data or as a stimulant for producing data. In the current debates concerning photography's role in social science research, these uses are the least controversial. The subject of greater contention is the analytic use of photographs; that is, when the researcher claims that the image stands by itself as an abstract statement or as an objective rendering of a setting or issue (Goffman, 1979; Trachtenberg, 1979; Harper, 1994). Many questions arise: Can photos taken by a researcher, or anyone else, capture the inner life of, say, a school? Can they grasp an essence that is elusive to other approaches? Do the photos that people take oversentimentalize what they are supposed to depict, or do they distort by concentrating on the stark or seamy side of life? Do they immortalize what is actually only a moment in an ongoing flow of events? Is the camera like a typewriter (Becker, 1978) that has nothing to say on its own? Is it only an instrument, dependent upon the skill and insightfulness of the one who is holding it? Or is there something about the relationship between the holder, the camera, and the understanding that is transcendent?

These are the questions with which qualitative researchers interested in photography must wrestle. In educational researchers' quest for understanding, photos are not answers, but tools to pursue them. The camera's invention and its extensive use has changed the way we view and experience our world. While we have discussed photography's uses in educational research, it is also important to see photography and the world of picture-takers as important subject matter for study in their own right. We have to understand how society affects and is affected by the photographic enterprise. Only when we do this more fully than we have to date can we explore in-depth the analytic worth of photographs. Photography can be an educational researcher's tool, but it must be understood as a cultural product and as a producer of culture.

Technique and Equipment

Do you have to be a good photographer to use photography in qualitative research? Yes and no. George Eastman's fortune was made on fulfilling the promise that "you push the button, we'll do the rest." In research, it is not quite that simple, but under certain conditions it might be close.

The question to be answered first is: "What are the pictures supposed to show?" If the goal is to have "inventory" photos of the research setting, very little skill may be required. If subtle events of interpersonal behavior must be captured, it might take quite a bit of discipline and practice to learn how to capture them with a camera. The key is to be able to specify ahead of time what the content of the desired photo will be. Anything that can be clearly specified can easily be photographed by anyone. The trick, then, is to know what you are looking for and, especially in exploratory stages of the research, to recognize what you are looking for when it appears.

The special photographic skill that is required when working with data more complex than the inventory is the ability to judge what a scene will look like when converted to a small, flat rectangle. This skill is particularly important when working in black and white media. Amateur snapshots abound in illustrations of how the translation from a real world to a 3″ by 5″ flat can go wrong. The obvious ones include cut-off heads, missing people, sun in the lens causing blacked-out foreground, or tiny people in a field of unwanted surroundings. It should be possible to overcome these errors simply by knowing what should be in the picture and then making sure it is actually in the viewfinder of the camera—and that very little else is.

At a slightly more complex level, you also have to develop a sense of what will "show up" in a photograph. The eye can isolate details in a way a picture cannot. Things that are subtle in color shading, texture, or brightness may not show up or may be exaggerated. Details that are small may not be resolved and decipherable on film. If they are likely to constitute important data, they should be photographed close up.

A research project certainly should not be your first experience shooting pictures. None of these skills is difficult to learn, but they must be learned. It would probably be enough, and well worth the time, for you to set up several exercises approximating the sort of pictures that you will want in the study. Specify what the picture should contain and then find a situation in which to try to shoot it. But do not settle for good pictures—demand of yourself that you get the pictures you set out to get. You cannot rely on accidentally good pictures for good research. The knack will come.

What kind of equipment does it take? The advice must unfortunately be the same as with tape recorders—it should be good. Since serious research usually is undertaken with at least a thought to eventual publication, the photographic data should be as good as possible. Since image quality deteriorates in reproduction, starting from bad negatives can be disastrous.

The final impediment to doing qualitative research with photography is the "model release." For publication, it is imperative that each recognizable individual in each picture sign a release that gives permission to publish his or her picture. Parents or guardians must sign one for minors. Steps should be taken to secure releases as soon as the project is underway, since the matter often turns out to be far more time consuming and difficult than anyone would suppose. In setting up a study and gaining access to a site, you will have obtained permission to visit and photograph, but this is not the same as the model release. Thus, unless releases also are obtained, you will wind up with a store of photographic data you cannot use.

Official Statistics and Other Quantitative Data

While conducting studies, the qualitative researcher often comes across quantitative data others have compiled. Schools, as we have said, keep and generate tremendous amounts of data. Teachers may choose to keep data for their own purposes. The administration collects data on racial composition, languages spoken, handicapping conditions, the number of athletic injuries, attendance counts, dropout rates, achievement scores, the number of acts of violence and suspension, and a host of other numerical computations. At times the qualitative researcher finds it useful to generate his or her own numerical data. What does a qualitative researcher think about and do with such material?

Quantitative data can have conventional uses in qualitative research. It can suggest trends in a setting—whether, for example, the number of students served has increased or decreased. It also can provide descriptive information (age, race, sex, socioeconomic status) about the population served by a particular educational program. These kinds of data may open up avenues to explore and questions to answer. Quantitative data are often included in qualitative writing in the form of descriptive statistics.

Statistical data also can serve as a check on ideas that you develop during research. You might learn through observation, for example, that while male trainees in a job-training program do not speak of training as important in their lives, female trainees do. You might compare this "working hypothesis" with official attendance records, assuming that these attendance records empirically indicate seriousness. You would not use attendance records to prove what you have found, but rather to explore the implications of your idea in that particular aspect of the program. If attendance records were not as high for women as men, you might be forced to explain this.

Looking at actual official statistics and comparing them to what subjects verbally report can be helpful in exploring perceptions. Recently, for example, a researcher who was studying the implementation of a new reading program often heard teachers make reference to how much the reading levels among the pupils had risen since the new program had been incorporated. When the researcher explored this statement she discovered that reading levels in the school had not gone up; teachers, in fact, had never seen data on reading levels. The enthusiastic support of the teachers for the new program was reflected in their reporting of the data, not in the data themselves.

While quantitative data collected by others (evaluators, administrators, other researchers) can be conventionally useful as we have described, qualitative researchers critically dispose themselves to the collection of quantitative data. It is not that the numbers themselves hold no value. Rather, the qualitative researcher tends to turn the compilation process on its head by asking what the numbers tell about the assumptions of the people who use and compile them. Rather than relying upon quantitative data as an avenue to accurately describe reality, qualitative researchers are concerned with how enumeration is used by subjects in constructing reality (Gepart, 1988). They are interested in how statistics support, or contradict, subjects' common-sense understandings.

Qualitative researchers are adamant about not taking quantitative data at face value. They see the social processes involved in numerical data collection and the effects of quantification on how people think and act as important subjects for study. This interest in studying the generation of numbers should not be confused with the study by statisticians of how to improve counting and estimation. The qualitative approach to quantitative data focuses on understanding how counting actually takes place, not on how it *should* take place.

The following describes eight ways of thinking about the quantitative data you may find in a school or human services organization (Bogdan, 1980; Bogdan & Ksander, 1980) to sensitize you to the qualitative perspective:

1. *The concept of "real rates" is a misnomer.* The process of quantification produces rates and measures. They do not appear "naturally" in the world. Rates and counts represent a point of view that subjects take toward people, objects, and events. In addition, because subjects take a numerical attitude toward certain categories of people, objects, or events does not mean there will be a natural consensus concerning how to arrive at rates and counts. Rates of acts of violence in schools, for example, are dependent on how the people who compile the figures at a given time and place define the phenomenon and go about their work. We cannot generate a rate of violent acts until we develop a perspective toward specific actions that deem them quantifiable or important to count. (See National Institute of Education, 1978, for an example of how school districts define violence differently.) A social scientist, a policy researcher, or a government official may arbitrarily choose one way to count and develop one set of conventions to arrive at a method of constructing a "real rate," but whatever is derived is the product of the assumptions used, the concepts employed, and the process that evolves. To claim to have the "true measure" is a claim for the supremacy of one definition and one method over the other and should not be confused with "truth" in the absolute sense.

What are the various ways that people define and quantify those things they are required to count? What factors seem to influence the definitions and the ways they proceed? Are there variations from data gatherer to data gatherer about how to proceed? How are understandings concerning what to count and how to count developed?

2. *Singling out people, objects, and events to quantify changes their meaning.* Quantification has the potential to make that which was once taken for granted salient and make that which was once amorphous concrete. Requirements to keep statistics on racial and ethnic backgrounds, for example, may increase the attention people pay to children's race, changing their ideas about who belongs in what category as well. Statistical data on minority or handicapped children, the number of athletic injuries, acts of violence, or incidence of drug use in schools does more than numerically portray phenomena; it changes how we experience them.

What specific effects does counting have on the meaning of events and people?

3. *Quantifying has a temporal dimension.* Any attempt to quantify has a history. Any generation or discussion of a measure or count of something is located at a particular historical moment. Numbers, in other words, do not stand alone, but are related to the social and historical contexts that generate them. Changes in reported rates—whether of attendance, drug use, achievement scores, or the number of children with learning disabilities—do not necessarily correspond to actual changes in behavior or to the characteristics of the people being counted. It is premature to make generalizations, but our observations of the counting of children with disabilities suggest to us that the greater our concern with a particular phenomena, the more we focus on it and the higher our rates will be. Sarason and Doris (1979), in their discussion of compulsory education and the rise in mental retardation, suggest that rates of mental retardation have to be understood in relation to our changing definition of who should be educated.

4. *Quantification involves many different participants and can only be understood as a multilevel phenomenon.* How an issue is viewed in Washington and how those at the national level go about measuring may not correspond with how it is thought about at the state or local level. Similarly, superintendents may interpret a directive differently from principals. Of course, the general public may receive data in a manner confounding to those who generated them. As one local newspaper writer put it: "One child is not necessarily one child the way the State Education Department does it.…The way educators count, one child can be a half of a child, a whole child, a child and a quarter, a child and four-tenths or in some cases, one child is actually two children" (Bogdan & Ksander, 1980, p. 303).

What is the original intention of initiating a count? How is the motivation and origin understood at the various levels that it passes through? How do people at the levels that receive data understand the meaning of what they get? How does that result correspond to what collectors understood they were doing?

5. *Both the person and his or her motivation for counting affect the meaning, the process, and the figures generated.* This assumption, while closely tied to the last, is separated to emphasize the important role played by those who initiate counting and the sanctions available to them. When federal funding for an organization, for example, is tied to serving certain categories of people, the tendency rises for these rates to be reached independent of actual changes in who is served and what is done. When the amount of money allocated to a school depends on generating counts, the counts will tend to move toward the levels that are most favorable to the agency seeking the funding. Increasingly, state and local governments are developing elaborate reporting systems because of orders to produce counts. These orders and their results deserve careful study.

Professionals' relationships to rate production are central because they often initiate counts and have a stake in rate production. A study of services to people who are blind reveals that the definition of legal blindness generally relied upon to produce counts of blind children, and which was devised by professionals, results in producing a category of people, the overwhelming majority of whom can see (Scott, 1969). The diagnostic category "learning disabled" illustrates the importance of studying who initiates counting. Some specialists report that up to 40 percent of all children are learning disabled while some professionals not associated with the specialty claim that "learning disability" is a contrived diagnosis.

What do people who generate counts understand as the consequences of their action? How does having funding attached to achieving certain rates affect counting? How do various professional groups affect counts? How do "lay" counts differ from professional counts?

6. *Counting releases social processes within the setting where the counting takes place in addition to and beyond the activities directly tied to counting.* Counting can shape what people consider important and meaningful and designate particular activities as expedient. Giving standardized tests at the end of a course of study, for instance, may change the content of the course and the activities that the class engages in during the year. Generating success rates can become the major activity of educational agencies.

How does counting affect the normal activities in which people engage in educational settings? What is the relationship between measuring success and being successful?

7. *People who produce data in educational settings are subject to social processes and structural forces similar to those that affect other work groups.* Studies of factory workers and other work groups have provided useful concepts such as quota restriction, gold bricking, self-aggrandizement, co-optation, and goal displacement to describe the effect of group processes and structural forces on work production. What concepts clarify the production of official data? Some commonly heard phrases among data collectors include *fudge factor, numbers game, massaging the data,* and *padding.* What do these terms mean? What underlying social processes and social forces act on those who generate data?

8. *Enumeration and its products have strong affective and ritualistic meaning in the U.S. educational system.* Other societies, attempting to explain everyday life, relied on religious systems. In the United States we rely on science, the symbol of which is the number. Counting outcomes and producing rates are synonymous with being rational. What is the symbolic meaning of counting to various people in the educational system? How are numbers used to communicate to the outside world? How are they used internally by administrators? What functions do numbers serve in addition to those we commonly say they do?

We do not advocate the termination of quantitative data collection; the U.S. educational system would collapse. Rather, our purpose is to suggest that the pervasive nature of quantification in educational organizations calls us to study counting and its ramifications from a qualitative perspective, one that moves us from a point of taking it for granted to one of studying it in context. This discussion of the quantitative data a researcher may come across in the course of a study is designed to sensitize you to a qualitative perspective on "hard data."

Concluding Remarks

We have described the qualitative approach to data as well as the various forms that qualitative data can take. We have not been exhaustive. Some people make extensive use of videotape equipment and film to pursue qualitative research; we have not covered their activities. Others inductively analyze themes and images of women and minority groups as presented in the mass media as well as in school textbooks. They also have been neglected. School yearbooks and literary magazines provide another area of data that we only touched upon in our discussion. While these and other types of data also exist, we shall move on, hoping that you have grasped the perspective that data are not only what one collects in the course of a study, but what things look like when approached in a "research" frame of mind. Being a good qualitative researcher is, in part, learning this perspective: Specific details are useful clues to understanding your subjects' world. Qualitative research involves holding objects and events up to the sensitive instrument of your mind to discern their value as data. It means having a grasp on the reason the objects were produced and how that affects the form as well as the information potential of what you are surveying. It also involves knowing when to discount certain pieces of data as being of dubious value and when to pursue them.

Remember the sign: "I am here to collect data. How does what I am doing relate to that goal?" If you have internalized the researcher's role, you must abide by that sign. There comes a point where you have enough data to accomplish what you have set out to do, and the explanation of why you remain is hollow. This is the time to say goodbye and get on to data analysis.

Chapter 5

Data Analysis

Data analysis is the process of systematically searching and arranging the interview transcripts, fieldnotes, and other materials that you accumulate to increase your own understanding of them and to enable you to present what you have discovered to others. Analysis involves working with data, organizing them, breaking them into manageable units, synthesizing them, searching for patterns, discovering what is important and what is to be learned, and deciding what you will tell others. For most projects, the end products of research are dissertations, books, papers, presentations, or, in the case of applied research, plans for action. Data analysis moves you from the rambling pages of description to those products.

The analytic task, interpreting and making sense out of the collected materials, appears monumental when one is involved in a first research project. For those who have never undertaken it, analysis looms large, something one can avoid, at first glance, by remaining in the field collecting data when that period should have ended. Anxiety mounts: "I didn't get anything good." "I've wasted my time." "This job is impossible." "My career will end with this mess of unanalyzed fieldnotes in my computer." These fears have crossed the minds of most of us the first time we faced analysis. While analysis is complicated, it is also a process that can be broken down into stages. Confronted as a series of decisions and undertakings rather than as one vast interpretive effort, data analysis becomes a more manageable process.

Our purpose in this chapter is to help you learn to handle analysis. Some have written about data analysis and we will refer you to them (Becker, 1970a; Cassell, 1978a; Lofland, 1971; Schatzman & Strauss, 1973; Spradley, 1980; Strauss, 1987; Miles & Huberman, 1994), but one complaint by novices about the qualitative research literature is that analysis has never received enough attention. This may be because no matter how much it is discussed in the literature, people who have not had experience doing it will never feel they know how, and consistently ask for more. The information we provide in this chapter is rudimentary and practical. We want to get you started. We provide some concrete suggestions on how to proceed to make analysis conceptually manageable as well as mechanically feasible. But if you want to learn how to do it, you have to take data and work with them, trying different approaches and styles as you go. There is no quick fix, no easy set of procedures to apply to all projects.

Before we start, we remind you of discussions in previous chapters. There are many different styles of qualitative research and there are a variety of ways of handling and analyzing data. It is useful to think of approaches to analysis as falling into two modes. In one approach, analysis is concurrent with data collection and is more or less completed by the time the data are gathered. This approach is more commonly practiced by experienced fieldworkers. If you know what you are doing it is most efficient and effective. The other mode involves collecting the data before doing the analysis. Because reflecting about what you are finding and making design decisions while in the field is part of every qualitative study, researchers only approach this mode, never following it in its pure form.

In our judgment, the beginning researcher should borrow strategies from the analysis-in-the-field mode, but leave the more formal analysis until most of the data are in. Problems of establishing rapport and getting on in the field are complicated and too consuming for beginners to enable them to actively pursue analysis. There is just too much to juggle at one time. In addition, new researchers often do not have the theoretical and substantive background to plug into issues and themes when they first arrive on the scene. To do ongoing analysis, one must have an eye for the conceptual and substantive issues that are displayed— something someone new to the field is not as likely to have as an old-timer.

While we recommend delaying attempts at full-fledged, ongoing analysis, some analysis must take place during data collection. You need to decide on a focus, for example. This is based on thinking and making judgments about your data—analysis. Without it, the data collection has no direction; thus the data you collect may not be substantial enough to accomplish analysis later. Although you always collect more data than you need or can ever use, a focus will keep the task manageable. After you complete a study or two, you can begin more formal analytic procedures earlier, employing them in the field.

Analysis in the Field

The following are suggestions to help you make analysis an ongoing part of data collection and to leave you in good stead to do the final analysis after you leave the field:

1. *Force yourself to make decisions that narrow the study.* As we said earlier, in most studies data collection is like a funnel. At first, you collect data widely, pursuing different subjects, exploring physical and social spaces to get a broad understanding of the parameters of the setting, subjects, and issues in which you are interested. After you have developed a research focus, based both on what is feasible to do and what is of interest to you, narrow the scope of data collecting. Do this after three or four visits or some initial interviews. The kinds of decisions you might make are: "I will focus on one third-grade class in this school." "I will explore more deeply women's memories of puberty." "My major concern will be how the children experience the program." "I will interview women who teach in large high schools." "My major focus will be on communication between teachers and students."

Enjoy the initial freedom of exploration, but force yourself to make decisions early. Choices are difficult, since everything is exciting and the world you study seems boundless.

You must discipline yourself not to pursue everything and to put some limits on your physical mobility, or else you are likely to wind up with data too diffuse and inappropriate for what you decide to do. The more data you have on a given topic, setting, or subjects, the easier it will be to think deeply about it, and the more productive you are likely to be when you attempt the final analysis.

2. *Force yourself to make decisions concerning the type of study you want to accomplish.* In Chapters 1 and 2, we discussed various types of qualitative studies: organizational case studies, observational studies, life histories, and so on. Some accomplished researchers belong to research traditions that favor one of these types over the others and they automatically pursue data directed at producing one of the types. Other experienced researchers are more eclectic but, nevertheless, make conscious decisions about what type of study they want to pursue. As a novice, you might not be associated with a particular tradition or may not have the knowledge to collect particular types of data. You should try to make clear in your own mind, for example, whether you want to do a full description of a setting or whether you are interested in generating a theory about a particular aspect of it. Are you interested in the minute details of interaction or are you concerned with more general social processes? While we recommend that you attempt to decide what type of study to pursue, we recognize that it may be difficult to accomplish in advance. While you can distinguish the different types, you may not feel that you have enough command over your project to do more than merely survive. Try to guide your work with some kind of model, but do not worry if you cannot.

3. *Develop analytic questions.* In our discussion of design, we mentioned that some researchers bring general questions to a study. These are important because they give focus to data collection and help organize it as you proceed. The questions you formulate are closely linked to the type of study you attempt. We suggest that shortly after you enter the field, you assess which of the questions you brought with you are relevant and which should be reformulated to direct your work.

When we began a study of a job-training program for the hard-core unemployed, we brought to the study the question: "What factors in the program effectively bring about changes in the trainees to heighten their employability?" After initial observations it became clear that the people in the program were not necessarily "hard-core unemployed," and that most of what went on in the program was unrelated to preparation for work. The first question was abandoned for: "How does this program continue when what goes on in it is so foreign to its official goals?" (Bogdan, 1971).

Examples of other organizing questions include one that a researcher asked after she started to spend time in a kindergarten class: "What do these children do in school each day?" In a study we did in an intensive care ward for infants in a teaching hospital, we started our fieldwork with no particular focus in mind, but soon organized our work around the question: "What is the nature of communication between parents and medical professionals on the unit?" Later that question was divided into three questions: "Who talks to parents about their children? What do they say? What do parents hear?"

Sometimes people who are new to qualitative research ask questions that cannot be answered very well by this approach. These questions are often a by product of early training in the quantitative tradition and are directed at finding the "cause" or rate of a particular phenomenon. One researcher, for example, who had years of experience as a nurse, was starting to do observations and interviews with recent heart attack victims who were enrolled in a patient-education program designed to reduce the risk of future heart problems. She was interested in the patients' compliance to the rules laid out for them in the training sessions. While the general interest in the program's relation to patient behavior was easily explored in a qualitative mode, she was misguided in stating two further questions: "Who was more compliant, men or women?" and "What were the differences in the rates of compliance?" Questions developed to guide a qualitative study need to be more open-ended and concerned with process and meaning rather than cause and effect.

In a study of a program in which instructional technologists encouraged teachers to use media more effectively, the question was: "What happened when media specialists attempted to get teachers to behave differently toward media?" In an interview study of people labeled "retarded," we asked: "How do people labeled retarded come to think about themselves?"

Qualitative researchers often make a distinction between substantive theoretical questions and formal theoretical questions. The questions we just listed are substantive; that is, they are focused on the particular setting or subjects you are studying. To change a substantive question to a formal theoretical question, change the wording; in most cases this can be accomplished by simply omitting phrases or adjectives (Glaser & Strauss, 1967, p. 80). "How does this program continue when what goes on in it is so foreign to its official goals?" becomes "How do programs that engage in activities so foreign to their stated goals continue to operate?" "What is the nature of communication between parents and medical professionals on the unit?" becomes "What is the nature of communication between parents and professionals?" "What happened when media specialists attempted to get teachers to behave differently toward media?" becomes "What happens when outside specialists attempt to change teachers' behavior?"

In research where you observe in a variety of settings and in studies in which you are employing theoretical sampling, the substantive questions will naturally change to theoretical questions. If you do a great deal of analysis in the field and develop these questions and answers as you move from site to site, you are generating what has been called *formal grounded theory* (Glaser & Strauss, 1967). As we have suggested, this sophisticated analysis while in the field is difficult for the beginner to accomplish. Most beginners will carry out a study within one setting or cohort of subjects. We suggest that you keep your questions at a substantive level for the purposes of guiding your data collection, but speculate in observer's comments and memos about the relation between substantive theory and formal theory. In the formal analysis, after you have completed data collection, you can speculate further. When writing up your findings you might, depending on your audience, attempt to link your substantive findings to formal theoretical issues, that is, reflect on what bearing your findings have on human behavior in general.

In addition to formulating questions, we find it useful to compose statements that capture the project's intent. The statements should be simple and limited to a sentence or two. Pretend an intelligent lay person who knows nothing of your interest or your field of study asks you, "What are you trying to find out in your research?" Examples of clarifying statements include: "I am trying to understand communication between staff and patients on a hospital ward." "I am trying to understand the changing ways young women think about their bodies as they progress from junior high school through college." You should work on being clear enough in your own mind to give a satisfactory answer that neither confuses nor bores the questioner. Work on such a statement; if you can come up with one, you are on your way to clarifying your own purposes—a key to analysis.

4. *Plan data-collection sessions in light of what you find in previous observations.* Regularly review your fieldnotes and plan to pursue specific leads in your next data-collection session. Ask yourself, "What is it that I do not yet know?" To answer this question, you will have to think about what you know already and what shape your study is taking. Decide if you want to spend more time in one place than another, arrange to see a specific activity, or plan to interview a particular subject with specific questions in mind. For example, in the neonatal study, after it was decided that the focus would be on communication between staff and parents, the researchers went out of their way to be at meetings where staff were discussing children with their parents. In conversations with parents, questions regarding what they knew and how they got to know it were raised.

While we suggest that you plan observation sessions to build on previous ones, these plans may fall through. You may go out into the setting only to find that it is impossible to do what you had hoped. While there is no way you can control what your subjects do in the field, the plans can help you focus and strengthen your project regardless of your ability to implement them.

5. *Write many "observer's comments" about ideas you generate.* Fieldnotes are supposed to contain observer's comments. As we discussed in Chapter 4, observer's comments are sections of the fieldnotes in which the researcher records his or her own thoughts and feelings. On first projects researchers usually do not spend enough time speculating. Rather than allowing the recording of detailed description to dominate your activities to the exclusion of formulating hunches, record important insights that come to you during data collection before you lose them. Whenever you feel strongly about an event witnessed or a dialogue engaged in, note the images that come to mind. When something occurs that reminds you of incidents in other settings, record these mental connections (this is particularly important in moving from substantive theory to formal theory). When words, events, or circumstances recur, mention it in observer's comments and speculate about meanings. If you think you have a breakthrough in understanding something that was previously obscure to you, record and elaborate on it. If you notice that certain subjects have things in common, point it out in observer's comments. The idea is to stimulate critical thinking about what you see and to become more than a recording machine. Figure 5-1 contains examples of observer's comments from the mainstreaming study that were helpful in analysis.

6. *Write memos to yourself about what you are learning.* After you have been in the field five or six times, force yourself to read over your data and write a one- or two-page summary of what you think is emerging. Develop links in that summary between observer's comments. Continue this practice of memo writing or summarizing regularly. These memos can provide a time to reflect on issues raised in the setting and how they relate to larger theoretical, methodological, and substantive issues.

The memo shown in Figure 5-2 was written after six observations at a mainstreaming program for "neurologically impaired" and "learning disabled" adolescents located in an

FIGURE 5-1   Examples of Observers Comments

The following are some examples of observer's comments taken from a study of the inclusion of children with disabilities into public school classrooms. If your notes have such paragraphs in abundance, final analysis will be easier.

O.C.: The principal of Fairview Elementary School refers to having regular (non-special education) teachers coming into this class for autistic children to teach music as "mainstreaming." I have never heard anyone at the university refer to mainstreaming in this way. It is as if the teacher is being mainstreamed into the class.

O.C.: Ben Shotland often has negative things to say about the district's efforts to mainstream, yet he does so well in his class with the children labeled "handicapped." He is up for tenure and may be feeling that pressure. He seems to be anti-administration, and what he says about mainstreaming may be a manifestation of his general dissatisfaction with the teachers' position in the school or with the administration.

O.C.: I found it unusual that the teacher said that the child going down the hall in the wheelchair was not disabled. What she meant was that the child was not receiving any special services and had not had an IEP written up on her. According to the administration, the child isn't disabled, but according to anyone who would see the child, you would think of her as disabled. I'll have to pursue the different perceptions of disability. Some kids appear to have nothing wrong with them; yet they are listed on the rolls as having disabilities. I'll have to pursue this further.

O.C.: This is the third time I've heard from different sources that the scheduling of mainstreamed children is done so that certain teachers do not have children with disabilities in their classes. How does this come about? How are they thought of by other teachers? It seems as if the school is divided between pro-mainstreaming and anti-mainstreaming forces.

O.C.: Mrs. May has little good to say about the workshop she attended to prepare her for taking children with disabilities into her class. Her emphasis on "What should I do?" rather than what is the nature of the children's problems seems to be an orientation shared by Mr. Reese, Mrs. Jones, and Sally Bartlett. Lowell Sharp and Minguel seem much more interested in the causes of the problem. It's interesting that those who are concerned with the here and now have never mentioned job mobility. The others are all taking university courses and talk about changing their fields. I wonder if my perceptions are true and if they are, what it all means.

urban high school. The form and content of such a memo can vary a great deal and we include this one only to show you an example of the many possibilities. Memos often make sense only to the people who are intimately involved in the research, thus parts of this memo may not be clear or may not have the significance they do to the author. As we discussed in Chapter 4, memos also contain material on fieldwork technique and research strategies. We include such an example in Figure 5-3. Additionally, memo writing may help you work through discouragement in the midst of a project, chart your own developing sophistication, and document the researcher's reflexivity. Figure 5-4 reflects such a memo written during the course of a student's doctoral research.

As your research proceeds, your memos may become more analytical. Some may be devoted to just one idea. Others may be more speculative "think pieces" linking your findings to other situations and data. You should not labor over these memos as you might when writing a formal paper. Use a free style, informal language, and let the ideas flow. You will have plenty of time to ponder over what you say when you get to the more formal analysis after you have completed data collection.

7. *Try out ideas and themes on subjects.* In Chapter 3 on fieldwork, we discussed key informants, subjects who are unusually perceptive and articulate. They can be used as resources in preliminary analysis. During preliminary observations in a study of inclusion, for example, you may notice teachers lining up for or against it. You might bring this up to a key informant by saying, "I've noticed that you can group teachers according to their pro and con stance on mainstreaming." See how the idea strikes the teacher. He or she may agree or disagree and explain why the way you are thinking is right or wrong. In the study of residents and interns on the infants' intensive care unit in a teaching hospital, we shared the scheme we developed to account for house staff's unofficial classification scheme of parents of the infants with selected informants. They pointed to "types" of parents we had not mentioned, as well as to the fact that we had been too categorical in making distinctions between parents and that a continuum better portrayed their thoughts about parents.

While you can use subjects for a resource, it is important not to defer to them completely. They have a stake in seeing things in a particular way that might interfere with their abilities to help clarify and analyze. One perceptive doctor in the teaching hospital study, for example, denied that making judgments about which infants were "nonviable" was problematic. He took the position that the specific nature of the criteria minimized individual judgment. Our fieldnotes were filled with references to the problematic nature of such decisions. His refusal to talk about this area did not mean that it was unimportant to explore; it just meant that he was not a good person to help us figure out that issue.

As we mentioned in the last chapter, it may be unwise to reveal how much you are learning to certain subjects because they may withdraw. Be selective in choosing helpers. While not everyone should be asked, and while not all you hear may be helpful, key informants, under the appropriate circumstances, can help advance your analysis, especially to fill in the holes of description.

8. *Begin exploring the literature while you are in the field.* While there is some debate about when someone doing a qualitative study should begin a review of the literature (Glaser, 1978), we believe that after you have been in the field for a while, going through the substantive

FIGURE 5-2 Fieldnote Memo

A number of themes, ideas, and areas for further investigation have emerged already. I will list them.

1. Students' use of the class and their label in negotiating a place in the school. Some kids at some times do not want to be associated with the program because they say they are ashamed to be in special education. Phil and Pam want the door closed when they are in the room, but they talk about negotiating with teachers whose classes they are taking in ways that indicate that being associated with the program lets them get certain advantages. It provides them with the opportunity to withdraw from certain activities. Phil's remark during the discussion about the military draft was that if they wanted to draft him he would tell them he was handicapped but he would not tell a girl he wanted to take out. That gets at some of the selective use of "disability." Alfred's discussion about how the kids in the program would be thought of as having an inferior brain but now they are thought of as having something particularly wrong with them is related to this. I'll have to look out for material on how kids use the labels and the class and when they choose to identify with them and when not.
2. Teachers' use of the concept of mainstreaming. When I first started this study I thought that regular class teachers would or would not want to be involved with disabled children on the basis of their feelings and experiences with "labeled" kids. While this seems to be true in some cases, a lot of the disposition to the program seems unrelated to the particulars about it or the population served. Some teachers feel that the administration is in general not supportive and they approach what they consider "additional" problems with the disposition that "I have enough." When I say "the administration," I mean the central office, those with whom they see as determining the outcome of the contract bargaining. Others concentrate on the principal and feel that he works hard to make things work for them so if he wants them to get involved in a new effort, they will. This needs a lot of working out but it may be fruitful to pursue looking at what one's position is on mainstreaming and how it is talked about as being a manifestation of conflict and competing interests in the school. Also, this reminds me of how particular teachers think of the various special education classes. Marge was telling me that she likes kids with learning disabilities because they aren't trouble-makers like those in the resource room who have emotional disturbances.
3. Categories of kids with disabilities. In a very short time I have gotten a lot of stuff on how the teacher perceives the various categories. I just mentioned Marge's comment but teachers who head up the programs have their own way of classifying the kids. Mr. O'Rourke, in describing "his kids," said that there were three kids that really didn't belong in the program. Two were there because parents had forced them in (one is "too smart" for the program—the

Continued

FIGURE 5-2 *Continued*

other is "too slow") and the other was there because he knew the kid from last year and there was nothing else for him. Then there are kids who never come. There are twelve kids on the books. If three don't belong and three aren't regularly in attendance, that leaves six. Raises questions concerning counting who the program serves. Then there are kids who are referred to as "really having problems." Kids that are going to "make it." Kids that they are "worried about." Kids that "won't be here after the end of the year or after they turn sixteen." "Nice kid" and "off-the-wall" are also terms that I am hearing. I'll have to be more systematic in getting at this and how the regular class teachers classify the students as compared to the special education students. There is some indication that this may be different. Also how the psychologist classifies the kids compared to the teachers should be interesting to look at.

4.   The relationship of the program to the structure and milieu of the school. I have already got a number of items in my notes referring to college and the academic press of the school. Two people have described the school as consisting of two types of kids: very high achievers and very low achievers. I am told that the high achievers are the kids of professional families living in the area immediately around the school, while the low achievers are mainly the inner-city kids, many of whom are on welfare. This is an interesting perception. There must be a lot of students here who don't fit those two categories. I wonder how this perception of who the students are affects what teachers do, if it does affect them. Where do the kids in the L.D. program fit? I am also told and have observed that, while there isn't hostility between blacks and whites, friendship patterns are pretty much along racial lines. White kids eat together in the cafeteria. Black and white kids mix, it seems, when the blacks are of professional backgrounds and the whites are too. The children in the L.D. program are rich and poor, black and white. It is important to explore how racial and economic status patterns in the school at large are reflected in the program for kids with learning disabilities.

literature in the area you are studying will enhance analysis. What are some of the crucial issues in the literature? What past findings have a bearing on your setting? How does your perspective differ from what you read? How does it agree? What has been neglected in the literature? In addition to reading in the substantive area of your study, just reading widely can help in analysis. We have found that it is very helpful for researchers to read qualitative studies in unrelated fields, because it makes them familiar with how others have worked with their data and it can provide models for their own work. The danger in reading literature while you are conducting your study is that you may read and find concepts, ideas, or models that are so compelling they blind you to other ways of looking at your data. Try to avoid jamming your data into preformed conceptual schemes. The reading you do should provide you with stimulation rather than be a substitute for thinking. It is perfectly honorable to do research that illustrates others' analytical schemes, but try to distance yourself enough to formulate concepts of your own or to expand the work of others.

FIGURE 5-3   A Methodological Memo

Memo

The Interviewer as Chameleon

Date: March 31, 1981

Teachers are so different from one another! Even though I hear so many common perspectives among them, I am always surprised, spending the amount of time that I do at Vista City, at how different these teachers are. Interviewing these teachers and establishing rapport with them means that the researcher really has to be like a chameleon during the interviews. On the one hand you don't want to pretend things that you don't feel, but on the other hand, in this quest to understand this other person's point of view, I find myself interacting and behaving differently in each interview. When I compare my interviews with Brigit and Bill yesterday, I almost see myself as two different people. With Brigit, I would ask her a question and she would give me a long answer. I would shake my head, say "uh-huh," and be very interested in her comments. The interview wasn't formal, but it was task-centered and straightforward.

My interview with Bill was much more casual. He swore when he talked and really observed no protocol at all. I found myself picking up his tone when he spoke. He continually said things like, "fuck this," and "fuck that." I sort of fit in with his mode, as I had with Brigit's mode, and said that something was "shitty." I don't think Bill had as much at stake in the interview as Brigit did, and that might account for some of the difference in his tone.

I take from this that the interviewer acts like a chameleon in an interview. I need to adapt (somewhat) to the different styles of the people that I'm interviewing in order to have a good interview. I think this strategy actually enables me to ask more challenging kinds of questions. If you adapt to their style, they can see you as a friend, and you can challenge some of the things they say. They seem to be willing to answer these challenges as one person to another, rather than as an insider to the outsider. Of course, you have to be careful with this too. If you try to be what you are not, people will see you as a phony. That's why it's more of a stretch than a contortion, I think.

---

9. *Play with metaphors, analogies, and concepts.* Nearsightedness plagues most research. We get involved collecting data in a particular place and become so captured by the particulars, the details, that we cannot make connections to other settings or to the wide experiential array we carry with us. Ask the question, "What does this remind me of?" about different aspects of the setting.

In the study of integrating students with disabilities into public schools, we mentally compared what we were seeing to what we knew of attempts at racial integration to see similarities and differences. In a more adventurous frame of mind, we unburdened ourselves of a historical time frame. In a national study that involved observing people counting the number of children with disabilities in particular Head Start programs, we wondered how people in Salem in the 1600s might have gone about taking a census of the witch population. Our subjects resorted to empirical indicators, expert judgment, and self-nomination—perhaps not very different methods from those used in Salem. Seen from this perspective, professionals can diagnose children even when symptoms are contrived. The diagnosis becomes reified and the symptoms fall by the wayside whether one is diagnosing witches or emotional disturbance. While this may sound far out, it enlarges the way you think about your research problems.

Another way to expand analytic horizons is to raise concrete relations and happenings observed in a particular setting to a higher level of abstraction. We have already mentioned that changing the wording of a statement is one way of doing this. Another way is to make up short phrases to capture the spirit of the generalization you are developing. In observations we did of a training program for the hard-core unemployed, for example, we noticed that the trainees with the most skills, the most talent, and the most potential to obtain jobs received the most attention from the program staff. Playing with that relationship, we developed the phrase the "teacher's pet principle" to describe the phenomena where the least needy got the most services.

On a pediatric ward in a teaching hospital, we noticed that house staff not only diagnosed the children, but sized up the parents as well. On the basis of their judgments of parents, they decided what to tell them about the condition of their children and how they would involve them in the treatment. We developed the phrase "diagnosis of the third party" to capture the idea that doctors judge others besides their patients. After you come up with such a phrase, you must stipulate under what circumstances and in what other settings it is likely to occur. This process helps you think more deeply about various aspects of your setting and how it compares with other settings. It is through this process that an idea becomes a concept.

10. *Use visual devices.* A technique of analysis that has received increased attention is the use of visual devices (Strauss, 1987; Miles & Huberman, 1994). Graphics and charts such as diagrams, continua, tables, matrices, and graphs can be employed in all stages of analysis from the planning to the finished product.

We have found it helpful early in a research project to draw visual representations of the possible components of a study for purposes of clarifying the choices to be made. These rough sketches are very informal—more like doodling than architectural blue prints. This is what we do in participant observation studies. We start by drawing circles to designate the various categories of people we have come across in our initial visits. For example, in a study of a residential juvenile detention facility there would be circles for the inmates, the residential staff, the professional staff, the outside consultants, the administrators, the state government officials, visitors (friends and family of the inmates), and the friends and families of the staff and on and on. We might even have circles for the lawyers involved in the negotiations about sentencing and other people in the judicial system. When we discover that particular categories represented by a circle really consist of people with different perspectives—the inmate circle is composed of first-timers and repeat offenders and they have very different points of view—we draw separate circles for each or draw circles within

FIGURE 5-4 A Personal Reflection Memo

Memo: The Little Voices in My Head

by Trace Haythorn

A fascinating process has begun to emerge as I interview folks. I feel as I interview that I actually have multiple voices engaged in the process. Primarily is the voice of the individual sitting across from me. She/he is speaking toward me, and thus I am working to focus on that particular voice. My focus is often broken by the other voices:

- the voice of anticipation is listening carefully to what the interviewee is saying, and crafting new questions to push for my own clarity and understanding of the interviewee's meaning(s);
- the voice of the research agenda brings pre-formed questions related to the general research question;
- the voice of prior experience works to integrate the data of prior interviews and observations as well as my own knowledge. This voice tends to be very outspoken and takes a great deal of energy to manage during interviews, believing that the energy it has to offer is most important and relevant, not realizing that it often squelches the meanings the current interviewee is constructing;
- the voice of good methodology sounds like a strange hybrid of Bob Bogdan and Sari Biklen, constantly reminding me of good questions and responses that get at good data;
- the voice of anxiety is the squeaky voice deep within that keeps telling me I'm missing important things and that I really have no business doing this research in the first place because I am so profoundly unqualified, intellectually inadequate, etc. (I really hate this voice); and
- the voice of practicality which watches the clock, measures how much time the interview is taking and always worries how long the tape will take to transcribe.

Obviously, some of these voices are far more important to spend time with, but it's very easy to mistake one for another in the midst of an interview. My goal is to ultimately integrate those voices that assist me in my research and work to attend to the other voices appropriately without letting them disrupt the research/interview process.

circles. We then put arrows from the various circles pointing to the other circles. These arrows represent perspectives—the perspective of the people represented by the circle the arrow is coming from on the people the arrow is pointing to. So the inmates circle has an arrow pointing to the professional staff representing the inmates' perspectives on them and the professional staff circle has an arrow pointing to the inmates. (This is designated by an arrow with two heads.) We attempt to cluster the categories of subjects' circles, placing together those having the most contact. We also place other shapes in our drawing, representing objects or places or processes that are significant to the various categories of people, and we use arrows to indicate their perspectives on those objects, places, or processes. Thus, in the juvenile detention study, we might have a rectangle symbolizing the high school and another symbolizing work. We try to arrange the whole thing to provide a diagram of all the components and their relationships to each other. We then look at the diagram and ask: What categories of subjects are we most interested in? What about them engages our interest? If we are interested in their relationship with others, which others? What other places and objects are meaningful to the subjects and should they be included in our study or not? We cross out circles, arrows and other symbols that we are not interested in and underline those we are.

In studies where you are interested in what happens to a person, or a relationship, organization, or some other human group over time, drawing flow diagrams can be helpful in figuring out what you are doing. Some will find such diagramming a waste of time or something they automatically do in their own heads without the aid of a pencil. For others, it is a useful way of laying out dimensions of the study and thinking through priorities and design. Use such an approach if it works for you.

Visuals vary in sophistication from rough stick figures drawn on a piece of scrap paper to very carefully drawn professional models. Some visual devices are mere scribbles in fieldnotes that express relationships or arrange insights you are gleaning. Such primitive doodling often helps you to visualize complexities that are difficult to grasp with words. They can help summarize your thinking for presenting findings to others (colleagues, dissertation committee members). Some researchers never use such devices, while others employ them often, even including formalized models in their manuscripts.

More Tips for Analysis in (and out of) the Field

There are three general points to make before moving on to the next section, "Analysis after Data Collection." Like some of the ideas and procedures we described under the heading, "Analysis in the Field," these points carry importance for both ongoing and final analyses.

The first point, alluded to earlier, deserves further attention. *Do not be afraid to speculate.* The lack of confidence one usually feels on the first research attempt often makes one too cautious about forming ideas. Worries about getting details and facts straight can hold a researcher down. We do not suggest that the facts and the details are not important, since ideas must be grounded in the data, but they are a means to clear thinking and to generating ideas, not the end. As C. Wright Mills reminds us, "Facts discipline reason; but reason is the advance guard in any field of learning" (Mills, 1959, p. 205). Barney Glaser, a central figure in the development of qualitative analysis, tells us that good ideas contribute the most to the science of human behavior. "Findings are soon forgotten, but not ideas" (Glaser, 1978, p. 8).

Newcomers to qualitative research often feel guilty when they speculate because they have been taught not to say anything until they are sure it is true. Speculation is, however, productive for this research approach. It helps you take the chances needed to develop ideas. You do not have to prove ideas in order to state them; they must be plausible given what you have observed. Do not put off "thinking" because all of the evidence is not in. Think with what data you have.

The second suggestion we have concerns venting (Glaser, 1978). Ideas and understanding will come to you on a regular basis as you go about your research. You are likely to become excited by this creative process. It can be exhilarating. Mulling over ideas creates energy you may want to vent. There are two ways of doing this: talking about the ideas with friends and colleagues or writing memos, observer's comments, and, later, a text. We do not want to sound antisocial when we suggest that talking things over with others may hinder analysis. We do warn you, however, that talking about your analysis can reduce the energy needed to do the hard work of putting your thinking down on paper. Said once, an idea may no longer compel you to record it; it becomes "something everybody knows," in the public domain. Data analysis must include time when you are alone with your computer. Write it down and then talk about it.

Finally, we suggest that while you review your data during the collection phase of research you jot down lots of ideas. Start a separate file on wild and crazy ideas and other speculations or write additional comments into your notes while you are reviewing them. (If you do this, make sure you indicate on the comment that it was added later and give the date. This helps you track your thinking.) If you are reviewing hard copy, make lots of comments in the margins of your fieldnotes and transcripts. Circle key words and phrases that subjects use. Underline what appear to be particularly important sections. When working from hard copy it should look used—covered with lines and notations, bent edges, and coffee stains. We suggest using a pencil so that you can erase confusing notations later.

Analysis after Data Collection

You have just finished typing the fieldnotes from your final observation of the study and you proceed to file them. There, facing you, is all the material you have diligently collected. An empty feeling comes over you as you ask, "Now what do I do?"

Many experienced observers know what to do; they take a break. They let the material sit, take a vacation, or do things they have neglected because they were consumed by the data collection, and then come back to it fresh and rested. There is a lot to say for not tackling analysis immediately. You can distance yourself from the details of the fieldwork and get a chance to put relationships between you and your subjects in perspective. You will get a new enthusiasm for data that may have become boring. Also, you get a chance to read and mull over other ideas. However, taking too long a break has drawbacks. It can be a stalling tactic to put off the hard work ahead. It also can cause you to lose touch with the content of your notes. The most serious drawback is that the need to return to the field to collect additional data may arise and if the break has been too long returning can be a problem. Subjects are difficult to locate or have changed positions, or the setting is not the same as when you left it.

Discussions of how long breaks should be and the advantages of putting data aside are esoteric to those who have deadlines to meet, assignments for course requirements, dates on contracts, and appointments to share findings.

Developing Coding Categories

Imagine a large gymnasium in which thousands of toys are spread out on the floor. You are given the task of sorting them into piles according to a scheme that you are to develop. You walk around the gym looking at the toys, picking them up, and examining them. There are many ways to form piles. They could be sorted according to size, color, country of origin, date manufactured, manufacturer, material they are made from, the type of play they encourage, the age group they suit, or whether they represent living things or inanimate objects.

Such an activity approaches what a qualitative researcher does to develop a coding system to organize data, although the task is more difficult the settings are more complex, the materials to be organized are not as easily separated into units, the setting is not void of people, nor are the classification systems as self-evident or clear-cut.

As you read through your data, certain words, phrases, patterns of behavior, subjects' ways of thinking, and events repeat and stand out. Developing a coding system involves several steps: You search through your data for regularities and patterns as well as for topics your data cover, and then you write down words and phrases to represent these topics and patterns. These words and phrases are coding categories. They are a means of sorting the descriptive data you have collected (the signs under which you would pile the toys) so that the material bearing on a given topic can be physically separated from other data. Some coding categories will come to you while you are collecting data. These should be jotted down for future use. Developing a list of coding categories after the data have been collected and you are ready to mechanically sort them is, as we shall discuss, a crucial step in data analysis.

When we discussed the toys in the gymnasium, we mentioned some schemes that might be used in sorting. The schemes included, for example, the manufacturers and the color. The signs (or the coding categories) for manufacturers would say Mattel, Fisher Price, Creative Playthings; the signs for colors would be pink, blue, red, yellow, and multicolored. If you were in the gym and you were told what the purpose of sorting the toys was—let us say, for example, that you were told they wanted piles so they could be sent back to the manufacturer—the task of developing codes would be considerably easier (by manufacturer). Developing coding systems in qualitative research faces similar parameters. Particular research questions and concerns generate certain categories. Certain theoretical approaches and academic disciplines suggest particular coding schemes. It is far beyond the scope of this book to lay out all the coding categories and theoretical approaches that might be used to develop coding systems. What we will do is provide a list of families of codes to suggest some ways coding can be accomplished.

We have made up the families or kinds of codes we will present for the purpose of this discussion. They do not represent universally defined coding conventions. The families overlap. Do not be concerned with which family the individual codes you develop fit under. Our purpose is to help you understand what codes are and some specific ideas for coding possibilities, not to present an exhaustive scheme from which you can mechanically borrow.

Under each coding family, we will define what we mean by the type, discuss what kinds of data can be sorted by it, discuss when this family of codes is most often used, and then provide an example of a unit of data that might be appropriately coded under categories representing the family.

With certain studies you, as a researcher, may have particular concerns and may draw upon one of the types mentioned almost to the exclusion of others. In other studies, categories are mixed. Remember that any unit of data (a sentence, paragraph, etc.) may be coded with more than one coding category from more than family. The coding families presented should provide you with some tools for developing coding categories that will be helpful in sorting out your data.

Setting/Context Codes

This term refers to codes under which the most general information on the setting, topic, or subjects can be sorted. Material that allows you to place your study in a larger context is found under such codes. In most studies one code is sufficient to cover this material. Under such codes much of the descriptive literature (pamphlets, brochures, yearbooks) produced about the setting, subject, or topic can be placed, as well as local newspaper articles and other such media coverage. In addition, general statements that people make describing the subject, the setting, and how the setting fits in the community can be coded here. Also, descriptive statistics and other quantitative data that describe the setting can be coded. Particular codes in this family might be labeled: "Descriptions of Elementary Schools"; "Midcity High School." The particular coding label would depend upon your subject.

Following is an example of data that can be coded under such a category. It is a statement made by a principal, describing his school to a researcher on the first day of the project:

> Johnson High has 850 students. Some 90 percent of them go to four-year colleges. The community we serve is mostly upper-middle-class professionals. They have had good educations and that's what they want for their own children. We spend more money per pupil than any other high school in this region. We have more merit scholars than any other. As far as football, well that's another story. We've been having a tough time fielding a team. Let me give you a list of our college placements. I'll also give you a brochure describing our philosophy, goals, and programs.

The material given to the researcher would also be coded under the setting/ context code.

Definition of the Situation Codes

Under this type of code your aim is to place units of data that tell you how the subjects define the setting or particular topics. You are interested in their world view and how they see themselves in relation to the setting or your topic. What do they hope to accomplish? How do they define what they do? What is important to them? Do they have a particular orientation that affects how they define participation (religious, political, social class, feminist, right-to-life)? You may be looking at various participants: students, pupils, and administrators, as well as parents. You might have a coding category for each type of participant. There may be other distinctions between participants that could be the basis of coding categories. Some "Definition of the Situation" codes in a study of women's perceptions of their own elementary school experiences included "Feminist Awareness," "Image of Present Self," and "Influences on Interpreting Past" (Biklen, 1973).

An example of data that fit in this family is the following statement made be a teacher, which was coded under "teachers' views on their work":

For me, teaching is my life. I don't separate the two. When I take a shower, I think, "What if I present the material this way, rather than the way I did it last summer?" Sometimes I spend twenty minutes in the shower without realizing it. My husband thinks I'm crazy but he's that way too. We're not big on parties or on vacations; work is really the substance of our lives.

Perspectives Held by Subjects

This family includes codes oriented toward ways of thinking all or some subjects share that are not as general as their overall definition of the situation but indicate orientations toward particular aspects of a setting. They include shared rules and norms as well as some general points of view. Often perspectives are captured in particular phrases subjects use. In the study of the intensive care unit of the teaching hospital, the following two phrases were often used. They capture shared understandings and become codes for sorting data. "You can never tell" (referred to not being able to predict what will happen to the patient). "Be honest but not cruel" (referred to understanding that you should inform parents but not in words that might upset them).

The following is a unit of data taken from the study that was coded under "You can never really tell."

I was with Carol, an intern. She was working on "the Hopkins baby," trying to start an I.V. Joan, a nurse, came in and said to me, "If you want to see what this is all about, come out here." I followed her into the hall and there were three of the nurses standing by the nursing station, standing over a little girl who was toddling around. Next to her was a woman I supposed was her mother. She had on a nice print dress. The little girl was dressed in stretch pants and matching top. Joan said to me in a low voice, "She's doing fine. In for a check-up. She was no bigger than the Hopkins baby when she first came in. We didn't think she would make it. Look at her—see, you can never tell with these kids."

Subjects' Ways of Thinking about People and Objects

This family of codes gets at the subjects' understandings of each other, of outsiders, and of the objects that make up their world. Teachers, for example, have definitions about the nature of the students they teach. There are types of students in teachers' eyes. In a kindergarten study, a researcher found that teachers saw children as being either "immature" or "ready for school." In addition, children were categorized according to how they were dressed and the teacher's assessment of the child's home environment. "Teachers' view of students" was a coding category in that study. In our study of the intensive care unit for infants in a teaching hospital, we found that professional staff categorized babies according to an elaborate scheme, with certain classifications relevant for certain stages in an infant's passage through the unit. Some of the categories referred to were: "feeders and growers," "nonviable," "very sick babies," "good babies," "chronics," "nipplers," and "pit stops." In the same setting, parents were seen as being "good parents," "not-so-good parents," or "trouble-makers." "Patients as seen by professional staff" and "parents as seen by professional staff" were coding categories in that study. Not only are people subject to classification; in one study of school janitors, different types of trash were made note of and classified.

The following is an excerpt from a study of an urban high school that contains material coded under a "subject's ways of thinking about people and objects"; in this case, "teachers' definitions of each other":

> Jody began talking about the other teachers in the school. She said, "You know the teachers here are O.K. I can't think of one that I wouldn't want to talk to. Of course there are differences. You've got the type that complains all the time—they think the kids are going to hell if they're doing fine. The kids aren't lousy. They usually won't do anything to help a kid that's not with it—here there is a group like that. They hang around together—all men—really conservative. Then there are the pluggers. They don't get discouraged and are willing to give it the extra mile...."

Process Codes

Process codes are words and phrases that facilitate categorizing sequences of events, changes over time, or passages from one type or kind of status to another. In order to use a process code, the researcher must view a person, group, organization, or activity over time and perceive change occurring in a sequence of at least two parts. Typical process codes point to time periods, stages, phases, passages, steps, careers, and chronology. In addition, key points in a sequence (e.g., turning points, benchmarks, transitions) could be included in the family of process codes (see Roth, 1963).

Process coding schemes are commonly used in ordering life histories. The coding categories are the periods in the life of the subject that appear to separate important segments. A life history of a person that emphasizes her education might include coding categories like: (1) early life, (2) moving to New Jersey, (3) the first day of school, (4) Mrs. Nelson, (5) elementary school after Mrs. Nelson, (6) the first weeks of Jr. High, (7) becoming a teenager, and (8) beyond Jr. High School. Notice that the codes suggested here reflect how the subject orders the sequence of her life. The codes do not reflect uniform lengths of time or other researcher-imposed periods. In developing life-history coding systems, the subject's classification scheme usually dictates the codes.

Process coding schemes are also commonly used to organize data in organizational case studies. Here, the change in the organization over time is the focus of interest. Similarly, studies of planned social intervention can be coded by a chronological coding scheme. Chronological coding is the mainstay of history.

While in some studies process coding categories dominate, in others they are merely one of a number of approaches used. In the study of a classroom, for example, the following headings suggest coding categories that might be used in addition to codes from other families: "stages in the career of a teacher," "the school year," "the school week," "steps of acceptance into an adolescent peer group," and "the process of dropping out of school."

An example of a unit of data that might be coded under the process heading "stages in the career of a teacher" follows:

> I've been here for five years now. While I don't feel I'm an old-timer like Marge and Sue, I'm not naive either. When I see those teachers coming in, I say to myself, "You'll learn. I did!"

Activity Codes

Codes that are directed at regularly occurring kinds of behavior are what we call *activity codes*. These behaviors can be relatively informal and lead to codes such as a "student smoking," "joking," or "showing films," or regularly occurring behaviors that are a formal part of a setting, such as "morning exercises in school," "lunch," "attendance," "student visits to the principal's office," "class trips," and "special education case conference." Units of data that might be coded under such headings are fairly obvious. The following is one such unit taken from a study of a special education program in an elementary school. It concerns a meeting about the placement of a child in a class for children with emotional disturbances.

> Although the meeting was supposed to start at 11, no one was in the room when I arrived at 11:05. (O.C.: This is the third such meeting I have attended and the others started ten minutes late with half the participants present.) The first person to arrive was Dr. Brown.

Event Codes

These kinds of codes are directed at units of data that are related to specific activities that occur in the setting or in the lives of the subjects you are interviewing. Event codes point to particular happenings that occur infrequently or only once. For example, in a study one of the authors did, which involved interviewing women about their experiences in elementary school, the onset of menstruation was an event mentioned by all the women (Biklen, 1973). The event became a coding category. In the course of participant observation studies, events that become coding categories are those that call forth a good deal of attention and discussion by subjects. Events that occurred prior to your research may be frequent topics. In some participant observation studies the following events became coding categories: "the firing of a teacher," "a teacher strike," "the riot," and "a school pageant."

An example of a unit of data coded under the event code, "the riot," is cited next. It is taken from a conversation with a teacher.

> The day we had the trouble there were more police cars than you've ever seen. Most of the kids didn't know what had happened. Sergeant Brown wasn't messing around. Things had gone too far. The school still hasn't gotten over it.

Strategy Codes

Strategies refer to the tactics, methods, techniques, maneuvers, ploys, and other conscious ways people accomplish various things. Teachers, for example, employ strategies to control students' behaviors, to teach reading, to get through the year, to get out of hall duty, or to get the classes they want. Students employ them to pass tests, to meet friends, or to negotiate conflicting demands. Principals use them to get rid of teachers, to open new positions, or to reduce absenteeism. The following is a quotation that might be coded under the strategy code "techniques to control class":

> Mrs. Drake walked into the class. No one was in his or her seat. They were all standing about talking, some loudly. Jamie had his radio on. Mrs. Drake said, in a speaking tone of voice but one which indicated she was annoyed, "Let us begin." She waited a second; nothing happened. Then she leaned over to Jason and said something that I

couldn't hear. He then said, in a loud singing voice, "Announcement! Announcement! I'm going to make an announcement!" Everyone stopped talking and looked at Jason. He said, "The class has commenced. Cool it." Everyone sat down. Leon said out loud, "Jason, my man, you should be drawing a salary." Mrs. Drake said, with a smile, "Haven't you heard?"

It is important not to impute motives to people's behavior or, if you do, to realize that you are. If you perceive behaviors as strategies and tactics, make sure to distinguish between your judgment and theirs.

Relationship and Social Structure Codes

Regular patterns of behavior among people not officially defined by the organizational chart are what we group under "relationships." Units of data that direct you to cliques, friendships, romances, coalitions, enemies, and mentors/students are what we mean by relationship codes. More formally defined relations, what social scientists refer to as *social roles, role sets,* and *positions,* represent another part of this coding family. The total description of relations in a setting refers to "social structure." Coding in this domain leads to developing a description of social structure.

The following unit of data is related to relationships and might be coded under a relationship/social structure code like "student friendships":

> The class came in from home room. A group of four boys—Tim, Harry, Peter, and Brian—stood by the door, half sitting on desk tops, talking. They did the same thing yesterday. Mary and Sue came in together and sat next to each other as did Beth and Allison. (O.C.: The boys seem to hang out in groups. Girls, on the other hand, seem to pair off. I'll have to check this out. Some kids have nothing to do with each other, while others are together regularly...)

Methods Codes

This coding family isolates material pertinent to research procedures, problems, joys, dilemmas, and the like. For most studies one code, "methods," will suffice. Some researchers, however, turn their research into a study of methodology, focusing, that is, on how to conduct research rather than on a substantive or theoretical topic in the setting (Johnson, 1975). In that case, all coding categories relate to methods. The various chapter headings and sections of this book could be codes in such a study. In fact, this book is a product of our own research experiences, and in preparing it, we have read over data that we and our students have collected. So, in one way, the divisions in this book are a coding system with which we have organized our data. As we suggested earlier, in any given study, more than one coding family is used. People who do methodological studies may use "process codes" to organize their data; the sequence of research activities are the codes (design, choosing a site, establishing rapport, analysis).

Usually observer's comments form the bulk of the units of data that are coded under "methods." The following is an example of an observer's comment from a study of a preschool program that might be coded with this label:

(O.C.: I feel so odd in this setting with all these three- and four- year-olds. I have no formal responsibilities, which makes me feel awkward. Yesterday, when we went on a trip to the museum, I tried to be like one of the children. I lined up, etc. This didn't work. I felt particularly uncomfortable when my little partner in line refused to hold my hand when I offered it. All the other partners were holding hands.)

Preassigned Coding Systems

As we discuss in Chapter 2 on design and evaluation research, researchers are sometimes employed by others to explore particular problems or aspects of a setting or a subject. In that case, the coding categories may be more or less assigned. In a study we conducted of including youngsters with disabilities, we developed a list of topics (Figure 5-5) about which those doing the research were expected to collect data. These later became the coding categories. Many evaluation research coding schemes are affected by and (at times) are a direct reflection of the agreement between the researcher's sponsors and the people conducting the research. Then the codes derive from the agreement.

Influences on Coding and Analysis

We have suggested categories for coding to give you ideas of what to look for when you code. These suggestions only offer hints for where to look. They do not, however, imply that analysis rises only from the data and not from the perspectives the researcher holds. Social values and ways of making sense of the world that can influence which processes, activities, events, and perspectives researchers consider important enough to code.

Different theoretical perspectives that researchers hold shape how they approach, consider, and make sense out of the data. Feminism, for example, considered as a loose set of social values, has changed how we consider gender as a category of analysis. Smith (1987) has argued that feminism has not only affected scruples and sensitivity in interviewing, as we suggested in Chapter 4, but more importantly, it has affected analysis, that is, what sense researchers make of the data.

Also, when we do analysis we are usually part of a dialogue about the topic we consider. Therefore, we may analyze and code against another way of considering our topic to which we object. One of the authors did a study of the perspectives of female elementary school teachers on their work. Her analysis was conducted against the backdrop of a sociological literature that dismissed the work women did as teachers because, measured against men, women did not appear to show commitment to their work (Biklen, 1995). So analysis is shaped both by the researcher's perspectives and theoretical positions and by the dialogue about the subject that one cannot help but enter.

The place of theory in the qualitative study is often difficult for novice researchers to locate. Some people do qualitative research guided by particular theories about, say, power or gender or conflict. These theories are influential before the data are collected, and researchers working in this mode frame their project in the light of these views. Other people doing qualitative research, are situated within particular paradigms, but do not name them, sometimes because they are not aware of them. Bosk's (1979) study of surgeons is situated within functionalist sociology, although this is never discussed or mentioned in the book.

FIGURE 5-5   Observation Guide for Inclusion Case Studies

The following are general areas in which you should collect data with some specific topics listed under each general area. We are interested in information in the area only if (and in ways that) it relates to mainstreaming and children with disabilities. For example, if the school has a reputation for being innovative in general, we are interested because it might tell us about the disposition of staff toward change.

DESCRIPTION OF THE SCHOOL
(TO PROVIDE A FEW PAGES, CONTEXT STATEMENT)

- Physical
- Historical
- Student population
- Neighborhood
- Teachers
- Special distinctions
- Reputation
- Well-known graduates or people affiliated with school
- Location

THE CLASS OR PROGRAM

- Location in school
- Its history—how and when it got started with children with disabilities (e.g., placement procedure, how child is assigned, teacher involvement, parent choice)
- Physical description of class use of space (e.g., learning centers, separate cubicles, etc.) adaptation of class space and equipment for handicapped child, things on walls, seating arrangements/location of teacher's desk, condition)
- Organization—including authority (decision making), dispersion of resource people, etc.
- Grade
- Inservice program and opportunities

THE TEACHER AND/OR OTHER PERSONNEL

- Style
- Physical description
- History as teacher
- Perspective on what he or she is doing, especially how he or she tries to integrate children with disabilities
- Perspective on including, children with disabilities, the administration, parents, etc. What affects successful inclusion?

Continued

FIGURE 5-5 *Continued*

- How he or she came to see things as he or she does
- Typical day
- Relationship to typical children and children with disabilities
- Additional personnel in classroom (aides, student teachers)
- Resource personnel relating to classroom (their role, perspective)
- Use of "special" teachers—art, music, gym—how they relate, perspective, importance to inclusive program
- Relation to other regular teacher peers (how viewed, team, support)
- Whom teacher perceives as supportive

CHILDREN DEFINED AS DISABLED

- How what they do is the same or different from what typical kids do
- Peer relations—what are they (sociometrics); how teachers affect
- Typical day
- Physical description
- Clinical description (severity of disability, independence)
- School and family history
- How they are treated and thought about by others in the class
- Physical location—where seated, etc., in relation to teacher, other kids
- Words others use to describe them
- How teacher defines child's progress (same/different from others), balance of social vs. academic goals
- IEP (see Curriculum)
- Amount and nature of contact with teacher (compare with typical)

TYPICAL CHILDREN

- Physical description
- Academic description
- Dress
- Background
- How they get along with each other and the teacher

CURRICULUM

- Content (materials used, any adaptive equipment, individualized?)
- Process (whole group, small groups, individualized, one-to-one, integrated, or disabled served separately)
- Amount of time spent with disabled vs. typical
- IEP (is there one, who wrote it, is it implemented, is it appropriate)

Continued

FIGURE 5-5 *Continued*

PARENTS

- Nature and amount of teacher contact with parents
- Parents asked about placement of child in mainstreamed program?
- Parent input into classroom and child's program
- Parent participation in IEP of disabled child
- Parent perspective on inclusion and success of program

PRINCIPAL AND OTHER SUPPORTIVE
AND ADMINISTRATIVE PERSONNEL

- Their part in and relationship to the program (including initiation, placement of child, parent contact, etc.)
- Their definition of the class and the program including if and why it is a success
- Description of things done or not done in support of the class or program (including materials, personnel resources, positive public relations, development of inservice opportunities)

This figure was compiled by Robert Bogdan and Ellen Barnes. Funds for this research were provided through a grant from the National Institute of Education.

Still others do qualitative projects, not clear at the beginning about what larger understandings either shape how they do their work or are significant for their data. They turn to particular theories that merged during data collection. One reason that it is difficult for students to learn from reading published studies when an author's theoretical views "kicked in" is because we are encouraged to write in a way that makes it seem as if the data and the theory are wedded in a seamless relationship. In what follows we look at two examples of how different projects connected with theory in their analysis.

> Example 1: Lesley Bogad was interested in media literacy. She calls herself a feminist, and wanted to study media literacy among adolescent girls. Her theoretical connections to feminism affected her early in the research in several ways. First, she was interested in questions of gender. Second, she felt that media had a significant influence on how girls construct gender. As she interviewed her informants, she saw that her assumptions about media literacy had been wrong. She had been defining media literacy too narrowly to reflect actual talk about different media forms. She found that media literacy involved more than talk about media themselves. She found that any definition of media literacy had to also include "literacies" about ideology, power, and social differentiation. These findings led her to believe that cultural studies, which emphasized these features, would best frame her research.

Example 2: Eckert (1989) was trained as a linguist and taught anthropology when she did her study of how adolescents take on particular social identities. She believed, before she began her study, that socioeconomic class was central to the process of identity formation, and that particular institutions reproduced people's class positions: "Schooling around the world is designed to perpetuate cultural and social systems through the preparation of young people for roles in those systems" (Eckert, 1989, p. 7). What she did not know was how class worked in social identity formation among high school students. Her research led her to argue that when students were in the working class, their family and neighborhood arrangements and participation led them to form groups with people of mixed ages, and segregated them from adults. She described the process by which an overwhelming number of working class youth become labeled as "burnouts." Middle-class students, on the other hand, tended to form same-age groups, also because of family arrangements, and were accustomed to having cooperative relationships with adults. These students tended to be labeled "jocks," and they were seen as the good kids. Each of these categories of students used the space of the school differently, and related to other students and adults differently. These two categories became very influential even when students did not fit either one specifically.

Each of these two projects engages theory at different moments in their projects. More accurately, each encounters theory in more and less complex ways at different times over the course of the project. At the same time, however, both researchers are surprised by their findings and learn from their informants about how they make sense of their worlds. Being theoretically engaged does not mean that gathering data is simply a process of filling in the blanks. Theory helps us to work through the contradictions we learn about. And contradictions take us deeper into the important parts of our data and expand theory.

The Mechanics of Working with Data

How do you physically handle your data after you have collected it? Remember, by "data" we mean the pages and files of descriptive materials collected in the process of doing fieldwork (interview transcripts, fieldnotes, newspaper articles, official data, subjects' written memoranda, etc.). Your own memos, think pieces, observer's comments, diagrams, and the insights you have gained and recorded should be handled in the same manner. By the mechanical handling of data, we mean the actual methods of physically sorting the material into piles, folders, or computer files in order to facilitate access to your notes. You organize them so as to be able to read and retrieve data as you figure out what there is to learn and what you will write. Techniques of mechanically working with data are invaluable because they give direction to your post-fieldwork efforts, thus making manageable a potentially confusing time. Having a scheme is crucial; the particular scheme you choose is not.

There are many different computer programs available for analyzing qualitative data and better software is being designed as we write. (See for example, HyperResearch, Nudist, Ethnograph, HylperQual, and Qualpro. For comprehensive reviews of specific programs and more details about their use see Weitzmann & Miles, 1994, Richards &

Richards, 1994; and Tesch, 1990). Some researchers working on small individual projects still prefer to do analysis without using one of the specially designed computer programs. We will describe the basic approach to mechanically sort the material. What we say should be applicable no matter whether you use a computer for analysis or not, and should be easily adapted for the particular computer program you use if you decide to go that way. There are many variations on this approach and exactly how you proceed depends on how detailed your analysis is, your personal preference, resources available to you (secretarial help, money, computer, time), the amount of data you have, as well as your goals.

We should mention that some researchers do little in the way of mechanically working with their data. They *eyeball* it, which means they look over the data and write from it from memory. This technique can be effective if there is a small amount of data and if you have limited goals, or if you are a genius, but even then we do not recommend this approach to you. It is difficult, if not impossible, to think deeply about your data unless you have the data sorted and in front of you.

We assume you have followed the suggestions in our discussion of fieldnotes, so your notes and transcripts have wide margins and the text is broken into many paragraphs.

The first step involves a relatively simple house-cleaning task: going through all the files and getting them in order. Most people like their files arrange. Similarly, the pages are usually numbered in chronological order according to when the data were collected, but if you have different types of data (from interviews, fieldnotes, official documents), you may want to order them in such a way as to keep similar kinds of material together. It does not make much difference. Your purpose is to facilitate locating data you may want. The important thing is to have a filing scheme that is not confusing. It is a good idea to make a clean copy of all your data before you analyze it to save. If you change the order of the data or otherwise alter it, you can always refer back to the stored original. In addition, the stored original can serve as a backup. Store it in a safe place.

After the data are ordered, take long, undisturbed periods and carefully read your data at least twice. We recommend undisturbed time because if your concentration is continually broken by other tasks, you are not as likely to get a sense of the totality of your data. Pay particular attention to observer comments and memos. While you are reading you should begin developing a preliminary list of possible coding categories. Keep a pad of paper beside you or a separate file you can access easily and as possible codes come to you jot them down. You should also write down notes to yourself which might include lists of ideas and diagrams that sketch out relationships you notice (Miles & Huberman, 1994).

In developing codes, look out for words and phrases subjects use that are unfamiliar to you or are used in ways to which you are unaccustomed. This special vocabulary may signify aspects of the setting important to explore. If the phrases will not make coding categories in themselves, take specific words and try to fit them together under some generic code. (For a good discussion of one way to do this, see Spradley, 1980.)

After generating preliminary coding categories, try to assign them (as abbreviations) to the units of data. Modify them and then read through your data once again, trying to assign the coding category abbreviations to units of data as you do so. If you are using a computer program specifically designed for qualitative analysis study the manual to learn how to assign codes to data. By "units of data" we mean pieces of your fieldnotes, transcripts, or documents that fall under the particular topic represented by the coding category. Units of data are usually paragraphs in the fieldnotes and interview transcripts, but sometimes they can be sentences or a sequence of paragraphs. Your first attempt to assign the coding categories to the data is really a test to discover the usefulness of the categories you have created. The coding categories can be modified, new categories can be developed, and old ones discarded during this test. It is important to realize that you are not attempting to come up with the right coding system, or even the best. What is right or best differs according to your aims. You might look at the data again after you complete more research projects and code them differently.

Try to develop a coding system with a limited number of codes, say thirty to fifty. The codes should encompass topics for which you have most substantiation as well as topics you want to explore. Play with different coding possibilities. After you have drawn up a new list, test them again. Speculate about what the new scheme suggests for writing possibilities. You might even try to outline a paper with the coding categories as topics or sections and see if they work for you.

You may experience indecision at this point. The data you have might be thin around your interests. Reformulate in light of what you have. You may come up with a list of codes that is extremely long. Try to cut that down. If you have over fifty major categories, they probably overlap. While it is difficult to throw away data or categories, analysis is a process of data reduction. Decisions to limit codes are imperative. And at some point—preferably about now in the analytic process—your codes should become fixed.

Codes categorize information at different levels. Major codes are more general and sweeping, incorporating a wide range of activities, attitudes, and behaviors. Subcodes break these major codes into smaller categories. In a study of career women's experiences of work and family life when they had children after thirty, the major code, "child care," also included five subcodes: history of, finances, negotiation of, preferences, and responsibility for. A study of the culture of gender and teaching included a major code of "collegial relations." The subcodes for this category, support, conflict, and transition—further classified teachers' relationships with each other. To develop subcodes, first settle on the major codes and then read through the material included within each code. If the code consists of data that would break down further for convenient handling, develop subcodes to take your analysis further (see Strauss & Corbin, 1990).

After you have developed your coding categories, make a list and assign each one an abbreviation or a number. Some people put the list in alphabetical order-related categories before abbreviating or numbering. This can be helpful because it facilitates memorizing the coding system. (See Figure 5-6, the coding system used in a study of a training program for the hard-core unemployed.) Now go through all the data and mark each unit (paragraph, sentence, etc.) with the appropriate coding category. This involves scrutinizing sentences carefully and judging what codes the material pertains to. It involves making decisions concerning when one unit of data ends and another begins. Often units of data will overlap and particular units of data will fit in more than one category. Thus many, if not most, units of data will have more than one coding abbreviation or number next to them. When you assign abbreviations or numbers, be sure to indicate exactly what sentences are encompassed by the code. We have included an example of coded hard copy fieldnotes (Figure 5-7) that indicates one method of doing this.

FIGURE 5-6   Codes Used in a Study of a "Hard-Core Unemployed" Training Program

1. Trainees' attendance
2. The training center (physical aspects, reputation, other programs)
3. Companies participating in the program
4. Staff definition of their involvement
5. Trainees as seen by the staff
6. Trainees as seen by company personnel managers
7. Jobs as seen by trainees
8. Trainees' perspectives on training, work
9. Trainees' views of staff
10. Trainees' views of other trainees and of self
11. Recruitment of trainees (how and why they are in the program)
12. Trainees' backgrounds
13. "Holdovers"
14. Trip to factories
15. The program's success (measuring success, how success is seen by various people)
16. Method (getting in, etc.)
17. "Hard core"
18. Joking
19. Follow-up
20. Relationships between trainees
21. "Lying"
22. "Dropouts"
23. Counseling
24. Referral meetings
25. Boredom
26. "Killing time"
27. Poverty programs
28. "On-the-job training"
29. History of the program
30. Trainees' troubles
31. Hustling
32. "The cost of working"
33. Children
34. Neighborhood living conditions
35. Big business involvement
36. "Counseling "
37. State employment service
38. Time (trainees definition of)
39. Rapping
40. Money
41. The director
42. The stolen television
43. The Chamber of Commerce
44. Training activities

When researchers work with hard copy they usually mark the original copy of notes with the coding categories, reproduce it on a copier, and then put the original away to serve as the unadulterated master copy.

When you use one of the qualitative data analysis programs, with the help of the program, you designate the boundaries or units of data and attach code symbols (abbreviations or numbers) to them. After you have placed the code symbols in their appropriate places in your text files, the computer will extract every word segment to which the same code was assigned. So, for example, if one of the codes in a study of a third-grade class is, "student friendship," every piece of data you have assigned that code will be extracted from the data with a command. You can review the extracted data on the screen or have them printed. When the data are extracted, the program will automatically indicate on each segment where it came from (the page and line in the text file). You can make a new file containing all the data coded a particular way and then work within that file doing sub-coding and other finer analysis.

Units of data can be assigned multiple codes, and coding segments can overlap each other. Segments of text can be simultaneously sorted into several different categories. Programs also count how many times each code occurred in the data files. These software

FIGURE 5-7   Hand-Coded Fieldnotes

Fieldnotes

Vista City Elementary School Teachers'

Lounge

Date: February 3, 1981

teachers'
work

Then I went down to the teachers' lounge to see if anybody might happen to be there. I was in luck. Jill Martin sat at the first table, correcting papers; Kathy Thomas was also there walking around and smoking. I said, "Hi Jill, hi Kathy. Okay if I join you?" "Sure," Jill said. "You and your husband have been to China, right?" I said, "Yes Why?" Jill then turned to Kathy and said, "Have you studied China yet? Sari has slides that she can show." Kathy said to me that she was going to study world communities, even though "they" had taken them out of the sixth-grade social studies curriculum

authority

"Now can you tell me who 'they' are?" I asked her. She said, "You know, 'them':'they'."

autonomy

Both Jill and Kathy were upset at how they had mandated what the teachers could teach in their rooms. "They" turned out to be the central office who had communicated the state's revised sixth-grade social studies curriculum. The state has "taken out all the things that we think are important" from the curriculum and has substituted the theme of "economic geography" for the sixth-graders to study.

doing your
own thing

Both Jill and Kathy think that "sixth-graders can't comprehend economic geography well," and think world communities of Africa and Asia are more important. They said they planned to teach what they wanted to anyway. Kathy said, "They'll come around one of these days." "Oh, Kathy, are you a rebel?" I asked. "No," she replied, "I'm just doing my own thing."

parents

After we chatted for a little while, Jill turned to me: "You're interested in what concerns us. I guess one thing is parents." She proceeded to describe a parent conference she had participated in

parents

yesterday afternoon with a child's parents and a child's psychiatrist. She said, "What really upsets me is how much responsibility they placed on me to change the child's behavior." They seemed to give lip service, she reported, to have "controls" come from the child when they said, "It's so difficult for parents to see that kids need to take responsibility for their actions."

programs eliminate the need for multiple paper copies or piles of special cards and folders filled with cut-up notes. If you prefer working on hard copy you can have all or any part of your data printed at any time. Data are easily re-coded so you can develop coding systems during analysis and change them as you proceed. New codes are easily added. Professors who teach qualitative research should be able to help you locate and choose a program. It is common for university computer centers to have this information; some even have qualitative analysis software packages available on networks.

We have outlined only the basic functions that computers can perform. There are more elaborate programs researchers use to examine the relationships between codes and develop more analytic abstractions as well as to formulate propositions and assertions. Some track the chain of reasoning of the researcher. Some claim to build and test theory. Some of this high tech software is controversial, with critics claiming that the programs are more sophisticated than the data and therefore subject to misuse and the creation of data analysis illusions. Novices beware! Explore these when you are more experienced and less likely to be taken in by their elegance.

Those who do not use computer software to help with analysis use a variation of the cut-up-and-put-in-folders approach. It was the way all data were handled before the age of good computer software. It is very similar to what the computer does but you have to do it all by hand and it is considerably slower and much more prone to error. It involves taking scissors and cutting up the notes so that the units of data can be placed in manila folders that have each been labeled with one code. In using this approach you would go through all the coded notes and place a code next to each coded unit of data that corresponds to the number of the page it is on so as to have a record of where it came from. Because some of the data units would be coded for more than one category, multiple copies of the notes were needed.

The technical advantages of using the computer are obvious when comparing what the computer can do with all the busywork that needs to be done using the cut-and-put-in-the-folder method. While this is true there are still mixed opinions on whether novice qualitative researchers should use the specially designed computer software programs. Some who have tried swear by them; others swear at them. The arguments about their use center around whether the time you spend learning how to do it is equal to the time you save. (There are other arguments; see Pfaffenberger, 1988; and Clark, 1987). If you are familiar with computers, are adept at learning how to use new programs, and the proper software is available, use a program to help you sort and retrieve on your first project. If your first project is major, for example a dissertation in which you expect to have hundreds of pages of notes and transcripts, use a program for the various mechanical aspects of data analysis. If you strongly believe that your first attempt at qualitative research will not be your last— that you will use it throughout your career—learn a program right away. If you are going to use a program, use one that those around you are familiar with and recommend.

Concluding Remarks

We have ended our discussion of data analysis rather abruptly. The actual process happens differently. Analysis continues into the writing stage, which we take up in the next chapter. If you are feeling stuck with piles of coded data, the next chapter will move you farther along toward the final product.

Chapter 6

Writing It Up

When the time comes to write up your research, there are many different ways to go about it. In fact, sitting before that computer, you may not know where to begin. What is most frightening is feeling out of control; that is, you do not know how to choose the right words, construct sentences, modulate active and passive voices, or organize your presentation so that the written product reflects your intentions. You can gain control, however, if you work on technique, and if you think about your writing as a series of discrete decisions rather than as one enormous undertaking that must be accomplished all at once.

One of the most important issues about writing is having something to say. If you do not know what you want to say, often you get sidetracked and hung up on peripheral concerns. Knowing what you want to communicate means that your efforts get channeled to that purpose. When your purpose or goal is unclear, all of your writing will reflect that lack of clarity.

Writing from qualitative data is somewhat easier than writing, say, a conceptual piece. The fieldwork and analysis produce files of coded description that provide a starting point—some words on the screen. Not only do you have the descriptive data in front of you, you have a host of observer's comments and analytic memos that may serve as beginnings of sections for your paper. You have a foundation you can revise and expand as you work toward the production of a finished report, paper, article, or book.

What you plan to produce with your data will affect what you write and how you organize your writing. If you are doing a dissertation, for example, you need to attend to certain conventions. Articles and research reports usually offer more stylistic freedom. There is room for choice and innovation, but whatever you write always needs a beginning, a middle, and an end. The beginning tells what you will do in the paper; it lays out the contents. The middle section develops, argues, and presents your findings. You discuss your insights, marshaling your data to convince the reader with evidence for what you claim. The conclusion may summarize what you have said, it may draw a few disparate points together, or it may suggest the implications of your findings for more research or practice; it is a tidying up, like dessert or coffee after the meal. (Some helpful classic handbooks on writing include

Baker, 1966; Kierzek & Gibson, 1968; Strunk & White, 1972; see also Friedman & Steinbert, 1989; Williams, 1990.)

While these are the bare bones of what a paper might look like, you may approach your task in a variety of styles and ways of organization. While sometimes what you must do is dictated by your assignment (i.e., you are assigned to undertake original research and write it up in the manner of a particular journal), usually within an assignment enough latitude exists for you to have some choices about how to proceed. The more you write, the better you will get, and the easier it will come to you.

Where do you start? You have already started. If you have followed our advice—if you narrowed your focus, looked for themes, made decisions about what type of study you are doing, wrote memos and observer's comments, and mechanically sorted the data and read in the literature—you are on your way (Wolcott, 1990; Atkinson, 1991). But what about the actual writing: the style, form, and content? In the sections that follow we construct the writing project as a series of choices. We describe some of the most important choices you need to make, and offer examples that illustrate alternative possibilities.

Writing Choices

The writing you produce depends on the choices you make about how to construct the piece, for whom to write it, and a number of other issues. You make these decisions whether or not you recognize them as such. You gain more control when you consider the different possibilities you have and consciously choose the option that looks like it will work for you. In what follows, we describe some of the decisions you will need to make. We have written about these choices as if they were separate from each other, but they really are not. Deciding whether or not you will cross disciplines when you write, for example, depends on your audience.

Decisions about Your Argument

A piece of good nonfiction writing has a clear focus. It states a purpose and then fulfills the promise. Coming up with a focus means deciding what you want to tell your reader. You should be able to state it in a sentence or two. We refer to this focus as an *argument*. The argument in a paper, chapter, or article is the point of view that the writer takes on the issue. Having an argument, which is central to all good academic writing, does not always mean being argumentative. It means that when someone reads your piece, he or she can say, "She says in this piece that talk shows about adolescent girls' experiences of sexuality always rely on experts to define the situation"; or, "He says in this piece that earlier in this century, you could buy post cards that pictured institutions that housed people with disabilities because the institutions were seen as important parts of the community"; or, "They argue that there are three major themes that characterize their study of high school mathematics students."

When you have an argument, you are making a point. Your writing should not take the reader on a tour of your changing perspectives on your topic. You want to avoid writing in a way that says, "First I thought this, and then I thought that, and then I realized that…" Your point is different from what motivates you (Williams, 1990, p. 98). Unless you are writing about how perspectives on data change, or unless you and your views are the topic of the paper, this tour of your coming to see the topic as you do is not strong enough to be your argument.

There are many types of arguments. One kind is a *thesis,* a proposition you put forth and then argue. The thesis can be born out of a comparison of what your research has revealed and what the professional literature says about the subject (e.g., "Researchers have taken the position that…" or "Our research has revealed another dimension…"). Or, it can contrast what practitioners claim and what your research has revealed (e.g., "The model of…presented in the manual takes quite a different form when implemented in the classroom."). The thesis might argue that the unforeseen consequences of a particular change instituted by outsiders is more important than the planned effect. The thesis is a good focus; it is argumentative and can build interest. But people who start arguments are often attacked. In developing a provocative thesis, there is a danger of overstating your case; you attack a position that no one would actually take. (This is called setting up a "straw man.") If you choose something to attack that has already been refuted, your statements sound droning. Academics are particularly critical of the trumped-up thesis. They take the assertion literally rather than as a matter of style. Use the thesis cautiously in writing for them.

An argument can also take the form of a *theme.* It lacks the overtly combative tone of the thesis, although it shares some of the "big idea" quality. A theme is some concept or theory that emerges from your data: "some signal trend, some master conception, or key distinction" (Mills, 1959, p. 216). Themes can be formulated at different levels of abstraction from statements about particular kinds of settings to universal statements about human beings, their behavior, and situations (Spradley, 1980). We presented some potential themes in our discussion of data analysis. The "teacher's pet principle" and "diagnosis of the third party" are potential themes that could serve as the focus for papers. Academic researchers interested in generating theory see the development of "generic themes" (Glaser & Strauss, 1967) as the most laudable goal for researchers. As Lofland puts it, a *generic theme* (frame) is "when the structure or process explicated is chosen and brought to a level of abstraction that makes it generally applicable rather than applicable only in a given institutional realm or ideological debate, or other localized concern" (Lofland, 1974, p. 103).

The *topic* provides a third possibility for an argument. Like the theme, the topic is pervasive in your notes, but it is more a unit of a particular aspect of what you were studying than an idea about it. A theme is conceptual; a topic is descriptive. We suggested some topics in our discussion of data analysis; for example, "What is a good teacher?" and "Communication on a Hospital Ward."

For the purposes of presentation, we have made the distinction between thesis, theme, and topic as examples of forms your argument can take. Arguments often are hybrids, having elements of all three. We have not stated all possible types; there are others. The argument of a paper, for example, might illustrate the usefulness of concepts or themes that others have developed. If you are involved in evaluation research, very often the argument responds to the question you agreed to explore when you entered the contract to do the work. No one, though, uses one type to the exclusion of the others.

Making a good decision about what type will work for your material will depend on how familiar you are with the field in which you are working. What is needed? (Of course, your decision may also be determined by what you are asked to do by your professor or contractor.)

If we do not have good descriptions of, for example, what a day in the life of a teacher is, a paper with this as a topical theme would be an important contribution to the study of teaching. If, on the other hand, you are working in an area where there is already good description in the literature, a theme or thesis as an argument would make your writing more valuable. Framing your argument around a well-known conceptual scheme that others have used in studies similar to yours may provide you with an easy writing solution and a good research experience, but it will not generate much interest. (No one would be interested in publishing it.) A theoretical theme paper might not be well received if you agreed to do an evaluation of a program's effectiveness for a particular contractor.

The type of argument you use also depends on your skills. The novice often cuts teeth arguing in the form of topics or themes. Most experienced writers, and people with broad backgrounds in research and in their substantive fields, tend to write with a thesis or theme, but they choose from the topical realm also.

Most crucial in deciding on what your specific thesis, theme, or topic will be is the data you have collected, analyzed, and coded. You cannot choose a focus in an area in which your data are thin. One simple way of finding a focus is to look over your coding categories and see which have yielded the greatest amount of data. All computer software designed for working with qualitative data provides a way of getting counts of the number of units of data as well as the total number of words you have under each code. If you have chosen the "folder method" of hand sorting the data, look through the folders and pick the fattest ones. If you have a few codes that have a lot of data under them, start reading through the data and see if they have some common thrust. Also, read over the memos you have written to see if you can make connections between codes, or if you have already noted themes.

While you start your writing with a search for a focus, what you first embrace may not work as you proceed with your writing. Your initial selection should be seen as a hypotheses that has to be tested. You have to see if it works. Expect false starts, reformulation, and refinement. Be open to discovery and to flashes of insight that were unattainable in the field or while doing analysis because you were too close to the data. At times a draft of the paper is needed before you see the light of a workable focus.

The title should reveal your focus. In "The Judged Not the Judges: An Insider's View of Mental Retardation" (Bogdan & Taylor, 1976), the authors presented the views of a person labeled "retarded" on special education and other aspects of programs for people labeled "mental deficient." "Be Honest but Not Cruel: Professional/Parent Communication on a Neonatal Unit" concerns what professionals tell parents of children who are patients on an intensive care unit for infants. "Be Honest but Not Cruel" is a perspective the staff share on the unit regarding communicating with parents. Although titles are decided after you finish writing, the attempt to come up with them before you start can facilitate your search for an argument.

Decisions about Your Presence in the Text

In the last ten years there has been a shift in preference of pronouns authors use to refer to themselves when writing qualitative research reports for academic journals or as scholarly manuscripts. The move has been from the less personal "we" or "the researcher" to the familiar "I." There are several reasons for this. One is the claim that the use of "I" is more honest and direct. Using "the researcher" is thought in many circles to be pretentious and is a device, which has since backfired, to gain authority. Another is that the use of "the researcher" connotes an objectivity that does not really exist. Since individual people with particular points of view designed and carried out the research, that should be reflected in the writing. Some authors still use the more formal style. Write in a voice you feel comfortable with but realize your taste might not match all your readers' dispositions.

Your presence in the text is also reflected in how much of your own situation you take up. Including the author's autobiographical, political, and self-reflections in qualitative research writing has gained in popularity in recent years (Ellis, 1995b, 1993; Krieger, 1991). Some authors see writing about themselves in papers and books as a way of separating themselves from or revealing to others their personal bias. Some see the reflective/confessional approach as more honest because it shows and tells the reader that you are aware of your own subjectivity. It also warns the reader to take it into account. Others, who may be part of the group they are studying (a teacher studying teachers), use the approach to help the reader develop a deeper understanding of the phenomena under study (Karp, 1996). In some qualitative circles, the confession is used as a new device to gain authority with the reader.

All confessions are not equally effective in winning reader confidence. Confessions can be read as shallow and as a reason for not valuing the work as well as a reason for honoring it (Patai, 1994). Although confessions can be effective, there are many ways of convincing a reader that you are being honest in addition to telling them who you are. Personal bias is an important thing to worry about, but it should not immobilize you or so dominate your writing that it gets in the way of writing about other things. While some authors have successfully developed researcher reflection into a genre (Linden, 1992), too much reflection can bore the reader and set a tone that the writer thinks he or she is more important than the subjects. Readers are not passive sponges taking in everything you say uncritically. They can be just as critical of self-proclaimed writers' confessions as they can be of ethnographies where the writer writes as if he or she is not present. Like any style of writing, confession works if you can make it work.

Decisions about Your Audience

How much should I write about methods? How detailed should my review of the literature be? How specific should I make my argument? What style should I write in? As with so many questions you might ask about writing, approach answering them by trying to imagine your reader. If it is a journal article you are writing, think: "What would the reviewers or the subscribers of the particular journal I would like to publish in want to know in order to feel comfortable with what I am saying?" "What questions would they have that I have left unanswered?" If you are writing for a particular professor or a dissertation committee, do the same, only think about what you understand their perspectives to be. In a way, it is like thinking qualitatively about writing. Always be specific about who you are writing for (Miles & Huberman, 1994).

Groups and even individuals subscribe to different conventions about writing. When you think of the audience you write for, you take into account the conventions by which they abide. Then, you can either honor those conventions, or flout them. But you have made the choice. You can decide how theoretical to be in your writing, how much you need to explain about a specific topic, whether or not your readers understand anything about cultural studies, for example, by writing for a specific audience.

What about your subjects? Shouldn't you write for them also? With the exception of some types of applied evaluation research, the potential audience for your article or book is not primarily your subjects. That does not mean you should not consider them, involve them, or that one or all of them might not read what you write. Although far from mainstream practice, some authors recommend and perform a brand of research where their subjects are as much partners in the enterprise as they are subjects. They may read drafts and even alter the text. Some are even co-authors. This raises some difficult issues regarding authority, censorship, control, representation and misrepresentation, and the value and viability of such research. We do not have room here to explore implications of this approach in detail. In general the conventions concerning your subjects and representing them is that the writer should try to present the subjects as they see themselves. You should go out of your way not to demean them in the tone of your writing or in the vocabulary you use to describe them. Use the words the subjects prefer in describing themselves (if your subjects are gay and they prefer to be referred to by that word rather than *homosexual,* abide by this preference). While your subjects are not your primary audience you need to keep them in mind—think about what how they might react if they read what you are writing. You often adjust what you say with them in mind not in the spirit of censorship because they might sanction you, but in an attempt to be honest and fair. Thinking about your subjects' reactions can make you more reflective and produce a better manuscript. Some authors share their writing with key informants and discuss it with them. On the other hand, often subjects do not give a hoot about what you write and will not spend the time laboring over a lot of words. In the end it is the researcher/author who has to stand behind what is produced. The researcher/author may not see eye to eye with the subjects on some items. The subjects may be divided among themselves. The subjects may want to appear in a more complimentary or heroic way than the author sees it. Sometimes, that means that the author has to hold his or her ground write in ways that may anger people. (One way of dealing with this is to write about how you see it as opposed to how they see it.)

While you must guard against demeaning and objectifying your subjects, be aware of the reverse tendency to romanticize them. Sometimes, the word *subjects* conjures up images of the holy innocent, oppressed and down-trodden, the salt of the earth. Some subjects are powerful with many resources. Subjects can turn out to be lying, cheating scoundrels who hurt people and do other vicious things. Be sensitive and honest; but there is no requirement that you be your subjects' public relations representative.

Decisions about Disciplines

When you write up your study, your vocabulary, way of considering the issue, and other concerns can either be done in a way that a specific discipline, such as sociology or anthropology, would approach it, or you can draw from a number of disciplines to frame your argument. If you stay within a discipline when you write, people in that discipline will be familiar with your vocabulary, and with the concepts you use, even if you apply them in innovative or new ways. Words like *role, career,* and *professionalism* are commonly used among sociologists. Those in the fields of educational administration or anthropology might more commonly use other terms or concepts. If you are doing your work within a particular discipline, you often use the vocabulary and concepts common to your peers without being aware of how influential they are.

You may find, however, that the common words of a discipline do not enable you to get at an issue deeply enough, or that your work is "interdisciplinary" (or transdisciplinary) rather than disciplinary. Amy Best (1997) found in her research on high school proms that both the language and concepts of cultural studies, an interdisciplinary field, suited the project better because they enabled her to better explain her data on young people's preparation for proms. Feminists came to believe early on that feminist research had to have some multi-disciplinary links. Your decision will be influenced by the audience you want to reach, and by the requirements of your graduate school program, your evaluation goals, or the journal you want to accept your article.

Decisions about the Introduction

Since all work needs an introduction, decisions you make about it are significant. We follow Becker's (1986c) advice to always write the introduction last, since you then know what you are introducing.

The introduction usually begins with the general background needed to understand the importance of the focus. Placing the paper in the context of the literature or some current debate is one strategy; stating the assignment that you are fulfilling is another. Often the introduction concludes with a description of the design of the rest of the paper. The discussion of research methods belongs in the introduction, but its length and specific location vary. When writing in a journalistic mode, you are not likely to include it. In research articles it is imperative that you tell you readers things such as the techniques you used, the time and length of study, the number of settings and subjects, the nature of the data, researcher–subject relations, checks on data, and other information that might help them evaluate the soundness of your procedures and the nature of your subject. Sometimes such information is provided in an appendix. This is especially true of books. Some important contributions to the methods literature can be found in the appendices of such classics as *Street Corner Society* (Whyte, 1955) and *Tally's Corner* (Liebow, 1967).

Some direct advice about the introduction: On the first page of any manuscript you write, directly and succinctly tell the reader what you are writing about. "What follows are the results of a participant observation study of elementary school children at play on school playgrounds." "This manuscript is the report of a two year study I conducted of teenage friendships in a suburban high school on the outskirts of a medium-size city in the midwest." Readers lose concentration if they do not have the larger picture to relate what they are reading to. We encounter the violation of this advice in at least a third of the manuscripts we read and often become extremely frustrated trying to follow the text. Sometime we read for twenty-five, even fifty pages, before we are told in a concrete way what the manuscript is about and why we are reading what is before us. By then we have forgotten what we have already read.

A good way to start a paper is to tell a brief story from your research that captures the essence of what the paper is about or something central to what you are studying. For example, in an article published on the neonatal study cited earlier, the authors start the paper thus:

The second time we visited an intensive care ward for infants (neonatal unit) we witnessed an event that foreshadowed the focus of the research reported here. A couple had come to visit their three-quarter-kg, critically ill, premature son. They were rural poor, in their early 20's and had driven 128 km that morning for the visit. They taped the carnation they bought at the hospital gift shop onto the heavy steel pole that held a heater over the open plastic box in which their child lay. Both stood near the child talking to each other and to the fragile infant, "You be home soon fella," the father said to his son. His mother added, "Everything's all ready for you." A nurse, standing within hearing distance, approached the couple and said, "Now, you have to be realistic, you have a very sick baby." That night the baby died. When the parents were told they were overpowered with grief. The mother said that the news took her completely by surprise. Staff/parent communication became the focus of our field research study of neonatal units. Specifically, we became interested in developing an understanding of: Who talks to parents about their child's condition? What do they say? What do parents hear? (Bogdan, Broun, & Foster, 1992, p. 6.))

Stories, as part of the introduction, can involve the readers early, ground them in a concrete way in the subject matter, convey some of the emotion of the setting, and provide a feel for what it might be like to be there. Such stories must be tied directly to the paper in order to be effective—tell the readers why you are telling it and how it is tied to the paper. While a few years back starting an article with a story might jeopardize your chances for acceptance in some academic journals, things have loosened up considerably in the last few years, with some journals encouraging more engaging styles and alternative formats.

Decisions about the Core of the Paper and Strategies for Communicating Evidence

You have a number of choices about how to organize the main part of your paper, the part we call the *core*. The core of the paper makes up the bulk of the manuscript and gets its direction from the argument. You proceed to do what you proposed to do in the introduction: advance your thesis, present your theme, illuminate your topic. The test of your argument is your ability to carry it through in the middle. You may find you do not have sufficient data to write the middle, a situation that forces you to enlarge or change your focus. You may discover, on the other hand, that you are flooded with data and have too much to write in the length of paper you had planned. Here the focus has to be narrowed.

In writing the middle, the argument keeps you on track. Everything that is included should be directly related to it. Cores have sections; parts that have headings. The test of whether to include each section is your answer to the question, "Does this section relate directly to my focus?"

The nature of the sections, what you include in them and how they relate to each other, grows out of further analysis of your coded data. After you have singled out a few coding categories embodied in your focus, you should begin working with them, reading them over, and looking for patterns, parts, or elements. You can treat them as you treated the whole when you mechanically sorted the data for the first time. The amount of the material will be much less and, therefore, easier to handle. It is the purpose of mechanical sorting to get the data in small enough files so that you can physically manage them.

In looking through data in a particular coding category, you should look for further divisions (subcategories). For example, one of your coding categories in a participant observation study of a classroom might be "teacher's definition of students." Reading through the material under this code, you might notice that the teacher used different phrases to describe the students. The teacher may have had a typology in mind—a classification system of "kinds of students": "good students," "brats," "poor souls," "dropouts," "pests," and "trouble-makers" might be phrases you notice repeating. You can work on developing the teacher's classification system. Here "teacher's definition of students" is the cover term; "kinds of students" is the subcategory coding system, with phrases such as "good students" being the "sub-codes" (Spradley, 1980). These categories can become the major and minor headings for different sections of your paper.

You can do the kind of analysis that we just discussed from many different types of coding categories. "Kinds of" subcategory coding systems are commonly used, but others, such as "steps in," "ways to," "parts of," "results of," "reasons for," "places where," "uses for," and "characteristics of" can be used to work coding categories as well. The subcategories system is a tool that can help you further organize the data because it facilitates thinking through how the sections in the core will look. The middle of your paper, for example, might present the typology and its elements. But do not become obsessed with developing typologies. It is one way to proceed. With a thesis as a focus, your sections might take a different form—a point-by-point presentation of the aspects of your study that support your thesis.

Whatever the specific content of the middle, each section should be structured in a way similar to the entire manuscript. Each should have a beginning, a middle, and an end. The beginning tells you what the section contains and links it to the focus and the parts that come earlier. The middle provides what the introduction promised, and the conclusion summarizes what was in the section, linking it again to the focus and providing a transition to the next section. To keep section content relevant, you ask whether what you are writing relates to what you said you were going to do in the beginning of the section.

There are several ways of considering what qualitative researchers do when they write up a study. Spradley (1979) calls it a *translation*. This way of understanding suggests that what researchers do is to take what they have seen and heard and write it down on paper so that it makes as much sense to the reader as it did to the researcher. Alternative modes of conceptualizing this process suggest that the translation metaphor is too close to portraying the researcher as an empty vessel transposing the informants' perspectives on paper for the reader (Clifford & Marcus, 1986). Clifford (1986) argues that the writer can capture "partial truths" which are shaped not only by the evidence but also by the language the writer uses.

The evidence makes the generalizations take hold in the reader's mind. The qualitative researcher, in effect, says to the reader, "Here is what I found and here are the details to support that view." The job involves deciding which evidence to use to illustrate your points; it is a balancing act between the particular and the general. Your writing should clearly illustrate that your generalizations (actually summaries of what you saw) are grounded in what you say (the details that, taken together, add up to the generalizations). Let us look more specifically at some choices you have for balancing the particular and the general: the use of quotations and how to lead into examples.

A good qualitative paper is well documented with description taken from the data to illustrate and substantiate the assertions made. There are no formal conventions used to establish truth in a qualitative research paper. Your task is to convince the reader of the plausibility of your presentation. Quoting your subjects and presenting short sections from the fieldnotes and other data help convince the reader and help him or her get closer to the people you have studied. The quotations not only tell what they said, but how they said it and what they are like.

In the following example, the author of an article on how Italian immigrants experience schooling in Canada mixes quotations from informants with her own description and analysis within the same paragraph:

> For children who have learned to respect school and to take their academic responsibilities seriously, the experience of total immersion in a foreign language environment is nothing short of devastating. "I felt like a piece of wood," says a fifteen-year-old boy. And a thirteen-year-old, from Cantanzaro: "It was as if I couldn't understand that I didn't understand English and couldn't get their messages in my corner." Even the simplest question was torture: "The teacher would ask me my name and I was afraid to say my name because they said it so much different from how I would say my name, and it was awful." This from a twelve-year-old girl from Molise. (Ziegler, 1980, p. 265)

The quotations and the author's interpretations intertwine to form a flowing paragraph that nicely modulates the particular with the general.

Another way to present data is to make a statement and illustrate the statement with several examples. Frequently, this way of illustrating abstract material is chosen in more formalized research, as in a dissertation. What follows is an example of this style from a dissertation based on interviews with adult women recalling their elementary school experiences. The particular example is from a chapter on their recollections of their teachers.

> Another bit of evidence subjects used to evaluate their teachers was whether the teachers' concern and interest in their job was visible to their students. Teachers were judged as poor if students felt that they did not like children or teaching:
>
> "The teacher I had the following year was a Mrs. Lolly. And she just didn't enjoy kids at all. She was really a mistake for the teaching profession." (#104)
>
> "Second grade was a young woman who was pregnant and I guess she was just not up to teaching at that stage of her life and she had two or three favorites, both boys and maybe one girl, and she and I got along horribly." (#320)
>
> "Fourth grade, Miss Aldan. I don't know what to say about Miss Aldan. Again, she was a woman who was in the role of teaching without caring a lot about it and she made it very boring. She had a monotone voice and she would go on and on. I did a lot of daydreaming." (#325)

Each of the examples offers a slightly different aspect of the general point to be illustrated (Biklen, 1973). In this case, the data are separated from the generalizations. In the previous example, the particular and the general were alternated. In the examples we used to illustrate how to intersperse the particular with the general, you can also see how to lead into data. Again, you can intermix analysis and example (as in the discussion of Canadian schooling) or you can set the examples off from the general statements. In either case, you must always indicate for what purpose you are using the data. The following are a few examples to give you an idea of the variety of ways you can lead into presenting description and quotations.

In this excerpt, the author relies on the "as so-and-so said" method, which she then reinforces with another example:

> But in her position as traffic cop she was limited to dealing with that which was observable. As Mrs. Preston said furiously to Lewis when he talked back to her on the playground, "I don't care what you think. Just don't say it and don't look it." Or Mrs. Crane, "I wish Joe wouldn't always insist on the last word. If he would just not argue I could ignore him." As long as the pupil conformed outwardly, as long as he did not defy her directly, the teacher could be in control. (McPherson, 1972, p. 84)

You will also notice that after the author presents the example she rounds it out with a concluding interpretation. This concluding sentence can either reinforce the interpretation or offer a slightly newer twist.

The next example indicates another method of presenting data—the use of the colon. The colon implies that the material presented after it will illustrate the preceding sentence(s):

> The observer, too, has had impact on the system. Geoffrey has been reluctant to be as punitive as he sometimes sees himself being. Geoffrey himself admits this in his notes:
> "When problems arise in class, such as Pete's behavior, the fact that an observer is there seems to affect my behavior to a greater degree than normally. Starting tomorrow, conscious though I may be of what he thinks, I am going to behave as I normally would, or as close to that as I can." (9/11) (Smith and Geoffrey, 1968, p. 61)

In this example, the participant observer in the class, Louis Smith, records an entry from the teacher's (Geoffrey's) diary as an example of data. With the use of the colon, the transition does not have to be as carefully constructed as it would were one to depend on sentence construction.

Another way to present data is to incorporate them directly into the text, so that they almost become part of a story you are telling. In this technique, you incorporate dialogue and description directly into the narrative. To the reader it appears as if you are telling a story; you are much less distanced from the material you are presenting. The following example reflects what the author learned after interviewing children in jail, in this case, "That kid (who) will end up killing somebody":

> Bobbie Dijon was always the tallest girl in her class; only a few boys were taller. Some of the children laughed at her in the third and fourth and fifth grade. But by the time she was twelve, she was so strong and so big, nobody ever teased her for they feared that Bobbie would haul off and pound them with her fists, which she was known to do. It was not, her teachers said, that she was a tough girl, or a bad girl. There was a tough

part of her, but it was a small part that lived inside her, content not to show itself unless seriously provoked. (Cottle, 1977, p. 1)

In this example, the descriptions gained in the interviews are not isolated and presented separately in the narrative; they flow with the story line to create an atmosphere of informality of presentation.

Clearly, there are many different ways to incorporate examples from your data. Relying on more than one means will give variety to your writing. At the same time, to achieve control over your writing you need to make certain that your style reflects your intent in writing, the audience for whom the piece is intended, and most importantly, what you want to convey.

We said that your paper should be well documented with data taken from your fieldnotes and other materials. That does not mean you should include large sections of data with no discussion or clear reason for their incorporation. Some novices get so intrigued with the richness of their data that they think what they are is self-evident and important to the reader as is. They say they do not want to ruin the feel of the description or the subjects' statements. The reader is often left cold. Writing and using quotations is hard work. Presenting raw fieldnotes is usually a cop-out from taking that next step of refining your thinking and sharing with the reader the intricacies of what you have learned.

There is a place for pure narrative in reporting qualitative research. It is most often used in presenting first-person life histories. In that case, the whole manuscript may be virtually the subject's own words with the author providing only a short introduction and perhaps the conclusion. But even with first-person life histories, the material is carefully edited and rearranged prior to publication.

Decisions about the Conclusion

You must conclude. What choices do you have? You can do a number of things. Often the argument is incisively restated and reviewed. The implications of what you have presented can be elaborated. Many research reports end with a call for further research. There is nothing that does not need further research; it is this belief that makes a researcher's life meaningful. But psychiatrists think that more people should have therapy, and television manufacturers think that people should buy more TVs. The sincerity of your belief does not erase the fact that you are dealing with a cliché. It is a dangerous cliché because this trite conclusion can substitute for a definitive statement of what you have come to understand and why the work is important. The call for more research is often a tactic used by writers when they have run out of steam, when they do not have enough energy to finish the trip to the end of a uniformly good paper. In the conclusion, the end is in sight; keep at it.

Sometimes qualitative researchers become myopic in their writing. They fail to step back and think and write about how what they are studying is part of the larger social units in a society. When writing up findings, especially in the conclusion, you should remind the reader that what you are presenting is only a piece of the puzzle, a close-up of one aspect of one segment of a larger world. For example, in studying the neonatal unit of a hospital, one could be mislead into believing that decisions about health care, about who should live and who should die, how we should allocate our health care resources were only made on hospital wards. In the conclusion of the published paper on the study we have discussed throughout this book, the authors specifically confront the reader with the idea that the unit had to be understood in the context of the medical care system in the United States of America. They pointed out how this system emphasized cure and crisis intervention rather than prevention. They also mentioned how an economic analysis was not done or who, if anyone profited, from the high technology approach used on the unit studied. Smith (1987) has been particularly important in pointing out how in our research we need to link peoples' perspectives and micro studies to the systems in which they are enmeshed. If this is not a part of your study design, you need to warn your readers of the limitations of what they are reading.

More Writing Tips

Call It a Draft

Hopefully some of our discussion of what makes a manuscript has given you some suggestions on how to proceed. Breaking the task down into manageable parts about which you make decisions is very important. First try to come up with a focus, then begin an outline of the core. Try writing a section. Tell yourself that what you are writing is not the final product, but that you are just working on a draft. Force yourself to start, putting your thoughts down on paper. You can always rewrite and change later. Calling something a "draft" can be a device to relieve tension, a way to suspend your overly critical reading of what you have written, a way of putting aside your feelings of inadequacy. Often "drafts" are easily converted into final products by some editing and erasing of words.

Styles of Presentation

Qualitative researchers are blessed in not having a single, conventionalized mode for presenting findings (Lofland, 1974; Richardson, 1994). Particular schools of qualitative research produce manuscripts with a distinct style; you can identify them by the particular phrases they employ. Diversity, however, reigns. You might want to choose a particular school to associate with, like groups who do "ethnographies," "constitutive ethnographies," or "micro-ethnographies," to refer to a few types. Study the school's style and model your writing after it (Van Maanen, 1988; Richardson, 1990b). This technique is a good one to follow if you are unsure of your abilities to develop your own style. With practice, your own mode of presentation will emerge.

Styles of presentation can be visualized on a continuum. At one end of this continuum you find the more formal or traditional ways of organizing a presentation. These styles may be didactic. At the other end of the continuum you find more informal and nontraditional modes of writing. Articles using these styles may tell a story first and draw conclusions only at the end; they are inductively presented. Let us look at what you would be choosing were you to work toward either end of this continuum.

There are some established formats in which to present information. If you choose one of them your form will require you to cover certain materials and organize them so as to touch certain bases. If, for example, you choose to do a micro-ethnography, you will focus on intimate behaviors in a single setting. In your research efforts you narrow in on more specific aspects of interactions in order to break down the setting further and further. To write out this micro-ethnography, you can take advantage of this organizing factor, this continual breaking down and dissection of events, using it to organize your written presentation. (Some good examples of micro-ethnographies include Florio, 1978, and Smith & Geoffrey, 1968.)

Similarly, in a macro-ethnography, you lay out the whole realm of a complex situation, making sure to cover all aspects that have relevance to your theme. It is not as if simply choosing a particular format automatically organizes the paper for you, but rather that you can take advantage of the particular conventions of these modes of qualitative research to order your presentation.

In more traditional forms of presentations, the findings or points of view are usually presented didactically. The author announces near the beginning what the paper, chapter, book, or dissertation will argue and then proceeds to show the readers by presenting key aspects of the perspective, documenting it with examples from the data. In this style, interestingly enough, the data are discovered inductively, but presented deductively, so the author must make a real effort to show that he or she did not collect data to prove a point of view already held.

A good example of a style that clearly depends on the deductive method of presentation is the illustration of some existing theory. The theoretical perspective may have been chosen after data collection was completed because it seemed to explain what the researcher found (see, for example, McPherson, 1972). There are many examples of theory illustration in contemporary qualitative research in education conducted in Great Britain (see, for example, Sharp & Green, 1975). What has been called "labeling theory" is also a popular concept of illustration (see Rist, 1977b).

At the more nontraditional and informal end of the continuum are modes of presentation that might be called *portrait writing* or *storytelling* (Denny, 1978b). These kinds are more controversial in academic settings, and if you were to attempt one of them for a formal paper at your university, you would be well advised to check with your instructor ahead of time to see if it is acceptable. Reading this kind of research is almost like reading a story; the writer creates atmosphere. In his book on busing, for example, Cottle portrays the feelings of people involved in both sides of the busing issue in Boston. He helps readers understand conflicting perspectives. In the following example a parent reacts to the news that his son will be bused:

> If Ellen McDonough was upset by the news, her husband Clarence, a tall handsome man with reddish curly hair and a long straight nose, was outraged. "They did it to me," he yelled one evening when I visited their home. "They went and did it to me, those goddam sons of bitches. I told you they would. I told you there'd be no running from 'em. You lead your life perfect as a pane of glass, go to church, work forty hours a week at the same job, year in year out, keep your complaints to yourself, and they still do it to you." (Cottle, 1976a, pp. 111–112)

The author has drawn a portrait in words.

Much of the material in fieldnotes makes good dialogue for plays and short stories (Reinharz, 1992; Paget, 1990; Turner, 1982; and Richardson, 1994). Some have even advocated for qualitative research poetry (see Richardson, 1993, 1994, and Schwalbe, 1995 for a critique). Others are practicing performance science (McCall & Becker, 1990). Our discussion of writing has not included this form of presentation. The possibility of using qualitative data in these ways is exciting. But as a novice you should master more traditional forms first.

Overwriting

First drafts often suffer from being overwritten: They are too wordy and contain more than the reader could possibly be interested in knowing. Authors have a tendency to think that everything is important, and it may be to them, but not to the reader. It is most difficult for a writer to throw away something he or she has written. Start a file for sentences, paragraphs, and sections that you have written in the process of producing a paper, but have not used. Read through your manuscript ruthlessly looking for material to put in this file. Try to make your paper short. Although the initial fear of the writer is that there is not enough to say, the concern of the reader is often that it goes on and on. If the paper gets to be over forty pages, you probably should have written two papers, or you are on your way to a book. Try to decide roughly how long the paper is going to be and then make a decision about focus and the core, shooting for that limit. Go through your draft looking for words and sentences that can be eliminated without changing the meaning, or that through elimination will make meaning clearer (Becker, 1986c).

We have often been given papers to read that are very long and told by the author that the reason for the excessive length is because the text is based on qualitative data. This is not a legitimate reason. Often long papers are documents that have not been worked on long enough. They are drafts rather than finished products. It is often easier to write longer papers than shorter ones. Get back to work.

Say it once! Another item related to overwriting: Tell the reader what you have to say once, clearly, and be done with it. Do not repeat again, again, again, and again the same point over and over again. Novice writers often give the impression that they are either insecure in making their point or think their readers are dense. Whole paragraphs, even sections, are just rewordings of points made earlier. Only repeat when you are elaborating on a point or are making transitions. But even here acknowledge the repetition: "As I said earlier…" "This supports and elaborates a point I made earlier." "Summarizing what I have said so far…" When you engage in needless repetition you bore readers, numbing them so that they lose the attention they need to absorb the important things you have left to say.

"Yes. But…?"

In writing up qualitative research you present your point of view, your analysis, your explanation, and your rendering of what the data reveal. The discerning reader might be skeptical. Their response is "Yes. But…" Even if you illustrate your discussion with quotations from the data and in other ways present evidence for the plausibility of your analysis, people will have questions: "Isn't there an alternative explanation for what you have found?" "That is your way of presenting it, what about this as an alternative?" "Did all the subjects express that point of view all the time?"

It is important that you raise questions the reader might have and address them in your paper. This is usually done in the core. Present alternative points of view and discuss why the one you chose was more consistent with the data. If there are subjects with a minority point of view that you did not discuss, mention them. You should pretend you are your paper's worst critic—raise all the tough questions and then deal with them one by one. Whatever style you choose, make sure that it permits you to confront alternative explanations for your findings.

Keep It Simple Up Front

Do not give the reader too much complex and/or detailed information too soon. The writer is familiar with the material he or she is presenting and often forgets that the reader is not. Start where the reader is, not where you are. Be simple and direct in the first sections of a manuscript, laying the necessary ground work for the reader to understand the more complex and detailed arguments and information later. If you want the very sophisticated reader to appreciate your knowledge and understanding of complex matters, reserve such information for later. You also might consider footnotes or appendices for such material. Keep the manuscript moving.

Whose Perspective Are You Writing From?

In qualitative research you often report the subjects' ideas, perspectives, ways of thinking. Studies often involve different categories of subjects—students, teachers, administrators—and each category has variations within it with regard to how the subjects see things. You, as the researcher and writer, have ideas about the subjects' ideas. We usually call your perspective on their perspective analysis. It is crucial when you are writing to make clear whose perspective you are writing from—theirs or yours. And if you are writing from your subjects' perspective, you also need to clarify which subjects. In addition, when you write, you have to watch imputing motives to your subjects based on observed behavior. For example, you can observe a teacher talking to a child and asking the child to sit in the corner, but you cannot say why that was done without consulting with the teacher and getting deeper into his or her thinking. You cannot say the teacher was punishing, or controlling, or setting an example, or protecting the child, based just on the observation (although if you are able to listen to the teacher talking to the child, you may know more). If you do this, you are substituting your way of thinking for their way of thinking. Be on your guard against this in your writing.

Jargon and Code

Our personal preference is for clear writing, writing that engages people not only in your specific field, but also those who may not know much about the substantive issues you discuss, but who are interested in the larger concerns you address. So when we write about using jargon, clichés, platitudes, truisms, and code words, we are also writing about the importance of considering your audience.

Jargon refers to a highly specialized or technical language (e.g., subject positions, symbolic interaction). *Clichés* are words that denote ideas that have lost their originality and force through overuse (e.g. multi-cultural, role,). *Platitudes* are hackneyed statements that have an air of significance or profundity but have lost their meaning through overuse and imprecise use (e.g., burn out, strategic planning). *Truisms* are words that are so self-evident that they need not be stated (e.g., Society is complex, power is pervasive). Watch out for the commonplace, ideas that are so well known that there is no reason to repeat them (e.g., teaching is difficult, all children have the potential to learn).

We are on dangerous grounds providing examples that we think fit the above definitions (Katz, 1995). While there may be quibbles over whether we placed the correct phrases under the right headings, there are deeper issues at stake. To some extent one person's jargon, cliché, platitude, or truism is another's significant concept (Hewitt, 1995). Take the phrase *strategic planning,* or *social construction,* or the word *discourse.* While they may be esoteric to the layperson, they have been used in precise ways by particular academic specialties and serve as important means of communicating. But they have also been applied widely and used by many in different ways so as to blur their meaning. In addition, they are regularly substituted for words that are easier to understand in the game of academic abstraction. Do they fit the definition of jargon or should they be considered basic and sacred social science concepts that have been misused? We do not advocate a ban on such words, only caution when using them. Particularly be concerned when you find yourself using the same abstract words over and over again—more than once in a paragraph, several times on a page, more times in a paper than there are pages. If you are attracted to particular concepts or ideas try to understand them, internalize what they mean and their implications, and then write from that perspective, but perhaps using your own words. If you are going to use words and phrases that your reader is not familiar with or phrases that are so widely used that their meaning is not clear, discuss your vocabulary with the reader and tell what you mean by certain words and phrases. When you define concepts, do not rely entirely on the quotations from those who have coined the words. Say it in your own words clearly so that your reader gets your understanding and you are sure you know what you mean.

What in one situation is jargon, in another is a kind of code. Sometimes, we use words in our writing that serve as a kind of code word. When we say "raced and classed identities," for example, these words become code words that are shorthand for announcing rather than describing that our identities are intertwined with race and class in deep, specific, and lingering ways. Or when we talk about "academic" writing—the word *academic* serves as a kind of shorthand to refer to how academics are taken with appearing as intellectual, or how academics live in an "ivory tower." Code words are useful, important, and also sometimes irksome. They are important because, like other codes, they signal to your readers a particular way of presenting yourself, and your political, activist, or theoretical affiliations. In addition to being a signal, they also stand in as shorthand for longer and more detailed descriptions of the thing you are discussing. And sometimes it is important to speak in this kind of code.

There are also limitations. When readers see the same code words again and again, they sometimes slide over them because they have become too familiar, or clichéd. They may also begin to signal meanings that you do not intend because the words have taken on more assumptions than you mean. And, readers who do not know the code will not be able to communicate well with you. These are some of the decisions you make when you write.

On Giving Voice

In the last decade or so the expression "giving voice" has come to be associated with qualitative research. The expression comes from feminist and other liberation movements and refers to empowering people who have not had a chance to tell about their lives to speak out so as to bring about social change (for examples of problematizing the concept of voice see Ellsworth, 1989; Lather, 1991b; McWilliam, 1994; Orner, 1992). In addition it has been used to refer to making these voices available in written form.

In the beginnings of qualitative research, researchers recognized and wrote about how their work allowed people to be heard who might other wise remain silent. The anthropologist Oscar Lewis, reflecting on his famous studies of poor Hispanic families done in the 1950s and 1960s stated: "I have tried to give a voice to a people who are rarely heard" (Lewis, 1965, xii). Early Chicago school sociologists made similar statements in regard to their studies of juvenile delinquents, hobos, and immigrants. Howard Becker in, "Whose Side are We On," written in the sixties, pointed to the political nature of giving the perspectives of people who are not privileged equal status with those who are normally on the higher end of the hierarchy of credibility. While qualitative research provides readers with access to the world of people they would not otherwise know and to some extent allows these people's stories to be told, the subject never really tells his or her own story. Although you might attempt to, and to some degree succeed at, conveying to a reader what it is like to be the person you are studying, you are always the one doing the telling. The romanticized view of purely giving voice is not an accurate description of what researchers do.

General Advice

- Try to write in the active rather than passive voice.
- The dictionary and the thesaurus are important tools. Often the difference between being clear and vague lies in the choice of a word. If you feel that you are not saying what you want, look up the words to see if they can be replaced by something more precise.
- Try to get into writing groups or have a writing partner who reads your work (as you read theirs) with an eye for constructive feedback (Stall, Thompson, & Haslett, 1995). Beware of people who only compliment your writing. Try to assess how readers really react to your writing (Schwalbe, 1995). Try to listen rather than defend yourself—a very difficult thing for writers to do. People who really care about your development will engage you and discuss the good and the bad.
- Read well-written qualitative research articles and books. This process will enable you to gain a sense of the variety of modes of presentation, as well as provide models of good writing. As we have said, the variety is enormous, ranging from the traditional presentation of research in a more formal mode to more nontraditional examples. Read widely to see how authors present data, how they construct their arguments, how they arrange their sentences, and how they organize their formats. When we think of con-

trasting but well-written examples of qualitative research, at the more formal end are Charmaz, 1991; Chase, 1995; DeVault, 1991; and Karp, 1996. In a somewhat more nontraditional (that is, personal and impressionistic) style are the works of Thomas Cottle, (Cottle, 1976a, 1976b, 1977) and Robert Coles's series on *Children of Crisis* (see, for example, Coles, 1964, 1977).

Many authors have said that writing helps them to think. That is not, however, the only reason for writing. Most write for a product—a manuscript to share with others. While your first research efforts may be for your professor, there is no reason to stop there. Seek a broader audience. Do not let your status as a novice researcher keep you from thinking about publishing your paper.

Criteria for Evaluating Writing

We have offered an abundance of advice in this chapter about writing. In the last chapter we did the same for how to go about analysis. Although we have written about them as if they were separate, in practice writing and analysis are part of the same process. The quality of the final product of a qualitative study—the dissertation, report, article or book—depends on the researcher's ability to integrate and deliver both simultaneously.

In the advice we have given for writing and analysis we have hinted at criteria to judge the quality of the final product, but we have not explicitly described them. When you read something based on qualitative research, how do you judge it? What do you mean when you say a piece of scholarship is well or poorly done? How do people who are knowledgeable in qualitative research make judgments about manuscripts? This has been an illusive topic; only in the last decade or so have people addressed it (Lincoln, 1995). One of the difficulties in talking about it was moving the conversation beyond the language, concepts, and conventions that quantitative researchers use—objectivity, proper procedures, reliability, and validity. While there are no standardized criteria to evaluate a piece of qualitative research, and we doubt that there will ever be, below we describe some dimensions to think about in evaluating your own work and that of others. We discuss whether your work is convincing, readable, and makes a contribution.

Is It Convincing?

Do you believe what the author is saying? There are a number of strategies authors can employ to be convincing. First, they can give a specific account of the research procedures used and the nature of the data collected. How many subjects did you have? For how long did you interview or observe them? You are also convincing when you effectively display good data to illustrate and prove your points. We have discussed this point extensively in this chapter. Another effective strategy is to argue against alternative explanations. Your writing style and your skill at establishing the authority of your text also contribute to your ability to convince your readers. There are no simple answers here. As we just mentioned, telling about yourself, for example, can establish credibility on the one hand, but if not done well, or done to the wrong audience, it can undermine what you have to say.

Is the Author in Control of the Writing?

All of the strategies we have listed in this chapter offer authors opportunities to be in control of their writing. When you are in control of your writing, you make your writing do what you want it to do, rather than getting pushed in directions you may not want to go because your writing is not working for you. When you are in control of your writing, you can make sure that the style of writing fits the audience. You can write up the same data in a more formal way for a dissertation chapter, and more informally for an article in the *Phi Delta Kappan.* You can, in other words, shift styles of writing with the same data. You can write in a way that is easy to understand, or you can decide that you want to write for a more academic audience, and write more theoretically.

If you are in control of your writing, you can focus on developing a clear logic (this does not have to be a rationalist logic) that your readers can follow. You can develop the argument you want to make, and shift it around in drafts if it is not working for you the first time. Readers can tell if an author is in control of the writing. Readers can also ask whether or not the text is interesting and involving. If you are in control of your writing, you will be able to revise your work to make it read in these ways. Readers will remember stories you tell because the stories are interesting and they make your point. When you are in control of your writing, you can take the readers through your points at the pace you want, you can have the readers take scenic detours and always pull them back to the main road, and you can move from substance to theory to personal reflection as you write. Your readers will always know where they are.

Does It Make a Contribution?

You might read an article and say: "It is well written and I am convinced about what the author is saying but, so what?" When people evoke the "so what" question they are referring to the worth of the article in the larger sense of making a contribution to our understanding of human behavior. This dimension raises a number of questions; there are many ways a piece of writing can make a contribution. Usually the question of contribution has to be grounded in a more specific context: To what does it make a contribution? Is it to a particular body of literature, a particular research tradition, general understanding, a particular substantive field (i.e., nursing, special education), or our knowledge of human behavior? How does it make a contribution? Does it describe something that has never been described before, present voices that have never been heard, develop a grounded theory that is new, refute someone else's theory? In a small number of works the author's contribution jumps out at you and does not have to be explained. For the rest of us, the author needs to tell the reader how to read the manuscript: what do they think its contribution is, and how does it relate to what has been done previously?

Another issue that is perplexing to new researchers involves the theoretical or conceptual contribution of a text. What do you do if you give something you have written to a reader who responds by saying: "It is good, but your writing is not conceptual or theoretical enough."? Qualitative researchers usually make a distinction between descriptive and conceptual qualitative writing. A piece of research is never exclusively one or the other, but in general a piece of writing is said to be descriptive when it concentrates more on describing the details of the specific setting and people you study. Conceptual or theoretical writing offers more ideas about the meanings of what you are studying and it relates what you are studying to larger conceptual or theoretical issues. Articles can be theoretical in two different ways. First, they can overtly use ideas from other people's theories to work the data, or they can use the data to contribute to particular theories. Second, the writing itself can develop theory generated by the data. The contribution generates grounded theory inductively. When readers comment that your writing is not theoretical or conceptual, they are probably referring to either or both of these ways. Conceptual writing usually is organized around ideas and concepts rather than around descriptive properties of the particular issue you are studying. Good description can make an important contribution to our understanding, but readers expect ideas about the description too.

Texts

Up until recently, people who wrote ethnographies and other varieties of qualitative manuscripts were not conscious of the fact that what they said and how they said it was influenced by factors other than the data they collect. Who they are writing for, the historical time and particular genre they are writing in, political and social forces, and their own biographies all enter into the construction of the text. Such things as whether you write in the first or third person ("I" or "the researcher"), your description of methods employed, whose point of view you take, the structure of your argument, what metaphors you use, and the authority you appeal to can be understood as a matter of text construction rather than of some immaculate outpouring of the "scientific" approach to knowing. In the last decade, promoted by postmodern debate and the work of scholars in the field of cultural studies and literary criticism (particularly deconstructionists), social scientists have begun to study the texts they produce to understand more about "knowledge" production (in anthropology, see Marcus & Cushman, 1982; Clifford, 1983; Clifford & Marcus, 1986; in sociology, see Van Maanen, 1988; Denzin, 1989, 1994).

The focus on the text has made qualitative researchers more self- conscious about how values intervene in the creation of studies. This emphasis has also called attention to one of the most important tasks of the qualitative researcher: writing. Most books and articles on methodology previously emphasized fieldwork, or design. Postmodern social scientists have shown, however, that the "same" story can be written in different forms and hence become "different" stories (Van Maanen, 1988).

You can take this irreverence toward qualitative texts as undermining the legitimacy of social science writing—that ethnographies are not scientific, they are only fictions. But it also can be seen as an opportunity for broadening the choices of how to write. If we understand that writing up qualitative findings is an interpretive craft and that the text can take a variety of forms, researchers can be liberated from some of the conventions that inhibited their creative expressions (McCall & Becker, 1990; Becker, 1986c). Reflecting on social scientists' current interest in text deconstruction, some anthropologists have referred to the present state of human sciences writing as "an experimental moment" (Marcus & Fischer, 1986).

A Final Point about Getting Started

Many writers are big procrastinators. We find countless reasons not to get started. Even when we finally get ourselves seated at our desks, we always seem to find diversions: make the coffee, sharpen the pencil, go to the bathroom, thumb through more literature, sometimes even get up and return to the field. Remember that you are never "ready" to write; writing is something you must make a conscious decision to do and then discipline yourself to follow through. People often tell us that we are lucky; they say, "Writing comes so easily to you." Writing comes easily neither to us nor to many others; it is hard work (Becker, 1986c, DeVault, 1994). As one author put it, "writing is easy; all you do is sit staring at the blank sheet of paper until drops of blood form on your forehead." Some become more proficient at it because they have developed good work patterns, confidence, and skills, but it is never easy. Writing seldom comes naturally. Most people feel very self-conscious before they write: often their hands sweat and they experience anxiety (Woods, 1985). Keep reminding yourself that you have something to say. That may be enough motivation to overcome your hesitancy.

Chapter 7

Applied Qualitative Research for Education

Research is conducted for a variety of purposes and audiences. Scholars have traditionally categorized research into two broad types: basic and applied. In this scheme, *basic research* is represented as adding to our general knowledge with little or no concern for the immediate application of the knowledge produced. *Applied research* efforts are those which seek findings that can be used directly to make practical decisions about, or improvements in, programs and practices to bring about change with more immediacy (Schein, 1987). Applied research is more explicitly related to practice. It has a variety of audiences (teachers, administrators, officials, parents, students), but what all forms have in common is this concern with its immediate practical implications.

The title of this chapter might suggest that we uncritically accept the rigid, sometimes antagonistic, distinctions commonly made between basic and applied research. This tension between researchers of each type reflects some of the values embodied in the university and scientific communities, where basic research carries more prestige and holds higher status because it is seen as more "pure," as less contaminated by the complications of everyday life.

Both basic and applied research abound in the field of education. Education ideally should be a meld between theory and practice, but in many cases there is hostility where there should be cooperation. Educators face problems when theory and practice are too sharply divided; the contempt many teachers and teacher educators feel toward each other exemplifies this tension. In the university, the education department is often called the poor cousin of the liberal arts because it is considered an applied rather than a scholarly field. Education professors become defensive. One reaction is for the educational researchers themselves to antagonistically distinguish between applied and basic research, disassociating themselves from their practitioner colleagues.

We prefer to think of these two types of research not as conflicting, but as sometimes complimentary, sometimes intertwined, and not necessarily antagonistic. Some applied research adds to theory, to a pool of knowledge about human beings. Some basic research, like research on learning theory, may be immediately taken by someone and applied to a particular student or class. Sometimes experienced qualitative researchers can serve both applied and basic interests simultaneously; they can assume both stances. The data they collect may be used for both purposes. Of course, this does not mean that the same piece of writing can address both the practitioner and the theorist, but the material written and conceptualized for one purpose can be reworked for the other. In our own case, we have found ourselves returning to practical reports we have written for an evaluation contract and eyeing them with a more basic research frame of mind (Bogdan, 1976; Bogdan & Ksander, 1980). Similarly, much of what we have learned through doing basic research has practical applications and we have reformulated that information for those purposes.

When do people undertake applied qualitative research in education and the human services? Let us look at some occasions:

A federal agency funds ten school districts around the country to start experimental programs. They hire qualitative researchers to monitor progress and to provide the districts with feedback that might help them modify their activities.

A national women's organization wants to promote models of what works for girls in schools. They hire an educational research company to evaluate which programs work for girls. The researchers design a plan to study urban, suburban, and rural schools around the country that represent themselves as serving girls well (Research for Action, 1996).

University staff members in a student affairs office feel dissatisfied with how a new university policy that is supposed to affect morale is working. They decide to put together a subcommittee of three staff members who will interview all of the members of the office, and the students who work in the dormitories that the staff work with, to see what the problem is.

A parent leafs through an elementary school reading textbook while waiting for a conference with her daughter's teacher. The book's descriptions of girls as "no fun to play with" and as "sissies," and its pictures of girls standing idly by while boys jump, run, climb, and throw surprise her. She had no idea that girls (and boys) still were represented in such stereotyped ways. She calls together a group of community women and explains what she saw and her angry reaction. The group decides to study all of the textbooks used in the elementary schools in town. They decide that they will look systematically at descriptions, pictures, and content relating to girls and women in order to raise public consciousness about their findings.

These examples show the qualitative approach at work. Although the goals are different in each case, in addition to being useful in the here and now, they all focus on change. In the case of the researchers with the experimental programs, the change is a planned, purposeful, initiated innovation. The educational research company is evaluating policies that schools have implemented to improve the experiences of girls who attend their schools.

Change in the case of the student affairs staff at the university involves practitioners dissatisfied about their work lives. The mothers of the elementary school girls want gender equity in school readers. In these examples the impetus for change comes from different sources, the research itself depends on academic or amateur researchers, and the change may or may not be welcomed by officials.

Change is serious because the goal is to improve life for people. Change is complicated because beliefs, lifestyles, and behavior come into conflict. People who try to change education, be it in a particular classroom or for the whole system, seldom understand how people involved in the changes think. Consequently, they are unable to accurately anticipate how the participants will react. Since it is the people in the setting who must live with the change, it is their definitions of the situation that are crucial if change is going to work. These human aspects of the change process are what the qualitative research strategies discussed in this book study best. Their emphasis on the perspectives that people hold and their concern with process enables the researcher to sort out the complications of change. The qualitative orientation allows for the researcher to simultaneously deal with participants in change, whether in a single classroom or at the many different levels of the educational bureaucracy. The perspective directs us to see behavior in context and does not focus on outcomes to the exclusion of process.

We have organized our discussion in this chapter under three broad categories of applied qualitative research: evaluation and policy research, action research, and practitioner research. These distinctions serve our purpose by providing a useful way to organize our discussion, but each category should not be thought of as totally distinct, nor should our discussion be thought of as complete and comprehensive. As we shall see, categories in the real world are seldom as clear and unrelated as they are in books. The three types of applied research we refer to have their own relationship to change and are participated in by different people and for different reasons.

In evaluation and policy research, the researcher is most often hired by a contractor (a government agency or upper level administrator) to describe and assess a particular program of change they oversee in order to improve or eliminate it. Evaluation research is the best-known form of applied research. The product of such research is usually a written report (Guba, 1978; Guba & Lincoln, 1981; Patton, 1980, 1987; Fetterman, 1984, 1987). In policy research, the researcher is usually hired by a government agency or a private organization interested in some particular social problem, service, or aspect of the society. Typically, the task of the investigator is to conduct research that will provide information that will help people who have the authority to develop programs and make other policy decisions. The information is given to the contractor in the form of a written (or, less frequently, an oral) report.

Action research takes two different forms. In political action research, persons conducting the research act as citizens attempting to influence the political process through collecting information. The goal is to promote social change that is consistent with the advocates' beliefs. Using the data collected, they develop pamphlets, press conferences, speeches, congressional and legal testimony, TV shows, and exposés to influence change. In participatory action research, the research is done on a program or policy, like a literacy program for rural farmworkers (See Table 7-1), with the researchers and the literacy workers or the program staff collaborating on the design and process of research. People in the

TABLE 7-1   Applied Qualitative Research in Education

Research Type	Who the Researcher Serves	Purpose	Form of Data Presentation
Evaluation and Policy Research	Contractor	Describe, document, and/or assess a planned change. To provide information to decision makers.	Written reports. Oral presentations.
Political Action Research	Social cause	To promote social change	Pamphlet, press conference, congressional testimony, TV show, sociodrama, exposé, report
Practitioner Research	Learner or Program	To promote individual or group change through education	Training programs, workshop, curriculum, and plans for change

program, regardless of their status, participate in the different aspects of the research effort. The purpose is to improve the program or policy.

In practitioner research, the investigator is often a practitioner (a teacher, an administrator, or educational specialist) or someone close to practice who wants to use the qualitative approach to do what he or she does better. The person wants to be more effective in teaching or in clinical work, and aspects of the qualitative approach are used to reflect on how effective the person is and how he or she might improve. Or, a group of practitioners decide to do things differently. The recipients of change are the practitioners' immediate clients, students, or supervisors. The persons who engage in this form of research do not necessarily write reports. They translate them immediately into practical changes, they enter them into lesson books, or they reflect on the data to create training programs, workshops, and new curricula.

Some might charge that by including this broad range of activities under the rubric of research, we enlarge our definition so much that it loses meaning. We are encompassing more than most researchers would, especially with our inclusion of action and political action research. Clearly these are at variance with traditional research in a number of regards and deserve special consideration. However, our purpose here is not to adorn these activities with the title of "research" as much as to speak to the value of pursuing the qualitative perspective in these areas.

Up to this point, our discussion in this book has been based on the assumption that the reader is learning to conduct qualitative research and is undertaking a first study. One's first study is rarely applied. Learning the techniques before the application is attempted is most effective. Up to now we have, therefore, neglected applied and emphasized basic research, but the differences are not all that great. Most of what we have already presented directly applies to or can be modified for applied research. Some particular problems and differences do arise. In this chapter we examine each of the types of applied research, elaborating and discussing these particular concerns. We present case studies in two of the categories to amplify different aspects of the approach. In the discussion sections which follow each case, we respond to similar questions asked of each case in order to show how research strategies get modified or stretched for applied research. The questions in each case include the following: Who designed the study? Who was on the research team? What was the purpose of the study? What did people want from the study? What was the relationship of the researcher to the "client"? What were the researchers' assumptions about the research site, and the topic? Who wrote the report? Was the research effective? What was meant by "effective" in the particular situation? These questions address central concerns about the participants, purpose, relationships between groups, the assumptions, and the results.

Evaluation and Policy Research

Head Start: Description of a Case Study

Head Start, the nationally funded early childhood education program, was ordered by Congress, in 1972, to increase to at least 10 percent the number of handicapped children served in each program. Head Start program directors around the country received the directive which, among other things, broadly defined what was meant by "handicapped children," and set the fall of 1973 as the date for compliance. The goal of the mandate was to increase the services available to children with disabilities and to promote their inclusion in programs with typical youngsters. The federal agency for the program wrote an RFP (Request for Proposal) to look at the effectiveness of the mandate. They wanted to know if Head Start programs had complied. A company bid on the work and received the contract. The research was organized into two parts that were carried out more or less autonomously. The major thrust of the first part consisted of mailing questionnaires to program directors asking them the number and types of handicapped children they presently had in their programs and how this compared with the composition of the program the year prior to the mandate. On the basis of that data it was reported that the number of handicapped children had doubled since the regulations went into effect and at least 10.1 percent of the children attending Head Start programs now had handicapping conditions.

A second aspect of the research consisted of a series of on-site visits to Head Start programs by teams of observers using a qualitative approach. Using an open-ended design, they went to the projects, observing and talking to parents and staff. The initial observations consisted of data collection around a number of general questions such as, "How was the mandate experienced by Head Start staff and parents?" and "What, if anything, had changed as a result?" The qualitative teams concluded that the number of handicapped children recruited had not notably increased; rather, there had been a change in how the children were defined. They suggested that the conclusion that Head Start now served 10.1 percent was misleading. The report took the form of a narrative that discussed a number of propositions concerning the mandate's effect. These included an account of the confusion generated by the term "handicap," how staff perceived the mandate in light of their general view of "orders from Washington," programmatic variations in compliance (from "paper compliance" to "active recruitment efforts"), as well as the unanticipated consequences of the mandate (from the labeling of children who previously were not labeled to a general improvement in individualization in programming for all children).

The funding agency was unhappy with the qualitative report. They wanted to know the facts: "What was the percentage of handicapped youngsters being served by Head Start?" The funders wanted the report to Congress to be clear and unambiguous, and, as the researchers also learned, they wanted the findings to be complimentary to Head Start.

Head Start: Discussion of a Case Study

The qualitative section of this evaluation was designed by the researchers in light of the government's request for narrative data. The research team consisted of a professor and graduate students who traveled to the different sites to interview the directors and observe the programs. The purpose of the study was to evaluate whether or not Head Start had been successful in including children with disabilities into their programs nationwide. But as the case makes clear, the funders wanted to deliver a report to Congress that found "successful" compliance with the new regulations. In this case, the researchers had been hired through a public competition through the RFP, so they did not have a personal relationship with the funding agency. This is one of the most common kinds of relationships between researchers and their clients. The research team thought qualitatively about the project, so they assumed that the different people involved in the project would have varying perspectives on what the problem was and how to respond to it. They were also in the field of disability studies so they thought of people with disabilities as human beings with preferences and outlooks. The professor wrote the report in collaboration with graduate students and then delivered it to the funding agency.

These responses suggest some of the tension points in doing qualitative research. The goals of the funders and the researchers may be at stake, and applied research is always conducted in the world in the midst of change. Also, contradictions may exist between the stated and hidden goals of the project. All of these pressure points usually result in the need for more negotiation in the applied research report.

In addition to the points made above, the Head Start experience illustrates a number of aspects of the qualitative approach to evaluation and policy research. These characteristics reflect the qualitative approach in general as discussed in Chapter 1. The data that are collected tend to be descriptive, consisting of people's own words and descriptions of events and activities. The presentation of findings also employs description. The research tends to be conducted in the places where programs are actually carried out. While usually not as extensive as in basic research, the researcher spends time with those he or she is evaluating on their own territory. The analysis and design proceed inductively. Rather than starting from predefined goals or goals extrapolated from official program descriptions, the researcher describes the program as he or she observes it working. There is an emphasis on process—how things happen—rather than whether a particular outcome was reached: and there is a concern with meaning—how the various participants in the program see and understand what happened. Here people at all levels and all positions in the program provide data concerning what the program meant to them. Administrators' views of what was supposed to happen or what went wrong are given neither more nor less weight than what the staff think of what happened. The emphasis is on telling what happened from many points of view and on the unanticipated as well as the hoped for consequences of the intervention.

Getting Funds

How do you get to do evaluation and policy research? As the example suggested, the most common way is through the RFP (Request for Proposal) route. You write a proposal to an agency that has requested that evaluation work be done and compete with other applicants for the contract.

One problem for qualitative researchers seeking funding is research design. Some RFPs that come out of Washington give a clear message: Qualitative researchers need not apply. The specific nature of the research questions exclude the qualitative approach from consideration. Those interested in seeking funding have to spot the signs and know that to pursue these funding sources is futile.

While some agencies are clearly antagonistic to qualitative research, they are becoming fewer in number. Some have expressed a real interest and commitment to the qualitative approach. It is to these groups that proposals should be submitted. One problem even here, however, is that proposal reviewers for these receptive agencies may not have been trained in qualitative approaches and, therefore, do not understand important aspects of qualitative design. How do you educate such reviewers? How do you go about describing your research methodology and research questions in detail when your inductive approach requires that the specifics of how you proceed evolve in the course of the research? We addressed this question briefly in Chapter 2 by suggesting that you might conduct a pilot study before you write a proposal so that your design is clear. Obviously, this does not work in evaluation. RFPs have to be responded to quickly. Yet reviewers without extensive training tend to be skeptical if a would-be researcher cannot depict in detail a study's progress beforehand, show his or her command of the technology to be employed, indicate clearly what contribution the findings will make, and indicate on the basis of what criteria the treatment will be considered effective. Obviously, you cannot satisfy such a reviewer, but you can address this challenge by conducting a broad-based and substantive review of the literature before you write a proposal, using your review to generate a list of fairly specific questions that you will use to begin your research.

You can discuss how you will proceed in relation to those questions, but make it clear that the design may change if the questions lack usefulness. Be more explicit than you might normally be about data analysis and other such procedures so that the proposal reviewer unfamiliar with the approach can gain a concrete sense of what is entailed. Remember that writing a research proposal to conduct a qualitative study and doing qualitative evaluation call for two separate approaches. The proposal represents a hypothesis on how to proceed in order to give the reviewer an idea of what you will accomplish. It is not a rigid blueprint of how you will conduct the research. When you enter the site, you may want to act as if you know little about schools so that your mind is fresh; but when you write a proposal, you want the reviewer to see you as a competent, knowledgeable person who will make a contribution to improving educational practices.

Relations between the Contractor and the Researcher

What puts evaluation and policy researchers in a different position than most other investigators is that their services are contracted for payment. They are guided not only by the cannons of research, but by the contractor's expectations as well. While not inevitable, and certainly avoidable through careful negotiation and explicit understanding, the researcher's standards concerning rigorous and well-conceived research can conflict with the contractor's expectations. "Hired hands" have an obligation to the contractor that they must balance with the responsibilities of a researcher. Here we sketch some of the areas of disagreement contractors and qualitative researchers often face, and we offer some suggestions on how to avoid or handle them.

1. *Ownership of the data.* If not agreed upon specifically before the study begins, who owns and has access to the field notes and other qualitative data can become a source of disagreement. It is understandable that the people who have paid you should consider these materials theirs, but research ethics suggest an opposing position. Subjects should be protected from the scrutiny of people who may make decisions about their future, and what transpires between the researcher and subjects is confidential. In order to collect rich data, subjects should feel that what they say to you will not be attributed to them in reports or in your conversations with others. For them to think that what you say will go directly to people in authority will skew their responses.

2. *Making program goals an object of study.* The canons of good qualitative research design suggest that research should not be conducted to answer specific questions such as, "Is the program successful or not?" The contractor who insists that you answer the question "Is the program working well?" has to be satisfied with the answer, "That depends on how you look at it." Some contractors feel violated when the goals of the program are questioned. After all, they feel that as the administrators, they establish the goals. They want you to make judgments about their goals because that is why they pay you.

There are several ways to avoid this conflict. First, the best cure is prevention. Make it as clear as possible at the outset of your research that the focus of your work is description or documentation rather than judgments of success and failure. In other words, try to reiterate in your agreement that your goal is not to provide information on whether the program is good or bad (Everhart, 1975).

3. *The hierarchy of credibility.* The qualitative researcher, taking all sources of data as important, often shakes up the hierarchy of credibility in an organization. This can be a source of contention between the contractor and the researcher. Sometimes reports juxtapose, say, a high school principal's view of a school with the students' views. Students' perspectives appear as credible as the principal's and often sound as logical. Authority and organizational structure symbolize to some that the words of people at the top are more informative and accurate than the words of those at the bottom, even when the people at the top are telling us about those at the bottom. To present the views of the "other side" in a credible way can make authority figures defensive and angry at the messenger with the conflicting news.

Qualitative researchers can present views of those holding different hierarchical positions tactfully. Researchers who want their work to be seriously considered, therefore, must monitor how they present their findings, avoiding inflammatory language on the one hand, and obsequious public relations writing on the other.

4. *"All you do is criticize."* The qualitative approach to evaluation and policy research critically examines organizational practices, but that does not mean that it has to be overly negative in its tone. Many times organizations are not doing what they say they are doing or what their goals indicate they should be doing. What they actually do, however, may be both substantive and laudable. Contractors often get upset with reports that only emphasize what is wrong, with no attempt to present accomplishments. All people perform better with positive reinforcement. You do not have to lie to be helpful, but an optimistic and positive tone is not a compromise.

5. *Contractor-enforced limits.* Qualitative researchers are dedicated to seeing subjects in context. When they study a program, they want to see how it relates to the larger organization of which it is a part. At times contractors put limits on what can be studied. The limits can sometimes exclude the higher echelons of an organization from scrutiny. When evaluation tasks are narrowly defined to include only the internal operations of a program, the evaluation report can present a distorted view. It may blame the victims of upper level organizational bumbling. Contractors may become upset when the investigator strays too far from the specific program, but this avenue of investigation may be important. Negotiating broad access to programs when the research undertaking is still under discussion can protect the researcher from this source of conflict.

6. *Who owns and gets the report?* Evaluation and policy research can be a double-edged sword for contractors. Often they do not want the unintended consequences or actual workings of an organization to be publicly revealed. Sometimes they want to conceal certain knowledge even from organizational members. Who should get the final report? Does someone own it? This can be a particularly touchy issue. Again, establishing an agreement with the sponsor may forestall later problems. We would advise you, however, not to sell off too many of your rights (to publish, reproduce, and the like).

The reports that evaluation and policy researchers write have political implications and can affect funding, people's livelihoods, and the services they receive. It takes good judgment and a great deal of tact and integrity to conduct such research without making enemies. As veteran researcher J. W. Evans (1970) writes, "It should be clear that the lot of the evaluator is destined to be a harassed and controversial one and those who contemplate a career in this field should be aware of this."

It is important for an evaluation or policy researcher to be aware of potential problems and to attempt to avoid some of them by careful pre-study planning and discussion. But researchers have a number of needs that make them vulnerable to pressure from contractors and other special interest groups that may lead them awry in their work. The first of these needs is money. Therefore, a good safeguard for keeping your integrity intact is to avoid contract research if you are (or will become) dependent on the research revenues for a livelihood. To put it another way, you can only afford to do evaluation or policy research if you can afford not to do it.

The Research Site

We have discussed how researchers should handle themselves at the research site in Chapter 3. Our discussion of demeanor, developing rapport, interviewing skills, and the like are relevant here. Because the setting is an evaluation or policy site, however, other issues arise.

When you are being paid to evaluate a program, you must evaluate a specific one and give feedback about the particular program to the agency that hired you. People feel uncomfortable being evaluated. They have something at stake. Some subjects may feel more confident about what they do and, therefore, participate and share information with you more willingly. Other subjects might feel more threatened in an evaluation and give much more circumspect responses. Informants may fear that you will give them a bad report and that they will loose funding or their jobs.

What are some of the things you can do to reduce discomfort? First, you can communicate clearly to those with whom you spend time that you are there to learn from them—how they feel about what they do and what they see as strengths and weaknesses. If you are at a particular school to study how its "back-to-basics" program is working, for example, it is important to know what teachers think about back-to-basics. You must communicate this to the subjects. You are not at the site to decide whether back-to-basics is "good"; you are there to gather subjects' views.

What may put some people at ease is making it clear that you are not ruled by "the hierarchy of credibility" (Becker, 1970a) in that organization. You take people seriously; you will listen to students as well as teachers, teachers as well as principals, and principals as well as the superintendent. Your demeanor should suggest that you value the perspectives of everyone involved.

It is also important to subjects that you are not a spy. They want to know that their names will not be identified and that their identities will in other ways be camouflaged. Problematically in evaluation research, you are at a particular site and your contractor may know which site you are at; thus, your subjects lack a real cover. Camouflaging individual participants is made much more difficult and people will feel less comfortable. There is no way to minimize the difficulty of this situation.

Feedback

When a qualitative research team studied a group of teachers using audiovisual equipment, they handed their first report to the teachers at the same time they gave it to the administrators. When the teachers saw that the fieldworkers' intent was to understand their perspective on technology, they became eager to share their views. In this situation, the evaluators gave feedback to those at the site during the course of the program. This form of evaluation is called, in evaluation lingo, *formative*. It means that the purpose of the evaluation is to improve an ongoing program through continuous reporting of the evaluators' findings. Information is shared with participants quickly, more informally, and in a spirit of congeniality. The evaluators may meet with subjects on a regular basis, present findings, and discuss the implications for change.

A second kind of evaluation is called *summative*. It has traditionally been the most common type. Here an evaluation is completed and then a final report is issued to the contractor. These reports are used to make decisions concerning reorganization of the program and the allocation of resources. In this sort of evaluation, feedback is rarely provided as the research proceeds. Because it is a more formal kind of evaluation with long-term implications, there are more opportunities for tensions to arise between an evaluator and project participants. For the qualitative evaluator, feedback is an essential methodological concern. Since one purpose of the research is to construct the multiple realities participants experience, the researcher needs to find ways to check with informants whether or not these constructions reflect the world as they see it. The qualitative approach demands that one rely on feedback as a research strategy. The implication is that qualitative researchers may feel more comfortable when engaged in formative evaluation.

The Audience

Evaluation and policy research, as we have said, is applied because it is used to provide information to practitioners or policy makers so that they may educate better. As such, the primary audience for the evaluation research report is the group that hires the researcher, whether that be a school, an individual education program, a federal agency, or a job-training center. Because the written report is supposed to encourage or lead to some kind of action, rather than simply provide more reading, the report must be written in a way that accomplishes this. It should be short rather than ponderous and simply worded rather than filled with jargon. Although qualitative researchers should have little trouble with most of these suggestions, the nature of qualitative data may mean that brevity does not come easily for those who do not depend on statistical renderings, tables, charts, and lists. Qualitative reports are, of necessity, filled with examples and descriptions. This naturally tends to lengthen them. One strategy qualitative evaluators have employed is to have a page of recommendations in the report that can be lifted out and sometimes distributed separately.

Timetables

"Ethnography is like fine wine—it needs aging and careful preparation," said Steve Arzivu, an educational anthropologist from California. This perspective has been a dominant one in qualitative fieldwork in education, particularly among people who have used participant observation. Along these lines, some qualitative researchers have suggested that one should plan twice as much time to write a report as it took to gather the data (Wolcott, 1975). The qualitative researcher who sees himself or herself as an artist rather than as a technician needs time to contemplate and muse. But the evaluation and policy researcher is supposed to provide information quickly—findings that are of immediate value.

It is our experience that qualitative research need not always take that long. We have completed evaluation studies from start to finish in less than four months. While our final report was not a publishable monograph of enduring quality, it was well received and helpful to those who hired us. Research styles in the applied qualitative mode are flexible. It is important to set realistic timetables for your goals, but your goals may be less modest than fine wine. While it is important to be explicit in your research report about the amount of time spent at the site, it is not necessary to make every study a major, lifelong undertaking. While some have condemned "blitzkrieg ethnography," the practice of rushing through qualitative research (Rist, 1980), at certain times findings that are reported cautiously and honestly may be useful.

A Values-Based Approach to Policy Research

We have given you an overview of the topics of evaluation and policy qualitative research. Now we want to discuss an approach we have found effective in overcoming some of the difficulties discussed earlier in doing meaningful applied research. This approach illustrates how changing historical circumstances may lead to different ways of contributing to meaningful social change and how so-called applied research can make a contribution to theory. The approach is "optimistic evaluation and policy research" (Bogdan & Taylor, 1990)

Since the Center On Human Policy at Syracuse University was founded in 1971, staff there have used qualitative research methods to study the lives and experiences of people with disabilities. Much of the center's research has had an evaluation/policy focus—applied qualitative research. In the 1970s the researchers at the center concentrated on institutions for people labeled mentally retarded and mentally ill and documented abusive and dehumanizing practices. Toward the latter part of the 1970s and into the 1980s, the center evaluated strategies and practices to integrate students with disabilities into regular school programs (Biklen, 1985; Taylor, 1982). More recently, the center devoted attention to community integration for people with severe developmental disabilities. Beginning in the late 1980s the center started to study practices and policies used by public and private agencies to integrate people with disabilities into the community (Taylor, Biklen, & Knoll, 1987; Taylor, Bogdan, & Racino, 1991; Taylor, Bogdan, & Lutfiyya, 1995).

When center researchers began their work on community integration, they were skeptical about past evaluation and policy studies. As they saw it, most evaluation and policy studies failed to provide useful and positive information to practitioners because they asked the wrong questions (Gustavsson, 1995). The mainstay traditional approaches rest on the question "Does it work?" Researchers had approached the topic of integration asking: "Does integration work?" or, put a slightly different way, "Is integration efficacious for people with disabilities?" There had been numerous studies of the efficacy of community programs and deinstitutionalization. Some studies showed that integration helped disabled people and others showed that it does not. But the staff at the center knew that it had been documented that people who believe in integration could develop programs and make them work. Besides, as the center staff saw it, whether people with severe disabilities should be integrated into society is a moral question rather than an empirical one. It is a question of values, not data. It is an issue similar to that of slavery. If there were social scientists around immediately prior to the Civil War would we ask them to tell us if freeing slaves was efficacious? Some policies are made regardless of the immediate implications for the people who experience them. They represent a change in consciousness.

As the researchers at the center concluded, the question, "Does integration of people with severe and profound disabilities work?" was not the right one to ask (Gustavsson, 1994). It is a skeptical question rather than an optimistic one. They wanted their research to help frame issues in ways that people can visualize the future. Their interests were in discovering how people were getting integration to work. "What does integration mean?" and "How can integration be accomplished?" were their questions. They wanted their research to help conscientious practitioners—people who are leading the reforms in the direction of integration—to advance their efforts at social change. They believed in being systematic and rigorous in data collection and analysis, in the importance of critical inquiry, and in the analytic power of bracketing assumptions. They also wanted to help bridge the gap between the activists, on the one hand, and the empirically grounded researchers, on the other. The approach they developed has implications for researchers who have strong opinions about the issues they study, whatever they are, and who want to contribute to social change and remain researchers as well.

The center staff have been successful in selling the approach to federal funding agencies. Not only have their proposals been funded but practitioners use their findings as well. Their work is widely read by those trying to be effective in integrating children and adults with disabilities into schools and communities.

Below we discuss in more detail our optimistic approach to research. More specifically we concentrate on a three year study center staff did of agencies across the country that had as their stated goal to help children and adults who are labeled "severely developmentally disabled" (people with severe mental retardation and multiple disabilities) live in the community.

More on the Study

As part of this project, they were funded to study eight programs per year. They looked at programs such as small group homes as well as more innovative approaches to community integration such as supporting people in their own families and homes. One observer went to each site and spent two to four days on location. In total they collected data on 40 programs. The field workers were all experienced in qualitative research and had been formally trained in the approach. While two to four days is not enough time to do a thorough traditional participant observation study, observers took extensive field notes, conducted tape-recorded interviews, and collected official documents and other material from agency files. In addition to turning in field notes and transcripts, each researcher wrote a 20- to 60-page case study describing the program he or she visited and highlighting agency practices and dilemmas.

Selecting Sites

Given the nature of the research questions, and the optimistic approach people at the Center use, they chose agencies to study in an unusual way. Because of the interests of policy makers and officials in generalizability, most national evaluation studies, even those employing qualitative data gathering and analysis, use some variation of random sampling techniques to select programs to study.

In their research, they were not interested in learning about average or supposedly representative programs. They knew that many "community programs" are as segregated from the community as institutions. In fact, a random sample of community programs might tell very little about integration. Rather than select a random sample of programs, they consciously tried to find places that could teach them about how people with severe disabilities *can* be integrated into the community. They started with only a vague definition of integration. Since they had studied total institutions extensively in the past, they knew that they were not looking for places that cut people off from the wider society. However, they treated the concept of integration as problematic; something to be investigated rather than assumed. They wanted to learn about how agencies committed to reversing the historical pattern of exclusion of people with severe disabilities define and accomplish integration.

While they used a variety of strategies to solicit nominations of integrated programs, including announcements in professional newsletters, national mailings, and reviews of professional literature, the most successful strategy was a variation of the "snowballing" technique. They started by identifying "key informants" and asking them to describe agencies that are doing a good job in integrating people with severe disabilities as well as other people who might know of programs. Key informants had two characteristics: first, while they ranged from disability rights activists to university researchers to parents and professional leaders, they shared a philosophical commitment to integration; second, they were people who have the opportunity to travel around the country evaluating or consulting with programs, and hence had first-hand knowledge of different agencies.

After compiling a list of nominated programs, they conducted in-depth phone interviews with each site in an attempt to further screen for positive examples. Based on these interviews, they selected eight agencies to visit each year. While they attempted to select agencies where they expected to find sincere efforts to integrate people into the community, the sites varied widely from one another in terms of the types of services they offered, where they were located, and how they were administered.

They found tremendous differences in the nature and quality of life of the people served in the programs they visited. Some met their expectations by providing positive examples of integration, others did not. By comparing agencies they were able to develop a clearer understanding of what integration means and a deeper appreciation of innovative agencies.

Field Relations

They experienced no problems gaining access to sites or obtaining the cooperation of agency officials and others affiliated with the programs. People went out of their way to accommodate them by arranging for visits to homes, scheduling interviews with staff, clients, family members, and other agencies, and providing reports and documents.

The level of cooperation reflected, to some extent, the nature of the agencies themselves. Many viewed their mission as working toward a society in which people with severe disabilities are accepted. They saw themselves as a positive example and wanted to spread the word.

The researchers' approach explains their cooperation too. Researchers told them that they had been nominated as innovative or exemplary. They were flattered, especially those in small agencies that had not gotten much attention. They welcomed researchers with open arms. Some even received phone calls from administrators requesting that their agency be part of the study.

Ironically, the positive approach leads many officials and staff to be more candid about their dilemmas then they otherwise might be. Most are just as likely to talk about their problems and struggles as to boast about their successes.

Analysis and Dissemination

Each researcher prepared a case study of the agency he or she visited. The case studies provided an overview of the agency, a description of innovative approaches, and a discussion of problems and dilemmas faced by the agency in accomplishing their work. The visits focused on the lives of at least two people served by each agency, thus the reports illustrated approaches and practices through their impact on people's lives.

The Center on Human Policy staff shared the case study with the agency and discussed it with those involved. They published short articles based on each case study in newsletters of local, state, and national professional and parent associations. These told the "story" of the agency.

Most of the reports and articles focused on the positive aspects of the agencies. In addition to demonstrating that people with disabilities, including those with severe disabilities, can lead decent lives in the community, the reports and articles legitimate positive efforts. In several cases the reports have been used by agencies to defend themselves against state bureaucracies attempting to stifle their creativity. When the reports focused on negatives of less-than-exemplary agencies, the agencies were given the choice as to whether they would remain anonymous.

As researchers, they were interested in patterns that transcend individual cases. Since the site visits yield not only reports and articles, but field notes and interview transcripts, they had thousands of pages of data that could be analyzed from different perspectives. Part of the analysis which has been helpful to practitioners focused on describing the "state of the art" in serving people with severe disabilities in the community; for example, the movement away from group homes to supporting children in families and adults in their own homes. Through concrete examples they illustrated how this is accomplished. They also pointed practitioners to conceptual issues which need to be thought through in order for effective community support programs to develop. For example, early formulations of deinstitutionalization and community living did not clearly distinguish between "being in the community" and "being part of the community." Being in the community points only to the physical presence; being part of the community means having the opportunity to interact and form relationships with other community members. They described services where practitioners understand this distinction and are active in helping people with disabilities have meaningful relationships with other community members.

Through their analysis, public speaking, workshops, and writing, they were attempting to paint a picture of a more positive future for people with severe disabilities and to point to some way in which this future might be realized.

Theoretical and Conceptual Understanding

While the "optimistic approach" might be considered too intertwined with practitioners to be related to basic research, they were also developing sensitizing concepts and grounded theory that go beyond practical application to the field of disability. They were seeing that what appears to be very practical and applied research yields basic findings that contribute to more academic disciplines such as sociology and anthropology, and to merging theory and practice. By taking this "optimist approach," they were guided to data that they might have overlooked; namely, the acceptance of people who are demonstrably different by those who are not.

For a quarter of century social scientists studying disability and deviance have concentrated on stigma and the labeling and rejection of people with physical, mental, and behavioral differences. The social science of deviance has become the sociology of exclusion. For sure, many atypical people are made outcasts by the social processes conceptualized and documented by labeling theorists. By becoming so engrossed in stigma and exclusion, however, they have overlooked caring relationships that exist between people who are different and typical people. In the Center's research they found many such relationships and have been able to describe them in detail (Bogdan & Taylor, 1989). Going into the field with an optimistic outlook helped to put these relationships into bold relief—something that had been neglected in the sociology of deviance. Acceptance has emerged as one of the central themes in their work (Bogdan & Taylor, 1987; Bogdan, 1992). The research not only offers practical ideas and suggestions by which practitioners can do better work. It offers lessons in how to do social science as well.

We have talked at length about the work at the Center on Human Policy not because we think others should adopt it as is, or because we think it is the best approach to applied research. Rather, we think it provides one example of how a group of researchers have worked to overcome some of the difficulties in doing meaningful evaluation and policy work. You should ask yourself: "How might I apply the discussion to my own work, and approaching the issues I am concerned with?" But more importantly, ask: "What kinds of innovative procedures and tactics might I invent and use to make my applied work creative and useful?"

Action Research

Action research reflects neither of the premises that only people with years of training, employed by universities, research corporations, or government agencies can conduct research, or that research must always be nonpartisan, serving no particular cause. From our perspective, research is a frame of mind—a perspective people take toward objects and activities. Outside the academy, people in the "real world" also can conduct research—research that is practical, directed at their own concerns and, for those who wish, a tool to bring about social change.

In recent years the split between academic research and action research has narrowed. Whyte (1991), for instance, has argued that "it is important, both for the advancement of science and for the improvement of human welfare, to devise strategies in which research and action are closely linked" (p. 8). He calls the research he and his colleagues do *participatory action research.* He calls for the involvement of "low ranking" members of organizational hierarchies to be involved in designing the research, whether it is about agricultural improvement strategies, industrial employee relations, or company evaluations. His work is professional research, but he does not rely on professional experts in design or process. Feminist research, as well, often straddles the line between academic and action research. The anecdote we described at the beginning of the chapter about the mother who was upset at the depiction of girls in reading texts was an ordinary person outside the academy who conducted research because she was invested in improving the lives of girls. But feminists in and out the academy also conduct partisan research on such topics as domestic abuse, homophobia, sexual harassment, rape, and discrimination. They are invested in a vision of social justice when they do this research (see Reinhartz, 1992, Chapter 10 for more examples).

Recent work in post-modernism and research also challenges the whole notion that some work is non-partisan and other work is partisan. As we discussed in Chapter 1, all researchers design their work from a particular perspective, and this perspective is a form of partisanship. All of these issues we raise suggest that the notion of applied and basic research is not as useful as it once was. At the same time, a short discussion of some of the issues particular to action research might be useful. We earlier suggested two kinds of action research. The first was *participatory* action research, where participants in a program or institutions together design and implement a research project in order to make recommendations for changing practice. The second was *political* action research where citizens do research to work for social change with regard to issues of power. We start our discussion with a case of participatory action research.

The Case of It Not Adding Up: Description

At a fall meeting of a high school PTA, a school we call Hamilton High (it is the same site researched in Grant, 1988, so we give it the same pseudonym), parents from most of the different racial and ethnic groups the school serves complained about the mathematics program (Biklen et al., 1992). The organized concern was sparked by the widespread low or failing scores on the state-wide mathematics' exams the previous spring. A task force formed, consisting of two teachers, four parents, and a student. The committee assumed that there was no single mathematics problem at Hamilton High, that how the problem was defined would depend on who you were—student, teacher, parent—and the nature of your involvement with the mathematics program. So the committee planned to interview all of the parties— students, teachers, parents, and administrators. The teachers reported back to the committee that the math teachers did not feel that they could speak freely to parents, so three graduate students of Biklen, who was on the committee, were recruited to help with the interviewing. In the end, Biklen and her students did all of the interviewing, Biklen doing parents, and the students dividing up teachers, administrators and students.

The committee found that teachers, parents, and students often agreed on what the problem was, although they proposed different remedies. There was also agreement that the problems with math were not just about math but reflected the school culture as a whole. If the "culture of coolness" squelched risking the wrong answer in many classes, it would also apply to math class. The lack of administration support felt by teachers, students, and parents also influenced teaching and learning in the mathematics classroom. The committee organized its report around four themes and recommended changes based on their findings.

First, parents, teachers, and students agreed that mathematics was not like other subjects. Math was not connected to the world in the same way that English or social studies are because students could not bring skills of talking and listening from daily life that they could in the other classes. Math was also unlike other classes, informants said, because of how it is constructed. Students saw mathematics as a series of steps that must be learned. Miss one and you could be in trouble. All the teachers agreed that most students saw math as a series of steps, and some teachers wished this were not so.

Mathematics, at Hamilton High, is also constructed by the shared view that it is socially acceptable both to dislike math and to admit failure with it. Some parents easily confessed their own difficulties with mathematics in a way they would never do with literacy. They also worried that they might pass along this fear to their children. Mothers spoke particularly to this when they made comments like, "I hope I don't pass along my inabilities to my daughter." At the same time that it is socially acceptable to dislike math and have problems with it, not doing well at math makes students feel as if they are not smart. This is because the obverse is also true: if you are smart in math you are seen as smart in general.

Second, the explanations the parties used to account for problems with math differed according to what position they were in. Teachers wanted students to like math, wanted those who were not doing well to do better, and wanted good students to be stimulated. They thought the math classes were too large, the administration too unsupportive, and the students burdened with bad habits learned in elementary school where "they don't learn to think but only to follow the rules." They worried about the motivation of students who did not do well in mathematics. They wanted questions that were "thought provoking" rather than ones they categorized as shallow like, "I didn't get that last step." So they wanted more tracking, or what they named "appropriate placement," so that kids who asked thoughtful questions were in classes with other kids who asked thoughtful questions.

Students agreed with teachers that classes were too large. But most said that teachers did not "like" too many questions. They praised teachers who "explained things well." They divided students into those who "got it" and those who did not. All the students who did not get it expressed frustration about it. "I get frustrated when the teacher makes everything sound so logical and it isn't to me." Upper-class students not in advanced math classes did not like sitting in classes with freshman or sophomores, especially when the younger students "got it" and they did not. All students said that they wanted to be in classes where they did not have to cover up what they did not know.

Parents were critical of the teachers. They worried when teachers labeled their children as "uninterested" or "not good in math" because this categorizing damaged their kids' "self-esteem." They did not want teachers to give up on their children.

Third, students, teachers, and parents all wanted better relationships with each other. Teachers wanted more time to get to know students outside of class so they could know them as persons, not just as pupils who performed at a particular level in their classes. Parents wanted better relations with the teachers. And students wanted better relationships with other students in their classes. They praised those teachers with whom they had close relationships. All the parties saw good relationships as central, but all agreed that building relationships took time.

Fourth, each group commented on homework. Teachers felt it was key that students do at least one-half hour of homework a night, and think about it. Students also agreed homework was important, but did not want to do it if teachers did not correct it. Parents worried when they could not help their children with their homework.

In addition to these four themes, parents also remarked on how larger issues of identity worked. White mothers of girls worried about passing on gender-based fears of math to their daughters. African American mothers worried about how race worked in relations between white math teachers and their black sons. Math was part of these larger issues.

As in the Headstart study we discussed first, the findings did not pinpoint a single problem, and they suggested that the issues were deeper than the math department. The recommendations covered a number of areas including less tracking, the importance of expecting that kids can do math, strategies to lessen the distinction between math and the humanities, forming study groups, having a math clinic in the school and so forth. But the primary recommendation was about communication. Teachers, parents, students, and administrators had to talk—and argue—with each other on an ongoing basis about these problems and all of their hopes. We had talked to all of the parties, but they had not talked to each other.

The Case of It Not Adding Up: Discussion

In response to the questions posed earlier, we comment on this case. The study was designed by a parent in the committee who taught at the university in response to the concerns of all of the parents and teachers who were on the committee. The parents wanted to make sure their voices were heard. The committee was supposed to be the research team, but most committee members declined to do the actual research because they were so busy, so Biklen and her graduate students did the actual interviewing. The committee had a multi-racial make-up. The purpose of the study was twofold. First, it was to find out why so many people were troubled about students' performance in mathematics, what criticisms were of the program from the perspectives of the different parties involved, and what people wanted to change. The second purpose was for a group of people involved in the school to take an activist stance, to "do something" about the problem. People wanted the study to produce a list of recommendations that could be implemented. The study indeed produced a long list of twenty recommendations, not all of which were liked equally well by all the different groups involved. In this case, the relationship of the researcher and the client was both personal and informal. No money changed hands in this research. Parents were concerned about their children, the committee members were all connected to each other through friendship, or being parents of young people in the same school, or teaching those young people, or being one of them herself. In this case, each of the committee members had different and sometimes conflicting assumptions about the issues. Two of the parents wanted teachers to be more accountable and wanted African American parents to be more involved in their children's schooling. One of the parents was a mathematics educator who wanted the school to adopt the NCTME (National Council of Teachers of Mathematics Education) guidelines about teaching mathematics. Biklen assumed that the perspectives of the different parties involved should be studied, and that doing a narrative, descriptive evaluation would be most valuable. The recommendations, to some extent, satisfied each of the committee members. Biklen wrote the report in consultation with the other committee members who read drafts and offered suggestions for revisions.

Political Action Research

Lois Gibbs, a woman with a high school education who was scared to speak in public, was worried over the illness of her son at the 99th Street Elementary School, which had been built over the Love Canal near Buffalo, New York, which the Hooker Chemical Company had used for toxic waste disposal. She interviewed neighborhood residents and kept a record of her observations of patterns of illness in families. Her research propelled other housewives who were worried about their families' health problems to start a Homeowners' Association. Her research identified that the toxin-related illnesses clustered around homes built on old drainage areas and ditches that radiated out from the Canal. The Homeowners' Association was able to persuade the state to buy out the families who had been affected (Antler & Biklen, 1990).

In this example, as in all political action research, the research was undertaken in order to precipitate change on some particular issue. The researchers themselves took an activist role, whether they were mothers concerned about their family's health, on toxic waste disposal (Levine, 1980b) or, in another case, professors concerned about the treatment of people with mental retardation locked away in the back wards of large state institutions (Blatt & Kaplan, 1974). Action research is always concerned with questions of importance.

In their concern with these issues, action researchers always assume that the research will reflect their own values. Scholarly research, as we have said on many occasions, also reflects values. When scholars employing the qualitative approach are concerned about some social problem, they might study it and write a book expressing the point of view of some powerless group. The values of these writers are also clearly reflected in their work, but, while it is valuable research, it is not action research because it is not tied directly to a plan for change.

We must make the point here that research always has political consequences. Research derives its meaning from, and its importance in, the purposes for which it is collected and the uses to which it is put. We tend to notice that the research serves some particular goal, however, when the purpose challenges some aspect of the status quo, not when it supports it. Many people in bureaucracies also collect data and conduct research with a particular goal in mind: to document how well they are doing in order to obtain continued funding, for example. This is a common function of organizational research. Sometimes the data collected may reveal that some slight reform might be desirable. Therefore, funds are needed for the agency so that it can perform better. It is no accident that organizations annually present reasons to show why they need more money and why they accomplished so much with what they had.

You are probably asking: "Is action research objective?" This question is important to clarify, particularly if you are a graduate student in an academic setting where concern with objectivity in research is high. Objectivity is often defined as giving equal weight to all the information one gathers, or as having no point of view when one undertakes research. In journalism, objectivity has traditionally meant getting both sides of the story (Wicker, 1978). Action researchers believe that objectivity is related to your integrity as a researcher and the honesty with which you report what you find. Let us look at a few examples of how action researchers themselves have discussed it.

An action research manual for people interested in investigating and monitoring state schools for people with mental retardation comments on objectivity in the context of preparing descriptive reports:

> These reports are not intended to yield an "objective" view of a facility, if "objective" means devoting equal attention to the positive and negative aspects of a facility. Institutional brochures, press releases, and public statements always paint a positive picture of the setting. As a monitoring strategy, descriptive reports should be oriented to violations of legal and moral rights—things that are seldom reported and need to be changed. Given this orientation, the observer should report his or her observations as honestly, completely, and objectively as possible. (Taylor, 1980)

While the action researcher in this example is clearly an advocate for the rights of institutionalized people, it is the advocacy role that acts as the stimulus to undertake research on living conditions. But the reportage of those conditions is governed by the concern to be honest, to describe in detail what one has seen, and to be exact.

Jessica Mitford, the famous muckraking journalist, says that she is not objective, if objectivity means having no point of view. She strives to be accurate and underscores its importance in her research:

> Accuracy is essential, not only to the integrity of your work but to avoid actionable defamation. It can be ruinous to try to tailor the evidence to fit your preconceptions, or to let your point of view impede the search for facts.
>
> But I do try to cultivate the appearance of objectivity, mainly through the technique of understatement, avoidance where possible of editorial comment, and above all letting the undertakers, or the Spock prosecutors, or the prison administrators pillory themselves through their own pronouncements. (Mitford, 1979, p. 24)

Mitford's bias is always clear to the reader, but she never distorts her informant's words or lies in other ways. One must never lie.

Another way of looking at objectivity reminds us of "the hierarchy of credibility" that we have discussed. Tom Wicker described objectivity in journalism in relation to the use of official sources. Until the 1960s, he suggests, journalism that did not rely on official sources was considered subjective. But the experiences of many journalists in Vietnam contributed to changing this view because reporters developed skepticism of what government officials told them. When reporters began to travel among Vietnamese people and low-ranking U.S. officials in the provinces, they did not get the same optimistic picture about how the war was going: "These reporters began to engage in the most objective journalism of all—seeing for themselves, judging for themselves, backing up their judgments with their observations, often at risk of life and limb, and the government's wrath. Under this scrutiny, the claims of generals, ambassadors, spokesmen began to appear hollow and inflated" (Wicker, 1978, p. 8). From Wicker's point of view, reporters gained in objectivity when they stopped relying exclusively on official sources (what they were told) and began firsthand involvement with their social world. For action researchers, objectivity means being honest, going to the source to gather data, and eliciting the views of those involved in the issue.

What Action Research Can Do

When action researchers collect data for a social cause, they do so to change existing practices of discrimination and environmental endangerment. Action research accomplishes this in several ways:

1. The systematic collection of information can help identify people and institutions that make the lives of particular groups of people intolerable. Geraldo Rivera, for example, exposed the conditions at Willowbrook State School in New York in order to change the way people with disabilities were treated (Rivera, 1972). Critics of services for people with retardation have often noted that institutions are built in isolated spots away from communities to limit public access to them. Rivera used the television camera to increase public access.
2. It can provide us with information, understanding, and hard facts to make arguments and plans more credible to large audiences and gives points to negotiate when it is time

for decisions to be made. Testimonies before legislatures on the dangers of corporal punishment in schools, for instance, are strengthened if details of interviews and observations are included.

3. It can help to identify points in the system that can be challenged both legally and through community action.

4. It allows people to understand themselves better, increases their awareness of problems, and raises commitment. To know the facts first hand is to have one's consciousness raised and dedication increased about particular issues. Geraldo Rivera, for example, underwent tremendous personal change after covering the Willowbrook story. He never again wants to do the lighthearted stories he once did: "Because of the response to Willowbrook, and the responsibility I feel for the children of state schools, I feel great guilt if I'm not wrestling with some profound issue" (Rivera, 1972).

5. Action research can serve as an organizing strategy to get people involved and active around particular issues. The research itself is an action. This was the case with Lois Gibbs and Love Canal, as well as with the women who studied the stereotyped textbooks. As C. Wright Mills (1959) wrote, the first step in social change is to locate others in the same position.

6. It helps you to develop confidence. It is difficult to act forcefully toward some goal when you rely on feelings without data to support your views. Data gathering helps you to plan strategy and develop community action programs.

Action research strengthens one's commitment and encourages progress toward particular social goals.

The Action Research Approach to Data

When you conduct action research, you must think about the process as research and you must call the evidence you collect data. If you approach the task as a researcher and ask "research questions," you force yourself into a frame of mind where you undertake your work more systematically. This may sound like a game of semantics, but asking yourself, "What research do I need to do?" makes the job much more serious than asking yourself, "What should I know about this?"

Action researchers are thorough in their search for documentary materials. Much of the material you may need is not secret and can be found in libraries, courthouses, and law offices. If you are working on a corporal punishment case in a community school, for example, you might read through the town's newspapers for the past fifty years to find how corporal punishment was handled in the past.

The facts never speak for themselves. As you look through records and materials, you must continually ask, "What can I do with this material that will make my case compelling?" While all researchers attempt to solidly document their views, the action researcher must also present recommendations for change. Consequently, you must always ask yourself how to make your material compelling enough to encourage others to act.

A particularly compelling kind of documentary material is less accessible to the public. These are documents from the trade journals, newsletters, and magazines of the particular group under investigation (see Mitford, 1979). Advertisements about psychotropic drugs in mental health journals, or school security systems in school administrator magazines, or articles in newsletters of southern private schools may all provide compelling examples of particular points of view. This is primary data.

Another compelling kind of data for action researchers is consumer testimony. People who have been cheated or discriminated against or who have suffered can speak forcefully about their concerns. The Children's Defense Fund's study of children excluded from school mostly against their will, for reasons such as pregnancy, retardation, "attitude," and bed-wetting, provided powerful documentation because it let the children's words be heard. Action researchers often build on the qualitative strategy of eliciting consumer perspectives, even when the people are retarded, very old, or very young—people who we usually assume cannot speak for themselves. These people can become part of the movement rather than objects to be served by it. It is a humanizing process.

When Geraldo Rivera conducted his expose of Willowbrook, he interviewed for a news broadcast Bernard Carabello, a twenty-one-year-old with cerebral palsy who, wrongly diagnosed as retarded when he was three, had spent the next eighteen years of his life at Willowbrook. Rivera recalls his interview with Bernard as the most dramatic moment of the exposé. Difficult to understand, but struggling to communicate, Bernard recounted his desire to go to school to learn to read and described how much worse conditions got every time there was a budget cut (Rivera, 1972). Bernard symbolized, for the viewers of the six o'clock news, the individual, particular humanity of an institutionalized person. Consumer testimony like this also counteracts the typical administrative stance that outsiders do not know what "it's really like here."

Another characteristic of action research data is that, as we just illustrated, they are often gathered and used to expose. While this is not true of all action research, action research in the muckraking tradition attempts to expose corruption, scandal, and injustice. This strand is particularly noticeable when action research is undertaken in large institutions such as schools, hospitals, government bureaucracies, or mental health facilities. In the muckraking tradition, unlike evaluation research, for instance, one does not seek to maintain confidentiality about the site but to expose it. An evaluation researcher is usually concerned with rapport with informants and does not want to endanger it. In action research, on the other hand, one's goal must be to expose the practice in order to change it. If you want to change the policy of busing in a particular community, affect corporate involvement in curriculum development in a certain school, or affect some other single institution or practice in a specific geographic area, you can not choose anonymity as a tactic.

If your goals are more nationally oriented, you must make a more sophisticated tactical decision about revealing names. After you have collected a number of specific instances of a social problem around the country, for example, you may decide to reveal generally where these instances occurred (which parts of the country or which schools), but your focus is no longer on those individually responsible for some unjust practice. Rather, you seek to inform people that this national problem occurs everywhere.

In this kind of research stakes can be high. People's jobs and ways of life are at stake, both those who are subject to unjust practices and those who work in or preside over the bureaucracies that perpetuate them. For these reasons, it is particularly important to be systematic, thorough, and rigorous in your data collection. If it is some practice in a school that is of concern, be certain to visit the site over a period of time to document your concern. Your observations, like any participant observation notes, must be described in detail.

If, as an action researcher, for instance, you plan to investigate some incident or pattern of treatment in a residential setting for people with retardation, you can facilitate the systematic recording of field notes if the facility is visited by teams of parents (or other monitoring groups) who collect and compile their notes.

These strategies are not different from those we described earlier in the book; it is just that because many people will find the social-change goals so threatening, it is vital to be honest, accurate, and thorough in accomplishing these goals. While data gathering may take longer, you leave yourself less open to challenges of distortion and libel, and in the long run, you may reach your goals more quickly.

An additional problem that action researchers may face is the charge that they do not have degrees or formal research training and, therefore, their data need not be taken seriously. When Lois Gibbs, the housewife who became a leader in the Love Canal struggle, first took the data about environmental patterns of poisoning to doctors, they dismissed it by saying it had only been collected by housewives (Levine, 1980b). If you are systematic, thorough, and grounded in evidence that has been gathered first hand, like Lois Gibbs you will be able to counteract this in the long run.

Action Research and the Qualitative Tradition

Action research, both participatory and political, like evaluation and policy research, builds upon what is fundamental in the qualitative approach. It relies on people's own words, both to understand a social problem and to convince others to help remedy it. And, instead of accepting official, dominant, and commonly accepted understandings such as "schools educate" or "hospitals cure," it turns these phrases on end and makes them objects of study. Because the primary goals of applied research are action, training, and decision making, some differences from basic research exist.

The roots of action research are deep. As our chapter on the history of qualitative research in education suggested, qualitative methods arose in a time of social turbulence. Muckraking journalism preceded the social survey, whose goals were to uncover the major problems people faced in the communities of the industrializing United States, and then to present the data so that people would act to stop water pollution, urban slum expansion, or the tracking of the poor in schools. We find these same efforts emerging again in the 1930s, when photographers like Dorothea Lange and Lewis Hine used photography to reveal the depths of poverty and despair in Depression-era America. In the 1960s, we saw action research again in the form of groups such as the National Action Research Against the Military Industrial Complex (NARMIC), which focused on U.S. military policies. The eighties and nineties witnessed action research in such areas as environmental disasters (e.g., Love Canal), medical policies (e.g., the overuse of cesarean section for childbirth, research on AIDS), and social problems (e.g., mistreatment of homeless people).

Qualitative research has always included both basic and applied work. During some historical periods these strains intertwined; at other times, they separated. Recently, a well-known educational anthropologist said that the role of the ethnographer in relation to social change is "to raise to the level of articulated, documented description what insiders and participants feel but cannot describe and define" (Hammersley, 1992, p. 102).

Practitioner Uses of Qualitative Research

Putting applied or action research towards getting teachers to be more reflective about their practice is not new; it has been written about since the 1950s (Zeichner & Gore, 1995). More recently, the question has been: What should teachers be reflective about? There has been an explosion of literature on this question, with answers ranging from how to collaborate (Oja & Smulyan, 1989), empowerment (Brunner, 1995), democracy (Noffke, 1995), and social justice (Zeichner, 1996). Because there are so many places to turn to learn about how to do applied research as a practitioner, and because the line between applied and theoretical research in education is growing more vague (see, for example, Ellsworth, 1989), we touch on a few of the key issues.

As our discussion of the theoretical roots of qualitative research emphasizes, teachers view what is going on in the classroom from a very different perspective than their students. Likewise, the principal sees the school differently than the teacher (or the parents, the custodian, the school nurse, or social worker). Not only do people in different positions in an organization tend to have different views, but there is great diversity among those occupying similar positions. All teachers do not view students similarly; the teacher's particular experiences, background, and out-of-school life flavors his or her particular view. As we go about living our lives, we make assumptions about how other people think (or assume they do not think), and we do this on the basis of little or no evidence. Often clichés substitute for real understanding. Thus we hear that certain students are not doing well at the university because "they are lazy," or "they didn't come from a good high school," or "they think they know it already," or "they are used to having it handed to them on a silver platter." Unpopular principals are seen as "too afraid to act," or "more interested in getting promoted than supporting us," or "being over the hill."

When practitioners employ the qualitative approach, they systematically try to understand the different people in their subject schools as they see themselves. The approach requires that educators be more rigorous and observant in collecting information in order to recognize their own points of view and to break through the stereotypical images that may govern their behavior toward others. In addition, the perspective calls for noticing patterns of behavior and features of the physical environment in order to be more analytical about regularities that may unknowingly govern their lives.

The belief that practitioners can improve their effectiveness by employing the qualitative perspective is rooted in the way the qualitative approach views change. When approached with an innovation to try in their classes, some teachers say, "It won't work. It doesn't fit the real world." We do not dispute that many innovations do not make sense and that the teachers are often right. But many practitioners take the "real world" as an unalterable given, as existing out there almost beyond their influence. Many see their situations as nonnegotiable. In this framework, people do not feel that they actively participate in shaping and creating meaning. The theoretical perspective that underlies qualitative research takes a different view. Reality is constructed by people as they go about living their daily lives. People can be active in shaping and changing the "real world." They can change, and they can affect others. Teachers and their students define the real world together as they interact each day in their classrooms. While what is possible is negotiated within the limitations of such things as the school hierarchy, availability of resources, and common-sense cultural understandings, how teachers and students come to define each other and what educational environments are like becomes transactional (Sarason & Doris, 1979). Our belief in the usefulness of the qualitative perspective to practitioners is related to seeing all people as having the potential to change themselves and their immediate environment, as well as becoming agents of change in organizations in which they work. Qualitative research skills can play a part in helping people to live in a world more compatible with their hopes by providing tangible information on what it is like now.

The qualitative approach can be incorporated into educational practice in several ways. First, it can be used by individuals (teachers, instructional specialists, counselors) who have direct contact with clients (in schools the clients are students) in order to be more effective. Second, when the qualitative approach becomes part of prospective teachers' educational training, it facilitates becoming a more astute observer of the total school environment and helps make the process of learning to become a teacher a more conscious effort. Third, qualitative research can be incorporated into the school curriculum so that students go out and actually do interviewing and participant observation studies.

Employing Qualitative Research to Improve Your Teaching

How can practitioners incorporate qualitative perspectives in their daily activities? How can they add research to their agenda? Of course, practitioners are busy people; they cannot be expected to keep detailed notes of everything they see or hear, nor do they have the luxury of pursuing leads and having access to the wide variety of participants that a researcher might have. But teachers can act like researchers as part of their role. While they never keep detailed field notes, they can be more systematic in writing down their experiences. Writing notes in a specific notebook helps in collecting data. While they cannot interview people like a researcher does, they can turn the conversations they might normally have into more productive information-gathering sessions. Incorporating the qualitative perspective means nothing more than being self-conscious, actively thinking and acting in ways that a qualitative researcher does. What are some of the things that you might do differently if you assume this stance?

Incorporating this perspective would mean that you would begin taking yourself less for granted and more as an object of study. You become more reflective. Watch yourself as you go about being an educator. Where do you walk? Where do you stand? How is your room arranged? With whom do you spend most of your time? How is your day structured? Who do you avoid? What is your perspective on your work? What parts of the day do you dread? To what parts of the day do you look forward? How does what you do match what you thought you would be doing or what you would like to do? What obstacles do you define as standing between what exists and what you would like it to be? Are there certain people with whom you feel particularly ineffective? What do you think about them? What do you think they are thinking?

What benefits are there for teachers who use the qualitative approach in this clinical manner? Because teachers acting as researchers not only perform their duties but also watch themselves, they step back and, distanced from immediate conflicts, they are able to gain a larger view of what is happening. A teacher participated in a study where she was asked to be a participant observer of one child in her classroom. The child she picked to observe was one that she "usually had difficulty with." She observed the child closely and kept a journal on what she heard and saw. By the end of the project, their relationship had "improved enormously." She came to "like" the boy, realizing to her surprise that earlier she did not. This feeling, she recounted, developed because she began to understand what the world looked like to her student and how he made sense out of what he saw. She came to see where their ways of thinking converged and where they conflicted.

This example reflects one particular problem a teacher chose to confront, but it represents a good model for using the qualitative approach to improve teaching effectiveness:

Step 1: Pick a problem on which to focus: a troubled relationship with a student, a particular habit of yours you want to change, or a specific style you want to nurture.

Step 2: Keep detailed notes on the issue, recording observations and dialogue whenever possible. Attempt to emphasize interactions that happen around this issue. Record what the student does and says to you and others. Write down when you exhibit the behavior you want to change and with whom you exhibit it. What are students' reactions to it? Detail class occurrences when the style you want to nurture is in play. Do you notice any students reinforcing this behavior?

Step 3: When you finish your long-term accounting of events, look through your data for any patterns that emerge. Ask questions about what stands out. Why did I react that way when the student requested information? What was going on in the class when I exhibited that behavior? And so on.

Step 4: Use the data to make decisions if necessary. Sometimes the research process itself may improve the situation (as in the case of the teacher whose developing respect for her student eased her relationship with him). At other times, however, you may need to use your knowledge to plan. Perhaps you should share, privately, some of what you have discovered about your relationship with a student with that individual. Perhaps you can hold a class meeting with students, or talk with other teachers, or ask a consultant for specific advice. The decision making is specific to individual circumstances.

The Qualitative Approach and Teacher Education

The qualitative approach requires researchers to develop empathy with people under study and to make concerted efforts to understand various points of view. Judgment is not the goal; rather, the goal is to understand the subjects' world and to determine how and with what criteria they judge it. This approach is useful in teacher-training programs because it offers prospective teachers the opportunity to explore the complex environment of schools and at the same time become more self-conscious about their own values and how these values influence their attitudes toward students, principals, and others.

We have found that future teachers with whom we worked often were unaware of the values and beliefs they brought to the classroom. Although values influence everyone's work and can strengthen teaching and interactive abilities, awareness of what these values are helps us see how they shape our attitudes toward students (and other educators). People become more aware of how they participate in creating what happens to them. As part of a preservice training experience of prospective primary and secondary school teachers, one of the authors used the qualitative research approach extensively.

As part of the training, the students spent time each week in a school. The qualitative approach was employed to help them sort out conflicting perspectives about schooling and to stimulate them to question their own assumptions about what schools are like. We trained them in some strategies of participant observation and, as part of their fieldwork, required them to conduct small-scale research in the classroom or school in which they were located. We organized their "field notes" by providing a list of general "research" questions. They wrote on one question as a focus for each set of notes. This list of "observer's questions" included questions such as:

How has the teacher organized the class?

What does the teacher you are observing mean by the term *discipline* and how does he or she act upon this meaning?

How would you characterize the atmosphere in your classroom?

How do teachers in your school feel about their jobs?

What kinds of students are most highly valued in the class you observe?

How are educational problems analyzed by the staff? (These may include reading problems, discipline problems, or the like.)

How is blame affixed? Where are solutions sought?

These questions were designed around the particular course content. You can design questions around other foci. The goals of these observer's questions were: (1) to increase students' abilities to describe before they evaluated, (2) to create a higher level of self-consciousness about their own values and perspectives, and (3) to encourage them to see more clearly the perspectives of those in different roles in the school.

We found that emphasizing the concept of "perspectives" as a means of looking at school life enabled the students to question the set of assumptions they brought to the teacher's role. Some of these potential educators, for example, assumed that students were difficult for teachers because they came from poor or low-income families or that "cultural" problems caused pupils to become deviants in the classroom. Observations can help university students to distance themselves from the behavior that occurs in the school or classroom.

The qualitative perspective demands that the person whose perspective the student seeks to understand speak on his or her own behalf. It means that students must listen to their words unfiltered through popular educational theories such as "cultural deprivation" or mental health metaphors such as "hyperactive." Systematic fieldwork enables students to begin to see how power is distributed, the kinds of pressures teachers face, the level of support an administrator provides, or the way students make sense out of school life. We underscore that the purpose here is to help students stand back from their own preconceived notions of school life—first to examine them and second to see school through others' eyes.

As the following two examples indicate, the use of the qualitative approach enabled student teachers to broaden their conception about educational "truths." A student observing at an early childhood education center felt at the beginning of the semester that the children were not disciplined. One day she saw Betsy snatch a doll away from another little girl who was playing with it. The little girl who lost her doll started to cry. When the teacher approached the two girls and asked Betsy why she had taken the doll, Betsy replied, "Because I wanted it," and ran away. When the observer tried to stop Betsy in order to get the doll and return it to the child, she was told by the teacher, "Let her go. I'll get another doll for Jo Ann." Upset at what she perceived as a lack of discipline, she decided to interview the teacher later about these actions. The teacher explained to the observer that she felt it was not always appropriate to have an adult step in to defend a child's right to some object. By doing this, the teacher explained, she felt the child might become dependent on the teacher to protect his or her rights. "It is very important, I feel, that the child learns that she, rather than the teacher, must defend her own rights. She must learn this or learn to always come up with the short end of the stick. What we need to do is to teach her the skills to defend her territory, so to speak, if the situation calls for it." The observer came to understand the teacher's perspective. Where first she had seen only chaos, she later began to discern method. She may not have heartily approved of this method, but she revised her view of what was occurring. In other words, her perception of reality changed.

Understanding a teacher's perspective is only one goal, however; sometimes students learned that relying on their own descriptions clarified for them what accepting the teacher's point of view at face value could not. In this example, an observer accepted the teacher's comment that the children in her class were "very easily distracted due to their short attention spans." The student's notes at first appeared to lend credence to this evaluation: "I observed the following during lesson time. One of the Indian children wasn't even paying attention to what the teacher was saying. All she did was to look out the window or fidget with her braids." Later in her notes, however, the student commented on another aspect of classroom life: "Some children in the class can't speak any English. They can't comprehend what the teacher says. The Indian girl is an example of this. She just came to the United States a short while ago and does not yet speak any English." The student then documented how her perspective on what was happening in this classroom changed.

We have been describing a way that the qualitative perspective can be employed in teacher-education programs. The qualitative method helps educators become more sensitive to factors that affect their own work and their interactions with others. Used pedagogically, the qualitative approach can be incorporated in in-service education, as well as in workshops and informal training sessions. An educational anthropologist, for example, was funded to train Chicano teachers to be ethnographers. The goal of the project was to heighten the teachers' awareness about how cultural factors influence their own and their students' behavior. In order to accomplish these goals, the teachers were placed in field situations very unlike their own. They had to gain entry, establish trust, and go through all the stages a fieldworker usually encounters in their attempt to understand this different "culture." The program stimulated soul-searching and also helped them learn to analyze the agencies and structures that they and their students had to continually confront.

The qualitative approach, applied pedagogically, is neither therapeutic nor a human relations technique. It is a research method that seeks to describe and analyze complex experiences. It shares similarities with human relations methods in that, as part of the data-gathering process, one must listen well, question closely, and observe details. But its goals are not therapeutic. The symbolic interactionist emphasis on understanding how many people in a situation make sense out of what is happening to them encourages an empathetic understanding of different people's points of view. The qualitative researcher's focus on "how things look and feel down under" (Becker et al., 1961) offers the opportunity to bring disparate and often unsought points of view out in the open.

A p p e n d i x

Examples of Observational Questions for Educational Settings

School Environment

Physical Environment

What is the nature of the school architecture?

How large is the building?

Is the building large enough to adequately accommodate the students?

How old is the building? In general, what is its condition?

Are there fences and walls around the school?

What are the grounds around the school like?

What is the general appearance of the facility?

Are entrances to the building accessible to students or teachers with disabilities?

Can people in wheelchairs enter the building?

In what section of the community is the school located?

What is the nature of that section?

What transportation facilities are available to and from the school?

Are entrances clearly marked so that new visitors can easily find the office?

What is the temperature in the school?

Is it adequately heated in the winter and cooled in the summer?

Can the temperature be controlled in individual rooms?

Can windows be opened or are they permanently shut?

What is the nature of the ventilation system?

What doors are present in the school?

How is the space arranged in the school as a whole?

How do teachers define their space?

Do teachers and other staff think of some space as their private territory?

Do students have private, locked places to keep their personal belongings?

Which students are located in the best places in the school?

Are students allowed (encouraged) to decorate the rooms and/or hallways?

What is the nature of these decorations?

Are any parts of the building inaccessible to someone in a wheelchair?

Are there elevators or ramps if the school is on different levels?

Do objects and furniture in the building stay constant so that blind students can find their way around?

Are bathroom doors and cubicles wide enough for a person in a wheelchair to enter?

Are the lavatories clean and free of odor?

Are there soap and towels in the lavatory?

Are there doors on the stalls to ensure privacy?

What is the nature of the graffiti (if any)?

What kind of audiovisual equipment is available?

Where is it stored?

How is it procured?

Do some people hoard equipment?

What happens to broken equipment?

Is the equipment used frequently?

Do staff members eat with students?

How much time is given for students and staff to eat?

Is it enough time for a leisurely meal?

What is the dining atmosphere?

How is food served?

On what vessels?

What eating utensils do students use?

What kind of food is served?

How is it served?

Do staff members talk negatively about students' food in front of them?

Are there any school lunch programs in which certain children do not pay?

How is this handled? Is there any stigma attached to getting free lunch?

What are the rules and regulations of the cafeteria?

How is the cafeteria arranged?

What do the children talk about at lunch?

Are children allowed to sit where they wish for lunch?

What do teachers think about cafeteria duty?

What do teachers and other staff members talk about at lunch?

What are the seating arrangements in the teachers' eating place?

Is it the same every day?

Economic, Social, and Cultural Environment

What is the reputation of the school in the community (good, tough, dangerous)?

What exactly do people mean when they say those things?

What are some of the major problems the school has faced over the past five years?

How do various staff people react to outside criticism?

What sort of things is the school criticized for by outsiders?

What is the racial composition of the school?

How does the racial composition compare with other schools in the area?

How do teachers, administrators, students, and parents feel about the racial composition?

Has there been or is there pending controversy over the racial composition of the school?

How are minority group students and teachers distributed in the school?

Do classes tend to be balanced or do minority students tend to wind up in the same class?

What is the nature of the relations between different ethnic groups in the school (do groups tend to stick together or is there integration)?

What are the words that members of different ethnic groups use to describe other ethnic groups? Themselves?

What is the socioeconomic composition of the school?

What kind of tax base supports the school?

Semantic Environment

To what extent, if any, do staff members use familiar nouns like *boy, kid, fella,* or *girl* when talking to students? In what tone are these said and under what circumstances?

Are students ever referred to by some behavioral or physical characteristic (i.e., *slow poke, big mouth, Miss pretty*)?

What nicknames do staff members give students?

What clichés do staff members use when talking about students? Some examples might be "give them an inch and they'll take a mile," and "spare the rod and spoil the child."

What nicknames do students have for staff?

What nicknames do students use for the various activities, objects, and places (i.e., in one school, lunch was known as the "pig out")?

What words do students use in referring to staff in private? What do kids call each other?

To what extent do program titles such as "counselor" or "rehabilitation" actually reflect activities in the school?

What words and phrases are used in the school that you have not heard before?

Are they unique to the school? What is their meaning?

Does the staff use an esoteric vocabulary to refer to activities, behavior, objects, and places instead of more mundane words that might better be used to describe the phenomena?

Can staff members define or intelligently discuss the esoteric vocabularies they employ?

What, specifically, do staff members mean by "behavior modification," "counseling," and "occupational training"?

How do teachers describe their school? How do students describe their school?

Human Environment

Teachers

What do teachers complain about?

What do they praise?

How do teachers explain low achievement on the part of students?

How do teachers explain high achievement on the part of students?

Do teachers have favorites? What are they like?

Do teachers distinguish between "my time" and "school's time"?

How do teachers think of sick days and vacation?

What do teachers define as unprofessional behavior?

How are girls treated differently from boys?

Are there assumptions about what boys can do and what girls can do?

What about the images of boys and girls and men and women in the textbooks?

How does what staff say reflect their assumptions about what is appropriate behavior for boys and girls?

Who are the most popular teachers in the school?

What seems to make them popular among teachers? Among students?

Who are the most disliked teachers in the school?

What seems to make them disliked?

Other Staff

What are the various titles of the people who work in the school?

What are the jobs of the various specialists?

How can you tell what positions people hold?

What are the specific qualifications for various staff positions?

What training do staff members receive before assuming their responsibilities?

What reasons do staff members give for working in the school ("I like children," "pay," "convenience")?

What do various staff members think of their jobs?

How are the various specialists (counselor, instructional technologist) thought of by students, teachers, parents, and administrators?

What goes on in the library?

To whom does the librarian define the books as belonging?

What do various staff members consider the most important aspect of their work?

What do various staff members like? Dislike? What are their reasons?

Do any particular staff members "sit around" more than others?

What rules and regulations do staff ignore?

Who comprises the janitorial staff?

What do they define as their job?

How does the administration define them?

How do the students define them?

The teachers?

What is the nature of the relationship between the janitors and others in the school?

What do the janitors think about various teachers? About students?

Where do the janitors stay?

What do they talk about?

Do janitors have any student helpers?

Who are the helpers?

Staff Members and Students: Communication

Do staff gossip about students? About each other?

If they do, what is the nature of that gossip?

To what extent are students teased? By staff? By each other? What about?

To what extent are students cursed? By staff? By each other? What about?

To what extent, if any, do students suffer other verbal indignities or put downs?

Is the students' time treated as valuable or do staff members break appointments with them and keep them waiting?

To what extent, if any, do staff members raise their voices when talking to certain students?

To what students is this done?

To what extent, if any, are students ignored by staff?

To what extent, if any, are students treated as if they were not there?

Under what circumstances?

How do staff and students talk about Fridays (TGIF?) and the other days of the week?

Is the tone of the school different on different days?

What about during different times of the year?

How is the end of the term thought of?

Does the nature of the work differ at different times of the year?

How do staff members measure their success in the school?

How do students measure success?

What are the goals staff members say they are working toward?

How do they see their activities related to these goals?

Are students and various staff members asked if they mind having outsiders observe them or walk through their work areas?

Do staff members knock on doors before entering rooms?

Do you think it would be difficult for you to keep your sense of dignity if you were a student at the school?

How do staff members view the students? As capable human beings? As babies? As dangerous?

To what extent does the staff stereotype students?

To what extent does the staff recognize the students' past experiences and family backgrounds?

How are these things treated?

Do staff members act differently in front of visitors? How?

To what extent do students purposely try to give staff a hard time?

How do they do this and what do they think about it?

Do students mock staff members?

If so, what form does this mocking take?

How do students communicate between classes?

Do students approach staff more than the staff approaches students?

To what extent is there free and open communication between the students and the staff?

Do staff hide information from students and vice versa?

What sort of things?

What do students think of the staff?

What does the staff think of students?

What are the names used for various achievement groups (bluebirds)?

What types of extracurricular activities are available?

Who participates in them? Staff? Students?

What type of achievements are most awarded in the school? Athletic? Academic? Other?

How much decision-making power do students have?

Students

How often and when do students have the opportunity for physical exercise?

Do some students receive more physical exercise than others? What students and why?

What kind of activities do the students enjoy doing? Dislike doing?

What do students and staff wear?

Does dress tell you anything about status systems or informal groups? What about hairstyles?

What do the children in the class fight about?

Who seem to be the most popular children in the class? For what reasons?

The least popular? For what reasons?

How do the school monitors behave? How are they selected?

When various children are troubled, whom do they look to for support?

What is the number, if any, of the students on behavior-modifying drugs?

What was the role of the school in having the children put on that treatment?

How do various people in the school feel about having modifying drugs?

Is medication ever used as a substitute for a program?

Administration

How long has the current principal been in that position and how do people talk about the previous principal?

How do teachers act when the principal enters the room?

What do administrators define as unprofessional?

How do administrators check on teachers?

What are the styles of administrators?

Are there school-wide assembly programs? What are they like?

How is the administration thought of by the staff? By the students?

How do classes move through the building?

What is the daily, weekly, and monthly school schedule?

What are the variations from room to room?

To what extent do student and staff needs rather than the school schedules determine the course of daily life?

To what extent are basic needs like eating and using the toilet done *en masse?*

To what extent are places provided for students and staff to be alone and not under surveillance?

What are the formal and informal dress regulations for students? For other staff?

To what extent, if any, do students have access to such things as the bathroom, the phone, the outdoors?

Who uses the loudspeaker and for what purposes?

What criteria does a student have to meet (age, residence) to be eligible to attend the school?

How are the classes organized—who decides who goes into what classes?

How is the decision made?

How is participation in special programs and events (trips, plays) distributed among students? Equally? As rewards?

Does participation in these events reflect class or ethnic distinctions?

Who determines the content of these activities?

Do students participate in the planning?

How does what is done at each grade level differ?

Are the different grades (rooms) decorated differently? How?

To what extent, if any, are pupils moved from one class to another without being consulted or without their prior knowledge?

What is the nature of student records?

Do records contain a place for parents' grievances?

Do records emphasize idiosyncratic episodes rather than a general picture of the whole person?

Are items entered into the records that are defamatory and discrediting to the student?

If so, is the student given opportunities to respond to these remarks?

Are the students' records discussed in public by the staff members?

Do parents have easy access to files containing information about their children?

Parents

What communication occurs between the school and parents?

Are parents consulted in decisions affecting their child?

What rules pertain to visitors?

Is there a PTO?

What does the PTO do?

How many people attend a typical meeting? What "kind" of people attend?

What are the programs for the PTO?

How are parents' complaints handled?

What literature or instructions are given to parents and guardians by the school?

What is the nature of that literature?

How often do parents have contacts with the school and what is the nature of those contacts?

What is the extent and the nature of the volunteer program?

Are there any conflicts between the staff and the volunteers?

Over what?

What jobs do volunteers do?

What is the school's visiting policy?

Are visitors a common occurrence in the school?

What are the school's open houses like?

Is the view of the school presented during open houses an accurate representation of the school on a regular day?

Learning Environment

Learning Situation

What decorations adorn the classroom?

Are students interacting with each other?

Will they be praised or penalized for such interaction?

What is the ability range of the class as measured by objective tests and past grades?

What are children complimented for?

Are the classrooms spacious or crowded?

In good physical condition or run down? Somber or cheerful? Barren or busy?

Which of the students in the class have performed well in terms of past measure of achievement? Poorly?

Are these accurate reflections of ability?

What is the average class size?

Is there provision for interest centers in the classroom?

Are all students engaged in the same task at the same time?

Do the students readily volunteer answers in discussion?

Do they talk to each other as well as to the teacher?

Does classroom procedure optimize cooperation or competition?

How often do students work on group projects?

How well do students work independently or on long-range assignments?

How much experience have they had in working in small groups?

Are the seats and desks in the class moveable and are they moved?

How do students perceive they will be rewarded for effort?

Are all students responsive to the reward system?

Is the class heterogeneously or homogeneously grouped?

If the latter, what is the criterion for such grouping?

Teacher–Student Relationships

How many dittos does the teacher use in class during the day?

Do students have free time when their work is finished?

Has the teacher prepared materials for use during free time?

What kinds of group work activities are provided?

What role does the teacher play during group activities?

Where is the teacher's desk located in the room?

What are the teacher's movements during the day in relation to his or her desk?

What kinds of curriculum materials are used (i.e., texts, other readings, games, etc.)?

Does the main instructional activity revolve around the use of texts, with other materials used for "enrichment"?

What kinds of teaching devices are on the walls, ceilings, and so on.?

What images of people do they portray? How are classroom chores divided?

How is the class paced?

What individualized teaching–learning occurs? For whom?

Which students have most contact with the teacher?

Which students have least contact with the teacher?

Which students are touched most and least by the teacher?

Discipline and Control

Can students choose where they sit?

How prominent is control in the day-to-day operation of the school?

Of different classrooms?

What restrictions are placed on students' mobility in the school?

What methods of control are used by staff?

What is the nature of punishment in the school?

How and when are punishments given?

How are requests made by students?

What tone of voice do staff use when addressing students?

What kinds of things do administrators purposely turn their backs on?

What do teachers purposely turn their backs on?

What is the nature and extent of corporal punishment?

Is the physical integrity of students and staff guaranteed in the school?

Is there danger of assault?

Is there an independent complaint system through which students can bring grievances against the staff for problems?

Are threats made to students?

What are typical threats?

How many students express hostility?

What student behaviors elicit punishment?

Which staff members have the authority to discipline students?

To what extent do the punishments and rewards of the school approximate punishment and reward systems in the larger world?

References

Acker, S. (Ed.). (1989). *Teachers, gender and careers.* New York: Falmer Press.

Adams, R. N., & Preiss, J. J. (Eds.). (1960). *Human organization research.* Homewood, IL: Dorsey Press.

Adler, P. A., & Adler, P. (1987). *Membership roles in field research.* Newbury Park, CA: Sage.

Adler, P. A., & Adler, P. (1991). *Backboards & blackboards: College athletes and role engulfment.* New York: Columbia, 1991.

Adler, P. A., & Adler, P. (1994). Observational techniques. In N. K. Denzin, & Y. S. Lincoln (Eds.), *Handbook of qualitative research.* Thousand Oaks, CA: Sage, pp. 377–392.

Agar, M. H. (1986). *Speaking of ethnography.* Newbury Park, CA: Sage.

Alloula, M. (1986). *The colonial harem.* Minneapolis: University of Minnesota Press.

Allport, G. (1942). *The use of personal documents in psychological science.* New York: Social Science Research Council.

Altheide, D. L., & Johnson, J. M. (1994). Criteria for assessing interpretive validity in qualitative research. In N. K. Denzin, & Y. S. Lincoln (Eds.), *Handbook of qualitative research.* Thousand Oaks, CA: Sage, pp. 485–499.

American Sociological Association (1989). *Code of ethics.* Washington, DC: American Sociological Association.

Anderson, N. (1923). *The hobo.* Chicago: University of Chicago Press.

Angell, R. (1936). *The family encounters the depression.* New York: Scribner's.

Angell, R. (1945). A critical review of the development of the personal document method in sociology 1920–1940. In L. Gottschalk, C. Kluckhohn, & R. Angell (Eds.), *The use of personal documents in history, anthropology, and sociology.* New York: Social Science Research Council.

Antler, J., & Biklen, S. K. (1990). Introduction. In *Changing education: Women as radicals and conservators.* Albany, NY: State University of New York Press, pp. xv–xxvii.

Anyon, J. (1984). Intersections of gender and class: Accommodation and resistance by working class and affluent females to contradictory sex-role ideologies. *Journal of Education 166*(1): 25–48.

Atkinson, P. (1990). *The ethnographic imagination.* London: Routledge.

Atkinson, P. (1991). Supervising the text. *Qualitative Studies in Education 4*(2): 161–174.

Back, L. (1993). Gendered participation: Masculinity and fieldwork in a south London adolescent community. In D. Bell, P. Caplan, & W. J. Karim. *Gendered fields: Women, men & ethnography.* London: Routledge, pp. 215–233.

Bacon-Smith, C. (1992). *Enterprising women: Television fandom and the creation of popular myth.* Philadelphia: University of Pennsylvania Press.

Bain, R. (1929). The validity of life histories and diaries. *Journal of Educational Sociology 3:* 150–164.

Baker, P. (1973). The life histories of W. I. Thomas and Robert E. Park. *American Journal of Sociology 79:* 243–261.

Baker, S. (1966). *The complete stylist.* New York: Crowell.

Ball, M. S., & Smith, G. W. H. (1992). *Analyzing visual data.* Newbury Park, CA: Sage.

Barker, R. D. (1968). *Ecological psychology.* Stanford, CA: Stanford University Press.

Barnes, E. (1978). *Peer interaction between typical and special children in an integrated setting: An observational study.* Unpublished doctoral dissertation, Syracuse University.

Barthel, D. (1988). *Putting on appearances.* Philadelphia: Temple University Press.

Bartlett, F. C., Ginsberg, M., Lindgren, E. S., & Thouless, R. H. (Eds.). (1939). *The study of society.* London: Kegan Paul, Trench, Trubner & Co.

Becker, H. S. (1951). *Role and career problems of the Chicago public school teacher.* Unpublished doctoral dissertation, University of Chicago.

Becker, H. S. (1952a). The career of the Chicago public school teacher. *American Journal of Sociology 57:* 470–477.

Becker, H. S. (1952b). Social-class variations in the teacher–pupil relationship. *Journal of Educational Sociology 25:* 451–465.

Becker, H. S. (1953). The teacher in the authority system of the public school. *Journal of Educational Sociology 27:* 128–141.

Becker, H. S. (1958). Problems of inference and proof in participant observation. *American Sociological Review 23:* 652–660.

Becker, H. S. (1963). *Outsiders: Studies in the sociology of deviance.* New York: The Free Press.

Becker, H. S. (1970a). *Sociological work.* Chicago: Aldine.

Becker, H. S. (1970b). The life history and the scientific mosaic. *Sociological work.* Chicago: Aldine.

Becker, H. S. (1970c). Whose side are we on? *Sociological work.* Chicago: Aldine.

Becker, H. S. (1978). Do photographs tell the truth? *After Image 5:* 9–13.

Becker, H. S. (1983). Studying urban schools. *Anthropology & Education Quarterly 14*(2): 99–106.

Becker, H. S. (1986a). Computing in qualitative sociology. *Qualitative Sociology 9*(1): 100–103.

Becker, H. S. (1986b). *Doing things together.* Evanston, IL: Northwestern University Press.

Becker, H. S. (1986c). *Writing for social scientists.* Chicago: University of Chicago Press.

Becker, H. S. (1995). Visual sociology, documentary photography, and photojournalism: It's (almost) all a matter of context. *Visual Sociology 10*(1-2): 5–14.

Becker, H. S., & Geer, B. (1957). Participant observation and interviewing: A comparison. *Human Organization 16:* 28–32.

Becker, H. S., & Geer, B. (1960). Participant observation: The analysis of qualitative field data. In R. Adams, & J. Preiss (Eds.), *Human organization research.* Homewood, IL: Dorsey Press, pp. 267–289.

Becker, H. S., Geer, B., & Hughes, E. (1968). *Making the grade.* New York: Wiley.

Becker, H. S., Geer, B., Hughes, E. C., & Strauss, A. (1961). *Boys in white: Student culture in medical school.* Chicago: University of Chicago Press.

Behar, R. (1990). Rage and redemption: Reading the life story of a Mexican marketing woman. *Feminist Studies 16*(2): 223–258.

Benney, M., & Hughes, E. (1956). Of sociology and the interview. *American Journal of Sociology 62*(2): 137–142.

Berger, P., & Luckmann, T. (1967). *The social construction of reality.* Garden City, NY: Doubleday.

Bertaux, D. (Ed.). (1981). *The life history approach in the social sciences.* Beverly Hills, CA: Sage.

Best, A. (1997). *Schooling and the production of popular culture: Negotiating subjectivities at the high school prom.* Paper presented at the annual meeting of the American Sociological Association, Toronto (August).

Bhaba, H. (1986). The other question: Difference, discrimination, and the discourse of colonialism. In F. Barker, P. Hulme, M. Iversen, & D. Loxley (Eds.), *Literature, politics, and theory.* London: Methuen.

Bhaba, H. (1990). *Nation and narration.* New York: Routledge.

Bhaba, H. (1992). Postcolonial authority and postmodern guilt. In L. Grossberg, C. Nelson, & P. Treichler (Eds.), *Cultural studies.* New York: Routledge, pp. 56–65.

Biklen, D. (1985). *Achieving the complete school.* New York: Teachers College.

Biklen, D., & Bogdan, R. (1977). Media portrayals of disabled people: A study in stereotypes. *Interracial Books for Children Bulletin 8*(6 & 7).

Biklen, S. (1973). *Lessons of consequence: Women's perceptions of their elementary school experience: A retrospective study.* Unpublished doctoral dissertation, University of Massachusetts.

Biklen, S. (1985). Can elementary school teaching be a career? *Issues in Education 3:* 215–231.

Biklen, S. (1987). School teaching, professionalism and gender. *Teacher Education Quarterly 14:* 17–24.

Biklen, S. (1993). Mothers' gaze through teachers' eyes. In S. K. Biklen, & D. Pollard (Eds.), *Gender and education.* National Society for the Study of Education Yearbook. Chicago: University of Chicago Press.

Biklen, S. (1995). *School Work: Gender and the cultural construction of teaching.* New York: Teachers College Press.

Biklen, S. with Mitchell, J., Patterson, J., Thomas, H., Tinto, P., & Yamini, A. (1992). *Hamilton High School mathematics task force report.* Unpublished document.

Biklen, S., & Moseley, C. R. (1988). Are you retarded? No, I'm Catholic: Qualitative methods in the study of people with severe handicaps. *Journal of the Association for Persons with Severe Handicaps 13*(3): 155–163.

Blase, J., Jr. (1980). *On the meaning of being a teacher: A study of teachers' perspective.* Unpublished doctoral dissertation, Syracuse University.

Blatt, B., & Kaplan, F. (1974). *Christmas in purgatory.* Syracuse, NY: Human Policy Press.

Bluebond-Langner, M. (1978). *The private worlds of dying children.* Princeton, NJ: Princeton University Press.

Blumer, H. (1969). *Symbolic interactionism: Perspective and method.* Englewood Cliffs, NJ: Prentice-Hall.

Blumer, H. (1980). Comment, Mead and Blumer: The convergent methodological perspectives of social behaviorism and symbolic interaction. *American Sociological Review 45:* 409–419.

Bogardus, E. (1926). *The new social research.* Los Angeles: Jesse Ray Miller.

Bogdan, R. (1971). *A forgotten organizational type.* Unpublished doctoral dissertation, Syracuse University.

Bogdan, R. (1972). *Participant observation in organizational settings.* Syracuse, NY: Syracuse University Division of Special Education and Rehabilitation.

Bogdan, R. (1976). National policy and situated meaning: Head Start and the handicapped. *American Journal of Orthopsychiatry 46*(2): 229–235.

Bogdan, R. (1980). The soft side of hard data. *Phi Delta Kappan 61:* 411–412.

Bogdan, R. (1983). Teaching fieldwork to education researchers. *Anthropology and Education Quarterly 14*(3): 171–178.

Bogdan, R. A. (1992). "Simple" farmer accused of murder: Community acceptance and the meaning of deviance. *Disability, Handicap and Society 7*(4): 303–320.

Bogdan, R. C. (1988). *Freak show: Presenting human oddities for amusement and profit.* Chicago: University of Chicago Press.

Bogdan, R. C., Brown, M. A., & Foster, S. (1982). Be honest but not cruel: Staff/Parent communication on neonatal units. *Human Organization 41*(1): 6–16.

Bogdan, R., & Ksander, M. (1980). Policy data as a social process: A qualitative approach to quantitative data. *Human Organization 39*(4): 302–309.

Bogdan, R., & Taylor, S. (1975). *Introduction to qualitative research methods.* New York: Wiley.

Bogdan, R., & Taylor, S. (1976). The judged not the judges: An insider's view of mental retardation. *American Psychologist 31:* 47–52.

Bogdan, R., & Taylor, S. (1982). *Inside out: The social meaning of mental retardation.* Toronto: University of Toronto Press.

Bogdan, R., & Taylor S. J. (1987). Toward a sociology of acceptance: The other side of the study of deviance. *Social Policy,* pp. 34–39.

Bogdan, R., & Taylor, S. J. (1989). Relationships with severely disabled people: The social construction of humanness. *Social Problems 36*(2): 135–148.

Bogdan, R., & Taylor, S. (1990). Looking at the bright side: A positive approach to qualitative policy and evaluation research. *Qualitative Sociology 13*(2): 183–192.

Bolton, R. (Ed.). (1989). *The contest of meaning: Critical histories of photography.* Cambridge, MA: MIT.

Borsavage, K. (1979). *L. L. McAllister: Photo artist.* Burlington, VT: Robert Hull Fleming Museum.

Bosk, C. (1979). *Forgive and remember.* Chicago: University of Chicago Press.

Botkin, B. A. (Ed.). (1945). *Lay my burden down: A folk history of slavery.* Chicago: University of Chicago Press.

Brent, E., Scott, J., & Spencer, J. (1987). Computing in qualitative sociology: Guest column. *Qualitative Sociology 10*(3): 309–313.

Briggs, C. L. (1986). *Learning to ask: A sociolinguistic appraisal of the role of the interview in social science research.* New York: Cambridge University Press.

Bronfenbrenner, U. (1976). The experimental ecology of education. *Educational Researcher 5*(1): 1–4.

Brown, R. H. (Ed.). (1995). *Postmodern representations: Truth, power, and mimesis in the human sciences and public culture.* Urbana, IL: University of Illinois Press.

Bruner, E. M. (1993). The ethnographic self and the personal self. In P. Benson (Ed.), *Anthropology and literature.* Urbana, IL: University of Illinois Press, pp. 1–26.

Bruner, L. (1995). The death of idealism? Or, issues of empowerment in the preservice setting. In S. Noffke, & R. Stevenson (Eds.), *Educational action research: Becoming practically critical.* New York: Teachers College Press, pp. 31–42.

Bruni, S. (1980). *The class and them: Social interaction of handicapped children in integrated primary classes.* Unpublished doctoral dissertation, Syracuse University.

Bruyn, S. (1966). *The human perspective in sociology.* Englewood Cliffs, NJ: Prentice-Hall.

Bryman, A. (1988). *Quality and quantity in social research.* Boston: Unwin Hyman.

Burgess, R. G. (1984). *In the field: An introduction to field research.* London: Allen & Unwin.

Burgess, R. G. (1985). *Issues in educational research: Qualitative methods.* Philadelphia: Falmer Press.

Burleson, C. W. (1986). *The panoramic photography of Eugene Goldbeck.* Austin, TX: University of Texas Press.

Burnett, J. H. (1978). Commentary on an historical overview of anthropology and education: A bibliographic guide. In The Committee on Anthropology and Education, *Anthropology and education: Report and working papers.* New York: National Academy of Education, pp. 62–69.

Campbell, D. (1978). Qualitative knowing in action research. In M. Brenner, P. Marsh, & M. Brenner (Eds.), *The social contexts of method.* New York: St. Martins, pp. 90–112.

Carey, J. T. (1975). *Sociology and public affairs, the Chicago school.* Beverly Hills, CA: Sage.

Carini, P. (1975). *Observation and description: An alternative methodology for the investigation of human phenomena.* North Dakota Study Group on Evaluation Monograph Series. Grand Forks, ND: University of North Dakota.

Carspecken, P. (1996). *Critical ethnography in educational research.* New York: Routledge.

Case, C. (1927). A crisis in anthropological research. *Sociology and Social Research 12*(1): 26–34

Cassell, J. (1978a). *A field manual for studying desegregated schools.* Washington, DC: The National Institute of Education.

Cassell, J. (1978b). Risk and benefit to subjects of fieldwork. *The American Sociologist 13:* 134–144.

Cassell, J., & Wax, M. (Eds.). (1980). Ethical problems in fieldwork [Special issue]. *Social Problems 27*(3).

Casella, R. (1997). *Popular education and pedagogy in everyday life: The nature of educational travel in the Americas.* Unpublished Ph.D. dissertation, Syracuse University.

Casey, K. (1993). *I answer with my life: Life histories of women teachers working for social change.* New York: Routledge.

Cazden, C., John, V., & Hymes, D. (Eds.). (1972). *Functions of language in the classroom.* New York: Teachers College Press.

Center for Law and Education (1978, September). Corporal punishment. *Inequality in Education 23.*

Chang, H. (1992). *Adolescent life and ethos: An ethnography of a US High School.* London: Falmer Press.

Chaplin, E. (1994). *Sociology and visual representation.* New York: Routledge.

Charmaz, K. (1991). *Good days, bad days: The self in chronic illness and time.* New Brunswick, NJ: Rutgers University Press.

Chase, S. (1995). *Ambiguous empowerment: The work narratives of women school superintendents.* Amherst, MA: University of Massachusetts Press.

Children's Defense Fund. (1974). *Out of school in America.* Washington, DC: Author.

Christian-Smith, L. (1988). Romancing the girl: Adolescent romance novels and the construction of femininity. In L. Roman, L. Christian-Smith, & E. Ellsworth (Eds.), *Becoming feminine: The politics of popular culture.* London: Falmer Press, pp. 76–101.

Christian-Smith, L (1990). *Becoming a woman through romance.* New York: Routledge.

Clark, C. M. (1987). Computer storage and manipulations of field notes and verbal protocols: Three cautions. *Anthropology & Education Quarterly 18:* 56–58.

Clifford, J. (1983). On ethnographic authority. *Reflections 1*(2): 118–146.

Clifford, J. (1986). Introduction: Partial truths. In J. Clifford, & G. Marcus (Eds.), *Writing culture: The poetics and politics of ethnography.* Berkeley: University of California Press, pp. 1–26.

Clifford, J. (1988). *The predicament of culture.* Cambridge, MA: Harvard University Press.

Clifford, J., & Marcus, G. E. (Eds.). (1986). *Writing culture: The poetics and politics of ethnography.* Berkeley: University of California Press.

Clough, P. T. (1992). *The end(s) of ethnography: From realism to social criticism.* Newbury Park, CA: Sage.

Coles, R. (1964). *Children of crisis.* Boston: Little, Brown.

Coles, R. (1977). *Privileged ones.* Boston: Little, Brown.

Collier, J., Jr. (1967). *Visual anthropology: Photography as a research method.* New York: Holt.

Collins, R., & Makowsky, M. (1978). *The discovery of society* (2nd ed.). New York: Random House.

Computers and qualitative data [Special issue]. (1984). *Qualitative Sociology 7*(1 & 2).

Cooley, C. H. (1926). The roots of social knowledge. *The American Journal of Sociology 32:* 59–79.

Corbin, J., & Strauss, A. (1990). Grounded theory method: Procedures, canons, and evaluative criteria. *Qualitative Sociology 13:* 3–21.

Coser, L. (1979). Two methods in search of a substance. In W. Snizek, E. Fuhnnan, & M. Miller (Eds.), *Contemporary issues in theory and research: A metasociological perspective.* Westport, CT: Greenwood Press, pp. 107–118.

Cottle, T. (1976a). *Barred from school.* Washington, DC: New Republic.

Cottle, T. (1976b). *Busing.* Boston: Beacon Press.

Cottle, T. (1977). *Children in jail.* Boston: Beacon Press.

Cressey, D. (1950). Criminal violation of financial trust. *American Sociological Review 15:* 738–743.

Cressy, P. (1932). *The taxi-dance hall.* Chicago: University of Chicago.

Cronbach, L. (1975). Beyond the two disciplines of scientific psychology. *American Psychologist 30*(2): 116–127).

Cronbach, L., & Suppes, P. (Eds.). (1969). *Research for tomorrow's schools.* New York: Macmillan.

Cronbach, L., et al. (1980). *Toward reform of program evaluation.* San Francisco: Jossey-Bass.

Curry, B. K., & Davis, J. E. (1995). Representing: The obligations of faculty as researchers. *Academe* (Sept.–Oct.): pp. 40–43.

Cusick, P. A. (1973). *Inside high school: The student's world.* New York: Holt, Rinehart & Winston.

Dalton, M. (1967). Preconceptions and methods in *Men who manage.* In P. Hammond (Ed.), *Sociologists at work.* New York: Anchor.

Daniels, A. K. (1983). Self-deception and self-discovery in field work. *Qualitative Sociology 6*(3): 195–214.

Daniels, J. (1997). *White lies: Race, class, gender, and sexuality in white supremacist discourse.* New York: Routledge.

Davis, A., & Dollard, J. (1940). *Children of bondage.* Washington, DC: American Council on Education.

Davis, A., Gardner, B. B., & Gardner, M. R. (1941). *Deep south.* Chicago: University of Chicago Press.

Davis, A., & Havighurst, R. J. (1947). *Father of the man.* Boston: Houghton Mifflin.

Decker, S. (1969). *An empty spoon.* New York: Harper & Row.

Denny, T. (1978a). *Some still do: River Acres, Texas.* (Report #3 in Evaluation Report Series). Kalamazoo, MI: Evaluation Center, Western Michigan University, College of Education.

Denny, T. (1978b). *Story telling and educational understanding.* Paper presented at meeting of the International Reading Association, Houston, Texas. (ERIC Document Reproduction Service No. ED 170 314)

Denzin, N. (1978). *The research act* (2nd ed.). New York: McGraw-Hill.

Denzin, N. K. (1989). *Interpretive biography.* Newbury Park, CA: Sage.

Denzin, N. K. (1994). The art and politics of interpretation. In N. K. Denzin, & Y. S. Lincoln (Eds.), *Handbook of qualitative research.* Thousand Oaks, CA: Sage.

Denzin, N. K. (1995). The poststructural crisis in the social sciences: Learning from James Joyce. In R. H. Brown (Ed.), *Postmodern representations: Truth, power, and mimesis in the human sciences and public culture.* Urbana, IL: University of Illinois Press, pp. 38–59.

Denzin, N. K., & Lincoln, Y. S. (1994). Introduction. In N. K. Denzin, & Y. S. Lincoln (Eds.). *Handbook of qualitative research.* Thousand Oaks, CA: Sage, pp. 1–17.

Denzin, N. K., & Lincoln, Y. S. (Eds.). (1994). *Handbook of Qualitative Research.* Thousand Oaks, CA: Sage.

Deutscher, L. (1973). *What we say/what we do.* Glenview, IL: Scott, Foresman.

DeVault, M. L. (1991). *Feeding the family.* Chicago: University of Chicago Press.

DeVault, M. L. (1990). Talking and listening from women's standpoints: Feminist strategies for interviewing and analysis. *Social Problems 37*(1): 96–116.

DeVault, M. (1994). Speaking up, carefully. *Writing Sociology 2*(1): 1–3.

Devine, E. T. (1906–1908). Results of the Pittsburgh survey. *American Sociological Society: Papers and Proceedings 3:* 85–92.

Dexter, L. A. (1956). Role relationships and conceptions of neutrality in interviewing. *IP American Journal of Sociology 62*(2): 153–157.

Dicken, D. R., & Fontana, A. (Eds.). (1994). *Postmodernism & social inquiry.* New York: Guilford.

Didion, J. (1979). *The white album.* New York: Simon & Schuster.

Dobbert, M. L. (1982). *Ethnographic research: Theory and application for modern schools and societies.* New York: Praeger.

Dollard, J. (1935). *Criteria for the life history.* New Haven, CT. Yale University Press.

Dollard, J. (1937). *Caste and class in a southern town.* New York: Harper.

Donovan, F. (1920/1974). *The woman who waits.* New York: Arno Press.

Douglas, J. (1976). *Investigative social research.* Beverly Hills, CA: Sage.

Dowdell, G. W., & Golden, J. (1989). Photographs as data: An analysis of images from a mental hospital. *Qualitative Sociology 12*(2): 183–214.

Du Bois, W. E. B. (1967/1899). *The Philadelphia negro: A social study.* New York: Benjamin Blom, distributed by Arno Press.

Duneier, M. (1992). *Slim's table.* Chicago: University of Chicago Press.

Durham, M. S. (1991). *Powerful days.* New York: Stewart, Tabori & Chang.

Duster, T., Matza, D., & Wellman, D. (1979). Fieldwork and the protection of human subjects. *The American Sociologist 14:* 136–142.

Easterday, L., Papademas, D., Shorr, L., & Valentine, C. (1977). The making of a female researcher: Role problems in fieldwork. *Urban Life 6:* 333–348.

Eckert, P. (1989). *Jocks & burnouts: Social categories and identity in the high school.* New York: Teachers College Press.

Edgerton, R. (1967). *The cloak of competence.* Berkeley: University of California Press.

Eddy, E. (1967). *Walk the white line.* Garden City, NY: Doubleday.

Eddy, E. (1969). *Becoming a teacher.* New York: Teacher's College Press.

Edwards, E. (Ed.). (1992). *Anthropology and photography 1860–1920.* New Haven, CT: Yale University Press.

Eisner, E. (1980). *On the differences between scientific and artistic approaches to qualitative research.* Paper presented at the meeting of the American Educational Research Association, Boston.

Eisner, E. (1991). *The enlightened eye: Qualitative inquiry and the enhancement of educational practice.* New York: Macmillan.

Eisner, E., & Peshkin, A. (Eds.). (1990). *Qualitative inquiry in education: The continuing debate.* New York: Teachers College Press.

Ellis, C. (1991). Sociological introspection and emotional experience. *Symbolic Interaction 14:* 23–50.

Ellis, C. (1993). Telling a story of sudden death. *Sociological Quarterly 34:* 711–730.

Ellis, C. (1995a). Emotional and ethical quagmires in returning to the field. *Journal of Contemporary Ethnography 24*(1): 68–98.

Ellis, C. (1995b). The other side of the fence: Seeing black and white in a small southern town. *Qualitative Inquiry 1*(2): 147–167.

Ellsworth, E. (1988). Illicit pleasures: Feminist spectators and *Personal Best.* In L. Roman, L. Christian-Smith, & E. Ellsworth (Eds.), *Becoming feminine: The politics of popular culture.* London: Falmer Press, pp. 102–119.

Ellsworth, E. (1989). Why doesn't this feel empowering? Working through the repressive myths of critical pedagogy. *Harvard Educational Review 59*(3): 297–324.

English, F. W. (1988). The utility of the camera in qualitative inquiry. *Educational Researcher 17*(4): 8–15.

Erickson, F. (1973). What makes school ethnography "ethnographic"? *Anthropology and Education Quarterly 4*(2): 10–19.

Erickson, F. (1975). Gatekeeping and the melting pot. *Harvard Educational Review 45:* 44–70.

Erickson, F. (1986). Qualitative methods in research on teaching. In M. C. Wittrock (Ed.), *Handbook of research on reaching* (3rd ed.). New York: Macmillan, pp. 119–161.

Erikson, K. (1962). Notes on the sociology of deviance. *Social Problems 9:* 307–314.

Erikson, K. (1976). *Everything in its path.* New York: Simon & Schuster.

Evans, J. W. (1970). Evaluating social action programs. In L. Zurcher, & C. Bonjean (Eds.), *Planned social intervention.* Scranton, PA: Chandler.

Evans, W. (1973). *Photographs for the Farm Security Administration, 1935–1938.* New York: Da Capo Press.

Everhart, R. (1975). Problems of doing fieldwork in educational evaluation. *Human Organization 34*(2): 205–215.

Everhart, R. (1977). Between stranger and friend: Some consequences of "long term" fieldwork in schools. *American Educational Research Journal 14*(1): 1–15.

Fabian, J. (1983). *Time and the other: How anthropology makes its object.* New York: Columbia University Press.

Fancher, R. E. (1987). Henry Goddard and the Kallikak family photographs. *American Psychologist 42*(6): 585–590.

Farber, P., & Holm, G. (1994). Adolescent freedom and the cinematic high school. In P. Farber, E. Provenzo, Jr., & G. Holm (Eds.), *Schooling in the light of popular culture.* Albany, NY: State University of New York Press, pp. 21–40.

Faris, R. E. L. (1967). *Chicago sociology, 1920–1932.* Chicago: University of Chicago Press.

Federal Writers' Project (1939). *These are our lives.* Chapel Hill, NC: University of North Carolina.

Ferguson, D. (1994). Is communication really the point? Some thoughts on interventions and membership. *Mental Retardation 32*(1): 7–9.

Ferguson, P., Ferguson, D., & Taylor, S. (Eds.). (1992). *Interpreting disability: A qualitative reader.* New York: Teachers College Press.

Fetterman, D. M. (Ed.). (1984). *Ethnography in educational evaluation.* Newbury Park, CA: Sage.

Fetterman, D. M. (1987). Ethnographic educational evaluation. In G. Spindler, & L. Spindler (Eds.), *Interpretive ethnography of education.* Hillsdale, NJ: Lawrence Erlbaum, pp. 81–108.

Fielding, N. G., & Fielding, J. L. (1986). *Linking data.* Newbury Park, CA: Sage.

Fields, E. (1988). Qualitative content analysis of television news: Systematic techniques. *Qualitative Sociology 11*(1): 183–189.

Filstead, W. (Ed.). (1970). *Qualitative methodology.* Chicago: Markham.

Finch, J. (1984). "It's great to have someone to talk to": The ethics and politics of interviewing women. In C. Bell, & H. Roberts (Eds.), *Social researching.* London: Routledge and Kegan Paul, pp. 70–87.

Finders, M. (1997). *Just girls: Hidden literacies and life in junior high.* New York: Teachers College Press.

Fine, G. (1987). *With the boys.* Chicago: University of Chicago Press.

Fine, G. A., & Glassner, B. (1979). Participant observation with children. *Urban Life 8*(2): 153–174.

Fine, G. A., & Sandstrom, K. L. (1988). *Knowing children: Participant observation with minors.* Newbury Park, CA: Sage.

Fine, M. (1988). Sexuality, schooling, and adolescent females: The missing discourse of desire. *Harvard Educational Review 58*(1): 29–53.

Fine, M. (1993). Over dinner: Feminism and adolescent female bodies. In S. Biklen, & D. Pollard (Eds.), *Gender and education.* 92nd Yearbook of the National Society of the Study of Education. Chicago: University of Chicago Press, pp. 126–154.

Fine, M. (1994a). Working the hyphens: Reinventing self and other in qualitative research. In N. K. Denzin, & Y. S. Lincoln (Eds.), *Handbook of qualitative research.* Thousand Oaks, CA: Sage, pp. 70–82.

Fine, M. (1994b). Dis-stance and other stances: Negotiations of power inside feminist research. In A. Gitlin (Ed.), *Power and method.* New York: Routledge, pp. 13–35.

Firestone, W. A. (1987). Meaning in method: The rhetoric of quantitative and qualitative research. *Educational Researcher 16*(6): 16–21.

Florio, S. E. (1978). *Learning how to go to school: An ethnography of interaction in a kindergarten/first grade classroom.* Unpublished doctoral dissertation, Harvard University.

Fontana A., & Frey, J. (1994). Interviewing: The art of science. In N. Denzin, & Y. Lincoln (Eds.), *Handbook of qualitative research.* Thousand Oaks, CA: Sage, pp. 361–376.

Fonow, M. M., & Cook, J. (1991). Back to the future: A look at the second wave of feminist epistemology and methodology. In M. M. Fonow, & J. Cook (Eds.), *Beyond methodology: Feminist scholarship as lived research.* Bloomington, IN: Indiana University Press, pp. 1–15.

Fordham, S. (1996). *Blacked out: Dilemmas of race, identity, and success at Capital High.* Chicago: University of Chicago Press.

Foster, M. (1992). African American teachers and the politics of race. In K. Weiler (Ed.), *What schools can do: Critical pedagogy and practice.* Albany, NY: State University of New York Press, pp. 93–127.

Foster, M. (1993). Self-portraits of black teachers: Narratives of individual and collective struggle against racism. In W. Tierney, & D. McLaughlin (Eds.), *Naming silenced lives: Personal narratives and the process of educational change.* New York: Routledge, pp. 155–175.

Foster, M. (1994). The power to know one thing is never the power to know all things: Methodological notes on two studies of Black American teachers. In A. Gitlin (Ed.), *Power and method: Political activism and educational research.* New York: Routledge, pp. 129–145.

Fox, D. M., & Lawrence, C. (1988). *Photographing medicine: Images and power in Britain and America since 1840.* New York: Greenwood Press.

Freire, P. (1968). *Pedagogy of the oppressed.* New York: Herder and Herder.

Fried, A., & Elmaii, R. (Eds.). (1968). *London (Excerpts from Life and labour of the people in London).* New York: Pantheon.

Friedman, S., & Steinbert, S. (1989). *Writing and thinking in the social sciences.* Englewood Cliffs, NJ: Prentice-Hall.

Fuchs, E. (1966). *Pickets at the gates.* New York: The Free Press.

Fuchs, E. (1969). *Teachers talk.* Garden City, NY: Doubleday.

Gans, H. (1967). *The Levittowners: Ways of life and politics in a new suburban community.* New York: Pantheon Books.

Garfinkel, H. (1964). *Studies in ethnomethodology.* Englewood Cliffs, NJ: Prentice-Hall.

Garfinkel, H. (1967). *Studies in ethnomethodology.* Englewood Cliffs, NJ: Prentice-Hall.

Geer, B. (1964). First days in the field. In P. Hammond (Ed.), *Sociologists at work.* Garden City, NY: Doubleday.

Geer, B. (Ed.). (1973). *Learning to work.* Beverly Hills, CA: Sage.

Geertz, C. (1979). From the native's point of view: On the nature of anthropological understanding. In P. Rabinow, & W. Sullivan (Eds.), *Interpretive social science.* Berkeley: University of California Press, pp. 225–242.

Geertz, C. (1973). Thick description: Toward an interpretive theory of culture. In *The interpretation of cultures.* New York: Basic Books.

Geiger, S. (1986). Women's life histories: Method and content. *SIGNS 11*(2): 334–351.

Georges, R. A., & Jones, M. O. (1980). *People studying people: The human element in fieldwork.* Berkeley: University of California Press.

Gepart, R. P., Jr. (1988). *Ethnostatistics: Qualitative foundations for quantitative research.* Newbury Park, CA: Sage.

Gerth, H., & Mills, C. W. (1978). *Character and social structure.* New York: Harcourt Brace.

Giroux, H., & Simon, R. (1989). Popular culture as pedagogy of pleasure and meaning. In H. Giroux, & R. Simon (Eds). *Popular culture, schooling, and everyday life.* New York: Bergin & Garvey, pp. 1–30.

Glaser, B. (1978). *Theoretical sensitivity: Advances in the methodology of grounded theory.* Mill Valley, CA: Sociology Press.

Glaser, B., & Strauss, A. L. (1967). *The discovery of grounded theory: Strategies for qualitative research.* Chicago: Aldine.

Glass, G. (1975). A paradox about excellence of the schools and the people in them. *Educational Researcher 4:* 9–13.

Glesne, C., & Peshkin, A. (1992). *Becoming qualitative researchers.* White Plains, NY: Longman.

Goetz, J. P., & LeCompte, M. D. (1984). *Ethnography and qualitative design in educational research.* New York: Academic Press.

Goffman, E. (1959). *The presentation of self in everyday life.* Garden City, NY: Anchor.

Goffman, E. (1961). *Asylums.* Garden City, NY: Anchor Books, 1961.

Goffman, E. (1979). *Gender advertisements.* New York: Harper.

Gold, R. (1958). Roles in sociological field observations. *Social Forces 36:* 217–223.

Goldman, R., & Papson, S. (1994). The postmodernism that failed. In D. R. Dickens, & A. Fontana (Eds.), *Postmodernism & social inquiry.* New York: Guilford, pp. 224–254.

Goode, D. (1992). Who is Bobby? Ideology and method in the discovery of a Down syndrome person's competence. In P. Ferguson, D. Ferguson, & S.

Taylor (Eds.), *Interpreting disability: A qualitive reader.* New York: Teachers College Press, pp. 197–212.

Goode, D. (1994). *A world without words: The social construction of children born deaf and blind.* Philadelphia: Temple University.

Gordon, H. (1997). *The monkey on my shoulder is not a nigger: Reconstructing images of the African American male.* Unpublished paper.

Gouldner, H. (1978). *Teachers' pets, troublemakers, and nobodies.* Westport, CT: Greenwood Press.

Graebner, W. (1990). *Coming of age in Buffalo.* Philadelphia: Temple University Press.

Graham-Brown, S. (1988). *Images of women: The portrayal of women in photography of the middle east 1860–1950.* London: Quartet.

Grant, G. (1979). Journalism and social science: Continuities and discontinuities. In H. Gans, N. Glazer, J. Gusfield, & C. Jenks (Eds.), *On the making of Americans: Essays in honor of David Riesman.* Philadelphia: University of Pennsylvania Press, pp. 291–313.

Grant, G. (1988). *The world we created at Hamilton High.* Cambridge, MA: Harvard University Press.

Greene, M. (1978). *Landscapes of learning.* New York: Teachers College Press.

Groce, N. (1985). *Everyone here spoke sign language.* Cambridge, MA: Harvard University Press.

Guba, E. G. (1978). *Toward a methodology of naturalistic inquiry in educational evaluation.* CSE Monograph Series in Evaluation, 8. Los Angeles: Center for the Study of Evaluation, University of California.

Guba, E., & Lincoln, Y. (1981). *Effective evaluation: Improving the usefulness of evaluation results through responsive and naturalistic approaches.* San Francisco: Jossey-Bass.

Guba, E., & Lincoln, Y. (1982). Epistemological and methodological bases of naturalistic inquiry. *Educational Communication and Technology Journal* 30: 233–252.

Guba, E. G., & Lincoln, Y. S. (1994). Competing paradigms in qualitative research. In N. K. Denzin, & Y. S. Lincoln (Eds.), *Handbook of qualitative research.* Thousand Oaks, CA: Sage, pp. 105–117.

Gubrium, J. (1988). *Analyzing field reality.* Beverly Hills, CA: Sage.

Gustavsson, A. (1994). Beyond the reformer's perspective and able-centrism. In B. Qvarsell, & B. L. T. van der Linden (Eds.), *The quest for quality.* Stockholm, Sweden: Peogogiska Institutionen.

Gustavsson, A. (1995) Preface. In A. Gustavssan, (Ed.), *Disability and integration.* Stockholm, Sweden: Department of Education, Stockholm University, pp. 3–8.

Gutman, J. M. (1974). *Lewis Hine, 1974–1940: Two perspectives.* New York: Grossman.

Hallden, G. (1994). Establishing order: Small girls write about family life. *Gender and Education* 6(1): 3–17.

Hammersley, M. (1992). *What's wrong with ethnography?* London: Routledge.

Hamilton, D. (1994). Traditions, preferences, postures in applied qualitative research. In N. K. Denzin, & Y. S. Lincoln (Eds.), *Handbook of qualitative research.* Thousand Oaks, CA: Sage, pp. 60–69.

Haraway, D. (1991). Situated knowledges: The science question in feminism and the privilege of partial perspective. In *Simians, cyborgs, and women.* New York: Routledge.

Harding, S. (Ed.). (1987). *Feminism and methodology.* Bloomington, IN: Indiana University Press.

Harper, D. (1994). On the authority of the image: Visual methods at the crossroads. In N. K. Denzin, & Y. Lincoln (Eds.), *Handbook of qualitative research.* Thousand Oaks, CA: Sage, pp. 403–412.

Harrison, S. (1931). *The social survey.* New York: Russell Sage Foundation.

Haskins, J. (1969). *Diary of a Harlem schoolteacher.* New York: Grove Press.

Heath, S. B. (1983). *Ways with words: Language, life and work in communities and classrooms.* Cambridge, UK: Cambridge University Press.

Heider, K. G. (1988). The Rashomon effect: When ethnographers disagree. *American Anthropologist 90:* 73–81.

Helling, I. K. (1988). The life history method. In N. K. Denzin (Ed.), *Studies in symbolic interaction.* Greenwich, CT: JAI, pp. 211–243.

Henry, J. (1955a). Culture, education and communications theory. In G. Spindler (Ed.), *Education and anthropology.* Stanford, CA: Stanford University Press, pp. 188–207.

Henry, J. (1955b). Docility, or giving teacher what she wants. *The Journal of Social Issues* 11(2): 33–41.

Henry, J. (1957). Attitude organization in elementary school classrooms. *American Journal of Orthopsychiatry 27:* 117–123.

Henry, J. (1963). *Culture against man.* New York: Random House.

Herndon, J. (1968). *The way it spozed to be.* New York: Simon & Schuster.

Herriott, E. (1977). Ethnographic case studies in federally funded multi-disciplinary policy research: Some design and implementation issues. *Anthropology and Education Quarterly 8*(2): 106–115.

Hertz, R., & Imber, J. (1993). Fieldwork in elite settings. *Journal of Contemporary Ethnography* (Special Issue of the Journal devoted to research with elites.) *22*(1).

Hewitt, R. (1995). Salvaging jargon. *Writing Sociology 3*(1): 1–3.

Hill, R. J., & Crittenden, K. (1968). *Proceedings of the Purdue symposium on ethno-methodology.* Lafayette, IN: Institute for the Study of Social Change, Purdue University.

Hochschild, A. R. (1983). *The managed heart: Commercialization of human feelings.* Berkeley: University of California Press.

Hollingshead, A. B. (1949). *Elmstown's youth.* New York: Wiley.

Holm, G. (1994). Learning in style: The portrayal of schooling in *Seventeen* magazine. In P. Farber, E. Provenzo, Jr., & G. Holm (Eds.), *Schooling in the light of popular culture.* Albany, NY: State University of New York Press, pp. 41–58.

Holm, G., & Farber, P. (1994). Education, rock-and-roll, and the lyrics of discontent. In P. Farber, E. Provenzo, Jr., & G. Holm (Eds.), *Schooling in the light of popular culture.* Albany, NY: State University of New York Press, pp. 41–58.

Holstein, J., & Gubrium, J. (1994). Phenomenology, ethnomethodology and interpretive practice. In N. Denzin, & Y. Lincoln (Eds.), *Handbook of qualitative research.* Thousand Oaks, CA: Sage, pp. 262–272.

Howe, K. R. (1988). Against the quantitative–qualitative incompatibility thesis or dogmas die hard. *Educational Researcher 17*(8): 10–16.

Hughes, E. (1934). Institutional office and the person. *American Journal of Sociology 43:* 404–413.

Hughes, E. C. (1971). *The sociological eye.* Chicago: Aldine.

Hurley, F. J. (1972). *Portrait of a decade: Roy Stryker and the development of documentary photography in the thirties.* Baton Rouge, LA: Louisiana State University Press.

Hyman, H. (1954). *Interviewing in social research.* Chicago: University of Chicago Press.

Ianni, F. (1978). Anthropology and educational research: A report on federal agency programs, policies and issues. In the Committee on Anthropology and Education (Eds.), *Report and working papers.* National Academy of Education, pp. 427–488.

Ives, E. (1974). *The tape-recorded interview: A manual for field workers in folklore and oral history.* Knoxville, TN: The University of Tennessee Press.

Jackson, P. (1968). *Life in classrooms.* New York: Holt, Rinehart & Winston.

Jacob, E. (1987). Qualitative research traditions: A review. *Review of Educational Research 57*(1): 1–50.

Jacoby, R. (1995). Clarifying seditious thought. *Writing Sociology 2*(4): 1–3.

Jahoda, M., Deutsch, M., & Cook, S. (1951). *Research methods in social relations (Part 1).* New York: Dryden.

James, A., & Prout, A. (Eds.). (1990). *Constructing and reconstructing childhood: Contemporary issues in the sociological study of childhood.* London: Falmer.

Janesick, V. J. (1994). The dance of qualitative research design. In N. K. Denzin, & Y. S. Lincoln (Eds.), *Handbook of qualitative research.* Thousand Oaks, CA: Sage, pp. 209–219.

Johnson, J. M. (1975). *Doing field research.* New York: The Free Press.

Journal of Educational Sociology, 1927 *1*(4).

Journal of Educational Sociology, 1927 *1*(7).

Junker, B. (1960). *Fieldwork.* Chicago: University of Chicago Press.

Karp, D. A. (1996). *Speaking of sadness: Depression, disconnection, and the meaning of illness.* New York: Oxford.

Katz, S. (1995). Learning the (T)ropes. *Writing Sociology 2*(3): 1–3.

Kellner, D. (1991). Reading images critically: Toward a postmodern pedagogy. In H. Giroux (Ed.), *Postmodernism, feminism, and cultural politics.* Albany, NY: State University of New York Press, pp. 60–82.

Kellogg, P. (1911–1912). The spread of the survey idea. *Proceedings of the Academy of Political Science 2*(4): 475–491.

Kelly, J. G. (1969). Naturalistic observations in contrasting social environments. In E. P. Willens, &

H. L. Raush (Eds.), *Naturalistic viewpoints in psychological research.* New York: Holt, Rinehart & Winston, pp. 183–199.

Kennard, M. (1990). Producing sponsored films on menstruation: The struggle over meaning. In E. Ellsworth, & M. Whatley (Eds.), *The ideology of images in educational media.* New York: Teachers College Press, pp. 57–73.

Kiang, P. N. (1995). Bicultural strengths and struggles of Southeast Asian Americans in school. In A. Darder (Ed.), *Culture and difference: Critical perspectives on the bicultural experience in the United States.* Westport, CT: Bergin & Garvey, pp. 201–225.

Kierzek, J., & Gibson, W. (1968). *The Macmillan handbook of English.* New York: Macmillan.

Kincheloe, J. L., & McLaren, P. L. (1994). Rethinking critical theory and qualitative research. In N. K. Denzin, & Y. S. Lincoln (Eds.), *Handbook of qualitative research.* Thousand Oaks, CA: Sage, pp. 138–157.

Kohl, H. (1967). *36 children.* New York: New American Library.

Komarovsky, M. (1940). *The unemployed man and his family.* New York: Dryden.

Komarovsky, M. (1946). Cultural contradictions and sex roles. *American Journal of Sociology 52:* 184–189.

Kozol, J. (1967). *Death at an early age.* New York: Bantam.

Kozol, W. (1994). *Life's America.* Philadelphia: Temple University Press.

Krathwohl, D. R. (1988). *How to prepare a research proposal.* Syracuse, NY: Syracuse University Press.

Krieger, S. (1985). Beyond "subjectivity": The use of the self in social science. *Qualitative Sociology* 8(4): 309–324.

Krieger, S. (1991). *Social science and the self: Personal essays on an art form.* New Brunswick, NJ: Rutgers.

Krueger, E. T. (1925a). The technique of securing life history documents. *Journal of Applied Sociology 9:* 290–298.

Krueger, E. T. (1925b). The value of life history documents for social research. *Journal of Applied Sociology 9:* 196–201.

Lancy, D. (1993). *Qualitative research in education.* New York: Longman.

Langer (1978). *Private worlds of dying children.* Princeton, NJ: Princeton University Press.

Langness, L. L., & Frank, G. (1981). *Lives: An anthropological approach to biography.* Novata, CA: Chandler & Sharp.

Lareau, A. (1987). Social class and family–school relationships: The importance of cultural capital. *Sociology of Education 56* (April): 73–85.

Lareau, A. (1989). *Home advantage: Social class and parental intervention in elementary education.* London: Falmer Press.

Lather, P. (1988). Feminist perspectives on empowering research methodologies. *Womens Studies International Forum 1*(6): 569–581.

Lather, P. (1991a). *Getting smart: Feminist research and pedagogy with/in the postmodern.* New York: Routledge.

Lather, P. (1991b). Deconstructing/deconstructive inquiry: The politics of knowing and being known. *Educational Theory 41*(2): 153–173.

Leacock, E. (1969). *Teaching and learning in city schools.* New York: Basic Books.

LeCompte, M. D. (1987). Bias in the biography: Bias and subjectivity in ethnographic research. *Anthropology & Education Quarterly 18:* 43–52.

Lesko, N. (1988). *Symbolizing society: Rites and structure in a Catholic high school.* London: Falmer Press.

Levine, M. (1980a). Investigative reporting as a research method: An analysis of Bernstein and Woodward's *All the President's Men. American Psychologist 35:* 626–638.

Levine, M. (1980b). *Method or madness: On the alienation of the professional.* Invited Address, Division 12. Meeting of the American Psychological Association, Montreal.

Lewis, O. (1965). *La vida.* New York: Vintage.

Liebow, E. (1967). *Tally's corner.* Boston: Little, Brown.

Lightfoot, S. (1978). *Worlds apart: Relationships between families and schools.* New York: Basic Books.

Lincoln, Y. (1995). Emerging criteria for quality in qualitative and interpretive research. *Qualitative Inquiry 1*(3): 275–289.

Lincoln, Y. S., & Denzin, N. K. (1994). The fifth moment. In N. K. Denzin, & Y. S. Lincoln (Eds.), *Handbook of qualitative research.* Thousand Oaks, CA: Sage, pp. 575–586.

Lincoln, Y. S., & Guba, E. G. (1985). *Naturalistic inquiry.* Beverly Hills, CA: Sage.

Lindeman, E. C. (1925). *Social discovery.* New York: Republic.

Linden, R. R. (1992). *Making stories, making selves: Feminist reflections on the Holocaust.* Columbus, OH: Ohio State University Press.

Lindesmith, A. R. (1947). *Addiction and opiates.* Chicago: Aldine.

Livingstone, S., & Lunt, P. (1994). *Talk on television.* London: Routledge.

Locke, L. F., Spirduso, W. W., & Silverman, S. J. (1987). *Proposals that work: A guide for planning dissertations and grant proposals.* Newbury Park, CA: Sage.

Lofland, J. (1971). *Analyzing social settings.* Belmont, CA: Wadsworth.

Lofland, J. (1974). Styles of reporting qualitative field research. *The American Sociologist 9:* 101–111.

Lofland, J. (1976). *Doing social life.* New York: Wiley.

Lorber, J. (1988). From the editor. *Gender and Society* 2(1): 5–8.

Lutz, C., & Collins, J. (1993). *Reading National Geographic.* Chicago: University of Chicago Press.

Lutz, F., & Gresson, A. (1980). Local school boards as political councils. *Educational Studies 2:* 125–143.

Lynch, M., & Peyrot, M. (1992). A reader's guide to ethnomethodology. *Qualitative Sociology 15*(2): 113–122.

Lynd, R. S., & Lynd, H. M. (1929). *Middletown.* New York: Harcourt Brace.

Lynd, R. S., & Lynd, H. M. (1937). *Middletown in transition.* New York: Harcourt Brace.

Lyon, D. (1992). *Memories of the southern civil rights movement.* Chapel Hill, NC: University of North Carolina Press.

Mac An Ghaill, M. (1994). *The making of men: Masculinities, sexualities and schooling.* Buckingham, GB: Open University Press.

Maccoby, E., & Maccoby, N. (1954). The interview: A tool of social science. In G. Lindzey (Ed.), *Handbook of social psychology* (vol. 1). Cambridge, MA: Addison-Wesley, pp. 449–487.

Mace, H. O. (1990). *Collector's guide to early photographs.* Radnor, PA: Wallace-Homestead.

Maines, D. R., Shaffir, W., & Turowetz, A. (1980). Leaving the field in ethnographic research: Reflections on the entrance–exit hypothesis. In W. B. Shaffir, R. A. Stebbins, & A. Turowetz (Eds.),

Fieldwork experience: Qualitative approaches to social research. New York: St. Martin's.

Malinowski, B. (1922). *Argonauts of the western Pacific.* New York: Dutton.

Malinowski, B. (1960). *A scientific theory of culture and other essays.* New York: Oxford University Press.

Marcus, G. E. (1994). What comes (just) after post? In N. K. Denzin, & Y. S. Lincoln (Eds.), *Handbook of qualitative research.* Thousand Oaks, CA: Sage, pp. 563–574.

Marcus, G. E., & Fisher, M. M. (1986). *Anthropology as cultural critique: An experimental moment in the human sciences.* Chicago: University of Chicago Press.

Marcus, G. M., & Cushman, D. (1982). Ethnographies as texts. *Annual Review of Anthropology 11:* 25–69.

Martin, E. (1987). *The woman in the body.* Boston: Beacon Press.

Mascia-Lees, F. E., Sharpe, P., & Cohen, C. B. (1989). The postmodernist turn in anthropology: Cautions from a feminist perspective. *Signs 15*(1): 7–33.

Matthews, F. (1977). *Quest for an American sociology: Robert E. Park and the Chicago school.* Montreal: McGill-Queens University Press.

May, E. T. (1988). *Homeward bound: American families in the cold war era.* New York: Basic Books.

McAdoo, H. (1976). *Oral history and educational research.* Paper presented at the meeting of the American Educational Research Association. (ERIC Document Reproduction Service No. ED 171 83 1)

McCall, G. J., & Simmons, J. L. (Eds.). (1969). *Issues in participant observation.* Reading, MA: Addison-Wesley.

McCall, M. M., & Becker, H. S. (1990). Performance science. *Social Problems 3* 7(1): 117–132.

McCracken, G. (1988). *The long interview.* Newbury Park, CA: Sage.

McDermott, R. (1976). *Kids make sense: An ethnographic account of the interactional management of success and failure in one first grade classroom.* Unpublished doctoral dissertation, Stanford University.

McDermott, R. P., Gospodinoff, K., & Aron, J. (1978). Criteria for an ethnographically adequate description of concerted activities and their contexts. *Semiotica 24:* 245–275.

McIntyre, D. (1969). Two schools, one psychologist. In F. Kaplan, & S. Sarason (Eds.), *The psycho-educational clinic: Papers and research studies.* Boston: Massachusetts Department of Mental Health, pp. 21–90.

McLaren, P. (1994). *Life in schools.* 2nd Edition. New York: Longman.

McLaughlin, D., & Tierney, W. G. (Eds.). (1993). *Naming silenced lives: Personal narratives and the process of educational change.* New York: Routledge,

McPherson, G. (1972). *Small town teacher.* Cambridge, MA: Harvard University.

McRobbie, A. (1991). *Feminism and youth culture.* Boston: Unwin Hyman.

McRobbie, A. (1994). *PostModernism and popular culture.* London: Routledge.

McWilliam, E. (1994). *In broken images: Feminist tales for a different teacher education.* New York: Teachers College Press.

Mead, G. H. (1934). *Mind, self, and society.* Chicago: University of Chicago Press.

Mead, M. (1942). An anthropologist looks at the teacher's role. *Educational Method 21:* 219–223.

Mead, M. (1951). *The school in American culture.* Cambridge, MA: Harvard University Press.

Mehan, H. (1978). Structuring school structure. *Harvard Educational Review 48:* 32–64.

Mehan, H. (1979). *Learning lessons.* Cambridge, MA: Harvard University Press.

Mehan, H., & Wood, H. (1975). *The reality of ethnomethodology.* New York: Wiley.

Meltzer, B., & Petras, J. (1970). The Chicago and Iowa schools of symbolic interactionism. In T. Shibutani (Ed.), *Human nature and collective behavior.* Englewood Cliffs, NJ: Prentice-Hall.

Meltzer, B., Petras, J., & Reynolds, L. (1975). *Symbolic interactionism: Genesis, varieties and criticism.* London: Routledge and Kegan Paul.

Mercurio, J. A. (1972). *Caning: Educational rite and tradition.* Syracuse, NY: Syracuse University.

Mercurio, J. A. (1979). Community involvement in cooperative decision making: Some lessons learned. *Educational Evaluation and Policy Analysis 6:* 37–46.

Merriam, S. B. (1988). *The case study research in education.* San Francisco: Jossey-Bass.

Merton, R. K., & Kendall, P. L. (1946). The focused interview. *American Journal of Sociology 51:* 541–557.

Messerschmidt, D. A. (1984). Federal bucks for local change: On the ethnography of experimental schools. In D. M. Fetterman (Ed.), *Ethnography in educational evaluation.* Newbury Park, CA: Sage, pp. 89–114.

Metz, M. H. (1978). *Classrooms and corridors: The crisis of authority in desegregated secondary schools.* Berkeley: University of California Press.

Michael, L., & Peyrot, M. (1992). Introduction: A reader's guide to ethnomethodology. *Qualitative Sociology 15*(2): 113–121.

Michaels, P. (1994). *The child's view of reading: Understandings for teachers and parents.* Boston: Allyn & Bacon.

Middleton, S. (1987). Schooling and radicalization: Life histories of New Zealand feminist teachers. *British Journal of Sociology of Education 8*(2): 169–189.

Middleton, S. (1993). *Educating feminists: Life histories and pedagogy.* New York: Teachers College Press.

Miles, M., & Huberman, M. (1984). *Qualitative data analysis.* Beverly Hills, CA: Sage.

Miles, M. B., & Huberman, A. M. (1994). *Qualitative data analysis: An expanded source book* (Second Edition). Thousand Oaks, CA: Sage.

Mills, C. W. (1959). *The sociological imagination.* London: Oxford University Press.

Mischler, E. G. (1991). *Research interviewing: Context and narrative.* Cambridge, MA: Harvard.

Mitford, J. (1971). *Kind and usual punishment.* New York: Knopf.

Mitford, J. (1979). *Poison penmanship.* New York: Knopf.

Moffatt, M. (1989). *Coming of age in New Jersey.* New Brunswick, NJ: Rutgers University Press.

Moore, G. A. (1967). *Realities of the urban classroom.* Garden City, NY: Anchor.

Morgan, D. L. (1988). *Focus groups as qualitative research.* Newbury Park, CA: Sage.

Morris, V. C., & Hurwitz, E. (1980). *The Heisenberg problem: How to neutralize the effect of the observer on observed phenomena.* Paper presented at the meeting of the American Educational Research Association, Boston.

Morrow, V. (1995). Invisible children? Toward a reconceptiualization of childhood dependency and responsibility. *Sociological studies of children* (JAI Press) *7:* 207–230.

Morse, J. M. (1994). Designing funded qualitative research. In N. K. Denzin, & Y. S. Lincoln (Eds.), *Handbook of qualitative research.* Thousand Oaks, CA: Sage, pp. 220–235.

Musello, C. (1979). Family photograph. In J. Wagner (Ed.), *Images of information.* Beverly Hills, CA: Sage, pp. 101-118.

National Institute of Education (1978). *Violent school-mate schools: The safe school study report to the Congress.* Washington, DC: Author.

Noffke, L. (1995). Action research and democratic schooling: Problematics and potentials. In S. Noffke, & R. Stevenson (Eds.), *Educational action research: Becoming practically critical.* New York: Teachers College Press, pp. 1–10.

North, L. V. (1909, March 6). The elementary public schools of Pittsburgh. *Charity and the Commons 21:* 1175–1191.

Oakley, A. (1981). Interviewing women: A contradiction in terms. In H. Roberts (Ed.), *Doing feminist research.* London: Routledge and Kegan Paul, pp. 30–61.

O'Barr, W. (1994). *Culture and the ad: Exploring otherness in the world of advertising.* Boulder, CO: Westview Press.

Odum, H. (1951). *American sociology: The story of sociology in the United States through 1950.* New York: Greenwood.

Ogbu, J. (1974). *The next generation: An ethnography of education in an urban neighborhood.* New York: Academic Press.

Oja, S. & Smulyan, L. (1989). *Collaborative action research: A developmental approach.* London: Falmer Press

Olesen, V. (1994). Feminisms and models in qualitative research. In N. K. Denzin, & Y. S. Lincoln (Eds.), *Handbook of qualitative research.* Thousand Oaks, CA: Sage, pp. 158–169

O'Neal, M. H. (1976). *A vision shared.* New York: St. Martin's.

Orner, M. (1992). Interrupting the calls for student voice in "liberatory" education: A feminist post-structuralist perspective. In C. Luke, & J. Gore (Eds.), *Feminisms and critical pedagogy.* New York: Routledge, pp. 74–89.

Oyler, C. (1996). *Making room for students: Sharing teacher authority in Room 104.* New York: Teachers College Press.

Paget, M. (1990). Performing the text. *Journal of Contemporary Ethnography 19*(1): 136–155.

Patai, D. (1994). Sick and tired of scholars' nouveau solipsism. *The Chronical of Higher Education,* February 23, p. A52.

Patton, M. Q. (1980). *Qualitative evaluation methods.* Beverly Hills, CA: Sage.

Patton, M. Q. (1987). *How to use qualitative methods in evaluation.* Newbury Park, CA: Sage.

Peters, C. C. (1937). Research technics in educational sociology. *Review of Educational Research 7*(1): 15–25.

Peshkin, A. (1986). *God's choice.* Chicago: University of Chicago Press.

Pfaffenberger, B. (1988). *Microcomputer applications in qualitative research.* Newbury Park, CA: Sage.

Plummer, K. (1983). *Documents of life: An introduction to the problems and literature of a humanistic method.* London: George Allen & Unwin.

Popkewitz, T. S. (1984). *Paradigm & ideology in educational research.* New York: Faber.

Porter-Gehrie, C. (1980). The ethnographer as insider. *Educational Studies 2:* 123–124.

Porter-Gehrie, C., & Crowson, R. L. (1980). *Analyzing ethnographic data—Strategies and results.* Paper presented to the meeting of the American Educational Research Association, Boston.

Pratt, M. L. (1985). Scratches on the face of the country; Or, What Mr. Burrow saw in the land of the Bushmen. *Critical Inquiry 12* (Autumn): 119–143.

Pratt, M. L. (1986). Fieldwork in common places. In J. Clifford, & G. Marcus (Eds.), *Writing culture.* Berkeley: University of California Press, pp. 27–50.

Pratt, M. L. (1992). *Imperial eyes: Travel writing and transculturation.* New York: Routledge.

Preskill, H. (1995). The use of photography in evaluating school culture. *Qualitative Studies in Education 8*(2): 183–193.

Press, A. (1991). *Women watching television: Gender, class, and generation in the American television experience.* Philadelphia: University of Pennsylvania Press.

Provenzo, E., & Ewart, A. (1994). *Reader's Digest* and the mythology of schooling. In P. Farber, E. Provenzo, Jr., & G. Holm (Eds.), *Schooling in the light of popular culture.* Albany, NY: State University of New York Press, pp. 85–102.

Psathas, G. (Ed.). (1973). *Phenomenological sociology.* New York: Wiley.

Punch, M. (1986). *The politics and ethics of fieldwork.* Newbury Park, CA: Sage.

Punch, M. (1994). Politics and ethics in qualitative research. In N. K. Denzin, & Y. S. Lincoln (Eds.), *Handbook of qualitative research.* Thousand Oaks, CA: Sage, pp. 83–97.

Quint, S. (1994). *Schooling homeless children.* New York: Teachers College Press.

Radway, J. (1984). *Reading the romance*. Chapel Hill, NC: University of North Carolina Press.

Ragin, C., & Becker, H. (Eds.). (1992). *What is a case?* New York: Cambridge University Press.

Raissiguier, C. (1993). Negotiating work, identity, and desire: The adolescent dilemmas of working-class girls of French and Algerian descent in a vocational high school. In C. McCarthy, & W. Crichlow (Eds.), *Race, identity and representation in education*. New York: Routledge, pp. 140–156.

Redfield, R. (1955). *The educational experience*. Pasadena, CA: Fund for Adult Education.

Reichardt, C. S., & Cook, T. D. (1979). Beyond qualitative versus quantitative methods. In T. D. Cook, & C. S. Reichardt (Eds.), *Qualitative and quantitative methods in evaluation research*. Beverly Hills, CA: Sage.

Reichardt, C. S., & Rallis, S. F. (Eds.). (1994). *The quantitative–qualitative debate: New perspectives*. San Franciso: Jossey-Bass.

Reinharz, S. (1992). *Feminist methods in social research*. New York: Oxford University Press.

Reinharz, S. (1993). Neglected voices and excessive demands in feminist research. *Qualitative Sociology 16*(1): 69–75.

Research for Action (1996). *Girls in the middle*. Washington, DC: American Association of University Women.

Richards, T. J., & Richards, L. (1994). Using computers in qualitative research. In N. K. Denzin, & Y. S. Lincoln (Eds.), *Handbook of qualitative research*. Thousand Oaks, CA: Sage, pp. 445–462.

Richardson, L. (1990a). Narrative and sociology. *Journal of Contemporary Ethnography 19*(1): 116–135.

Richardson, L. (1990b). *Writing Strategies: Reaching diverse audiences*. Newbury Park, CA: Sage.

Richardson, L. (1993). Poetics, dramatics, and transgressive validity. *Sociological Quarterly 34*(4): 695–710.

Richardson, L. (1994). Nine poems: Marriage and the family. *Journal of Contemporary Ethnography 23*(1): 3–13.

Richardson, L. (1994). Writing. In N. K. Denzin, & Y. S. Lincoln (Eds.), *Handbook of qualitative research*. Thousand Oaks, CA: Sage, pp. 516–529.

Riessman, C. (1987). When gender is not enough: Women interviewing women. *Gender and Society 1*(2): 172–207.

Riis, J. (1890). *How the other half lives*. New York: Scribner's.

Riley, J. J. (1910–1911). Sociology and social surveys. *American Journal of Sociology 16*: 818–836.

Rist, R. (1970). Student social class and teacher expectations: The self-fulfilling prophecy in ghetto education. *Harvard Educational Review 40*: 411–451.

Rist, R. (1973). *The urban school: A factory for failure*. Cambridge, MA: Massachusetts Institute of Technology Press.

Rist, R. (1977a). On the relations among educational research paradigms: From distain to detente. *Anthropology and Education Quarterly 8*: 42–49.

Rist, R. (1977b). On understanding the processes of schooling. In J. Karabel, & A. H. Halsey (Eds.), *Power and ideology in education*. New York: Oxford University Press.

Rist, R. (1978). *The invisible children*. Cambridge, MA: Harvard University.

Rist, R. (1980). Blitzkrieg ethnography. *Educational Researcher 9*(2): 8–10.

Ritzer, G. (1975). *Sociology: A multiple paradigm science*. Boston: Allyn & Bacon.

Rivera, G. (1972). *Willowbrook: A report on how it is and why it doesn't have to be that way*. New York: Vintage.

Roberts, J. (1976). An overview of anthropology and education. In J. Roberts, & S. Akinsanya (Eds.), *Educational patterns and cultural configurations*. New York: David McKay, pp. 1–20.

Roberts, J. (1971). *Scene of the battle*. Garden City, NY: Doubleday.

Roberts, J. I., & Akinsaiiya, S. K. (Eds.). (1976a). *Educational patterns and cultural configurations*. New York: David McKay.

Roberts, J. I., & Akinsanya, S. K. (Eds.). (1976b). *Schooling in the cultural context: Anthropological studies of education*. New York: David McKay.

Robinson, W. S. (1951). The logical structure of analytic induction. *American Sociological Review 16*: 812–818.

Rogers, C. (1945). The nondirective method as a technique for social research. *American Journal of Sociology 50*: 279–283.

Rogers, C. (1951). *Client-centered therapy*. Boston: Houghton Mifflin.

Roman, L. (1997). Denying (white) racial privilege: Redemption discourses and the uses of fantasy. In M.

Fine, L. Weis, L. Powell, & L. M. Wong (Eds.), *Off white*. New York: Routledge, pp. 270–282.

Roman, L. G. (1988). Intimacy, labor, and class: Ideologies of feminine sexuality in the punk slam dance. In L. G. Roman, & L. C. Christian-Smith with E. Ellsworth (Eds.), *Becoming feminine: The politics of popular culture*. London: Falmer Press, pp. 143–184.

Roman, L., & Apple, M. (1990). Is naturalism a move away from positivism? Materialist and feminist approaches to subjectivity in ethnographic research. In E. Eisner, & A. Peshkin (Eds.), *Qualitative inquiry in education: The continuing debate*. New York: Teachers College Press, pp. 38–73.

Rosaldo, R. (1989). *Culture and truth: The remaking of social analysis*. Boston: Beacon Press.

Rosensteil, A. (1954). Educational anthropology: A new approach to cultural analysis. *Harvard Educational Review 24:* 28–36.

Rosenthal, R., & Jacobson, L. (1968). *Pygmalion in the classroom*. New York: Holt, Rinehart & Winston.

Roth, J. (1963). *Timetables*. Indianapolis, IN: Bobbs-Merrill.

Rothman, D. J., & Rothman, S. (1984). *The Willowbrook wars*. New York: Harper and Row.

Rothstein, W. R. (1975). Researching the power structure: Personalized power and institutionalized charisma in the principalship. *Interchange 6*(2): 41–48.

Rowe, D. (1995). *Popular cultures: Rock music, sport and the politics of pleasure*. London: Sage.

Rubin H., & Rubin, I. (1995). *Qualitative interviewing*. Thousand Oaks, CA: Sage.

Rubin, L. (1976). *Worlds of pain*. New York: Basic Books.

Said, E. W. (1993). *Culture and imperialism*. New York: Alfred A. Knopf.

Saljo, R. (1994). Qualitative research on learning and instruction in Scandinavia. *Qualitative Studies in Education 7*(3): 257–267.

Sanjek, R. (Ed.). (1990). *Fieldnotes*. Ithaca, NY: Cornell University Press.

Sarason, S., & Doris, J. (1979). *Educational handicap, public policy, antisocial history*. New York: The Free Press.

Sarason, S., Levine, M., Goldenberg, I., Cherlin, D., & Bennett, E. (1966). *Psychology in community settings*. New York: Wiley.

Schaller, G. (1965). *The year of the gorilla*. Chicago: University of Chicago Press.

Schatzman, L., & Strauss, A. (1973). *Field research*. Englewood Cliffs, NJ: Prentice-Hall.

Schein, E. H. (1987). *The clinical perspective in fieldwork*. Newbury Park, CA: Sage.

Schmuck, P. (1975). Deterrents to women's careers in school management. *Sex Roles 1:* 339–353.

Schneider, J., & Conrad, P. (1980). *Having epilepsy*. Philadelphia, PA: Temple University Press.

Schoonmaker, M. (1994). *Videoasis: The character of viewing in a video community*. Unpublished doctoral dissertation, Syracuse University.

Schwalbe, M. (1995). A writer's data. *Writing Sociology 3*(1): 6.

Schwalbe, M. (1995). The responsibilities of sociological poets. *Qualitative Sociology 18*(4): 393–413.

Schwandt, T. A. (1994). Constructivist, interpretivist approaches to human inquiry. In N. K. Denzin, & Y. S. Lincoln (Eds.), *Handbook of qualitative research*. Thousand Oaks, CA: Sage, pp. 118–137.

Schwartz, D. (1989). Visual ethnography: Using photography in qualitative research. *Qualitative Sociology 12*(2): 119–154.

Schwartz, H., & Jacobs, J. (1979). *Qualitative sociology*. New York: The Free Press.

Schwoch, J., White, M., & Reilly, S. (1992). *Media knowledge*. Albany, NY: State University of New York Press.

Scott, R. W. (1965). Field methods in the study of organizations. In J. G. March (Ed.), *Handbook of organizations*. Chicago: Rand McNally.

Scott, R. (1969). *The making of blind men*. New York: Russell Sage.

Scriven, M. (1972). Objectivity and subjectivity in educational research. In L. G. Thomas (Ed.), *Philosophical redirection of educational research: The seventy-first yearbook of the National Society for the Study of Education*. Chicago: University of Chicago Press.

Sharp, R., & Green, A. (1975). *Education and social control*. London: Routledge and Kegan Paul.

Sharpe, J. (1993). *Allegories of Empire: The figure of women in the colonial text*. Minneapolis, MN: University of Minnesota Press.

Shaw, C. (1966). *The jack roller* (2nd ed.). Chicago: University of Chicago Press.

Shelly, A., & Sibert, E. (1986). Using logic programming to facilitate qualitative data analysis. *Qualitative Sociology 9*(2): 145–161.

Sherman, E., & Reid, W. J. (1994). *Qualitative research in social work.* New York: Columbia

Sherman, R. R., & Webb, R. B. (Eds.). (1988). *Qualitative research in education: Focus and methods.* Philadelphia, PA: Falmer Press.

Shumway, G., & Hartley, W. (1973). *Oral history primer.* Fullerton: California State University Press.

Shuy, R., & Griffin, P. (Eds.). (1978). *The study of children's functional language and education in the early years.* Final Report to the Carnegie Corporation of New York. Arlington, VA: Center for Applied Linguistics.

Shuy, R., Wolfram, W., & Riley, W. K. (1967). *Field techniques for an urban language study.* Washington, DC: Center for Applied Linguistics.

Sleeter, C. (1993). How white teachers construct race. In C. McCarthy, & W. Crichlow (Eds.), *Race, identity and representation in education.* New York: Routledge, pp. 157–171.

Smith, D. (1987). *The everyday world as problematic.* Boston: Northeastern University Press.

Smith, J. K. (1983). Quantitative versus qualitative research: An attempt to clarify the issue. *Educational Researcher 12:* 6–13.

Smith, J. K., & Heshusius, L. (1986). Closing down the conversation: The end of the quantitative–qualitative debate among educational inquirers. *Educational Researcher 15*(1): 4–12.

Smith, L., & Geoffrey, W. (1968). *The complexities of an urban classroom: An analysis toward a general theory of teaching.* New York: Holt, Rinehart & Winston.

Smith, L. M. (1992). Ethnography. In M. C. Alkin (Ed.), *Encyclopedia of Educational Research 2:* 458–462.

Smith, L. M. (1994). Biographical method. In N. K. Denzin, & Y. S. Lincoln (Eds.), *Handbook of qualitative research.* Thousand Oaks, CA: Sage, pp. 286–305.

Snedden, D. (1937). The field of educational sociology. *Review of Educational Research 7*(1): 5–14.

Solomon, B. (1996). Unpublished field notes. Syracuse University.

Sontag, S. (1977). *On photography.* New York: Farrar, Strauss and Giroux.

Spencer, D. A. (1986). *Contemporary women teachers.* New York: Longman.

Spindler, G. (Ed.). (1955). *Education and anthropology.* Stanford, CA: Stanford University Press.

Spindler, G. (1959). *The transmission of American culture.* Cambridge, MA: Harvard University Press.

Spindler, G. E. (Ed.). (1982). *Doing the ethnography of schooling: Educational anthropology in action.* New York: Holt, Rinehart & Winston.

Spradley, J. (1979). *The ethnographic interview.* New York: Holt, Rinehart & Winston.

Spradley, J. P. (1980). *Participant observation.* New York: Holt, Rinehart & Winston.

Squiers, C. (Ed.). (1990). *The critical image.* Seattle, WA: The Bay Press.

Stack, C. (1974). *All our kin: Strategies for survival in a black community.* New York: Harper & Row.

Stacey, J. (1988). Can there be a feminist ethnography? *Women's Studies International Forum 11:* 21–27.

Stainback, S., & Stainback, W. (1985). Quantitative and qualitative methodologies: Competitive or complementary? *Exceptional Children 51:* 330–334.

Stake, R. E. (1978). The case study method in a social inquiry. *Educational Researcher 7.*

Stake, R. E. (1994). Case studies. In N. K. Denzin, & Y. S. Lincoln (Eds.), *Handbook of qualitative research.* Thousand Oaks, CA: Sage, pp. 236–246.

Stall, S., Thompson, M., & Haslett, D. (1995). Creating a supportive writing group. *Writing Sociology 2*(3): 1–3.

Steffens, L. (1904). *The shame of the cities.* New York: McClure, Phillips.

Steffens, L. (1931). *The autobiography of Lincoln Steffens.* New York: Harcourt Brace.

Stewart, D. W., & Shamdasani, P. N. (1990). *Focus groups: Theory and practice.* Newbury Park, CA: Sage.

Stott, W. (1973). *Documentary expression and thirties America.* New York: Oxford University Press.

Strauss, A. (1987). *Qualitative analysis for social scientists.* New York: Cambridge University Press.

Strauss, A., & Corbin, J. (1990). *Basics of qualitative research: Grounded theory procedures and techniques.* Newbury Park, CA: Sage.

Strauss, A., & Corbin, J. (1994). Grounded theory methodology: An overview. In N. K. Denzin, & Y. S. Lincoln (Eds.), *Handbook of qualitative research.* Thousand Oaks, CA: Sage, pp. 273–285.

Strunk, W., Jr., & White, E. B. (1972). *The elements of style.* New York: Macmillan.

Stryker, R. E., & Wood, N. (1973). *In this proud land, America 1935–1943 as seen in the FSA photograhs.* Greenwich, CT: New York Graphic Society, Ltd.

Sussman, L. (1977). *Tales out of school.* Philadelphia, PA: Temple University.

Sutherland, E. (1937). *The professional thief.* Chicago: University of Chicago Press.

Swaminathan, R. (1997). *"The charming sideshow:" Cheerleading, girls' culture, and schooling.* Unpublished Ph.D. dissertation, Syracuse University, Syracuse, NY.

Tagg, J. (1988). *The burden of representation: Essays on photographies and histories.* Amherst, MA: The University of Massachusetts Press.

Taylor, C. (1919). *The social survey. Its history and methods.* Columbia, MO: University of Missouri. (Social Science Series 3).

Taylor, D. (1996). *Toxic literacies: Exposing the injustice of bureaucratic texts.* Portsmouth, NH: Heinemann.

Taylor, S. J. (1980). *A guide to monitoring and investigating residential settings.* Syracuse, NY: Human Policy Press.

Taylor, S. J. (1982). From segregation to integration. *The Journal of the Association for the Severely Handicapped 8*(3): 42–49.

Taylor, S. J. (1987). Observing abuse: Professional ethics and personal morality in field research. *Qualitative Sociology 10*(3): 288–301.

Taylor, S. J., Biklen, D., & Knoll J. (Eds). (1987). *Community integration for people with severe disabilities.* New York: Teachers College Press.

Taylor, S. J., & Bogdan, R. C. (1984). *Introduction to qualitative research and methods: The search for meaning.* New York: Wiley.

Taylor, S. J., Bogdan, R., & Lutfiyya, Z. (1995). *The variety of community experience.* Baltimore, MD: Paul H. Brookes.

Taylor, J., Bogdan, R., & Racino, J. (Eds.). (1991). *Life in the community: Case studies of organizations supporting people with disabilities.* Baltimore, MD: Paul H. Brookes.

Tesch, R. (1990). *Qualitative research: Analysis types and software tools.* London: Falmer.

Tesch, R. (n.d.). *Software for the computer-assisted analysis of text.* Mimeographed.

Thomas, N. (1994). *Colonialism's culture: Anthropology, travel and government.* Princeton, NJ: Princeton University Press.

Thomas, W. I. (1923). *The unadjusted girl.* Boston: Little, Brown.

Thomas, W. I., & Znaniecki, F. (1927). *The Polish peasant in Europe and America.* New York: Knopf.

Thomson, J., & Smith, A. (1877). *Street life in London.* London: Sampson, Low, Murston, Searle, & Rurington.

Thorne, B. (1980). "You still takin' notes?" Fieldwork and problems of informed consent. *Social Problems 27:* 271–284.

Thorne, B. (1993). *Gender play: Girls and boys in school.* New Brunswick, NJ: Rutgers University Press.

Thrasher, F. (1927). *The gang.* Chicago: University of Chicago Press.

Tierney, W. (1994). On method and hope. In A. Gitlin (Ed.), *Power and method.* New York: Routledge, pp. 97–115.

Trachtenberg, A. (1979). Introduction: Photographs as symbolic history. In *The American image: Photographs from the National Archives, 1860–1960.* New York: Pantheon.

Travers, R. (1978). *An introduction to educational research* (4th ed.). New York: Macmillan.

Trudell, B. (1990). Selection, presentation, and student interpretation of an educational film on teenage pregnancy: A critical ethnographic investigation. In E. Ellsworth, & M. Whatley (Eds.), *The ideology of images in educational media.* New York: Teachers College Press, pp. 74–106.

Turner, R. H. (1953). The quest for universals in sociological research. *American Sociological Review 18:* 604–611.

Turner, R. (Ed.). (1974). *Ethnomethodology.* Middlesex, UK: Penguin.

Turner, V. (1982). *From ritual to theatre.* New York: PAJ Publishing.

Turner, V. (1886). *The anthropology of performance.* New York: PAJ Publications.

Tyler, R. (Ed.). (1976). *Prospects for research and development in education.* Berkeley, CA: McCutcheon.

Valdes, G. (1996). *Con respeto: Bridging the distances between culturally diverse families and schools.* New York: Teachers College Press.

Vandewalker, N. (1898). Some demands of education upon anthropology. *American Journal of Sociology 4:* 69–78.

Van Maanen, J. (1988). *Tales of the field: On writing ethnography.* Chicago: University of Chicago Press.

Vidich, A. J., & Lyman, S. M. (1994). Qualitative methods: Their history in sociology and anthropology. In N. K. Denzin, & Y. S. Lincoln (Eds.), *Handbook of qualitative research*. Thousand Oaks, CA: Sage, pp. 23–59.

Wagner, J. (Ed.). (1979). *Images of information*. Beverly Hills, CA: Sage.

Waldorf, D., & Reinarman, C. (1975). Addicts—Everything but human beings. *Urban Life 4*(1): 30–53.

Walker, R. (1993). Using photographs in evaluation and research. In M. Schratz (Ed.), *Qualitative voices in educational research*. London: Falmer, pp. 72–92.

Waller, W. (1932). *Sociology of teaching*. New York: Wiley.

Waller, W. (1934). Insight and scientific method. *American Journal of Sociology 40*(3): 285–295.

Warner, W. L., & Lunt, P. S. (1941). *The social life of a modern community*. New Haven, CT: Yale University Press.

Warren, C. A. B. (1988). *Gender in field research*. Newbury Park: CA: Sage.

Wax, M. (1980). Paradoxes of "consent" in the practice of fieldwork. *Social Problems 27*: 265–272.

Wax, R. (1971). *Doing fieldwork: Warning and advice*. Chicago: University of Chicago Press.

Wax, R. (1979). Gender and age in fieldwork and fieldwork education: No good thing is done by any man alone. *Social Problems 26*: 509–523.

Webb, B. (1926). *My apprenticeship*. New York: Longmans, Green & Co.

Webb, S., & Webb, B. (1932). *Methods of social study*. London: Longmans, Green & Co.

Weiler, K. (1988). *Women teaching for change*. South Hadley, MA: Bergin Garvey.

Weis, L. (1990). *Working class without work: High school students in a de-industrializing economy*. New York: Routledge.

Weiss, L., Proweller, P., & Centrie, C. (1997). Re-examining "a moment in history": Loss of privilege inside white working-class masculinity in the 1990s. In M. Fine, L. Weis, L. Powell, & L. M. Wong (Eds.), *Off white: Readings on race, power, and society*. New York: Routledge, pp. 210–226.

Weitzman, E., & Miles, M. B. (1994). *Computer programs for qualitative data analysis*. Thousand Oaks, CA: Sage.

Wells, A. F. (1939). Social surveys. In F. C. Bartlett, M. Ginsberg, E. S. Lindgren, & R. H. Thouless (Eds.), *The study of society*. London: Kegan Paul, Trench, Trubner & Co, pp. 424–435.

Wells, M. C. (1996). *Literacies Lost: When students move from a progressive middle school to a traditional high school*. New York: Teachers College Press.

Werner, O., & Schoepfle, G. M. (1987a). *Systematic fieldwork: Volume 1, Foundations of ethnography and interviewing*. Newbury Park, CA: Sage.

Werner, O., & Schoepfle, G. M. (1987b). *Systematic fieldwork: Volume 2, Ethnography analysis and data management*. Newbury Park, CA: Sage.

West, C., & Zimmerman, D. (1987). Doing gender. *Gender and Society 1*(2): 125–151.

Whatley, M. (1991). Raging hormones and powerful cars: The construction of men's sexuality in school sex education and popular adolescent films. In H. Giroux (Ed.), *Postmodernism, feminism, and cultural politics*. Albany, NY: State University of New York Press, pp. 119–143.

Whyte, W. F. (1955). *Street corner society*. Chicago: University of Chicago Press.

Whyte, W. F. (1960). Interviewing in field research. In R. H. Adams, & J. J. Preiss (Eds.), *Human organization research*. Homewood, IL: Dorsey Press.

Whyte, W. F. (1984). *Learning from the field*. Beverly Hills, CA: Sage.

Whyte, W. F. (1991). *Participatory action research*. Newbury Park, CA: Sage.

Whyte, W. F. (1992). In defense of street corner society. *Journal of Contemporary Ethnography 21*: 52–68.

Whyte, W. H. (1979). On making the most of participant observation. *The American Sociologist 14* 56–66.

Wicker, T. (1978). *On press*. New York: Berkley Publishing.

Wiley, N. (1979). The rise and fall of dominating theories in American sociology. In W. Snizek, E. Fuhrman, & M. Miller (Eds.), *Contemporary issues in theory and research, a metasociological perspective*. Westport, CT: Greenwood, pp. 47–80.

Williams, J. (1990). *Style*. Chicago: University of Chicago Press.

Willis, D., & Dodson, H. (1989). *Black photographers bear witness: 100 years of social protest*. Williamstown, MA: Williams College Museum of Art.

Willis, P. (1977). *Learning to labor*. New York: Columbia University Press.

Willis, P. (1980). Notes on method. In Center for Cultural Studies (Ed.), *Culture, media, language*. London: Hutchinson, pp. 88–95.

Willis, P. (1990). *Common culture: Symbolic work at play in the everyday cultures of the young.* Boulder, CO: Westview Press.

Willower, D. J., & Boyd, W. L. (Eds.). (1989). *Willard Waller on education and schools.* Berkeley, CA: McCutchan.

Wilson, S. (1977). The use of ethnographic techniques in educational research. *Review of Educational Research 47:* 245–265.

Wirth, L. (1928). *The ghetto.* Chicago: University of Chicago Press.

Wolcott, H. (1973). *The man in the principal's office.* New York: Holt, Rinehart & Winston.

Wolcott, H. (1975). Criteria for an ethnographic approach to research in schools. *Human Organization 34:* 111–127.

Wolcott, H. (1977). *Teachers vs. technocrats: An educational innovation in anthropological perspective.* Eugene, OR: Center for Educational Policy and Management.

Wolcott, H. (1990). Making a study "more ethnographic". *Journal of Contemporary Ethnography 19(1):* 44–72.

Wolcott, H. (1995). Making a study "more ethnographic." In J. Van Mannen (Ed.), *Representation in ethnography.* Thousand Oaks, CA: Sage, pp. 79–111.

Wolcott, H. F. (1990). *Writing up qualitative research.* Newbury Park, CA: Sage.

Wolcott, H. F. (1992). Posturing in qualitative research. In M. D. LeCompte, W. L. Millroy, & J. Preissle (Eds.), *The handbook of qualitative research in education.* New York: Academic Press, pp. 3–52.

Wolcott, H. W. (Ed.). (1983). Teaching fieldwork to educational researchers: A symposium. *Anthropology & Educational Quarterly 14*(3): 171–212.

Wolf, R. L. (1979a). *An overview of conceptual and methodological issues in naturalistic evaluation.* Paper presented at the meeting of American Educational Research Association, San Francisco.

Wolf, R. L. (1979b). *Strategies for conducting naturalistic evaluation in socio-educational settings: The naturalistic interview.* Paper prepared for publication in the Occasional Paper Series, Evaluation Center, Western Michigan University.

Wood, P. (1975). *You and Aunt Arie: A guide to cultural journalism based on Foxfire and its descendants.* Washington, DC: Institutional Development and Economic Affairs Service, Inc.

Woods, P. (1985). New songs played skillfully: Creativity and technique in writing up qualitative research. In R. G. Burgess (Ed.), *Issues in educational research: Qualitative methods.* Philadelphia, PA: Falmer Press.

Yin, R. K. (1994). *Case study research: Design and methods* (3rd ed.). Thousand Oaks, CA: Sage.

Yin, R. K. (1989). *Case study research: Design and methods.* (2nd ed.). Newbury Park, CA: Sage.

Zeichner, K. (1996). Teachers as reflective practitioners and the democratization of school reform. In K. Zeichner, S. Melnick, & M. L. Gomez (Eds.), *Currents of reform in preservice teacher education.* New York: Teachers College Press, pp. 199–214.

Zeichner, K., & Gore, J. (1995). Using action research as a vehicle for student teacher reflection: A social reconstructionist approach. In S. Noffke, & R. Stevenson (Eds.), *Educational action research: Becoming practically critical.* New York: Teachers College Press, pp. 13–30.

Ziegler, S. (1980). School for life: The experience of Italian immigrants in Canadian schools. *Human Organization 39*(3): 263–267.

Zimmerman, C., & Frampton, M. (1935). *Family and society, a study of the sociology of reconstruction.* New York: D. Van Nostrand.

Znaniecki, F. (1934). *The method of sociology.* New York: Farrar and Rinehart.

Zorbaugh, H. (1929). *The gold coast and the slum.* Chicago: University of Chicago.

Index